The Art of Jewish Living

סדר ליל פסח The Passover Seder

Books in *The Art of Jewish Living* Series

Hanukkah

The Passover Seder

The Shabbat Seder

A Time to Mourn, A Time to Comfort:
A Guide to Jewish Bereavement and Comfort

In each generation, every individual should feel as though he or she had actually been redeemed from ***Mitzrayim****, as it is said: "You shall tell your children on that day, saying, 'It is because of what* ***Adonai*** *did for me when I went free out of* ***Mitzrayim****.'"*

The Passover Haggadah

The Art of Jewish Living
סדר ליל פסח The Passover Seder

By Dr. Ron Wolfson
With Joel Lurie Grishaver

A Project of
The Federation of Jewish Men's Clubs
and
The University of Judaism

Jewish Lights Publishing
Woodstock, Vermont

The Passover Seder
The Art of Jewish Living Series

1996 First JEWISH LIGHTS Publishing printing

The University of Judaism is an academic institution dedicated to the study and enhancement of Jewish life.

None of the photographic work for this project was actually done on Passover. The Passover settings were all simulated.

Photography: Jules Porter Photographers, Los Angeles
Typesetting and Design: Alef Type and Design, Los Angeles

10 9 8 7 6 5 4 3 2

ISBN 1-879045-93-1
LCCN 88-080181

Manufactured in the United States of America

Published by JEWISH LIGHTS Publishing
A Division of LongHill Partners, Inc.
P.O. Box 237
Sunset Farm Offices, Rte. 4
Woodstock, VT 05091
Tel: (802) 457-4000 Fax: (802) 457-4004

I am my beloved's
And my beloved is mine.

(Song of Songs 6:3)

For Susie, my beloved.

TABLE OF CONTENTS

ACT THREE—THE FEAST

ACT FOUR—REDEMPTION

PART TWO: PREPARING FOR PASSOVER

PREFACE

Few titles do as much justice to their subject as *The Art of Jewish Living*, of which the present volume is the second in the series. To my mind, the title conveys three essential truths about Judaism: First, that it is an intricate pattern of behavioral prescriptions and not a disembodied theological creed. Second, that the rhythm and ritual must be imbued with a sense of beauty and elevated to the level of an art form. And third, that it is a religious system addressed to the individual Jew, for Judaism is nothing if not participatory.

But the title implies a sociological fact as well. There are countless Jews today for whom Judaism as a way of life is inaccessible. Nurtured on an ethos of individualism and deprived as children of home example and formal education, they are unable to give Jewish expression to their resurgent religious feelings. They are the confused and forlorn members of "a generation without memory" (Anne Roiphe).

For such Jews, this creative and sensitive book, like its immensely successful predecessor *The Shabbat Seder*, offers abundant evidence that Judaism is still conquerable. Ron Wolfson has again unpacked the intimidating details of a complex Jewish ritual and assembled a galaxy of diverse and inviting models, something for every reader. In the process, he has enlivened a fixed and sacred ritual wih a spritely blend of individualization. The guiding philosophy of both books is to appropriate Judaism incrementally, one set of rituals at a time. Or as put by the Mishnah nearly two millennia ago: "Whosoever performs even a single commandment it shall go well with him, and his days shall be prolonged, and he shall inherit the land" (trans.-Blackman). The meaningfulness derived from one ritual will generate the incentive to internalize others. Indeed, for all serious Jews the conquest of Judaism is the labor of a lifetime.

For nearly a decade now The Federation of Jewish Men's Clubs has devoted itself with zeal and imagination to assisting those adult Jews ready to embark on that conquest. The educational materials it has produced—for learning Hebrew and celebrating Shabbat and Passover—are among the most appealing and effective access points into the world of Jewish living that I know. The network of Men's Clubs has become in consequence an active agent for raising the quality of observance throughout the Conservative Movement and lessening the gap between rhetoric and reality. The practice of Judaism, informed by knowledge and graced with beauty, is its best defense. I salute the Federation for its vision and accomplishments.

Ismar Schorsch
Chancellor
Jewish Theological
Seminary of America

FOREWORD

Seder nights are magic. They both transcend and unite history. Torah teaches us that the first Seder took place on the eve of the Exodus. It was a watch night filled with fear and anticipation. While the angel of death stalked the Egyptian firstborn, slave families gathered to eat the paschal lamb. Since then, our families have relived that evening more than three thousand times. For generations we have sat together to remember, retell, recreate, and relive that Exodus experience. Over time, the Seder has become more than an historic remembrance; it has evolved its own memories and significance. We cannot return to the lessons of that first Seder night in Egypt without its being enriched by the memories of our own Seder celebrations. As I sit to write of Seder traditions and customs, I return in my mind to Omaha. Such is the Jewish way. Family history and national history are interwoven. I cannot prepare to experience the spiritual liberation from Egypt without first returning in memory to Nebraska.

I remember vividly the Seders of my childhood. As a Jewish educator, I now consistently correct my students when they say "Seders." I insist that they use the proper Hebrew plural, *Sedarim*. Yet, in boyhood memory, they will always be "Seders."

First Seders were always at Bubbie and Zadie's (grandmother and grandfather). We were a big family: grandparents; four daughters, each of whom was married; four sons-in-law, who all worked in my grandfather's supermarket business; and nine grandchildren. Any pilgrimage to Bubbie and Zadie's was an important event, but on *Pesaḥ*, it was unique.

Seder was a dress-up affair: suits, ties, the works. I used to think that this was odd. It made sense to dress up when you went to synagogue, but not to Bubbie and Zadie's. It was also filled with tremendous anticipation. My Zadie, may he rest in peace, was a legend in his own time, known by virtually everyone in Omaha, and generous to a fault. We knew that come *afikomen* time, he would come up with something spectacular.

In twenty years of visiting my grandparents, I never once entered through the front door. Everyone came in through the back door, directly into the kitchen. And what a kitchen! It was by no means large, but what came out of that kitchen was absolutely amazing. My Bubbie, may she rest in peace, was a *balabuste* (homemaker) second to none, famous in her own right around town for her *mikhels* (specialties). Her mandel bread, fondly and widely known as "Bubbie's Cookies," were incredible wedges of flour and nuts, smothered in cinnamon sugar. She made them in huge quantities and stored them in an old roaster near the doorway between the kitchen and the dining room. First stop, after kissing Bubbie in the kitchen, was that roaster. Even on *Pesaḥ* before the Seder.

But, on *Pesaḥ*, there was a virtual avalanche of other goodies being prepared: chopped liver, homemade gefilte fish, roasts, turkeys, carrot *tzimmes* (stew), vegetables, salads, you name it. Best of all were the *gribines*. As a kid, I had no idea how they were made. But, the colander which held these delectable, crunchy tidbits was another favorite destination. What it has done to my cholesterol count, I don't want to know. (*Gribines* are the by-product of rendering chicken fat—deep-fried chicken skins.) A busy kitchen was no place for children; we were banished to the basement to play with our cousins until the Seder was to begin.

With some 19 family members and assorted guests (up to 35 people), it was impossible to seat everyone in their small dining room. So, tables and chairs were rented and set up in the long living room. The time when people arrived was the most chaotic. With all the tables, there was no place to sit and talk. The kitchen was too small for anyone but those actually preparing dinner, so people often ended up in bedrooms or on the sun porch—awaiting the start of the Seder.

Seder was usually called for 6:30, but we never got started until after 7:00; some family always came late. Usually one of the dads had to miss the first part of the Seder to watch the store. Finally, one of the parents would call down into the basement for all the kids to come up. By that time, all of our nice clothes were disheveled from furious games of kickball, "war," and other assorted opportunities to beat up on each other. We'd reluctantly trudge upstairs, only to be greeted by irate mothers who would quickly try to tuck in shirts, comb hair, and make us presentable at the table.

Seating everyone was not easy. With just inches separating the backs of the chairs from the furniture on the perimeter of the living room, there was a lot of sucking-in tummies to climb into those seats. Once the rest of us were settled, Zadie sat down at his big throne-like chair at the head of the table, we picked up our *Haggadahs*—Maxwell House of course (what would you expect from a family in the grocery business!)—and we would begin.

My Zadie was not what you would call a religious man, although in his own way, he was deeply sentimental and nostalgic. For him, the best part of the Seder was to see his "*ainekhlakh*" (grandchildren) ask the "*fier kashes*". One by one, as each of us became the youngest old enough to ask the Four Questions, he would nearly burst with pride as we stood at attention and sang or read these few words. I can still see his ruddy face, tears welling in his eyes, as he pretended to follow along in the text, but all the while soaking up our broken Hebrew singing or English reading.

I don't remember much more about the first part of our Seders. I do recall watching Zadie break the *matzah* for the *afikomen*, wrap it in a napkin, and stick it in his suit pocket, all with a sly smile towards the children. I'm sure he and some of the men said a few more parts, but I don't think it took more than thirty minutes before we were ready to eat.

I always knew it was time for the meal because the men could take off their jackets and loosen their ties. The women headed for the kitchen to help Bubbie who, by the way, never sat down at the Seder. During the reading of the *Haggadah*, Zadie would call out to her, "Sit, sit," and she would call back, "I'm listening, I'm listening." If I hadn't learned later that this could be different, I would have thought that it was part of the ritual that the hostess is not allowed to sit down until after the guests have left! Out came the fish, and then the soup with huge, fluffy *matzah* balls, followed in quick succession by all the other dishes. While I learned later that the original *Pesaḥ* meal in Egypt was eaten in haste, I suppose that we rushed through this huge dinner because it was late, and everyone was starved!

Sometime between the fish and the soup, Zadie would quietly get up and disappear. If we tried to follow him, he would shoo us back to the table. We knew what he was up to. As soon as we would eat "just two more bites" of turkey, we could look for the prized *afikomen*. The signal given, we madly dashed around the house, darting from lampshade to pillow cushion, frantically searching for the napkin. Zadie was a great *afikomen*-hider, so we'd come running back to him, begging for clues. He loved that, taking great satisfaction from hiding the treasure so well. Finally, one of us would find it, rushing back into the dining room screaming "I found it!" to the claps and cheers of parents, aunts, and uncles, and the disappointed silence of the other cousins.

Presenting the *afikomen* to Zadie, the finder always was first in the annual line-up of grandchildren to receive the long-awaited *afikomen* prize. Zadie was an equal-opportunity, everybody-gets-a-prize kind of Zadie, and this was the crowning moment of the evening for him. Every year, he had the bookkeeper at the store prepare for him nine envelopes, each one inscribed with the name of one of his beloved grandchildren. He would pull them out of the front pocket of his suit, struggle to read the name, and announce the recipient of the envelope. One by one, we would take the envelope from him, whereupon he would plant a big, wet, scratchy kiss on our lips. This was his *naches* (joy), the wet kisses and giving us those envelopes, each holding a brand-new $20 bill which the bookkeeper had acquired for him at the bank the day before.

Sometime between the end of dinner and dessert, we opened the door for Elijah, but I don't think we ever sang or said anything. We kids would then run back to the table to see if the level of wine in Elijah's cup had gone down. It always seemed to. Dessert was a true climax, a real double treat. In addition to Bubbie's *Pesaḥdik* cakes and cookies, every year we had watermelon for dessert. Watermelon—in mid-April in Omaha, Nebraska. Zadie would order it special from the produce dealer who had it brought in from Mexico or South America, just for us. I guarantee you, we were the only Jewish family in Omaha to have watermelon for Passover!

We'd sing "*Adir Hu*" and "*Ḥad Gadya*" and then the kids ran down to the basement for more kickball and general roughhousing, while the adults enjoyed dessert and shmoozing upstairs. The evening came to an end the same way each year—with somebody crying. As the hour got late and the interactions in the basement intensified, one of the kids inevitably got kicked in the head or some other part of the anatomy which resulted in screaming loud enough to bring one of the parents downstairs. That was the signal that enough was enough and we prepared to go home.

By now, Zadie had gone to sleep and Bubbie was just sitting down to eat something, but not before she had packed up four bundles of leftovers for each family to take home. She, too, would give each of us a big, wet kiss and we'd take off, my brothers and I blissfully falling asleep by the time we got home.

The second Seder was at our house and always a bit more manageable. There were only the five of us and guests. My mother would call the synagogue each year to get a list of Jewish boys living at Offutt Air Base nearby or to see if there were any Jewish kids at Boys Town who needed an invitation to Seder. Having guests in the house was exciting, and it served to calm us boys down during the ceremony.

I recall one Seder we had a famous non-Jewish guest. My mother had started the first Jewish braille group in a synagogue at Beth El in Omaha and was very active in volunteering her time to help the blind in Nebraska. The braille group's big project was to produce the first Hebrew-English braille edition of the Passover *Haggadah*. And, in her work with the Nebraska Foundation for the Visually Handicapped, she often met famous blind personalities when they came through Omaha.

One year, the outstanding blind jazz pianist George Shearing played an engagement in town during Passover. My mother met him a few days before the Seder and invited him. Never will I forget the excitment of having a famous personality in our home. Shearing was delightful, participating fully in the Seder ceremony, reading from the braille *Haggadah* my mother had worked so hard to produce. The next evening, Shearing invited all of us to attend his concert which he began by raving to the audience about the Seder experience in our home. He then proceeded to play a jazz variation of "*Dayyenu!*"

My father had grown up in an orthodox home, so he remembered much of the Seder ritual. However, as soon as we boys started learning the parts of the Seder in Hebrew school, we took over a major part of the service. We had a big, oversized edition of the *Haggadah* with dramatic pictures of Moses leading the people out of Egypt, and Egyptian charioteers drowning in the Reed Sea. By the time I was Bar Mitzvah, I was leading the Seder, assigning parts by writing in the names of the participants in the margins of my "leader's" *Haggadah*. Each year, I would search the pile of *Haggadot* to find that copy with all my notes, and each year, I'd erase some names and fill in others, depending on who was at the Seder and who could sing what.

We actually read most of the *Haggadah* at our family Seder. We sort of skimmed through the *Maggid* and I can't recall that we sang the *Hallel*, but it was certainly a more complete Seder than at Bubbie and Zadie's. And when meal time came around, well, my mother was no slouch at cooking. My brothers and I would search for the *afikomen*, happy at the much-better odds of finding it this night than the night before. All in all, pleasant memories of another wonderful Seder night.

One year, the inevitable happened. Zadie was sick and Bubbie had already begun to become a bit senile, and the family faced a major decision: who would host the big family Seder now? I didn't realize it at the time, but this was a critical moment of transition and transmission of Jewish tradition in our large extended family. If no one volunteered, we would each have our own small family *Sedarim* or none at all. The job fell to my mother, and, all of a sudden, we were hosting 35 people for Seder in our home.

By now, I was a teenage *macher* (leader) in United Synagogue Youth, as well as an experienced Seder leader and, with the help of my brothers, I became the organizer of the Seder. It was also a time when the older cousins in the family had begun to bring fiancees to the Seder table. This swelled our ranks and, sometimes, led to quite interesting complications.

I'll never forget the first time my wife Susie and her parents came to our Seder. We had been going steady for a couple of years and things looked very serious. My mother suggested I extend the invitation to her and her parents to "meet the family," and what better occasion than the Passover Seder. Susie's parents were thrilled, especially since they had come to America in 1950 from Berlin with only one other surviving member of their family. When they asked what they could bring, my mother demurred. They wouldn't accept that and offered to bring their specialty, homemade gefilte fish. Susie told me how excited they were to be able to impress the prospective in-laws and their large family with this very important part of the Seder meal.

Imagine their chagrin when they found out we were Litvaks! While all of my family was used to the rather bland gefilte fish balls common among people who trace their roots to Russia, Susie's parents' version tasted suspiciously sweet, as if sugar was added, and, horror of horrors, came wrapped in real fish skin. A few people were polite enough to pick at it, but not enough to satisfy Susie's folks who had spent several days "hocking" 55 pounds of carp and pike to create their masterpiece. It was a true test of our young love for one other, this realization that, as the song says:

"I say *kugle* and you say *keegle*,
I say *shule* and you say *sheel*;
kugle, keegle, shule, sheel—
let's call the whole thing off."

Well, thank God, we didn't call the whole thing off at all and today we make our own *Sedarim* in a happily "intermarried" Litvak/Palisher home!

The tradition requires that on Seder night, we reexperience the liberation from Egypt. We are to remember how our family suffered as slaves; we are to feel the exhilaration of redemption. We must retaste the bitterness and must rejoice as a family over our newfound freedom. We annually return to Egypt in order to be freed. We remember slavery in order to deepen our commitment to end all suffering; we recreate our liberation in order to reinforce our commitment to universal freedom. Every year, my personal escape from Egypt, my private path to liberation, goes through boyhood memories of Omaha. Kickball, *gribines*, Four Questions, and crossing the Reed Sea are permanantly interconnected.

The celebration of Passover begins on the first full moon of spring, the 15th of *Nisan* in the Jewish calendar. The corresponding date in the secular calendar varies from year to year. The Festival is celebrated for eight days by Conservative and Orthodox Jews outside the state of Israel and for seven days by Reform and Israeli Jews.

Pesaḥ is one of the three pilgrimage festivals (the others are *Sukkot* and *Shavuot*), occasions when Jews in ancient times would journey to Jerusalem in order to offer sacrifices in the Holy Temple. Passover begins with two days of *Yom Tov* (literally: "good day" or Festival)—a full holiday, followed by four days of *Ḥol ha-Moed* (intermediate days of the Festival)—a half-holiday, and concludes with two more days of *Yom Tov*. In the days of the Temple, it was unclear when exactly the new moon occured, so to be safe, the rabbis decreed that most Festivals outside Israel begin with two days of *Yom Tov*.

It is also important to understand that, because the Jewish calendar is based in part on a lunar cycle, Jewish days begin at sundown. This is why we begin the Passover holiday at night with the lighting of *Yom Tov* candles and the celebration of the Seder on each of the first two nights of *Pesaḥ*.

It is somewhat ironic that this holiday which celebrates freedom has, without doubt, the most restrictive rules of preparation and celebration of any Jewish festival. During the eight days of *Pesaḥ*, we are not to eat or even own any products which contain the slightest trace of *ḥametz*—leaven. Many families completely change over the entire kitchen—dishes, cooking utensils, cupboards, counters, and shelves—in order to ensure that no *ḥametz* will be eaten during the eight days of the holiday. The raised dough of self-pride is replaced with the flat *matzah* of humility.

The entire month between the celebration of *Purim* and the beginning of *Pesaḥ* is one of preparation. Special *Shabbatot* are marked in the synagogue prayer service. The entire household is cleaned, the pantry is depleted of *ḥametzdik* (Yiddish for "having to do with *ḥametz*") products and replaced with special *kosher l'Pesaḥ* ("fit for Passover") foods, and plans for the Seder celebration are made. It is undoubtedly one of the busiest times of the year in a Jewish household.

On Seder night, it is probable that more Jews come into contact with Jewish ritual practice than at any other single moment of the year. While less than 50% of North American Jewry belong to a synagogue, nearly 90% attend a Passover Seder. Perhaps even more significantly, the vast majority of Jews celebrate the Seder in a home; if not their own, then at a family member or friend. Children come home from college, families gather together from long distances, strangers are welcomed—it is a night of gathering, a night of remembering, a night which celebrates the birth and continuing renewal of Jewish peoplehood.

Thus, it is no surprise that the second volume of *The Art of Jewish Living* series should be *The Passover Seder*. Following in the footsteps of the first volume in the series, *The Shabbat Seder*, we have attempted to create a comprehensive guide to the celebration of Passover, with particular emphasis on the preparation of the home and the creation of a meaningful Seder ceremony. As with the previous text, we began our work by talking with families, real Jewish families who approach the celebration of Passover quite seriously. It should not be surprising that we discovered much that was similar and much that was different about their experiences of *Pesaḥ*. The basic components of celebration are the same. The "art" of Jewish living is in knowing how to compose one's own particular expression of the ritual in a way that is meaningful to oneself and one's family and friends.

The Art of Jewish Living: The Passover Seder text is the basis for a series of workshops on the celebration of Passover. Other resources which have been prepared for these workshops include:

The Art of Jewish Living: The Passover Seder Workbook, an interactive text designed for workshop participants which contains worksheets for those responsible for preparing the home for the holiday and for leading the Seder celebration. It also includes a variety of creative ideas to enhance the Seder experience.

The Art of Jewish Living: The Passover Seder Audiotape, an audiocassette featuring the traditional chants of the major portions of the Seder service.

The Art of Jewish Living: The Passover Seder Teacher's Guide, a detailed manual of suggested lesson plans and activities for teaching Passover workshops in adult education settings.

All of these materials are available from the Federation of Jewish Men's Clubs, 475 Riverside Drive, New York, New York, 10115.

A project of this magnitude cannot be imagined, much less completed, without the unwavering support of many individuals and institutions. It is my honor to recognize those who have made significant contributions in support of this effort:

Jules Porter, immediate past President of the Federation of Jewish Men's Clubs, continues to be the guiding light of *The Art of Jewish Living* project. A remarkable layperson, Jules has devoted a good portion of his incredible energies to bringing Jewish life back into the home. His contributions, public and private, have provided the direction, the resources, and the enthusiasm to hundreds of Men's Clubs chapters, to countless individuals, and indeed is to the Conservative Movement. His personal encouragement to me has been extraordinary and is deeply appreciated.

Rabbi Charles Simon, executive director of the FJMC, is a tireless and talented colleague and friend. Clearly one of the top young executives in Jewish communal life today, Chuck has enthusiastically guided the development of the AJL project, raising funds, garnering support, and moving the FJMC into the forefront of creative Jewish programming.

Mr. Jerome Agrest, International President of the FJMC, and Rabbi Joel S. Geffen, spiritual advisor to the FJMC, have been wonderfully supportive of this effort.

On behalf of the FJMC and the University of Judaism, co-sponsors of the AJL project, I am pleased to thank the following individuals and institutions for their support:

Milken Family Foundation, Encino, California
Arnold C. Greenberg, West Hartford, Connecticut
Mount Sinai Memorial Park and Mortuary, A community service of Sinai Temple, Los Angeles
The Susan and David Wilstein Foundation, Los Angeles
The Billy Rose Foundation, New York
Morris and Dorothy Niemerow (in memory of Harry Evans), Los Angeles
Bill and Sandy Goodglick, Los Angeles
Paul Newman, Detroit
The Morris and Betty Kaplum Foundation, New York
Joseph Muchnick, Washington, D.C.
Jack and Rae Gindi, Los Angeles
Maury, Georgina, and Zackary Sachs, South Salem, New York
The George Wasserman Foundation, Washington, D.C.
Irving Laker, Southfield, Michigan
Mr. and Mrs. Jerry Oren, Beverly Hills
Jules and Marion Porter, Los Angeles

The Art of Jewish Living series continues to enjoy the endorsement of Rabbinical Assembly of America, the Women's League for Conservative Judaism, and the Jewish Theological Seminary of America. I wish to especially thank Rabbi Joel Roth, chairman of the Law Committee and Standards of the Rabbinical Assembly who generously gave of his time to review the manuscript.

I am particularly honored that Dr. Ismar Schorsch, Chancellor of the Jewish Theological Seminary of America, graciously agreed to contribute the Preface to the volume.

I am also indebted to my colleagues at the University of Judaism who have supported my work: Dr. David Lieber, Dr. Elliot Dorff, Rabbi Ben Zion Bergman, and Dr. Eliezer Slomovic.

Special thanks are due the families and individuals whose comments illuminate this volume and who allowed us into their homes to share their experiences of Passover: Sally, Jerry, Adina and Gavi Weber; Rica and Victor Sabah; Carol, Dan, Benjamin, Mordechai, and Hannah Karsch; Marlene, Barry, Mark, Brad, and Michael Horwitz; Judith and Louis Miller; Keren and John Goldberg; Miriam Prum; and Linda, Lorin, Ari, and Yoni Fife. Quotations from Abby Kantor, David Coburn, Paula Peck, Yonina Dorph, and Matthew Gill are drawn from *Seder: A Passover Experience*, a slide-tape created by Torah Aura Productions, Los Angeles. All of these are wonderful models for anyone wishing to make Passover special in her/his life.

I am especially pleased that the outstanding production team which created the design for the AJL series again lent their considerable talents to this volume. Thanks to the staff of Jules Porter Photographers, particularly Lewis Gottesman, Tracy and Tom Zumpano, and, of course, Carolyn Moore-Mooso, copy editor extraordinaire, helped us to better write what we wanted to say. And, the creative whirlwinds of Alef Type & Design, Jane Golub and Alan Rowe, provided the technical expertise for which they and their firm are becoming justifiably well-known.

In 1969, I met Joel Lurie Grishaver in the pages of his first book, the landmark *Shema is for Real.* From the moment I opened the text, I knew that this man had a talent for creating the kind of innovative Jewish educational curricula I found sorely lacking in our field. It wasn't until I moved to Los Angeles in 1974 that I met Joel in person, he then a graduate student at Hebrew Union College—Los Angeles and I a graduate student at the University of Judaism. We have been good friends ever since. Collaborating with Joel is a roller-coaster ride through rabbinic literature, *Kabbalah*, and Tom Peters. He combines the keen eye of a terrific editor with an innate command of curricular design. It continues to be a great pleasure to work with this most creative whirlwind of a Jewish educator.

For my *mishpaḥa*, the writing of a book means many hours at the computer terminal, many evenings at the production office, and many weeks with little time for them. I want to thank Havi, Michael, and Susie for their patience, their encouragement, and their love. God (and the printer) willing, I'll be home for *Pesaḥ!*

Ron Wolfson
Los Angeles, California
Tu B'Shevat 5748
February, 1988

USING THIS TEXT

There are two major parts to this text. *Part I: The Passover Seder* presents an outline of the complete Seder ritual by dividing the elements of the *Haggadah* into an innovative format. *Part II: Preparing for Passover* offers a comprehensive guide to the preparation for Passover and for conducting the Seder experience. So, if you are interested in learning about the content and meaning of the Seder ceremony, turn to Part I. If, however, you want to begin with the information on how to organize and lead a Seder and how to make the home ready for Passover, turn to Part II.

To begin with, we hear from the families we interviewed for this project as they talk about the various steps of Passover preparation and celebration. We hope their insights and experiences with making *Pesaḥ* will resonate with those who are just learning to do so and for those who have experienced a Seder, but know very little about what it all means.

Our goal in *Part I: The Passover Seder* is to lead the reader through the *Haggadah*, step-by-step, in order to explain the purpose and process of each moment in the Seder experience. To this end, the chapters follow a consistent outline. Most of the chapters begin with a short essay about the particular step under discussion which sets the tone for the detailed information to come. The "Concepts" section offers a brief explanation of the major themes of the particular step. The "Objects" section discusses the various items required for each step and their requirements. The "Practice" section details exactly how the ritual is performed.

Next, the texts of the blessings are presented in a unique format which has proven quite successful in helping those unfamiliar with the original texts to understand their meaning. First, the texts have been divided into small word phrases and numbered in a linear fashion. Second, there are three columns of texts. From right to left, they are: 1) the Hebrew or Aramaic text, 2) the English translation of the text, and 3) the English transliteration of the text. This format allows those who are able to read the original language to work with it and English translation columns, while those who cannot read the original texts can work with the English transliteration and translation columns. This linear presentation should assist the learner in deciphering the meanings of the Hebrew and Aramaic words.

Please note that all the texts, both original and English, have been reproduced from the *Passover Haggadah: The Feast of Freedom*, edited by Rachel Anne Rabinowicz and published by the Rabbinical Assembly of America (1982). The transliteration scheme also generally follows that used by the Rabbinical Assembly in its new prayerbooks:

ai	= as in "I"—*Adonai*	= ah—doe—n'I
ei	= as in "hay"—*Eloheinu*	= eh—low—hay—nu
i	= as in "see"—*l'hadlik*	= leh—hahd—leek
o	= as in "low"—*shalom*	= shah—lowm
e	= as in "red"—*Elohim*	= eh—low—heem
a	= as in "Mama"—*bara*	= bah—rah
u	= as in "blue"—*vanu*	= vah—nu
kh	= as in the sound you make when trying to dislodge a fishbone from the roof of your mouth	
ḥ		= as above

A word about translations. The editor of the Rabbinical Assembly *Haggadah* has done an excellent job in writing a translation which is both faithful to the original text and yet easy to read at the table. It is not, however, an exact word-for-word translation of the original. Another concern is that of the near-universal use of masculine tense in the Hebrew and Aramaic texts. For example, God is always referred to in masculine terms. There is no easy solution to this problem. In having adopted the translations of the Rabbinical Assembly *Haggadah*, we have adopted their approach to the issue.

Following the texts, a section entitled "Practical Questions and Answers" poses and answers common questions about the steps in the Passover Seder.

A suggestion: have a copy of your *Haggadah* handy as you read through Part I so that you can discover how your text is translated and structured.

In Part II: Preparing for Passover, the chapters begin with the comments of our model families and then present the information on how to lead a great Seder and how to prepare the home for the holiday.

A "Selected Bibliography" only hints at the multitude of resources available for those interested in learning more about the Passover experience.

B'hatzlaḥah! We wish you "good success" on learning *The Art of Jewish Living.*

1
THE ART OF PASSOVER ON "MAKING" *PESAḤ*

One year, prior to *Pesaḥ*, my mother brought her mother to visit. My grandmother had never been on an airplane before, so this was really a very strenuous trip for her. I was very close to this grandmother. They couldn't stay for *Pesaḥ*, they left the day before the Seder, but I had one most extraordinary experience with them.

I don't come from an observant home, and in fact, my mother didn't come from an observant home either. My grandparents, who were first generation Americans, were not observant at all; they were very much assimilated. When I was going through this dramatic, intricate ritual of *kashering* ("making fit") my kitchen for *Pesaḥ*, my grandmother came and spent time with me. At this one moment, I saw that she had been standing for a long, long time, staring at me. I could feel the pressure of someone's eyes. I was busy moving around, and there she was, staring at me—almost in a daze. So finally I turned around to her and asked, "Grandma, what is it?" and she looked at me, paused, and then said, "You are my mother."

Carol Karsch

ON RECAPTURING THE PAST

A Story.

When the Baal Shem Tov had a difficult task before him, he would go to a certain place in the woods, light a fire, and meditate in prayer. And then, he was able to perform the task.

A generation later, the Maggid of Mazrich was faced with the same task. So, he went to the same place in the woods, but he had forgotten exactly how to light the fire as the Baal Shem Tov had done. He said: "I can no longer light the fire, but I can still speak the prayers." And so he prayed as the Baal Shem Tov had prayed, and he was able to complete the task.

A generation later, Rabbi Moshe Lev had to perform this same task. He too went into the woods, but he had not only forgotten how to light the fire, he had forgotten the prayers as well. He said: "I can no longer light the fire, nor do I know the secret meditations belonging to the prayers. But, I do know the place in the woods to which it all belongs and that must be sufficient." And sufficient it was.

But, when another generation had passed, Rabbi Israel Salanter was called upon to perform the task. He sat down on his golden chair in his castle and said: "I cannot light the fire. I cannot speak the prayers. I do not know the place in the forest. But, we can tell the story of how it was once done, and that must be sufficient." And sufficient it was.

Passover asks us to do one simple thing: tell the story. Tell the story of how a people, enslaved and oppressed, was brought out from bondage and made into a great nation by an Almighty God. The Seder night is our vehicle for telling this story. The *Haggadah* is our text. And, although we can no longer engage in the ancient sacrifices, and though we may not know the secret meditations of our ancestors, we can tell the story. "Tell your child on that very day that this is what the Lord did for me when I went out from Egypt"—this is the goal of the Passover Seder.

As we've talked to families about their memories of Passovers past, this story illuminates another truth about Passover observance today. There are those among us whose memories of Passovers past are weak, or perhaps even non-existent. For some, Passover was a ritual performed by grandparents and, like the Maggid of Mazrich, we no longer remember how to "light the fire," how to perform most of the ritual choreography—sometimes not even the most basic of the steps. For others, the words of the *Haggadah* are no longer fluent for us. Like Rabbi Moshe Lev, we know the place to go, but the words have failed us. And certainly, there are those of us who cannot perform the ceremony, do not know the words, and have even forgotten the Seder's meaning—except as an important family meeting time. Like Rabbi Israel Salanter, we try to tell the story in whatever way we can. Yet, without understanding the rituals or the words, even this very basic task is quite difficult to do in a way that is meaningful to us and our family.

Sally, Jerry, Adina and Gavi Weber

Sally and Jerry Weber come from radically different Jewish experiences. Jerry's memories of Passover in a "chaotically observant" home are filled with the difficulties of adhering to strict kashrut, a long traditional Seder at his grandfather's, and a stimulating mix of people, rituals, and conversations in his parent's highly political, very intellectual, semi-Socialist home. Sally is relatively new at Jewish practice, having grown up in a nontraditional home, learning most of what she knows about Passover from Jerry, reading, and a lot of experimentation.

Together, they have fashioned a totally involving, participatory Seder experience for their daughters Adina, 14, and Gavi, 11, family members, and many friends who eagerly await the yearly letter inviting them to the Weber Seder. Theirs is one of the few families we know which gives guests homework to do before coming to Seder. Since the guests and assignments always change, no two Weber Seders are ever the same. Although both work professionally in the Jewish community, the Webers are prototypical self-taught enlightened laypeople, ever searching for new and deeper ways to experience the wonder, the fun, and the intellectual stimulation of Seder night.

YOUR AUTHOR: Can you remember a favorite Passover story?

ADINA: Yes, I can remember one.

GAVI: One o'clock in the morning singing *Ḥad Gadya.*

ADINA: I remember this year my birthday was on the third day of Passover and I had kind of forgotten that. When it got to midnight Mom stopped everything and sang Happy Birthday.

GAVI: I don't know what year, it was a while ago, when somebody found the *afikomen* and then lost it. We had to start looking all over again.

ADINA: I remember that same year on my birthday I actually found it. It was a double-header.

SALLY: Oh, I've got a favorite one. A couple of years ago we opened the door for Elijah and who walked in? Elijah walked in. And Elijah was this seventy-year-old man straight off the Johnny Carson show—going from house to house because he knew people had so many questions. What questions did we have?

GAVI: How could you exist this long?

SALLY: That was hysterical.

For Elijah's side of the story, see page 215.

SALLY: We do a lot of stuff in our Seders. Being invited to our Seder means not just getting an invitation to come but an assignment. We give people questions that they have to prepare answers to, so there's a lot of intellectual interchange, there's a lot of joking around interchange. I think partly we invite people who sort of have different viewpoints—Jewish viewpoints, political viewpoints, life experiences—to come and share that. It really adds to the spice of the evening.

JERRY: It began, I think, about five or six years ago. We thought of it as an idea to kind of open the Seder to other people. I jokingly say, but it's also true, that now, running this Seder is practically like chairing a meeting because there are so many stimulating people. It's a way to both open up the *Haggadah* and to open up the experience to various kinds of viewpoints and various kinds of questions.

SALLY: We also found that people were also coming to the Seder with things to share. In '78, Mark Horwitz brought his flute unsolicited because he wanted to share something. We had a friend who is a professor of Yiddish who brought a poem about the Warsaw ghetto which he read in Yiddish.

JERRY: There was an unusual Seder where the Catholic family across the street was included with their oldest child who teaches at Louisville High; she's a sister of the order.

SALLY: One year my mother said she wasn't going to come to the Seder any more; that she was really, really uncomfortable at the Seder. She didn't feel it was the place for her. As I sort of pushed her on that, she said, "Your friends are all so knowledgeable and they have so many ideas and they bring so much to share—and I just don't come from that background." She thought that this all happened spontaneously. We had never assigned questions to the grandparents and she thought people just came and shared. The next year, we gave her a question. Her background is in art and we gave her a question about the nature of Jewish art, why the emphasis in Jewish art was on ritual objects rather than great cathedrals or oil paintings. She gave this fabulous talk and it really gave her a place at the Seder that she had felt excluded from.

Rica and Victor Sabah

Rica and Vic Sabah are Sephardic Jews whose Pesaḥ observance reflects the challenge of retaining ancestral customs in the midst of the majority Ashkenazic culture. Vic's parents came from Turkey, while Rica is descended from a family that has lived in Jerusalem for more than 500 years. Having grown up in a family with generations of rabbis, including a great grandfather who was chief Sephardic Rabbi of Palestine, Rica brings to her Passover celebration a rich heritage of Sephardic customs and ceremonies.

Yet, the Sabah family Passover observance is in the throes of transformation. Having sent their three children, Joshua, 26, Daniel, 23, and Jody, 21, to a synagogue school where the majority of classmates, teachers, and customs taught were Ashkenazic, Vic and Rica's celebration of Pesaḥ has evolved into a truly "integrated" Sephardic-Ashkenazic experience. Rica, a Jewish educator, and Vic, a real estate investor, both very active members of their synagogue and the broader Jewish community, await the birth of their first grandchild (from Joshua and his wife, Debbi), wondering about the future of their very rich Sephardic heritage in the next generation.

RICA: The other thing that happens during the Seder—and it doesn't happen every year, but I remember it in my grandmother's house—is that we take a little kid and give him a stick and a hobo bag with a *matzah*. He takes it on his shoulder, goes out and then comes back in sometime during the Seder. When he returns, there is a kind of skit—very simple. The group says, "*Mi Attah*" (Who are you?)—and he

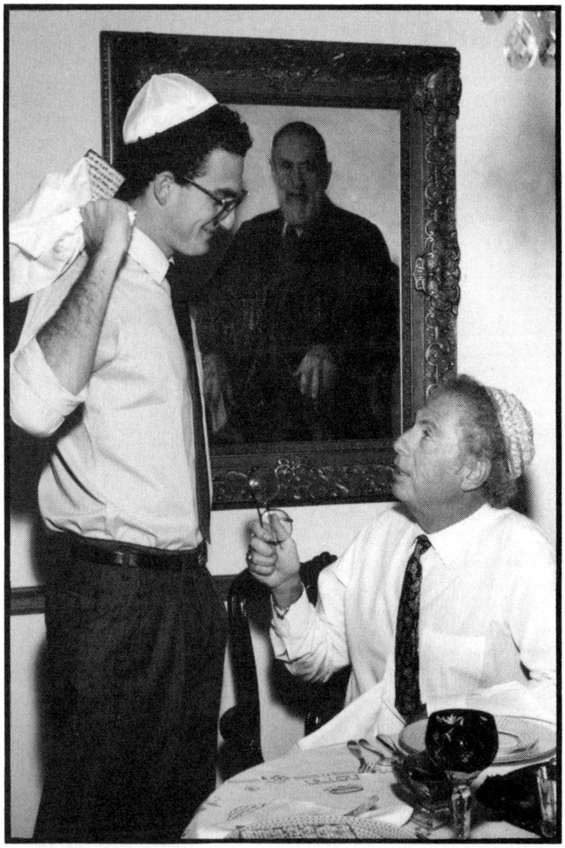

answers, "*Ani Yehudi*" (I am a Jew). They ask, "Where did you come from?" and he answers, "From the land of Egypt." They ask, "Where are you going?" and he answers "To the Land of Israel to be a free Jew."

VIC: We tend to keep in touch with Sephardic roots through the food, but seeing as most of the people at our Seder are not Sephardic we just keep a flavor of the Sephardic, just to keep in touch and to introduce them.

RICA: Besides the Seder, the important thing to me was to be able to give my children something so that they would continue the tradition the way that they can. When the kids were small, people would say to me, "How come you're not sending them to a Sephardic Temple?" It's hard enough to raise them as Jews. We're a minority in this society, and to raise them as a minority within a minority… It was more important to me to just give them a Jewish religion.

JODY: All my friends laugh at me.

RICA: Why?

JODY: When I say I'm Sephardic, they say, "What's a Sephardic?" "What's so Sephardic about you?"

RICA: In our tradition, we never eat the whole egg, and the egg is only a symbol on the table. When my girlfriend and I do the Seder together, she says, "Everybody should have an egg." This is something we go through every year. I just cut the eggs in half, because the only people who eat a whole egg are the people in mourning after a funeral. I think my mother would be very upset if I put a whole egg on the table and asked people to eat it.

Carol, Dan, Benjamin, Mordechai, and Hannah Karsch

In the desert of Arizona, we found the Karsches of Tucson, an incredibly involved family of five who have developed a Seder night which is communal, religious, political, and intellectual in nature—all at the same time. Dan, a past president of a Conservative synagogue, and Carol, a top lay leader in the local Jewish Federation, are experienced Seder-givers whose stated goal is to share what they know with younger, learning families. In a dynamic environment around the table, featuring important contributions by their three day school-Camp Ramah graduate children—Benjy, 19, Hannah, 17, and Mordy, 16—the Karsch family Seder is a mixture of traditional texts, liturgical poems, political protest, lessons from Rabbi Becker, and lively dialogue seeking to infuse meaning into the ancient ritual.

The Karsches are one of several families we spoke to who have "permanent" Seder guests. Each year, they share Seder with their close friends and next-door neighbors, the Shultzes, the family, plus college students in need of a home for Seder, a family interested in experiencing an elaborate Seder, and always a few non-Jewish friends, including local clergy and political figures.

HANNAH: When we have guests over, many times they're not as knowledgeable about the exact part of the *Haggadah*, but they ask their own questions, and in that way we stimulate more discussion—and other discussion that has to do with the Seder indirectly. And in this way, it makes each Seder different and distinct. And they're all enjoyable—I've never been to a boring Seder, and each year we come out with new knowledge.

MORDY: When we first start the Seder, my Dad will usually start out asking one of us—no, he'll start out with some of the first explanations, then he'll ask me or my brother or sister, and we'll give a whole bunch of explanations. Soon, the guests realize that that's the way we'll be doing it, and that there's so much to each part, and they'll add anything they know—later on they'll just say whatever they feel like saying.

BENJY: We have a *Haggadah*, I forget what it's called... but it's a good *Haggadah* and it has some good explanations that are the Rabbi Becker-type explanations.

MORDY: Rabbi Israel Becker is the orthodox rabbi here, Chafetz Chaim, and he taught at Tucson Hebrew Academy. I learned from him in fifth and sixth grade. We learned a lot of *gematria* (deriving meanings through numbers). We learned a lot of hidden, complicated meanings, and I retained a lot of it. I wrote a lot of it down. Rabbi Becker is a silent partner in our Seder.

BENJY: We used to footnote things when we said a "Rabbi Becker," we'd call it a "Rabbi Becker," or "*peirush Rabbi Becker.*"

DAN: Or "*mishigas Rabbi Becker.*"

BENJY: Last year I was having a piece of my back taken out and I was in the hospital, and just the way the timing worked out, it was during Passover. I was getting my operation two days before the Seder... I had the operation and then I was just in pretty bad shape and the day before the Seder I was very uncomfortable, so I told my mother not even to bring anything. But, she figures that I would feel better, and so right before Seder time, late in the evening she brought a Seder plate and she really brought a full spread... I rang the bell and called the nurse and asked for some salt water... I went through, I did the entire Seder, and didn't skip anything.

CAROL: We had all been very worried about him, and so the emotions that he had about having survived this were certainly emotions that we felt as well. And, I was mainly concerned about bringing him the food because I know Benjy's very observant with his *kashrut*... I wanted to be sure he had all the food, but in addition, just in case, I took him a whole Seder plate with all of the little ingredients in little zip-lock bags. You can tell with someone who's ill, if you're greeting them and they're starting to feel better, because there's a certain spark that returns, the *nefesh* (soul) really. I saw he was feeling better and he was able to sit up a little bit as we began to unveil these little gifts. It was very special. Then Benjy started to organize himself. I realized that by the time we got to the Four Questions that he was lingering over each prayer, nursing each one of the prayers, and it reminded me of stories in the Middle Ages. So I stayed for about an hour and a half and then I wanted to go back to the Seder that I had left. I got back there and they were more or less concluding, but it was really one of the most special experiences we ever had—very memorable.

Judith and Louis Miller

Judy and Lou Miller are our "empty-nester" Pesaḥ family. With their children out of the house and creating families of their own, Judy and Lou have nevertheless retained their role as Seder-givers for the ever-increasing Miller mishpaḥah.

The Millers have two Sedarim—the family Seder and the self-proclaimed "Super Seder." The family Seder is geared to their three adult children (Larry, 35, Phillip, 31, and Caryn, 28) and their spouses (Adrian, Judy, and Jerry), plus five grand-children under five. It's a no-frills affair, a straight run-through in deference to the number of small children around the table. The "Super Seder" is a more lei-surely, yet intensive experience to which are invited friends with significant Jewish knowledge who can appreciate the ex-tended discussions and commentaries which characterize the evening.

Lou, a successful businessman, has learned most of what he knows about Jew-ish practice as an adult and sees himself on an ever-deepening journey to in-creased Jewish knowledge and awareness. Judy comes from a family filled with Jewish tradition, celebration, and nostalgia. Together, they have created a home which is the spiritual center for their growing family and circle of friends.

JUDY: We had this big discussion on the process, the evolution of becoming more observant. He said, "The first thing you have to do is make the house kosher." I said, "Sure! That's easy for you to say—the first thing *I* have to do is make the house kosher—right!" I'm married twenty-five years, more than twenty-five years, and now all of a sudden, I've got to make this house kosher.

LOU: You can't really be observant unless you keep kosher.

JUDY: So I said, "Why don't we first try to really observe Shabbat? Let that be our first thing." But, he says, "You can't do one without the other. You've got to start with *kashrut*."

What we always did was get rid of all the *ḥametz*, I always took it out of the house. Always. In fact, my father, may he rest in peace, who scoffed at all this, he used to laugh at me. He used to make fun. I didn't have a kosher home and we weren't truly observant, so he couldn't understand. But, he used to love to come and be there on Passover and on every other holiday. I said, "You know, Dad, it makes me feel better." So, he said, "Okay."

LOU: From the time they were little kids, the kids never ate *ḥametz* that week. They always took *matzah* to school.

JUDY: They wanted it that way. For them it was something special, they never objected to it. They loved it. They always liked Passover. It was always a beautiful holiday for them...I think it was around January I said to him, "Okay, we'll make the house kosher. He got all excited and he was so happy... And I got a brand new set of dishes!

I start thinking about *Pesaḥ* the day after *Purim*. When I first start thinking about *Pesaḥ*, I start hyperventilating, I stop sleeping, and I start making lists. And, I keep thinking that there should be a master list. I say that every year. I keep thinking that each year that I'm going to improve something, that the method is going to get a little bit easier, that it will be a little better organized, but I blunder through it every year.

LOU: My theory is, there is an Orthodox family in Boston and they have the ultimate—a *Pesaḥ* kitchen.

JUDY: That's my dream.

LOU: I've decided that's second-rate. What you need is a *Pesaḥ* house. I also start thinking about *Pesaḥ* the day after *Purim.* I generally think of finding some new *midrashim* (commentaries) that I can discuss, finding some new twist to keep people's interest up, and trying to figure out a way to finish the Seder before eleven o'clock.

JUDY: I have the feeling he tries to make it last as long as he can.

LOU: I also think about the "Super-Seder", that's the one where all the people are semi-observant or know a little bit about it, and we can do a lot more with it. The other Seder you also have to have, is where the rest of the family comes, and you kind of *shlep* them through it.

Miriam Prum

Miriam Prum is a single woman facing and meeting the challenges of making Pesaḥ for herself, her family and her friends. A Jewish community professional, Miriam was born in Mexico City to a traditional, very European family in which Seder was an important, but male-oriented experience. Today, as a well-educated, liberated and highly observant Jew, Miriam has developed her own style of religious practice which she shares in two Sedarim, one for family and one for friends.

Miriam approaches Passover with tremendous energy and resolve. Recognizing that it's hardly easy to "make Pesaḥ" by oneself, she nevertheless throws herself into the holiday with total dedication. Surrounding herself with a close community of friends, both married and single, Miriam has discovered that being single need not be an obstacle to a full and meaningful Passover experience.

MIRIAM: Last year in the small Seder I had with my friends, it was wonderful. And it really worked very, very well.

At the "friends'-Seder" the Four Questions are usually sort of a joke—Okay, who's the youngest?" I think last year I was the youngest, so I did it. Sometimes we all do it together. It really depends on whether the youngest gets embarrassed about being the youngest....

My family tradition was that my grandfather handed the pieces of *afikomen* to all of us kids and the kids were supposed to hide it from him. At my "friends'-Seder" it goes the opposite where I or whoever does *afikomen* hides the *afikomen*. Usually, they try to steal it at some point....

Five years ago I started insisting on having the "family-Seder" because I really wanted my nephews and nieces to be at a Seder that was meaningful to them. And so I really started having the Seder and tried to focus the Seder around them. One of the things I love to bring to my Seder is from an issue of *Chicken Soup*, the song "Take Me Out to the Ball Game." I mean, my nephews love it. It's become a family tradition at *Pesaḥ*....

I think the hardest part is trying to do it all myself. And by all, I mean not just doing all of the cleaning and all of the cooking, but also all of the preparation for the Seder—and to read the *Haggadah* and read the commentaries and start formulating some of my own questions that I want to raise at the Seder.

Sometimes, I get so wrapped up in just taking care of the cleaning and cooking that I run out of strength by the time it's time to deal with the substance of the Seder...

Take Us Out of Egypt

A seasonal Seder song

(To the tune of: "Take Me Out To The Ball Game")

Take us out of Egypt
Free us from slavery.
Bake us some *matzot* in a haste.
Don't worry about flavor—
Give no thought to taste.
Oh, it's rush, rush, rush to the Reed Sea,
If we don't cross, it's a shame!
It's Ten Plagues down and you're out,
At the *Pesaḥ* History Game!

Linda, Lorin, Yoni and Ari Fife

Lorin and Linda Fife are an intermarried couple. Lorin comes from a very eclectic religious background which includes Mormon grandparents, a Methodist father, and a mother who belonged to the Christian Science Church. Lorin himself went to a Presbyterian Sunday School as a child. Having discovered an affinity for Judaism while reading a book on comparative religion when a Navy officer on his way to Vietnam, Loren's interest in Judaism intensified while dating Linda. Eventually, Lorin converted to Judaism and married Linda. Together they are building a Jewish family with sons Yoni, 8, and Ari, 4.

Linda has recently inherited the job of making Pesaḥ from her mother, and now the family Seder is held in her home. With two young children, the Fife Seder is very much a young family affair, filled with songs brought home from nursery and day school, enhanced by creative activities discovered by Linda, a Holiday Workshop Series teacher.

Last year, after an extended period of struggling over what holidays would be celebrated where, Lorin's parents attended Seder at his home for the first time. They found their son an accomplished, confident Jew, comfortable with his role as leader of an elaborate ritual. Although the religious differences between child and parents continue, Lorin's father and mother appreciated the very beautiful and meaningful ceremony of the Seder as celebrated by their son's family and friends.

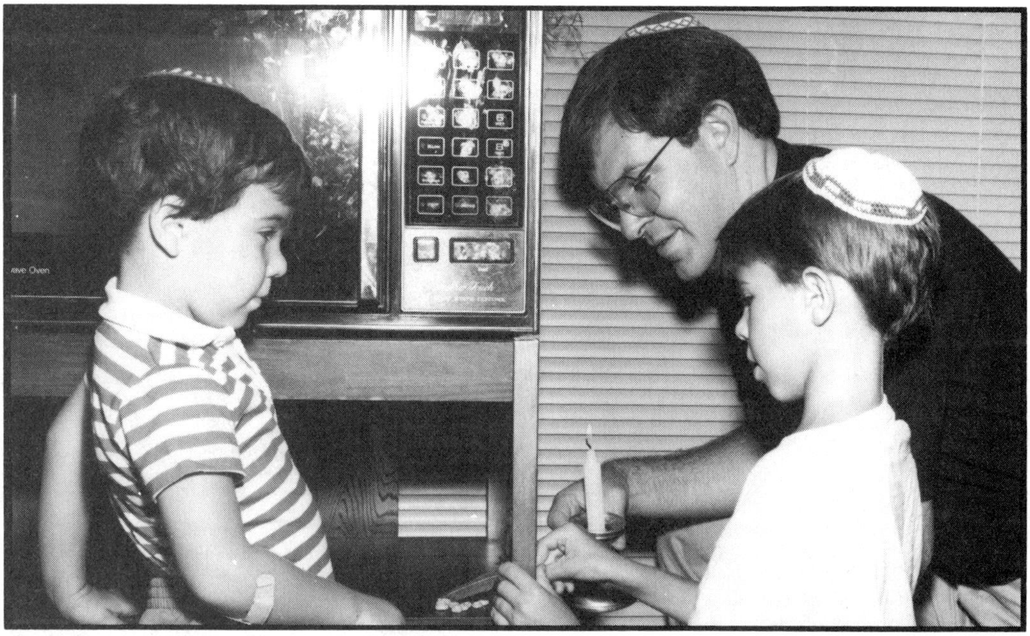

LINDA: My earliest memory of *Pesaḥ* is Seder at my parent's house. I remember we used to take in the Ping Pong table, and that's what people would sit around. We didn't change dishes... I remember my mother closed off certain parts of the cabinets. And I remember we never ate bread. But, we did have a fairly traditional Seder.

LORIN: I'm trying to think of the first Seder I attended. I guess it was right after we were first married. When we decided to make a Seder for ourselves, I did basically the same thing I had seen my father-in-law do for a number of times. I guess I learned something about Passover when I converted, but most of what I know came from observing someone else do it. After you've participated in a couple of Seders then, you know, you begin to have ideas about what you like—what works, what doesn't work. And, it helps to read a little about it, to develop your own knowledge about it.

LINDA: We've both found that as you grow, your needs change, and what you want out of a Seder changes, too. It's sort of an evolutionary process.

LORIN: This year, Yoni helped a lot. We sat next to each other at the Seder and he helped coordinate things. I would do the Hebrew and he would do the English. I think it's important for the kids to get involved. The more they do, the more they understand. The more they understand, the more comfortable they are.

Keren and John Goldberg

When faced with the task of hosting a Passover Seder for the first time as a single parent, Keren Goldberg turned to her friend, Melinda, who had hosted her for the past ten Sedarim. With Melinda's help, Seder with her 14-year-old son John and sixteen friends and relatives became a manageable, wonderful experience—even if the matzah balls were as hard as rocks!

Keren grew up in a Reform congregation which her father served as President. While her father expressed his Jewish commitment through communal leadership, Keren's mother provided the home with holiday celebrations throughout the year. Keren's former husband was not religious and, in the years they were married, they only attempted one Seder experience. Thus, when it came time to make Pesaḥ for herself and John, Keren sought out advice and help from her many friends with whom she had celebrated Jewish holidays in the years since her divorce.

An energetic arts administrator, Keren still glows with the memories of John's recent Bar Mitzvah, but wonders how she can maintain the warm Jewish feelings she and John have shared, together and with their friends, at Passover time.

KEREN: There are certain Jewish holidays that I have celebrated with the same friends for the last 10 or 11 years—every year. Usually, she does the Passover Seder and I do *Yom Kippur*. We decided for some reason that one particular year we would switch. I would do the Passover and she would do the *Yom Kippur*. I had done a Passover Seder before, so this wasn't my first time, but it was the first time I had done it in probably ten years.

There were seventeen of us. Actually, we were going to have less until about four days before Passover when the most amazing thing happened. All of a sudden I got a phone call from a man who is Israeli and who is in a family that I had met when I was in Mexico the summer before. We had met in the museum and just spontaneously developed this relationship. They said, "Guess what? We're here in Los Angeles and the whole family is here." And,

I said, "Well, you'll have to come to Seder." So they said, "We would love to." And four of them joined us. They said it was their first Passover in the 'diasporate.' That was how they described it.

JOHN: I cooked. I helped with the *matzah* balls. We had got the formulas for the different recipes mixed up and it was tough. They were terrible, like a rock.

KEREN: What happend to the *matzah* balls is that I didn't turn to my family, and get on the phone and say, "How do you make *matzah* balls?" I decided no, no, no—just to know, somehow there was sort of a genetic message inside. I was supposed to really know naturally how to make *matzah* balls, even though I'd never made them before in my life. So, you know, we added a little of this, a little of that. What could go wrong? I'd eaten *matzah* balls all my life, right? Right. And John was there, working away for hours. I was sure that we had a good thing going there, and we waited for that moment when the *matzah* ball soup was brought to everybody and we sat down and I waited for the first moments of...

JOHN: "Ooh" and "Ahh."

KEREN: ...first moments of "ooh" and "ahh." And there was a strange silence...

JOHN: (Laughter)

KEREN: ...and then I knew there was trouble. Even though people, of course, were very hungry.

KEREN: I think whether John makes a Passover Seder or not will be based a lot on the circumstances of his life between now and his mid-twenties. Because I think it depends on what the experience of Confirmation will be like for him. And it will also depend on the people that he becomes friends with during this critical period of his life, and especially the young women that he's around.

JOHN: Right.

KEREN: I would like him to do a Passover. I would like him to raise his children Jewish. I'd like him to be involved in something in his life that was Jewish. I'd like him to feel good about the fact that he's Jewish and proud of it, and I think that's harder and harder.

Marlene, Barry, Mark, Brad and Michael Horwitz

The Horwitz's are an all-American modern family that represents a link in the chain of Jewish tradition. Having moved from their birthplace in Chicago, Illinois, Barry and Marlene became active members of a major Conservative synagogue in the Los Angeles area, Valley Beth Shalom, with the intention of giving their three boys a good Jewish education. Little did they realize that their own observance and commitment to Jewish life would far exceed anything they ever dreamed of when they were teenagers in the Midwest.

Both active members of the Jewish community, Barry and Marlene have created a home filled with Jewish expression. Since both sets of parents moved from Chicago to live near them, their Passover Seder has become a three-generation affair. Mark, 20, is a senior at the University of California, Berkeley, and is feeling his way as a young Jewish adult in the 80's. Brad, 16, is an active leader in United Synagogue Youth, and Michael, 11, is a precocious Jewish day school student. Marlene is a para-rabbinic counselor at the temple, her mother, Eve Clapick, is a major force in the Women's League chapter, and Barry serves on the Board of Camp Ramah in California.

We interviewed all three generations of Horwitzes about their Seder experiences through the years. It became quite clear that their Seder has evolved into a ceremony which has improved and deepened from generation to generation.

EVE: Oh, my father used to conduct the Seder with such meaning. As kids, it seemed like we'd wait forever for dinner. We'd sit there and giggle, you know. And all he had to do was look at you. He didn't have to say anything.

We always did the Seder in Hebrew, no English at all. We didn't understand the Hebrew, but when he'd sing the songs, we would sing along with him. Certain melodies I'd even like to sing today, but the melodies now are entirely different.

We held the Seder at my parent's home for 40 years. When my mother died, the Seder was held at the home of my oldest and youngest sisters who never married—my father went to live there. They had an extremely kosher home. After my father died, then my husband Hy would run the Seder, but we still had it at Pearl and Sophie's.

BARRY: I remember the Seders at Sophie and Pearl's house when I was dating Marlene. That was in 1960. I'll never forget those Seders—there was no room to breathe! They had an apartment. You couldn't move the chairs forward or backward or sideways, and there were always 8 billion people...

MARLENE: That went on until 1974 when we moved to California. We started making Seders as soon as we got here.

EVE: And when we moved out, we joined their Seder.

MARLENE: The special part of Seder for me is having the family together. This year, both my brothers and sisters-in-law and all of my nieces and nephews and Barry's sister and her son and all of our parents were together. You see your family around the table, you see how the kids have gotten bigger...I really felt very good this year that we had the whole family around the table.

The Art of Jewish Living: The Passover Seder is designed to give you the skills and understandings to "tell the story" of Passover at your Seder in a way that is meaningful, beautiful, and enjoyable. We will teach you the structure of the Seder and the basic contents of the *Haggadah*, including the major Hebrew and Aramaic prayers, and offer advice on how to conduct the Seder in a fashion that involves those around the table. You will learn the meaning of the *Haggadah* texts and the precise method of conducting the ritual movements. You will learn how to edit your *Haggadah* and plan a Seder experience that will be participatory for all. You will learn how to prepare your home for the holiday and how to create family traditions that may last for generations. Finally, you will learn how to personalize your Seder ceremony so that it reflects both the tradition and your own interpretation of it.

2

סֵדֶר שֶׁל פֶּסַח

SEDER SHEL PESAḤ THE PASSOVER SEDER

I grew up with what today would probably be considered a fairly traditional Seder. There were differences, though. For instance, when *Ha Laḥma Anya* was said, there were immediately discussions as to whether this applied to all people or just to Jews. The whole *Haggadah* was read in Hebrew, but we would go around the room and talk about it...

...When I was 13 or 14, my parents, in what was a radical move, started inviting some non-Jews on a regular basis, some friends of theirs. My grandfather wasn't very happy about it, but my parents really held their ground and just told him, "You don't have to come if you don't feel comfortable." He came, and he sat, and we had the people we invited, who were often really stimulating to talk to and had things to say at a Seder, and really kind of opened it up...

Later, when I lived in Northern California, I was invited to some friends' house in San Francisco. A strange thing happened. I kind of took over the Seder. I didn't know that was going to happen. I had no idea. It was a period of time when I was probably at my lowest point of Jewish observance. Afterwards, the people who invited me said, "I'm sorry you have plans tomorrow night. We would really like you to come back."
Then I understood that the Passover Seder probably had the greatest impact on me of anything we did.

Jerry Weber

The Seder can perhaps best be described as a "talk-feast." Conducted around a table laden with the bounty of the earth, it is people spending a leisurely evening engaged in good talk and good food. For the rabbis who formalized its procedures, Seder was the pre-eminent vehicle of cultural transmission from one generation to the next. Long before printed books and formal schools, the yearly Seder night transformed every Jewish home into a classroom.

This remains true today. Nearly ninety percent of North American Jews attend a Passover Seder. And, while less than fifty percent of Jewish children are currently enrolled in any form of Jewish education, most of them have a yearly Seder experience. Seder night is perhaps the most potentially powerful opportunity for Jewish education we have.

What makes the Seder such a marvelous Jewish teaching opportunity?

1. **The Setting.**
   The Seder is traditionally conducted in the home, the foundation for all Jewish education. Research has clearly demonstrated that the family is the single factor with the greatest influence on Jewish adult religious identification. The Seder is the Jewish family-based religious experience *par excellence.*
2. **The Teachers.**
   The Jewish tradition has always seen the nurture and education of children as a parental responsibility. The Mishnah assumes that a father will circumcise his own son, a "hands-on" entering of a child into the Covenant. Likewise, it was assumed that parents would directly provide their children with a formal Jewish education. It was assumed that parents would sit and study with their children, and do far more than just drive carpool and help with homework. Only if the parents lacked Jewish knowledge themselves was it permitted to hire a professional to fulfill their responsibility.

   The Seder puts Jewish teaching back into the hands of the parents. We live in an era when most Jewish parents have abdicated this responsibility. We depend on the synagogue or religious school to teach our children what it means and how to be Jews. The Seder returns this power to parents, creating the setting and structure for them to "tell your children on that day, saying, 'It is because of what God did for me, when I went free out of Egypt.'"

   There are other teachers at the Seder as well. Family members, guests, even the children themselves all have teaching roles during the ceremony. One of the secrets of the power of the Seder is that everyone at the table is both teacher and student.
3. **The Lesson Plan.**
   The Seder even offers a sure-fire lesson plan, proven effective in millions of Jewish "Seder-classrooms" over thousands of years. It is called the *Haggadah.* This remarkable script provides the words of instruction, the way to perform the learning experiences, and the basic structure of the entire evening. Like any good lesson plan, this one is adaptable to individual needs and

circumstances. In the hands of a good teacher (Seder leader), the lesson comes alive to reach its goal of telling the story.

The job of the "good teacher" is to learn about the lesson plan, the *Haggadah*—to understand its contents, to become comfortable with its structure, and ultimately, to be able to edit it in a way that makes sense for his/her "students," the family and guests at the Seder. One of the major goals of this book is to help you do just that. And we begin by walking through the *Haggadah* in order to get a broad overview of the entire experience.

A TALK-FEAST IN 4 ACTS

One person's logical sequence is another person's chaos. One generation's obvious associations are another generation's random groupings.

Seder means order. The tradition understands the Passover table ritual as a fixed progression, 15 steps, a logical unfolding of the single most important Jewish lesson from the retelling of the single most significant Jewish experience. Yet, that logic, that progression, and that process are not at all obvious to the untrained.

As a child, I recall sitting at the Passover table in rapt attention—for about twenty minutes—or until the Four Questions had been asked. At some point during the Four Sons, my mind would begin to wander. By the time we were in the middle of the *Maggid*, with uncles and guests reciting what were to them meaningless paragraphs about the Israelites in Egypt who were alternately "few in number" and "numerous," "great and mighty" and "oppressed," I would begin flipping through the *Haggadah* to look at the pictures or to try to guess how long it would be until all the talking was over. A sense of relief would come with the popular singing of "*Dayyenu*" as I counted the pages until the meal, knowing full well that there was a good chance the intervening texts would be mostly skipped.

Most of the people at our *Sedarim* had at best only a vague understanding of the *Haggadah*'s structure. For them, as for me until I studied it in college, the *Haggadah* was a seemingly endless series of strange texts, trying to tell a story, but in ways which often seemed disjointed. It was no wonder that the attention span of the adults, let alone that of the children, was severely tested as we plowed through the *Haggadah*. It perked up only when familiar tunes or well-known passages were reached. Inevitably, as the evening wore on, someone would rather loudly drop the hint, "When do we eat?"

I suspect—in fact, I know—that my childhood experiences were not unique. Even without fully understanding the structure and sequence of the Seder, I experienced it as a successful, functional, learning experience. Even when my mind wandered, songs, activities, foods, and rituals drew me back into the Seder experience. This is its true genius.

In actuality, the *Pesaḥ* Seder is one of the most carefully constructed learning experiences ever created. In an amazing combination of aural and tactile learning tasks, the Seder has something for everybody—drink, food, symbols, prayers, songs, stories, philosophy, text study, simulations, ritual actions—all designed with one overriding goal: to take each person at the Seder table back to Egypt, to re-enact the dramatic Exodus story, to make each one of us feel as if she or he had actually been redeemed from *Mitzrayim*.

AN OUTLINE

The *Pesaḥ* Seder is a talk-feast in four acts. Four is an all-important number in understanding the *Haggadah*. There are Four Cups of Wine, Four Questions, Four Children, Four Verses in the Telling, and so on. If we view the Seder as a kind of dramatic talk-feast, the four acts represent a way to look at the *Haggadah* in its broadest form. They are:

ACT I: THE BEGINNING

In the first act, the scene is set. The Seder as talk-feast is introduced as it quickly becomes clear that at this table there will be not just food, but prayer, ritual, and song as well.

THE PROLOGUE: Even before the Seder begins, there are a number of activities which create the setting. A production of this magnitude cannot be staged without adequate preparation. Formal preparations include ridding the house of *ḥametz*, "*kashering*" the kitchen for Passover, setting the Seder table, and preparing the meal.

HADLAKAT NEROT (CANDLE LIGHTING): Before the Seder begins, the *Yom Tov* (Festival) candles are lit, signifying the beginning of the holiday.

KADESH, URḤATZ: We recite or sing an ancient mnemonic device, "*Kadesh, Urḥatz*," a listing of the fifteen steps of the order of the Seder service, a kind of "advance organizer" for the ceremony to come.

SCENE 1: ***KADESH*** (THE FIRST CUP OF WINE): The Festival *Kiddush* is chanted, praising God who sanctifies the people Israel and the Festival seasons, and thanking Him for enabling us to reach this time of celebration.

SCENE 2: ***URḤATZ*** (WASH HANDS): We wash hands as if preparing to eat, but without reciting a blessing.

SCENE 3: ***KARPAS*** (APPETIZER): A green vegetable, symbol of spring, is dipped in salt water, a reminder of the tears of our ancestors in Egypt. It is a kind of historic appetizer.

SCENE 4: ***YAḤATZ*** (BREAK THE MIDDLE MATZAH): The *matzah* is introduced silently. We break the middle *matzah* in order to hide one portion as the *afikomen*, the "dessert" of our meal, a symbol of the redemption yet to come.

CURTAIN: ***HA LAḤMA ANYA*** (INVITATION): We uncover the *matzot*, calling them the "bread of affliction," for as we are about to begin our story, our ancestors are enslaved in Egypt. We invite all who are hungry or needy to join in our *Pesaḥ* service. As Act I closes, we acknowledge our slavery, but hope for our freedom.

ACT II: MAGGID (THE TELLINGS)

Act II is the heart of the Seder experience. We tell the story of our Exodus from slavery to freedom four ways, in four different tellings. Each telling begins with a *Question*, to which an *Answer* is given, and for which we *Praise* God, the Hero of our story.

SCENE 1: **THE FIRST TELLING:** The *First Telling* begins with the famous Four Questions, traditionally asked by the youngest member of the Seder party. The answer, which is to begin with the degradation of our people and end with the glory of redemption, tells the story in one brilliant, concise sentence: "We were slaves to Pharoah in *Mitzrayim*, but *Adonai* our God brought us forth with a mighty hand and with an outstretched arm." But, this story deserves more than a one-sentence summary, so, we have three more versions to come. God is deserving of praise which we pronounce four times.

SCENE 2: **THE SECOND TELLING:** The *Second Telling* begins with the questions of the Four Children. Here, the *Haggadah* teaches us that to tell the story well, we must tell it differently to different types of learners. Although the questions are different, they all relate to the same central query: "What is this Passover service all about?" The answer in this telling goes back even earlier in Jewish history, back to our idol-worshipping roots. Yet, we recall the promise God made to Abraham to make his descendents a great nation. We praise God who kept His promise then and keeps His Covenant with us alive to this day.

SCENE 3: **THE THIRD TELLING:** The *Third Telling* offers the learner the core story of the Exodus as related in four verses from Deuteronomy. By exploring the meaning of these words, we embellish the answer, we flesh out the story of our liberation. The climax of this story is the awe-full series of Ten Plagues which God brought upon Egypt, convincing Pharoah to let the people go. We then praise God Who, if He had performed only this one act of kindness, "*Dayyenu*"—it would have been enough!

SCENE 4: **THE FOURTH TELLING:** The *Fourth Telling* returns to concrete symbols with questions about the *Pesaḥ*, *Matzah*, and *Maror*, the central symbols on the Seder table. The specific questions are answered, but once again, the key question is "Why do we do this ritual? Why do we tell this story?" The answer is directed to each person, individually: "Because in each generation, every individual should feel as if he or she had actually been redeemed from *Mitzrayim*." We are redeemed and therefore, we acclaim God with a new song, *Halleluyah*, and we praise *Adonai*, Redeemer of Israel.

CURTAIN: KOS SHEINI (THE SECOND CUP OF WINE): Act II comes to a close with the sanctification of the Second Cup of Wine, a reminder of God's promise to deliver us. We have told the Exodus story four times, we have relived the slavery and the liberation from bondage. We celebrate our redemption with a cup of wine.

ACT III—THE FEAST

The third act of the talk-feast is the feast itself. As with all Jewish holiday meals, there are ritual actions before and after the meal. On *Pesaḥ*, some of these rituals are common to any Jewish meal (washing hands, *Motzi, Birkat ha-Mazon*), while others are specific to the Passover celebration (*Maror, Korekh, Tzafun*). The importance of these rituals is to underscore the fact that this is no ordinary meal. In fact, it is no ordinary Festival meal. It is the *Pesaḥ* feast which we reenact today as our ancestors did on that fateful night in Egypt. To some observers, this is the climax of the Seder itself; we eat the *Matzah*, the *Maror*, and the *Korekh*-substitute for the paschal sacrifice, just as the Israelites did on the eve of the Exodus.

SCENE 1: **PREPARE TO EAT**

We actually began the preparation for the meal at the very beginning of the Seder with the *Kiddush*. Then, we washed without a blessing and ate an appetizer, the *Karpas*. Now, we continue the preliminaries to the feast by performing four ritual acts:

> ***ROḤTZAH***—we wash our hands and recite the blessing for this act which precedes the breaking of bread at every Jewish meal.
>
> ***MOTZI/MATZAH***—we praise God, first for the general blessing of bringing forth bread from the earth, and then for the specific blessing of *matzah*, the bread of freedom.
>
> ***MAROR***—we eat the bitter herbs, symbol of our former slavery.
>
> ***KOREKH***—we bind the *matzah* and *maror* together, just as Rabbi Hillel did at his Seder nearly 2,000 years ago, as a reminder of the paschal offering on Passover night.

SCENE 2: ***SHULḤAN OREKH*** (SET THE TABLE): The festive meal is eaten.

SCENE 3: ***TZAFUN*** (DESSERT): We find or redeem that which is "*tzafun*"—hidden, the *afikomen*. It is our dessert, the last morsel of food eaten at the Seder, a symbol of redemption.

SCENE 4: ***BAREKH*** (BLESSINGS AFTER FOOD): We praise God for providing us food, the Promised Land, the Feast of Unleavened Bread, Jerusalem, and all the goodness we have in our lives.

CURTAIN: ***KOS SH'LISHI*** (THE THIRD CUP OF WINE): The meal concludes with the Third Cup of Wine, another reminder of God's promise of redemption.

ACT IV: REDEMPTION

We have told the story of the Exodus. We have eaten the symbolic foods and the festive meal. Now, we celebrate our redemption, with praise for God the Redeemer and prayers for our ultimate redemption in Messianic times. We sing songs of praise, songs of joy, we recognize the harvest season, and we conclude with the final cup of wine and the prayer for our return to Jerusalem.

SCENE 1: ***SHFOKH ḤAMATKHA*** ("POUR OUT YOUR ANGER")
ELIYAHU HA-NAVI (ELIJAH THE PROPHET):

The fourth and final act begins on a controversial note. *Shfokh Ḥamatkha* is a late addition to the *Haggadah*, a remembrance of those enemies of religious freedom who have made the Jewish people their particular target. Some have set aside this time as a moment to remember the Holocaust, to recognize the plight of our brothers and sisters still subject to modern Pharoahs around the world, to celebrate the dawn of redemption in our day—the state of Israel. The redemption theme is then sounded by the lilting, hopeful strains of "*Eliyahu ha-Navi*," welcoming to the table Elijah the Prophet, harbinger of the Messiah.

SCENE 2: ***HALLEL*** (SONGS OF PRAISE) The recitation of *Hallel*, which began before the meal with *Halleluyah*, now continues with the remaining psalms of praise for God who redeems the people Israel.

SCENE 3: ***Z'MIROT*** (SONGS) With the formal requirements of the Seder completed, the mood turns even more festive with the singing of *Z'mirot*, songs which celebrate our rejoicing.

SCENE 4: ***SEFIRAT HA-OMER*** (COUNTING OF THE OMER) At the second Seder, we begin the forty-nine day countdown to the festival of *Shavuot*, the end of the spring harvest and the time marking the giving of the Torah at Mount Sinai. The *omer*, a sheaf of grain, is symbolically counted daily beginning tonight.

CURTAIN: ***KOS R'VI'I*** (THE FOURTH CUP OF WINE)
NIRTZAH (ACCEPTANCE)

The Seder now draws to a conclusion, marked by the Fourth Cup of Wine and a prayer that our Seder be accepted and the promise of our redemption be fulfilled. We end with the messianic hope spoken by generations of Jews for millenia—"Next Year In Jerusalem!"

The Historical Evolution of the Seder Experience

To fully understand how a Seder works, and to realize the full potential of your own family Seder, we need to examine both its structure and its history. In doing so, we can uncover three (or four) interlocking layers of structure. Once we understand their individual logic and structure, the overall Seder process becomes quite clear.

The First Passover. The Torah (Exodus 12:1-20) is very clear about the instructions given to *B'nai Yisrael* for the observance of the first Passover, *Pesaḥ Mitzrayim*, the Seder held during their last night as Pharaoh's slaves. Each family was to take a lamb, slaughter it at sunset, and use its blood to mark the two doorposts of the house. The meat, which had to be completely consumed that night, was to be roasted and then served with *matzah*—unleavened bread—and *maror*—bitter herbs. The Torah is very specific:

> This is how you should eat it:
> with your loins girded,
> your sandals on your feet,
> and your walking stick in your hand.
> And you shall eat it hastily—
> it is a *Pesaḥ* offering.

The first Seder had three key elements: the *Pesaḥ* offering, *matzah* and *maror*. In our Seder, at the very end of the *Maggid* section, in the last retelling of the Exodus saga, we come to Rabban Gamliel:

> Rabban Gamliel would say: "Those who have not explained three things during the Seder have not fulfilled their obligation. These three things are: the *Pesaḥ* offering, *matzah* and *maror*."

This first Seder was an act of protection. The blood from the lamb became the marking which protected Jewish homes. On the eve of the Exodus, the families of Israel stood dressed, walking sticks in hand, ready to leave. It was an event on the edge. It also set a direction for the next forty years, beginning a process of trusting God to be the Redeemer of the Jewish people. To our day, despite myriad changes and additions, the Seder remains rooted in the anticipation of that night—it continues to be an intertwining of history and ritual. This embryonic Seder of *Pesaḥ*, *matzah*, and *maror* still sits at the core of our present Seder.

At the end of this passage describing the instructions for the first *Pesaḥ* comes the *mitzvah* of annually observing *Pesaḥ*:

> This day shall be to you one of memory;
> you shall celebrate it eternally as a festival.
> Seven days you shall eat unleavened bread;
> on the very first day you shall remove leaven from your house…
> You shall observe the Feast of Unleavened Bread,
> for on this very day I brought your ranks out of the land of Egypt…
> And when your children ask you,
> "What do you mean by this rite?"

you shall say,
"It is the *Pesaḥ* offering to *Adonai*
because God passed over the houses of *B'nai Yisrael* in Egypt,
when God killed the Egyptians, but saved our families."

That night's history, ritual, and experience became part of the annual cycle of the Jewish year. It set the pattern for all Jewish celebrations, for as families recall and relive our history, we transmit our core values and beliefs to our children.

This same lesson is found in Rabban Gamliel's Seder (within our *Haggadah*), "*In each generation, every individual should feel as though he or she had actually been redeemed from Mitzrayim.*" This lesson is then supported with the biblical verse: "You shall tell your children on that day, saying, 'It is because of what *Adonai* did for me when I went free out of *Mitzrayim*.'" (Exodus 13:8)

Pesaḥ in the Land of Israel. *Pesaḥ* was not observed in the wilderness. During those forty years, the ritual lay in wait. Upon entering the Land of Israel, those born during the 40 years of wandering were circumcised. Then they were eligible to eat from the *Pesaḥ* sacrifice. The book of Joshua tells us (5:10-12):

While camped at Gilgal, in the plains of Jericho
B'nai Yisrael offered the *Pesaḥ*-offering
on the fourteenth day of the month, at sunset.
On the day after the *Pesaḥ*-offering,
on that very day,
they ate from the produce of The Land,
matzah and parched grain.
On the day after (the *Pesaḥ*-offering)
when they ate from the produce of The Land,
the *manna* ended.
B'nai Yisrael got no more *manna*;
that year they ate of the yield of the Land of Canaan.

The Exodus was over. It ended, as it had begun, with the celebration of a *Pesaḥ* Seder. What began as a watchnight, a night of fear and anticipation, ended in a celebration, a night of thanksgiving and further anticipation. The first *Pesaḥ* created 40 years of dependence; the second Seder at Gilgal established a new independence.

From the time *B'nai Yisrael* entered the Land of Israel, the observance of the *Pesaḥ*-offering became a national ceremony, with the service and cooking performed by the *Kohanim*, the priests. We assume, though the Torah is silent on the issue, that it was a regular practice as long as the Temple was in existence. In the book of Second Chronicles (30:21-22) we find a description of the *Pesaḥ* celebration of King Hezekiah:

B'nai Yisrael who were in Jerusalem
kept the Feast of *Matzah* seven days,
with great rejoicing;
The Levites and the *Kohanim*

> *praising Adonai* daily
> with powerful instruments for the Lord.

It seems that by the time the ritual in the Temple had been fully developed, a fourth element, the singing of hymns of praise—*Hallel*—had been added to this core Seder. In *Jubilees*, an extra-biblical book from this period, the eating of the *Pesaḥ*-offering and the singing of hymns of praise is connected to the drinking of wine. Josephus, the Jewish historian who recorded the wars with the Romans, adds to our understanding. In *Wars* 6:423-4, we are given this description:

> On the feast called Passover, at which they sacrificed from the ninth to the eleventh hour, a *fellowship-group* of not more than ten persons gathers around each sacrifice (*because feasting alone was not permitted*), while the companies often included as many as twenty.

Erev Pesaḥ was a major event in Temple times. Josephus tells us that 255,600 lambs were sacrificed, feeding 2,700,000 people. It was a rather large gathering. Even when tempered by the numbers given in the Bible, (II Chronicles, 30) we are still dealing with the cooking and serving of 2,000 bullocks and 17,000 lambs. Even on this smaller scale, this was no minor pageant. Yet, in contradistinction to other national events, the spirit of small family-like gatherings described at the original *Pesaḥ* in Egypt was retained. It is this familiar setting which became the core of the rabbinic Seder, and insured its survival.

The Rabbis' Seder. In chapter ten of the Mishnah (the Oral Law developed from biblical times which was codified around 200 C.E.) on *Pesaḥ*, we are taught the primal structure of the rabbinic Seder. At its heart are four elements: *Pesaḥ*, *Matzah*, *Maror* and *Hallel* (Songs of Praise).

> Rabban Gamliel would say: "Those who have not explained three things during the Seder have not fulfilled their obligation.
> These three things are: the *Pesaḥ* offering, *matzah* and *maror*."
> *Pesaḥ*—because the Lord passed over the houses of our ancestors in Egypt.
> *Maror*—because the Egyptians embittered the lives of our ancestors in Egypt.
> *Matzah*—because they were *redeemed*.
>
> Therefore we are obligated to give thanks, to praise, to glorify, to crown, to exalt, to elevate the One who did for us all these miracles and took us out of slavery into freedom, And let us say before that One, *Halleluyah* (Psalms 113:1ff)
>
> (*Shabbat* 10:5)

The Seder, as we know it, is essentially the creation of the same rabbis who created the Talmud, the *Midrash*, the Siddur, and most of what we know as modern Judaism. They lived in an era which experienced its own kind of holocaust. In the conflicts with the Roman Empire, thousands were killed, the Temple was destroyed; everything that had served as the core and the anchor of Jewish life was gone. In order to save Jewish life, it was necessary to reinvent every process and every ritual. In this transformation, prayer replaced sacrifice, the embryonic synagogue grew to replace the Temple, allegiance to the Torah and its laws replaced participation in a nation-state, and our strange mixture of ethnicity, ideology, faith, and legal strictures came to replace citizenship as the core of Jewish identity. While being rooted in the past, everything was reconceived and re-expressed. The *Pesaḥ* Seder is a classic example of this regeneration.

In recasting *Pesaḥ*'s opening pageant—the great public *Pesaḥ* offerings—into the Seder, two dramatic changes were necessary. First, with the prime setting—the Temple—gone, a new format had to be found. The center of *Pesaḥ* had always been the *Pesaḥ*-offering. Through this direct re-enactment of the last night in Egypt, memories easily became lessons about freedom and responsibilty. When the Temple was destroyed, it was no longer possible to sacrifice the *Pesaḥ* offering. Inspired by both common practice and by careful reading of the Torah, the rabbis returned the celebration to the home. An elaborate home-study, home-worship, home-eating experience was evolved to replace the public pageant.

Second, the meaning of *Pesaḥ* had to change. With the world in absolute chaos, with everything which had been significant destroyed, the simple Passover story needed interpretation. In its purest form, Passover was the story of how we slaves were given our own land. It was a classic folk tale, an oral tradition which explained "how things got to be the way they are." Having now lost that land (for the second time), the story of the Exodus evoked a sense of loss; it had become a source of pain and frustration. The Exodus now demanded new interpretation. No longer could *Pesaḥ* remain pure history. Instead, it became allegorical. Redemption, an old theme, took on new meaning. Beneath all the recollections there came a new understanding and a new hope: that which God had done, God could again do. This God makes and keeps promises. Having been redeemed from one Egypt, we could be assured that we would be redeemed from the next. The story of our ascent from slavery became more than the public pageant of a national celebration of independence; it grew into an affirmation of the possible, the wellspring of hope.

While the Seder was in formulation, Judaism was being subjected to high-pressure influence from Greek culture. Rabbinic Judaism evolved many of its own forms both as adaptions of and reactions against the Greek world. It is a common assumption that the Seder ritual grew out of the *symposia*, the elaborate talk-feasts held by the Greeks. In those evenings, wine, food, entertainment and dialogue were merged. While the Seder shares many of these elements, it is very much a rejection of the *symposia*'s self-indulgent values. The essence of the Seder is, in reality, the surrounding of the four primal Seder steps (*Pesaḥ Matzah*, *Maror* and *Hallel*) with the regiment of a ritual Jewish meal. All of these elements are woven together and made explicit by a *midrashic* exposition predicated on a close reading of selected portions of the biblical text.

The Seder shares a series of elements with an *Erev Shabbat* dinner: *Kiddush* (a *b'rakhah* [blessing] said over wine), a ritual hand-washing, a *b'rakhah* said over food eaten before any bread is eaten, *Motzi* (a *b'rakhah* said before eating bread) and *Birkat ha-Mazon* (the *b'rakhot* said after eating). In the Seder, each of these elements play a basic role as well as helping to establish or reveal portions of the Exodus saga. When they are put together with the elements of the Temple ritual, we have most of the Seder's fifteen steps.

The Seder begins with three steps: *Kiddush* introduces the holiday of *Pesaḥ* as sacred time. *Urḥatz*, a ritual washing of hands, prepares the participants for the experience which follows. *Karpas*, the third step, functions on two levels at once. It is paradigmatic of the Seder process. Overtly, *Karpas* is simply the eating of a vegetable (before the eating of any bread). Following basic rabbinic ritual procedure, a *b'rakhah* is said and the vegetable is eaten. However, something has been added—the dipping into salt water. It is an unusual act, one which formally prompts a question later in the Seder (number three out of four). It is also, however, a gesture which provokes immediate questions, questions which begin an associative process. The Seder provides no explanation of this unusual dipping ritual, but we need one. So, we search our memories. We build associations. We talk of the vegetable symbolizing spring and suggest that the salt water evokes the tears of suffering. By not explaining, the Seder forces us to explain. What we've done is make *midrash*. We've gathered information from other sources and applied it to formulate an explanation. The unclear ritual, a variation on a normal meal, has begun a process of questioning, recalling and explaining. This is the essence of the Seder. The progression of unclear rituals, of theme and variation on regular patterns, makes the meal a conversation.

The Core of the Rabbinic Seder. The true backbone of the rabbinic Seder can be found in the Torah. In the sixth chapter of Exodus we find a series of promises which God makes to Israel's family:

> I am the Lord
> I *will bring you out*
> from beneath the burdens of Egypt,
> I *will rescue you*
> from slavery to them,
> I *will redeem you*
> with an outstretched arm—with great judgments
> I *will take you* to Me as a people...

Here we find four promises, each another level of the liberation and redemption from Egypt. One verse later, we find a fifth promise.

> I *will bring you* into the land which I promised
> to give to Abraham, Isaac, and Jacob.

In the Mishnah, the first layer of the Talmud, the first rule given for the Seder involves the drinking of wine. We are taught:

> On the eve of *Pesaḥ*, from close to the time of *Minḥah*... (the afternoon prayer service), a person should not eat until after it gets dark.
> Even a poor person in Israel should not eat without reclining.
> And one should not drink less than four cups of wine, even if the funds come from public *tzedakah* (philanthropic) collections.

Pesaḥim 10:1

We are given no explanation of the four cups, though the remainder of chapter ten of Mishnah *Pesaḥim* does describe their function. The first is an opening sanctification, the *Kiddush*. The second is tied to the *Maggid* section of the Seder, and is used as a prop in the telling of the story. The third cup is part of the *Birkat ha-Mazon*, a regular feature of communal Jewish meals. The fourth cup is described in the Mishnah as "following *Hallel*," and forms the *Nirtzah*, the Seder's last formal step. These four cups provide another one of the Seder's frames, the first cup opening the Seder, the second concluding the telling of the Exodus saga, the third cup concluding the meal, and the fourth cup concluding the Seder.

When we search the *Gemarah*, the second layer of the Talmud, we find only a brief explanation:

> Said he (Raba) to him (R. Ḥanan):
> Our rabbis instituted four cups as symbols of freedom:
> let us perform a religious act with each.
>
> *Pesaḥim* 117b

From this passage we learn that the number four is intentional. We know that it has a symbolic purpose. And, we know that this symbolic intent provides a ritual framework. The *Gemarah* tells us no more. As with the dipping of the *Karpas*, we are left to search for explanation.

Over the years, various explanations have evolved: four cups to reflect the four kingdoms before the final redemption, (Daniel 7), four cups of punishment given to the evil, and four cups to match the four promises given to Israel in Exodus 6. It is this last explanation which has emerged as central. In two medieval codes of law, the *Shulḥan Arukh* (*Orekh Ḥayim* 481:1) and the *Mishneh Torah* (Laws of *Ḥametz* and *Matzah* 8:10) this explanation becomes the center of a legal question, the introduction of a fifth cup of wine to match the fifth promise, "I *will bring you* into the land."

In both those sources, the question is asked, "Should we pour and drink a fifth cup to match the fifth promise?" Rabbinic tradition provides no solution, so a compromise is introduced. A fifth cup is poured and not drunk. It is to serve as a symbol until the coming of the Messiah when all legal questions will be solved. The cup is left undrunk until Elijah the prophet returns to announce the beginning of the final redemption.

We have no way of knowing if the rabbis who organized the Seder really predicated the four-cup Seder framework on the four promises made in Exodus 6:6-7. Yet, the more one looks at the conjunction of biblical structures and the Seder's organization, the more it suggests that they did.

It really makes little difference to our perception of the *Pesaḥ* experience we have inherited. We know that our Seder is designed to be a spiritual journey. Every year we go on a trip from slavery to freedom. We do so through a progression of four cups we drink and one which we leave for Elijah. These cups and their accompanying rituals take us through God's four promises: we are brought out, rescued, redeemed, and taken as God's people. Yet, like the fifth cup (and like the freed Israelites facing forty years in the wilderness)—we wait. We are still in need of the fulfillment of the final promise, we are still waiting for the final redemption.

We have now come to understand most of the Seder's structure. An opening retelling of the *Pesaḥ* story is surrounded by two cups of wine and punctuated by *Karpas*, *Matzah*, *Maror* and *Pesaḥ*. The meal comes next, concluded by the finding of the *afikomen*, a Judaic reworking of the Greek pattern of after-dinner entertainment, and *Birkat ha-Mazon*. The third cup of wine, which concludes *Birkat Ha-mazon*, bridges the second half of the Seder centering on *Hallel* and other songs of praise. A final cup of wine concludes the Seder.

While all this seems logical and simple, we already know that rabbinic structures are quirky, filled with exceptions and variations which demand explanation. It is a literary style assimilated and adapted from the biblical text. The part of the Seder which seems most complex and most elliptical is the *Maggid*, the formal telling of the Seder story. While it contains some of the most famous portions of the Seder: the Four Questions, the Plagues, and *Dayyenu*, it also seems to be a chaotic assortment of diverse elements. Again, it is only by returning to the biblical text, and reading it with rabbinic eyes, that its arrangement becomes clear.

The rabbis noted these four biblical verses:

> *And when your children say to you:*
> "What does this service mean to you?"
> You should say to them:
> "It is the *Pesaḥ*-offering to God
> Who passed over the houses of The Children of Israel
> in Egypt when He struck down the Egyptians
> but saved our houses."
>
> Exodus 12:26-27

> *And you shall tell your son on that day*, saying:
> "It is because of that which the Lord did for me
> when I went out from Egypt."
>
> Exodus 13:8

> *And in the future when your child asks*, saying:
> "What is this?"
> You should say to him:
> "With a strong hand the Lord brought us out of Egypt
> from the house of slavery."
>
> Exodus 13:14

> In the future, *when your child asks you:*
> "What mean the testimonies, statutes, and laws
> which the Lord our God commanded you?
> You should say to your child:
> "We were Pharaoh's slaves in Egypt
> and the Lord brought us out of Egypt with a mighty hand…
>
> Deuteronomy 6:20-21

For them, the existence of four verses, each of which essentially says the same thing, was very problematic. In their view, God wrote the Torah, making it a perfect work. There should be no need to repeat, unless each repetition teaches us something new. Therefore, the rabbis were forced to conclude that each of these four different sets of instructions about teaching the *Pesaḥ* story had a different purpose. It was another time to make *midrash*. The rabbis quickly concluded that the Torah's purpose was to teach us that different children mandate different kinds of instruction. Those familiar with the Seder will quickly recognize that both this lesson, and these four questions, serve as the basis of the Four Children section of the *Maggid*, (though, as we shall see, the answers given in the Torah are not identical with those given in the *Haggadah*).

However, if we look closely at the entire *Maggid* section, we find an interesting pattern: four tellings of the *Pesaḥ* story, each with four elements: Four Questions, Four Children, Four Biblical Verses in the *Maggid*, and *Pesaḥ, Matzah, Maror*, plus a piece of *Hallel*. Most probably, the rabbis took the notion of four different ways of teaching very seriously, making it the core structure of the entire teaching portion of the Seder.

In Summary. Through our historical review of the Seder's evolution, we can begin to understand that the ceremony we know today is really a complex layering of simple structures. Like coral growing on a sunken vessel, its basic elements have grown and embroidered a basic core. At its heart are the three elements of *Pesaḥ Mitzrayim*, meshed with the songs of *Hallel* adapted from the Temple ritual. In transferring the *Pesaḥ* service from the Temple to the home, the rabbis surrounded these elements with the basic rituals of a formal religious meal: *Kiddush*, hand washing, a *b'rakhah* over vegetables preceding the eating of bread, *Motzi* and *Birkat ha-Mazon*.

Over these two elements was then spun a ***midrashic*** structure of rituals—some of which contain explanations—some of which demand explanations, texts and interpretations. All of these elaborations serve as echoes of the Torah's own interactive teaching style. Yet, the Seder's growth doesn't end here. The rabbinic Seder was again reworked in the Gaonic period. Portions were added to the text, to the ritual, and some reordering of the food elements was effected. In addition, the text and experience of the Seder has been constantly enriched by ongoing interpretation, individual creativity, and the growth of folk traditions. Seder night centers in the memory of the Jewish people's most formative experience, reexpressed by the rabbis in their search for ongoing survival and the final redemption. It speaks to our own search for freedom and redemption.

ACT ONE: THE BEGINNING

PROLOGUE: HADLAKAT NEROT
KADESH, URḤATZ

SCENE 1: **KADESH** (THE FIRST CUP OF WINE)
SCENE 2: **URḤATZ** (WASH HANDS)
SCENE 3: **KARPAS** (APPETIZER)
SCENE 4: **YAḤATZ** (BREAK THE MIDDLE MATZAH)

CURTAIN: **HA LAḤMA ANYA** (INVITATION)

As you might imagine, there is a significant amount of preparation to do before the actual Seder begins. There is the entire process of cleansing the house of *ḥametz*, culminating in the fascinating *Bedikat Ḥametz* ceremony, the steps in *kashering* the kitchen for the holiday, the setting of the table, the creation of the Seder plate, and so on. All of these steps will be discussed in detail later in the book. Suffice it to say that there is much to do. Let us begin with the Seder itself.

3

הַדְלָקַת נֵרוֹת

HADLAKAT NEROT
CANDLE LIGHTING

By means of that light which was created on the first day Adam was able to gaze and behold eternity from one end to the other.

Pesikta Rabbati 23:6

Moshe stretched out his hand over the heavens and there was gloomy darkness throughout all the land of Egypt, for three days.

A man could not see his brother, and a man could not arise from his spot for three days.

But for all the Children of Israel, there was light in their settlements.

Exodus 10:21-3
Translation from *Now These are the Names*,
Everett Fox

There are times when we need to be certain that "after" will be different than "before."

On the science fiction television show *Star Trek* they use a transporter. Instantaneously, one reality is shifted into another. Step into the transporter beam and things are immediately different. In the Jewish tradition we light candles. In blessing their beams, we recognize and invoke a transformation. We change our reality, making ordinary weekdays into sacred occasions. Candle lighting is the instant of transformation. With the lighting and blessing of candles, the holiness of Shabbat or a Festival becomes real. It becomes the new reality which we perceive and experience.

Candle kindling is a strange *mitzvah*. We use a *b'rakhah* formula which states, "who has sanctified us with His commandments and commanded us..." It is the formula used for all acts which the rabbinic tradition considered *mitzvot*—obligations. Yet, in searching the Torah, there is no command to kindle either Shabbat or Festival (*Yom Tov*) lights. Rather, it is a *mitzvah* which is considered *d'rabbanan*—a piece of rabbinic legislation, something passed on through the oral tradition and only later formalized as law.

When we search the Talmud, the basis and ruling for candle lighting is still somewhat obscure. The rabbis seem to take this obligation for granted, beginning their discussion not with, "Why do we light Shabbat or Festival lights?," but with "What kind of wicks, oils, and materials can be used for lighting these lights?" When we read further, we find very little material which explains why they are lit, and what we learn from doing it. Instead, we are given much in the way of "proper procedures."

> On *Erev Shabbat*, just before night,
> a person must say three things:
> Have the tithes been taken?
> Is the *Eiruv* prepared?
> Have the Sabbath lights been kindled?
> When it is doubtful whether it is night or not:
> it is too late to tithe,
> utensils may not be immersed,
> and the lights may not be kindled.
>
> *Shabbat* 34a

This Mishnah makes it clear that the kindling of Shabbat lights is something which must be done before the holiday begins. If there is any doubt about being in advance of the beginning of night, we must not light them. Any kindling of a flame during Shabbat would be an act of work and violation of the sanctity of the day. That is why candles are traditionally lit eighteen minutes before the actual beginning of evening and allowed to burn into the night.

In another portion of the Talmud, we are told that the Shabbat and Festival lights, unlike the Ḥanukkah lamp, must be kindled in the place where the meal is to be eaten. The implication is that unlike the Ḥanukkah lights which cannot be used for any practical purpose, these lights are designed to illuminate the dinner. It might seem logical, then, to think that these lights were designed to fulfill a practical rather than spiritual purpose. Often, the rabbis enact one law to prevent the breaking of a more stringent rule, a process they call *si'ag l'Torah*, "putting a fence around the Torah." In this case, lighting a light before sundown and placing it in the area where the meal is to be eaten serves to insure that other lamps aren't kindled during that evening's activities. However, other clues show us that Festival and Shabbat candles are more than a zone defense.

> On the eve of Shabbat, before sunset, they saw an old man holding two bundles of myrtle and running at twilight. "What are these for?" they asked him.
> "They are in honor of the Sabbath," he replied.
> "But shouldn't one be enough?,"
> One is for "Remember the Sabbath Day" (Exodus 20:8)
> and the other is for "Observe the Sabbath Day." (Deuteronomy 5:12)
>
> Said Rabbi Simon bar Yoḥai to his son,
> "See how precious the *mitzvot* are to Israel."
> This relaxed their minds.
>
> *Shabbat* 32b

While this passage concerns myrtles, the context of the *Gemorah* is that of Shabbat candles. Rashi explains: "The myrtle's fragrance is to beautify Shabbat and lend it cheer." The matching of the two branches with the two versions of the Shabbat command found in the two sets of the Ten Commandments is the same explanation applied to the Shabbat candles. For our purposes, this passage is one of many which suggest that the Festival and Shabbat candles have a proactive purpose, for they too, like the myrtle, are described as an act of honor.

Likewise, the act of candle lighting is connected to a spiritual process in other ways. We are told (*Shabbat* 23b) that one who lights candles regularly will have scholarly sons (who have seen the light). We are warned that a woman who does not light a candle (*ner*) may miscarry and lose the soul (*ner*) she is carrying. Finally, in the most revealing passage (*Shabbat* 22b), Rabbi Sheshet asks if we are lighting these Festival lights for God's sake. He answers: "God does not require light. During the forty years in the wilderness, Israel was only able to travel by God's light. The light is a testimony to humanity that God's light rests with Israel."

The kindling and blessing of candles is a rabbinic creation. It was part of the process of transferring Jewish religious life from public rituals in the Temple to ceremonies in the home. The Eternal Light, the Great Menorah, and the altar fires once symbolized God's presence—the closeness of the holy. In its place grew the ritual of a home flame which both signified and symbolized the beginning of a holy time. It brought a sense of God's closeness to each and every home. With that light, the reality that a different kind of time is beginning fills the home. It relaxes the mind and restores the soul. It directs us to make "after" different than "before."

CONCEPTS

CANDLE LIGHTING

Candle lighting is one of the central rituals in Jewish practice. As on the weekly Shabbat eve, candles are lit at the beginning of each day of *Yom Tov.*

Why the importance of candlelight? The light is symbolic of the joy of our celebration. For many, the kindling itself is an act of great meaning, the numbers of candles lit often representing beloved family members. It is also a time for personal prayer, the soft, whispered words of petition and thanksgiving privately spoken.

OBJECTS

CANDLESTICKS

As on Shabbat, a minimum of two candles are lit for Passover, although many families have lovely candalabra with three or more candles. There are no physical requirements for the candlesticks themselves, but brass and silver are popular materials. Elaborate or simple in design, short or tall, family heirloom or brand-new, the candlesticks simply need to hold the candles to be lit.

CANDLES

Two factors dictate the type of candles to be used. First, the candles should not be made of any material which might contain *ḥametz.* Pure paraffin wax candles (sometimes called "utility candles") are preferable. The candles should last for at least several hours, so do not use small birthday or Ḥanukkah candles. Long tapers are quite lovely and will last throughout the Seder. White is the traditional color for Shabbat and Festivals, although there is no specific legal requirement that stipulates this color.

HADLAKAT NEROT—
CANDLE LIGHTING

1. *Barukh attah Adonai*	1. Praised are You, *Adonai,*
2. *Eloheinu melekh ha-olam*	2. our God, King of the universe,
3. *asher kidshanu*	3. who has sanctified our lives
4. *b'mitzvotav*	4. through His commandments,
5. *v'tzivanu l'hadlik*	5. commanding us to kindle
6. *ner shel (Shabbat v'shel)*	6. the lights of (Shabbat and of)
7. *yom tov.*	7. the festival.

PRACTICE

The procedure for lighting the *Yom Tov* candles is as follows:

1. If you wish, bless your children using the traditional blessing (See *The Art of Jewish Living: The Shabbat Seder*, chapter 6) for this purpose and/or a personalized blessing for this time of year.
2. Place the candlesticks wherever you choose. Most families place the candlesticks directly on the Passover dinner table or nearby.
3. Put the candles into the candlesticks. If you have difficulty making them stay put, burn the bottom of the candle to allow some hot wax to drip into the receptacles. This should help the candles stick in the holders.
4. It is common practice to cover the head before lighting candles.
5. Unlike Shabbat candles, *Yom Tov* candles need not be circled with the hands three times, nor must the eyes be closed while chanting the blessing. The reason is that lights may be lit on the holiday itself, so there is no reason to employ the legal fiction of preparing the lights and then pretending they aren't there while reciting the blessing. In this case, candle lighting is like nearly all other ritual acts in Judaism—we say the blessing first, and then do the act. So, you recite the blessing and then kindle the wicks.

   On the other hand, many people are so conditioned to light candles as if they were Shabbat candles, it really would be acceptable if you light candles in that manner. First, light the wicks. Then, circle the flames with your hands three times, block your view of the candles, and then chant the blessing. Uncover your eyes and gaze upon the lights.
6. Do not say "Amen" at the end of the blessing. Although many people are used to saying "Amen" at the conclusion of a blessing, technically it is unnecessary. The word "Amen" literally means "so be it," a formal acknowledgement that one agrees with what has just been said. This was developed as a device for those unfamiliar with the prayers to nevertheless participate in

1. בָּרוּךְ אַתָּה יהוה
2. אֱלֹהֵינוּ מֶלֶךְ הָעוֹלָם
3. אֲשֶׁר קִדְּשָׁנוּ
4. בְּמִצְוֹתָיו
5. וְצִוָּנוּ לְהַדְלִיק
6. נֵר שֶׁל (שַׁבָּת וְשֶׁל)
7. יוֹם טוֹב.

the process of praying. If, however, you are reciting a particular blessing yourself, it is superfluous to say "Amen" to your own prayer.

7. At this point, it is traditional to say the "*Sheheḥeyanu*" prayer, thanking God for bringing us to this time. This is done on both of the first two nights of *Pesaḥ*. "*Sheheḥeyanu*" will be recited again as the concluding blessing of the *Kiddush*.
8. Spend a few moments in private prayer.
9. Wish everyone "*Ḥag Sameaḥ*" (Happy Holiday), or "*Ḥag Sameaḥ v'kasher*" (Happy and Kosher Holiday), "Good *Yom Tov*" (Good Holiday), or "*Gut Yontiv*" (Good Holiday) with an appropriate kiss, handshake, hug, etc.

A remaining question is: When are the candles lit? To answer this question, it is important to understand the differences between the *halakhah* (law) governing *melakhah* (work) on Shabbat and on *Yom Tov*. On Shabbat, absolutely no *melakhah* is allowed in order to guard the commandment to leave the environment completely at rest. Among the things prohibited is the lighting of fire; thus, the Shabbat candles are to be lit at least 18 minutes before sundown and no cooking is allowed during the day. In short, all preparations for Shabbat must be completed before the day begins.

On *Yom Tov*, the rules governing *melakhah* are modified slightly and allow certain latitude in preparing for the holiday on the day itself. One of these changes is to allow the use of fire on *Yom Tov* as long as it is transferred from a flame that was lit before the holiday began. For the rabbis, transferring an already existing flame, which they allowed on *Yom Tov*, was quite different from kindling a new flame. In fact, this explains why candles, a stove, even cigarettes can be lit on *Yom Tov* as long as the fire used comes from a flame that was lit before the holiday began.

To this end, observant families prepare a source flame before *Yom Tov* that will burn throughout both days of the holiday which can be used to transfer fire for other purposes. A gas pilot or two 24-hour candles (one is lit before *Yom Tov* and the second is lit from the flame of the first at the beginning of the second day) are common source flames.

Thus, the rules for candle lighting on *Pesaḥ* are:

1) When the first Seder falls on any night other than *Shabbat* (Friday nights), it is preferable to light the candles 18 minutes before sunset. If you forget to do so, since it is a *Yom Tov* you may light candles after dark by lighting (not striking) a match from a preexistent source fame and then kindling the lights. (Allow the match to burn itself out.)

At a second Seder which does not fall on *Shabbat* eve, since we are already into *Yom Tov* time, the candles should be lit by transferring a fire which is lit from an existing flame about one hour later than the previous night.

2) At a second Seder which falls on *Shabbat* eve, light the candles at least 18 minutes before sunset from an existing flame since no fire may be kindled on the Shabbat itself.

3) When the first or the second Seder falls on Saturday night, candles should not be lit until Shabbat is over, approximately 40 minutes after sunset. *Havdalah* will follow as part of *Kiddush*.

PRACTICAL QUESTIONS AND ANSWERS

Who should light the *Yom Tov* candles?

As with Shabbat candle lighting, both men and women are equally obligated to light *Yom Tov* candles. However, because traditionally the woman of the house was at home preparing for the Seder while the men were at the synagogue for the afternoon/evening service, it fell upon her to light the candles.

Today, when many women pursue careers outside the home and household responsibilities are being shared, many families are likewise sharing the candle lighting ritual.

How many candles should be lit?

At least two. However, many families light one for each family member. Children may also light their own candles. Use long fireplace matches so little fingers don't get burned.

What happens if we are invited to someone else's Seder?

You should light your own *Yom Tov* candles before leaving for the Seder. However, be very careful to place the candlesticks so that if the candles should fall over, the fire will not damage your house. More than one home has been destroyed or damaged by falling candles. Cut the candles down to a shorter length and/or place the candlesticks on kitchen tile or in the sink.

4

קַדֵּשׁ וּרְחַץ

KADESH, URḤATZ A MNEMONIC TO REMEMBER THE SEDER ORDER

When the kids were little we always had small family Seders, and then I guess they must have been 5 or 6 when my parents came in from Chicago and we had our first huge one. There must have been about thirty people there. Rachel, who is my youngest, just didn't know what to make of all these people. She started to sing Happy Birthday.

Abby Kantor

Just before the Seder starts, everyone is sort of milling around the table, and to start the service my Papa usually bangs on his wineglass and goes, "Sshhhhh." You know, it took years before I realized that the bang and the "Sshhhh" weren't parts of the Seder ritual.

David Coburn

In the *Midrash* (*Bereshit Rabbah* 41:5), we are given a glimpse of the way God teaches. The scene: the top of Mount Sinai. The event: the giving of the Torah.

> Rabbi Simeon bar Lakish taught: "...It was like the way that a rabbi teaches his disciple.
> Before the student has learned it, the teacher would recite it, and the student would repeat it. But, after the student had acquired the knowledge, the teacher would say to him, 'Come, we will both recite.' So it was with Moses. He began by reciting the Torah after his Creator, but after he had learned it, God said, 'Let us say it together.'"

Today, memorization has fallen out of favor, and the mnemonics which once served it have been all but abandoned. Memorization seems passé in our age of quick information retrieval and constantly expanding data bases. Ironically, only in the semiliterate street culture of "rap music" (and its cousins) and in the innocent word-play of our children does rhyme, the prime servant of memory, see major use as a conveyor of important messages. Yet, it was once the key to both learning and social cohesion.

In English, the idiom is "learning by heart," a taking within, a process of making information part of what keeps you alive. In Hebrew, the image is reversed; its idiom is "*b'al peh,*" literally a learning 'by mouth' or a learning 'out loud.' It was knowing something well enough to reteach it. In fact, knowing *b'al peh* is the essence of rabbinic Judaism. The rabbis saw knowing and teaching Torah *b'al peh* as the essential Jewish process. For them, Torah, God's ultimate truth, was always a twofold instruction. One was written, a *Torah she-b'ktav*, the words now found in the scroll we know as Torah and in the bound volume we know as the Bible. The other was a dynamic tradition of knowing by heart, interpreting, and reteaching; it was the Oral Law, *Torah she-b'al peh.* Talmud, *Midrash*, the *Haggadah* and all other rabbinic creations are products of the process of learning "out loud," repeating, and then reciting together. That is why the rabbis understood from the beginning that this was God's teaching method.

James Burke, the English popularizer of the history of human progress, has suggested that the invention of the printing press and the mass availability of printed information moved humankind away from its oral traditions. It is a process which changed society. In his book, *The Day the Universe Changed* he explains, "Printing changed the entire, backward-looking view of society, with its stultifying respect for achievements of the past, to one that looked forward to progress and improvement... If knowledge could be picked up from a book, the age of unquestioned authority was over. A printed fifteenth-century history expressed the new opinion: 'Why should old men be preferred to their juniors when it is possible, by diligent study, for young men to acquire the same knowledge?' The cult of youth had begun... Printing gave us our modern way of ordering thought. It gave us the mania for the truth 'in black and white.' It moved us away from respect for authority and age, towards an investigative approach to nature based on the confidence of common, empirical observation... In removing us from old mnemonic ways of recall and the collective memory of the community, printing isolated each of us in a way previously unknown, yet left us capable of sharing a bigger world, vicariously."

On Seder night, we jump through history. We relive the Exodus from Egypt through the words and tools of the rabbinic period. We return to an older time when parents earned their authority as God's representatives to their children by passing on truth and wisdom, word by word. The Seder evolved in a world without printing, a world where learning took place "out loud," where words were said, repeated, and then recited together. That which was known "by heart" was passed on "by mouth." So, the evening of reliving the Exodus begins with *Kadesh,Urḥatz*, a rhyming, sing-song chant of the fifteen steps which make up a Seder.

Francois Truffaut, a French filmmaker, made a movie of a Ray Bradbury novel, *Farenheit 451*. It involves a society in which books are banned. It is a culture in which firemen are empowered to burn books and rebels become "bookpeople," learning volumes by heart to keep them alive. It ends with a haunting scene which Truffaut added to the story. In an abandoned railroad yard, the "bookpeople" camp out and gather. They recite themselves, one for the other. In one corner we see a grandfather passing on the last chapter of his book, *Great Expectations*, to his grandson. With the last words spoken, repeated, and then recited together, the grandfather dies, having left a legacy.

On Seder eve, parents become teachers. Even before we begin, we chant together the evening's curriculum. We teach as God taught Moses, inviting our children to recite the order with us.

CONCEPTS

The basic structure of the Seder is remarkably similar in virtually every edition of the *Haggadah*, all 3,000 of them. In fact, the essential outline of the Seder has not changed much since it was codified in the Mishnah about 200 C.E.

To insure this uniformity, the rabbis concocted a mnemonic device to help people remember the order of the Seder. Before written texts of the *Haggadah* were available, this mnemonic was a great aid to those around the Seder table who had to recall the ritual and its texts by heart.

Kadesh, Urḥatz	קַדֵּשׁ, וּרְחַץ
Karpas, Yaḥatz	כַּרְפַּס, יַחַץ
Maggid, Roḥtzah	מַגִּיד, רָחְצָה
Motzi, Matzah	מוֹצִיא, מַצָּה
Maror, Korekh	מָרוֹר, כּוֹרֵךְ
Shulḥan Orekh	שֻׁלְחָן עוֹרֵךְ
Tzafun, Barekh	צָפוּן, בָּרֵךְ
Hallel, Nirtzah	הַלֵּל, נִרְצָה

The mnemonic is made up of the fifteen steps of the Seder service, listed in their order of appearance in the *Haggadah*. Each major step of the Seder has been given a name which refers to the basic purpose of the particular step. Thus, *Kadesh* is the name for the *Kiddush* blessings which sanctify the time of the Passover, *Karpas* refers to the vegetable which is blessed, and so on.

Notice the rhymes. This list has evolved, not to reveal the full structure of the Seder, but to make the major actions easy to remember. Therefore, while three of the Four Cups of Wine, the Four Questions, the Four Children, the Ten Plagues, *Dayyenu*, and the *Z'mirot* (songs) concluding the Seder are not listed here, the list still makes the progression clear. (The remaining cups of wine are tied to other Seder functions, and the other major "parts" are all part of the *Maggid* cycle). This sing-song chant with its easy rhyme serves as a mnemonic facilitating mastery of the structure of the Seder.

PRACTICE

Learn to chant this mnemonic device. Many children learn it in school. Perhaps yours can teach it to you and those assembled at the Seder itself.

Begin the Seder with the chanting of "*Kadesh, Urḥatz*." It is found at the front of most *Haggadot*. Some families have taken on the Sephardic custom of chanting the mnemonic up to the particular step of the Seder about to be celebrated. For example, when the family reaches *Maror*, before doing the *Maror* ritual, "*Kadesh, Urḥatz*" is chanted from "*Kadesh*" to "*Maror*," thereby announcing the next step in the Seder.

INNOVATIONS

Since this mnemonic is actually an outline of the Seder, some families prepare a large chart on poster board with each of the steps clearly listed. Other families prepare table cards (blank 3 x 5 index cards work well) listing the steps which are then placed at each table setting. This enables the leader to refer often to the list which helps the participants follow the order of the service. It also helps with those who are impatient, as in "Don't worry, we've just finished the *Maggid* and we have only five short steps until dinner!"

5

קַדֵּשׁ

KADESH SANCTIFICATION OF THE DAY

ACT I, SCENE 1

When we pass out the *Haggadot*, the different wine stains on each one remind me of Seders from the years past. Like the time that Harvey spilled his whole glass of wine over the book and now each page is red. And then there was the year when we used white wine instead of red wine, so the stains are multi-colored.

Abby Kantor

In school they try to fake it with grape juice and some people try to talk you into just sipping from the glass 'cause you're a kid. But, I know that the Jewish law wants you to drink four full glasses of wine. I've got to do my best to be a good Jew, don't I?

Matthew Gill

Often religious arguments seem silly to those on the outside. In *Gulliver's Travels*, Jonathan Swift postulates a war between Lilliput and its neighbor, fought over the right way to open a soft-boiled egg. We laugh, seeing it as a parody of the hairsplitting that often engrossed both civic and church life. For us, real religious questions are things like abortion, capital punishment, human rights—things which actually make a difference in the way that people live. We laugh at the way medieval theologians argued over the number of angels that could fit on the head of a pin, a kind of heavenly hairsplitting. Only, to them it wasn't so funny. Angels were only the example; the real issue was how powerful is "omnipotent"—a rather larger question. For them, their whole understanding of "free will," of the extent of God's influence and control over us, was the question really being argued. Sometimes, the symbolic really does inform the real.

In the Mishnah, we find a major argument between the schools of Hillel and Shammai over the right way to say *Kiddush*. The *Pesaḥ Kiddush* is made up of two parts: a one-line *b'rakhah* which is a blessing over the wine (*borei pri ha-gafen*), and a longer blessing, a *b'rakhah* over the holiday (*m'kadesh Yisrael v'ha-Z manim*). Hillel's and Shammai's schools argue over the correct order of these two *b'rakhot*. While our first reaction to such an argument may be to file it with discussions of the correct end from which to open a soft-boiled egg, or the pin-head stuffing record set by the angels' fraternity, close investigation reveals much about the purpose of the *Kiddush* and more about the meaning of holiness.

In the Mishnah (*Pesaḥim* 10:2) we find this brief record of that debate:

> The first cup of wine is poured for him.
> The **School of Shammai** says:
> One says the blessing over the day first
> and then says the blessing over the wine.
> The **School of Hillel** says:
> One says the blessing over the wine first
> and then says the blessing over the day.

In looking at this text, nothing is revealed. The Mishnah is only the most minimal record of the basic positions and decisions taken by the rabbis. Fortunately, most of the Mishnah is accompanied by a second work, a collection called the *Tosefta*, additions. Here we find the necessary explanations.

> The **School of Shammai** reasons:
> *That the blessing over the holiday goes first, because*
> the holiday *provides the occasion* for drinking the wine.
> *Also*, the day is already holy,
> while the wine becomes holy through the blessing.
> The **School of Hillel** reasons:
> *That the blessing over the wine goes first, because*

the wine provides ***the means*** for the sanctification of the holiday.
Also, it is always an obligation to bless wine,
while only some days receive blessings.
The ***halakhah*** (ruling) follows the words of the **School of Hillel.**

Something which is holy is something which is set apart, something which is recognized as special, as significant, as connected to the Divine. The argument between Hillel's and Shammai's schools is a debate over comparative holiness. It is also a debate over what makes something holy.

For the School of Shammai, holiness is something created by God. The day, whether Shabbat or a Festival, was "consecrated" by God and therefore is officially set aside as holy. That is why they can say, "the holiday ***provides the occasion*** for drinking the wine." For them, the fact that God set aside the day as sacred is the central concern. For them, "the day is already holy;" the ***b'rakhot*** over the day and wine are merely the human recognition of this truth.

Hillel's school understands holiness differently. For them, holiness is a potential, something which becomes active through human perception. That is why they reason, "it is always an obligation to bless wine, while only some days receive blessings." For them, wine, a mundane drink, always carries the potential to encounter the holy. That is why it must be blessed each and every day. Our standing relationship with wine becomes a bridge to recognize the unique holy potential of the days which God has set aside as sacred convocations.

Johnny Appleseed is a wonderful creation of American folklore. His "prayer" and his "***mitzvah***" have been taught to most scouting-type youth groups and in many schools. His reads:

The Lord is good to me
and so I thank the Lord
for giving me the things I need—
the sun, the moon, and the apple seeds.
The Lord is good to me.

Johnny Appleseed's "***mitzvah***" was that every act of eating an apple obligated one to plant an apple tree and provide future generations with apples. This was not a new conception. Ḥoni the Circle Maker, a pre-rabbinic teacher of the fifth century B.C.E., similarly devoted his life to filling the world with trees for future generations. Johnny Appleseed's prayer is the perfect School of Hillel ***Kiddush.*** Eating an apple triggers the recognition of God's creations. This recognition motivates an expression of thanksgiving and a call to ethical action. The ordinary apple triggers the kind of human behavior which is to be set apart and praised.

Kiddush begins the Passover. We lift a cup of wine, an ordinary natural product (manipulated by basic human engineering). In it, we recognize the Divine hand. Even though we grew, crushed and fermented the grapes, they would not have grown without "the sun, the moon, and the apple seeds"—so we thank the Lord.

However, unlike Johnny Appleseed, our relationship with God has a history. In thanking God, we remember that God has both done things for us and demanded things from us. Therefore, our ***Kiddush*** has a second half. ***Pesaḥ*** is the start. We were chosen, liberated, and contracted into a covenantal relationship. The day has been set aside as holy, as a time to retell the story and to celebrate the relationship. A simple glass of wine triggers the memory. Through it we recognize that a potential experience awaits us, and that by acknowledging it as holy, we can enter into all that Passover offers.

For the Jewish tradition, there is a connection between that which is simple and that which is symbolic. Through *Kiddush*, a glass of wine can actually change our perceptions of time and space.

Sometimes it is worth knowing how many angels can stand on the right end of an egg.

CONCEPTS

KIDDUSH SANCTIFIES THE DAY, NOT THE WINE

The word *Kadesh*, the name for this section of the Seder, comes from the Hebrew word "*kadosh*"—holy. "*Kiddush*" literally means "making holy" or "sanctification." But what is it we are sanctifying? Contrary to popular perception, we are not sanctifying the wine. Rather, we are sanctifying the day as a *Yom Tov*, a Festival. We are, in effect, setting this time apart as "holy." We sanctify the *Yom Tov* over wine because wine is a symbol of joy and happiness. It is also considered the drink of those who enjoy freedom.

KIDDUSH RECALLS THE EXODUS

The unifying theme of every *Kiddush* is the rememberance of the Exodus from Egypt. So central is this event in the memory of the Jewish people, it is recalled in every Shabbat and Festival *Kiddush*.

All revolutions reverberate to the original revolution—the Exodus from Egypt. Michael Walzer, in a fascinating book called *Exodus and Revolution*, points out that when a medallion was to be struck in the 18th century to celebrate the American Revolution, the theme Thomas Jefferson suggested was "Rebellion against tyranny is obedience to God." The saying was illustrated by a picture of the Jews passing through the Reed Sea.

KIDDUSH SANCTIFIES THE PEOPLE ISRAEL

It is interesting to note that unlike the Shabbat *Kiddush*, the memory of Creation (*zikaron l'ma'aseh v'reishit*) is not included in the *Yom Tov Kiddush*. Even when the *Yom Tov* falls on Shabbat, the words added in honor of Shabbat are "*shabbatot lim'nuḥah*," "Shabbat for rest," rather than recalling the theme of Creation. (It is true that the "*Vayekhulu*" paragraph which is also added in honor of Shabbat does refer to Creation, but in the body of the *Yom Tov Kiddush* itself, there is no mention of Creation.) The common understanding of this omission is that on *Yom Tov* we celebrate the particular creation of the Jewish people rather than the cosmic creation of the world.

KIDDUSH SPEAKS OF CHOSENNESS

A related theme of the Festival *Kiddush*, as in the Shabbat *Kiddush*, is chosenness. Here that theme is struck twice: "*asher baḥar banu mikol am v'rom'manu mikol lashon*"—literally: "who has chosen us from among all peoples and has exalted us above all languages." Then further: "*ki vanu vaḥarta*"—"for you have chosen us."

The idea of the Jews being a chosen people is not an elitist notion. Rather, it is the statement of an obligation: God chose us for the purpose of observing the Law and for receiving and caring for Shabbat and the sacred Festivals, including Passover. Likewise, the Jewish people's special relationship with God is based on our willingness to accept God's covenant, living up to the standards set by these laws.

KIDDUSH SANCTIFIES THE PASSOVER AND FESTIVALS

The *Kiddush* recognizes that God has "favored us with the Festivals for joy, seasons and holidays for happiness, among them this Festival of *Matzot*, the season of our liberation..." Here we thank God for the gift of the Festivals, and particularly for *Pesaḥ*. Interestingly, among the many names for *Pesaḥ*, the one used in the *Kiddush* is "*ḥag ha-matzot*," the Festival of Unleavened Bread. Why? Probably because this is the name given to the Festival in the Bible. Moreover, the term *Pesaḥ* refers to the specific ceremony of the paschal sacrifice which lasted only one night, while the Festival of Unleavened Bread lasted for the entire week. But notice that this term is immediately modified with another name for Pesaḥ—"*z'man ḥeruteinu*", the season of our liberation, connecting the ancient Festival of Unleavened Bread with the Exodus experience.

While there are several themes in the *Kiddush* of the Seder, as in all Jewish liturgy, the tip-off to the most important theme is in the "*ḥatimah*," the "seal," the concluding sentence of the *b'rakhah*. Here, the essential theme is repeated in the ancient formula: "*Barukh attah Adonai*..." In the case of the *Pesaḥ Kiddush*, *Adonai* is praised as the One who sanctifies the people Israel and the festive seasons.

HAVDALAH

Every Saturday night at the conclusion of Shabbat, Jews celebrate the beautiful ceremony known as *Havdalah*, literally "separation." The *Havdalah* marks the transition from the "sanctified" time of Shabbat to the "ordinary" time of the rest of the week. This is done through a very mysterious, even sensual, series of ritual acts involving wine, a special twisted candle, and spices.

When Shabbat is over and the next day is a *Yom Tov*, the rabbis wanted to mark the conclusion of Shabbat, but the transition was not from the normal "sanctified" time to "ordinary" time. Rather, in this case, the *Havdalah* marks the transition from one "sanctified" time—Shabbat— to another "sanctified" time—the *Yom Tov* Festival. Thus, when *Pesaḥ* falls on Saturday night, a slightly abbreviated and somewhat different version of the *Havdalah* ceremony is incorporated into the *Kiddush*.

Why the *Kiddush?* First of all, it is the first official ritual act of the Seder and therefore the first opportunity to make the distinction between Shabbat and *Yom Tov*. Second, we are already reciting the blessing for wine which is the first blessing of the regular *Havdalah* ceremony.

There are several differences between the regular *Havdalah* and this *Yom Tov* version. While the blessing for the lights of fire is included, we do not use the special twisted *Havdalah* candle. The reason is that candles have already been lit, and, in fact, we use the *Yom Tov* lights to examine our fingers or palms, thereby differentiating light and darkness. We also do not recite the blessing over spices. The use of spices was introduced during the Gaonic period (6th-11th centuries) to replace the "*n'shamah y'teirah*," "the additional soul" we are said to acquire during Shabbat, a kind of spiritual smelling salts to reinvigorate us for the week ahead. But, when moving from Shabbat to a *Yom Tov*, both representing "sanctified" times, this was deemed unnecessary.

In fact, the central paragraph of this *Havdalah* serves to distinguish between the levels of "sanctification" of Shabbat and the Festival—"*bein kodesh l'kodesh*." Practically speaking, as we have seen earlier, there are differences in the kinds of work that can be done on Shabbat and *Yom Tov.* Moreover, this *Havdalah* paragraph lists seven "distinctions:" 1) between sacred and profane, 2) between light and darkness, 3) between Israel and the nations, 4) between the seventh day (of resting) and the six days of creating, 5) between the sanctity of Shabbat and the sanctity of the Festivals, 6) between the sanctity of Shabbat as a "holy" day and the work days, and finally 7) separating and distinguishing God's people Israel through His holiness. Once again, the key to the paragraph's theme is in the concluding benediction: "Praised are You, *Adonai,* who differentiates between the sanctity of Shabbat and the sanctity of *Yom Tov.*"

SHEHEḤEYANU

The *Kiddush* concludes with the famous *Sheheḥeyanu* prayer, thanking God for giving life, sustaining us, and enabling us to celebrate (literally: "reach") this Festival. The *Sheheḥeyanu* is recited at the conclusion of *Kiddush* on both nights of the Seder. It is a fitting exclamation point to this first prayer of the Seder which establishes this time as special in our lives.

OBJECTS

The two items normally required for *Kiddush* are a cup and wine. At the Seder, the wine cup often rests upon a saucer or plate. There are two reasons, both very practical. One is that later in the Seder, we will spill out drops of wine onto the plate at the recitation of the Ten Plagues. The other is that with all the pouring of Four Cups of Wine, there are bound to be spills!

The cup used for *Kiddush* has traditionally been among the most beautiful of ritual objects found in the home. And certainly, the *Kiddush* cup used for the year can be *kashered* and used at the Seder table (unless it is made of china). However, there is to be an even more beautiful *Kiddush* cup set at the table for Elijah the Prophet. Thus, you may use a normal wine goblet for the purposes of *Kiddush.* As with candlesticks, there is no requirement that it be made of silver or crystal—any material is suitable. It should, however, hold at least 3.3 fluid ounces of wine, the minimum required for each of the four cups.

The wine itself must, of course, be kosher for Passover and made from grapes—the fruit of the vine. Traditonally, red wine is used, reminding us of the blood of the Hebrew infants who were drowned in the Nile by Pharoah. But, in the sixteenth century, the commentary *Oraḥ Ḥayim* suggested that red wine not be used because of the fear caused by the infamous blood libel—the outrageous and false accusation that Jews murdered Christian children in order to use their blood for the wine of the Seder. Now we may use either red or white wines.

A generation or two ago, many people made their own kosher-for-Passover wine. We know of one family which still uses some of "Bubbie's wine" to fill the Cup of Elijah each year, thus remembering their beloved grandmother at the Seder. Today, in an era when fine *kosher l'Pesaḥ* wines are available, many hosts place bottles of a variety of wines on the table and invite their guests to choose the wine they prefer. Some families purchase Israeli wines as a gesture of support for the Jewish state.

PRACTICE

This is the traditional way to say *Kiddush*:

1. The *Kiddush* cup and the wine cups of each individual are filled, preferably to the top. It is customary not to fill your own cup, but to have someone else fill it for you as a sign of freedom.
2. The *matzot* should be covered.
3. The *Kiddush* cup is raised and held in the dominant hand. Some hold the cup in the palm of the hand with fingers pointing up, as if God were pouring the wine into the cup.
4. On Shabbat, the *Vayekhulu* is said.
5. Some people introduce the blessing for wine with the words "*savrei ḥaveirai*"—literally "with the permission of friends" (or with the more traditional "*savrei maranan*"—"with the permission of our teachers"). This is a formal announcement that a blessing is about to be said.
6. Say the first blessing, *borei p'ri ha-gafen*—the blessing over the wine. Do not drink the wine yet. Remember, if you are saying the blessing, you need not say "Amen." Those who are listening say "Amen" acknowledging their agreement with the blessing.
7. Say the second paragraph, ending with *m'kadesh (ha-Shabbbat v') Yisrael v'ha-Z'manim*. This is the blessing that sanctifies the Jewish people and the Festival. Include the words in parentheses on Shabbat.
8. On Saturday night, say the *Havdalah*, consisting of two blessings. First, put down the wine cup and recite "*borei m'orei ha-aysh*" with the upper side of the hand facing the *Yom Tov* candles. Look at the fingers, thereby using the light while you say the blessing. Then, raise the wine cup again and say "*ha-mavdil bein kodesh l'kodesh*."
9. Say *Sheheḥeyanu*.
10. Sit (if standing) and drink the wine while reclining to the left.

KIDDUSH

On Friday night, begin with *Vayekhulu* and add the words in parentheses.

1. *Vayar Elohim et kol asher asa*	1. And God saw all that He had made,
2. *v'hinei tov m'ode,*	2. and found it very good.
3. *Vay'hi erev vay'hi voker.*	3. And there was evening and there was morning,
4. *yom ha-shishi.*	4. the sixth day.
5. *Vayekhulu ha-shamayim*	5. And the heavens were completed
6. *v'ha-aretz v'khol tz'va'am.*	6. and the earth and all they contain.
7. *Vay'khal Elohim ba-yom ha-shvi'i*	7. And God finished on the seventh day
8. *m'lakhto asher asa,*	8. the work which He had been doing.
9 *va'yishbot ba-yom ha-shvi'i*	9. And He rested on the seventh day
10. *mikol m'lakhto asher asa.*	10. from all the work which He had done.
11. *Vay'varekh Elohim et yom ha-shvi'i*	11. And then God blessed the seventh day
12. *vay'kadesh* oto,	12. and sanctified it,
13. *ki vo shavat mikol m'lakhto*	13. because on it He rested from all His work
14. *asher bara Elohim la'asot.*	14. which God created.

1. וַיַּרְא אֱלֹהִים אֶת כָּל אֲשֶׁר עָשֹׂה
2. וְהִנֵּה טוֹב מְאֹד,
3. וַיְהִי עֶרֶב וַיְהִי בֹקֶר
4. יוֹם הַשִּׁשִּׁי.
5. וַיְכֻלּוּ הַשָּׁמַיִם
6. וְהָאָרֶץ וְכָל צְבָאָם.
7. וַיְכַל אֱלֹהִים בַּיּוֹם הַשְּׁבִיעִי
8. מְלַאכְתּוֹ אֲשֶׁר עָשָׂה,
9. וַיִּשְׁבֹּת בַּיּוֹם הַשְּׁבִיעִי
10. מִכָּל מְלַאכְתּוֹ אֲשֶׁר עָשָׂה.
11. וַיְבָרֶךְ אֱלֹהִים אֶת יוֹם הַשְּׁבִיעִי
12. וַיְקַדֵּשׁ אֹתוֹ,
13. כִּי בוֹ שָׁבַת מִכָּל מְלַאכְתּוֹ
14. אֲשֶׁר בָּרָא אֱלֹהִים לַעֲשׂוֹת.

1. *Barukh attah Adonai*	1. Praised are You, *Adonai,*
2. *Eloheinu melekh ha-olam*	2. Our God, King of the universe
3. *borei p'ri ha-gafen.*	3. who creates the fruit of the vine.
4. *Barukh attah Adonai*	4. Praised are You, *Adonai,*
5. *Eloheinu melekh ha-olam*	5. our God, King of the universe,
6. *asher baḥar banu*	6. who has chosen us
7. *mikol am v'rom'manu mikol lashon*	7. and distinguished us
8. *v'kid'shanu b'mitzvotav.*	8. by sanctifying us through His commandments.
9. *Va-titen lanu Adonai Eloheinu b'ahava*	9. You have lovingly favored us with
10. *(Shabbatot lim'nuḥah u')*	10. (Shabbat for rest and)
11. *mo'adim l'simḥah,*	11. Festivals for joy,
12. *ḥagim u-z'manim l'sason,*	12. seasons and holidays for happiness,
13. *et yom (ha-Shabbat ha-zeh v'et yom)*	13. among them (this Shabbat and)
14. *ḥag ha-matzot ha-zeh,*	14. this day of *Pesaḥ,*
15. *z'man ḥeiruteinu*	15. the season of our liberation,
16. *(b'ahavah) mikra kodesh,*	16. (lovingly) a day of sacred assembly
17. *zekher litziyat Mitzrayim.*	17. commemorating the Exodus from *Mitzrayim.*
18. *Ki vanu vaḥarta,*	18. You have chosen us,
19. *v'otanu kidashta mikol ha-amim*	19. sanctifying us among all people by granting us
20. *(v'Shabbat) u-mo'adei kodsh'kha*	20. (Shabbat and) Your sacred Festivals
21. *(b'ahavah u-v'ratzon)*	21. (lovingly and gladly)
22. *b'simḥah u-v'sason hin'ḥaltanu.*	22. in joy and happiness.
23. *Barukh attah Adonai*	23. Praised are You, *Adonai,*
24. *m'kadesh (ha-Shabbat v')*	24. who sanctifies (Shabbat and)
25. *Yisrael v'ha-Z'manim.*	25. the people Israel and the Festival seasons.

1. בָּרוּךְ אַתָּה יהוה
2. אֱלֹהֵינוּ מֶלֶךְ הָעוֹלָם
3. בּוֹרֵא פְּרִי הַגָּפֶן.
4. בָּרוּךְ אַתָּה יהוה
5. אֱלֹהֵינוּ מֶלֶךְ הָעוֹלָם
6. אֲשֶׁר בָּחַר בָּנוּ
7. מִכָּל עָם וְרוֹמְמָנוּ מִכָּל לָשׁוֹן
8. וְקִדְּשָׁנוּ בְּמִצְוֹתָיו.
9. וַתִּתֶּן לָנוּ יהוה אֱלֹהֵינוּ בְּאַהֲבָה
10. (שַׁבָּתוֹת לִמְנוּחָה וּ)
11. מוֹעֲדִים לְשִׂמְחָה,
12. חַגִּים וּזְמַנִּים לְשָׂשׂוֹן,
13. אֶת יוֹם (הַשַּׁבָּת הַזֶּה וְאֶת יוֹם)
14. חַג הַמַּצּוֹת הַזֶּה,
15. זְמַן חֵרוּתֵנוּ,
16. (בְּאַהֲבָה) מִקְרָא קֹדֶשׁ,
17. זֵכֶר לִיצִיאַת מִצְרָיִם.
18. כִּי בָנוּ בָחַרְתָּ,
19. וְאוֹתָנוּ קִדַּשְׁתָּ, מִכָּל הָעַמִּים
20. (וְשַׁבָּת) וּמוֹעֲדֵי קָדְשְׁךָ
21. (בְּאַהֲבָה וּבְרָצוֹן)
22. בְּשִׂמְחָה וּבְשָׂשׂוֹן הִנְחַלְתָּנוּ.
23. בָּרוּךְ אַתָּה יהוה
24. מְקַדֵּשׁ (הַשַּׁבָּת וְ)
25. יִשְׂרָאֵל וְהַזְּמַנִּים.

HAVDALAH

On Saturday night, add:

1. *Barukh attah Adonai*	1. Praised are You, *Adonai,*
2. *Eloheinu melekh ha-olam*	2. our God, King of the universe
3. *borei m'orei ha-aish.*	3. who creates the lights of fire.
4. *Barukh attah Adonai*	4. Praised are You, *Adonai,*
5. *Eloheinu melekh ha-olam*	5. our God, King of the universe,
6. *ha-mavdil bain kodesh l'ḥol,*	6. who differentiates between sacred and profane,
7. *bain or l'ḥoshekh,*	7. between light and darkness,
8. *bain Yisrael la-amim,*	8. between Israel and other nations,
9. *bain yom ha-shvi'i*	9. between the seventh day
10. *l'sheishet y'mei ha-ma'aseh,*	10. and the six days of creating.
11. *bain k'dushat Shabbat*	11. (You made a distinction) between the sanctity of Shabbat
12. *lik'dushat yom tov hiv'dalta,*	12. and the sanctity of the Festivals,
13. *v'et yom ha-shvi'i misheishet y'mei ha-ma'aseh kidashta,*	13. and You sanctified Shabbat more than the other days of the week
14. *hiv'dalta v'kidashta*	14. distinguishing and hallowing
15. *et amkha Yisrael bik'dushatehkha.*	15. Your people Israel through Your holiness.
16. *Barukh attah Adonai*	16. Praised are You, *Adonai,*
17. *ha-mavdil bain kodesh*	17. who differentiates between the sanctity of Shabbat
18. *l'kodesh.*	18. and the sanctity of *Yom Tov.*
19. *Barukh attah Adonai,*	19. Praised are You, *Adonai,*
20. *Eloheinu melekh ha-olam*	20. our God, King of the universe,
21. *sheheḥeyanu,*	21. for giving us life,
22. *v'kiy'manu,*	22. for sustaining us,
23. *v'higiyanu*	23. and for enabling us
24. *la-z'man ha-zeh.*	24. to celebrate this Festival.

1. בָּרוּךְ אַתָּה יהוה
2. אֱלֹהֵינוּ מֶלֶךְ הָעוֹלָם
3. בּוֹרֵא מְאוֹרֵי הָאֵשׁ.
4. בָּרוּךְ אַתָּה יהוה
5. אֱלֹהֵינוּ מֶלֶךְ הָעוֹלָם
6. הַמַּבְדִּיל בֵּין קֹדֶשׁ לְחוֹל,
7. בֵּין אוֹר לְחֹשֶׁךְ,
8. בֵּין יִשְׂרָאֵל לָעַמִּים
9. בֵּין יוֹם הַשְּׁבִיעִי
10. לְשֵׁשֶׁת יְמֵי הַמַּעֲשֶׂה,
11. בֵּין קְדֻשַּׁת שַׁבָּת
12. לִקְדֻשַּׁת יוֹם טוֹב הִבְדַּלְתָּ,
13. וְאֶת יוֹם הַשְּׁבִיעִי מִשֵּׁשֶׁת יְמֵי הַמַּעֲשֶׂה קִדַּשְׁתָּ,
14. הִבְדַּלְתָּ וְקִדַּשְׁתָּ
15. אֶת עַמְּךָ יִשְׂרָאֵל בִּקְדֻשָּׁתֶךָ.
16. בָּרוּךְ אַתָּה יהוה
17. הַמַּבְדִּיל בֵּין קֹדֶשׁ
18. לְקֹדֶשׁ.
19. בָּרוּךְ אַתָּה יהוה
20. אֱלֹהֵינוּ מֶלֶךְ הָעוֹלָם
21. שֶׁהֶחֱיָנוּ
22. וְקִיְּמָנוּ
23. וְהִגִּיעָנוּ
24. לַזְּמַן הַזֶּה.

PRACTICAL QUESTIONS AND ANSWERS

Who should have a *Kiddush* cup?

Everyone who participates in the Seder should have his/her own wine cup. A central requirement of the Seder is to partake of four cups of wine representing the four promises of redemption made by God: "I will free you, I will deliver you, I will redeem you, I will take you to be my people." (Exodus 6:6-8).

Who recites the *Kiddush?*

The leader of the Seder generally leads the *Kiddush.* Traditionally, this role fell to the father, but both women and men are equally obligated to say the *Kiddush.* A woman most certainly can recite the *Kiddush* on her own behalf or on behalf of any males present.

Encourage participants of all ages to join in whatever parts of the *Kiddush* they know. They probably are familiar with *borei p'ri ha-gafen* and they may be able to join the leader from "*ki vanu vaḥarta*" in the *m'kadesh Yisrael v'ha-Z'manim.* Most people are familiar with the *Sheheḥeyanu.*

Is the *Kiddush* recited while standing or sitting?

The rabbis were undecided on this point, although the overwhelming sentiment seems to be on the side of sitting during *Kiddush.* While this might seem strange, remember that the Seder is a banquet, and we, as the guests of honor, are expected to spend most of the feast not only sitting, but reclining! Thus, even if you are inclined to say *Kiddush* while standing, you should sit down after *Sheheḥeyanu* and drink the wine while leaning to your left.

Why does someone else fill our wine cups for us?

This is a sign of people who are free. In ancient times, the leader had his cup filled by his servant or another person. It is a lovely custom to have participants fill each other's cups with wine as a reminder of the nobility of free people.

Why do we lean to the left?

Most people are right-handed, so leaning to the left leaves the right hand free to use for eating or drinking.

How much wine must be drunk?

Since this is the first of a minimum four cups of wine during the Seder, this question was taken quite seriously. According to strict interpretations of the law, a "*revi'it*" of wine (3.3 fluid ounces) is to be drunk each of the four times wine is required. Since this would result in a substantial amount of wine drunk, it was determined that if one drinks the majority of the "*revi'it*" (1 and 2/3 fluid ounces), the *mitzvah* would still be accomplished.

What should children drink?

Children should drink the four cups. There are at least three options: they can sip real wine, the wine can be diluted with grape juice, or you can serve them grape juice.

What if someone cannot drink wine?

If one finds the wine to be discomforting, then grape juice should be substituted.

Why are the *matzot* covered during *Kiddush?*

There is a tradition, at once both fanciful and serious, that we cover the *matzot* so that they are not embarrassed by all the attention lavished on the wine. After all, we had *matzah* in the desert, not wine! Covering the *matzah* is also a reminder of the dew-covered *manna* which fell in the desert during the Exodus.

Why do some *Haggadot* have hunting pictures next to *Havdalah*?

This is an interesting example of how a mistake can become incorporated into liturgical forms. In order to remember the proper order of the *Kiddush* when *Yom Tov* began on Saturday night, the mnemonic *YaKNeHaZ* was created. The Hebrew letters stand for 1) **Yud** = *Yayin* = Wine (*borei p'ri ha-gafen*), 2) **Kuf** = *Kiddush* = Sanctification of the people and the Festivals (*m'kadesh Yisrael v'ha-Z'manim*), 3) **Nun** = *Ner* = Lights (*borei m'orei ha-aysh*), 4) **Hey** = *Havdalah* = Distinction (*ha-mavdil bein kodesh l'kodesh*), and 5) **Zayin** = *Z'man* (time) = *Sheheḥeyanu* (*la-z'man ha-zeh*). *Ya-KNeHaZ* sounded to some like the German phrase "*Jag den Has*," meaning "hunt the hare." So, some medieval artists illustrated their *Haggadot* with a hare-hunting picture. The incongruity of such a picture is, of course, that hunting animals for sport is frowned upon in Judaism and the hare or rabbit is not a kosher animal to begin with.

6

וּרְחַץ

URḤATZ
THE FIRST WASHING OF HANDS
ACT 1, SCENE 2

One of our traditions is having the littlest kids at the table carry the bowl with water for the washing of the hands. The boy holds the bowl and the girl pours the water.

Vic Sabah

I'll never forget the way my Grandfather looked on Seder night. During the year whenever I saw him, he was dressed in his trousers and suspenders, but when we walked into the house on Seder—there he was dressed in all white. He was in his *kittel*, sitting on a chair with a huge cushion. When he sat at the table and washed his hands, it really reminded me of the kings in the storybooks we were reading.

Abby Kantor

We understand cleanliness; we don't understand purity. Cleanliness is the kind of washing that a surgeon does before an operation, the kind of scrubbing which has to do with fingernails and dirt behind the ears. Purity is more abstract. Cleanliness is logical—it's scientific. Purity is connected to the Divine.

"Cooties" is a technical term employed by children for describing a state of ritual impurity. You can "have cooties," "catch cooties" and "wipe cooties off." Still, "cooties" do you no real harm because they have to do with perception, not with physical reality. So too, with the world of "*tohorah*," Jewish ritual purity. The *Encyclopedia Hebraica* explains *tumah*, ritual impurity, this way: "a concept that a person or object can be in a state which, by religious law, prevents the person or object from having any contact with the Temple or its cult. The state is transferable from one object to another in a variety of ways, such as touching the object or being under the same roof with it. The state of impurity can be corrected by the performance of specific rituals, mainly including ablution, after which the person or object becomes pure once more until impurity is again contracted." In other words, *tohorah* is the state of having no ritual "cooties."

In the biblical tradition, three kinds of things create a state of *tumah*: leprosy, fluids from sexual organs, and dead bodies—the kinds of things that you really don't want to touch. *Tumah* could be caught by people, food, drink and utensils. When the rabbis went to work on this material, other things got added. Objects of idolatry became unclean, the Diaspora was declared unclean (except for paths taken by pilgrims coming to the Temple in Jerusalem) and, in a wonderfully creative insight—hands were able to become impure, while the rest of the body remained in a state of purity (*Pesaḥim* 19a-b).

This brings us to the washing of hands. In the Mishnah, (*Ḥagigah 2:5*) we read:

> One must wash hands before *eating ordinary (non-holy)* food,
> the food for tithes
> or the food set aside for the priests
> but for holy things (*such as the meat eaten from a sacrifice*)
> one must immerse them...

While the custom of handwashing may well have been influenced by the sanitary washing of hands common to the formal Greek meal, for the rabbis it was something else. *Tohorah* was originally a Temple issue. Most of the purity literature concerned the *Kohanim*, the priests, and established their state of readiness to perform sacred services. The rest of that original literature focused on the congregation, but also involved their ability to participate in the Temple ritual. Sacrifices were, for the most part, eaten, and one had to be "pure" either to cook or to eat. The radical implication of the above Mishnah is the establishment of a level of holiness to every act of eating, and the creation of every table as an altar, a point of divine service.

The rabbis were masters at lifting every biblical concept to higher levels. In looking at the extensive material on impurity they tried to lift the mundane to make it spiritually instructive. They looked at all the laws of *Metzorah*, the impurity of leprosy, "the leper", and in a brilliant wordplay, moved it from the medical to the ethical. They saw *Metzorah* (leprosy) as *motze shem rah*, "one who spreads evil gossip." It became very clear that one had to become pure from the pollution of gossip. Likewise, they taught that "murder makes the land impure," (*Mekhilta Shabbat* 1), and that "anyone who is arrogant causes the land to be impure." (*Yoma* 38b). They also taught that repentance and good deeds lead to purity (*Avodah Zarah* 20b) and that the study of Torah (just like water) can wash away impurity (*Shir ha-Shirim Rabbah* 1:2 no.3)

Lady Macbeth is the most famous handwasher of all times. In the fifth act she wanders the night, endlessly washing her hands. "Out, damned spot! Out, I say... Here's the smell of the blood still, all the perfumes of Arabia will not sweeten this little hand." Her quest is for purity, not cleanliness. It is not dirt that she is trying to wash away, it is not a hygenic purity she is seeking. For her, handwashing is a search for an internal cleanliness.

Every act of Jewish eating is a chance to approach the sacred. Every single piece of food provides a potential religious experience. To open ourselves to that opportunity, to elevate our table to an altar, we wash our hands. Our goal is not cleanliness. It is not the removal of ritual "cooties." Rather, it is a sense of preparation. We use our hands to make our spirit clean and ready.

Cleanliness is good for aesthetics. *Purity* is next to Godliness.

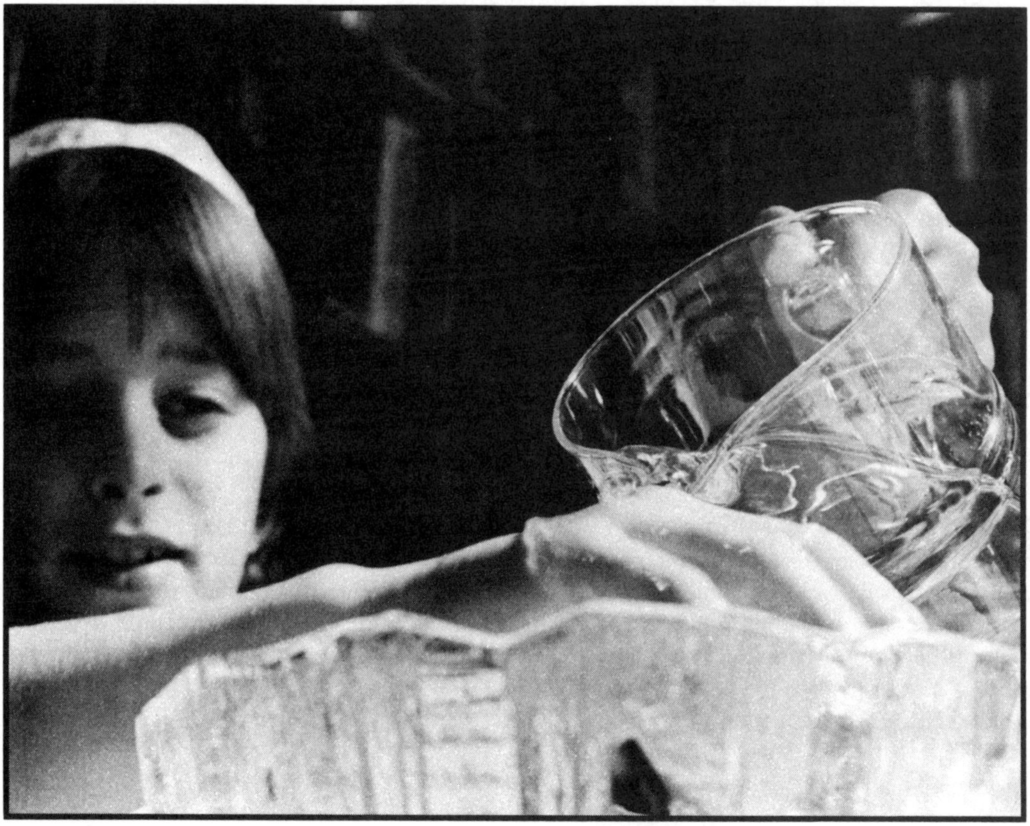

CONCEPTS

WASHING HANDS

There are two points in the Seder when we wash hands. *Urḥatz*, the first time, has the curious distinction of being one of four rituals during the Seder which has no blessing (the other three are *Yaḥatz*, *Korekh*, and *Tzafun*). Why?

In the Talmud we learn that during Temple times there was a law in effect which required hands to be washed before eating any food dipped into a liquid. Because this hand washing immediately precedes *Karpas* when we dip a vegetable in a liquid, the *Urḥatz* remains as a reminder of these times.

In the Talmud (*Pesaḥim* 115a) there is a long discussion over the necessity to recite a blessing during *Urḥatz*. Although the Talmud states: "Whatever is dipped in a liquid requires the washing of hands," some commentators believe that this washing is not required today. We are not obligated to follow the high standards of purity mandated in the Temple. Thus, the ***halakhah*** (law) which comes down to us is to wash with no blessing.

This practice is quite unusual for those accustomed to hearing a blessing associated with handwashing. It is an action designed to raise the curiosity level of children who are in the know; the first such act to stimulate the statement "How different this night is from all other nights!"

OBJECTS

Traditionally, this handwashing is done at the table by the leader. S/he uses a pitcher of water, a basin, and a towel. In some families, the leader and/or participants go to a sink to wash, using a cup to pour the water over the hands.

PRACTICE

The leader and/or participant takes a pitcher or cup of water and pours it over each hand. The hands are dried, no blessing is recited, and then the ***b'rakhah*** over *Karpas* is immediately recited. There should be no talking between *Urḥatz* and *Karpas* as they are considered one act. So, if there is to be an explanation of *Urḥatz* or *Karpas*, it should be made before washing.

PRACTICAL QUESTIONS AND ANSWERS

Who washes hands, the leader alone or all participants?

Some authorities feel that this washing is a special honor reserved for the leader who washes hands as a representative of all assembled. Since this washing is essentially symbolic, the participants consider the leader's washing a sufficient recognition of this symbol. Others feel that since everyone will eat the *Karpas* vegetable, everyone should wash hands at this point. Custom will dictate the practice in your family. One thing to keep in mind: if you have a large number of participants, this handwashing can take a good deal of time if everyone washes.

7

כַּרְפַּס

KARPAS
THE APPETIZER
ACT 1, SCENE 3

When they dip the greens at the Passover service, I think of the newness of beginning of Spring, of running barefoot up a green-grassed mountain—sort of like the beginning of *The Sound of Music.*

Paula Peck

One year we dipped the parsley in the salt water and it really tasted funny. Rachel and her friend Robin had switched all the salt water for sugar water—because they thought that freedom should taste sweet.

Abby Kantor

The *Random House College Dictionary* defines "tease" as "to irritate or provoke with persistent petty distractions, trifling, raillery, or other annoyance, often in sport." The interpersonal meaning of "tease" has its origins in the ancient craft of making fabric. This kind of "teasing" is found in the second definition, "to pull apart or separate the adhering fibers (of wool and the like), as in combing or carding." The third definition, "to ruffle (the hair) by holding it at the ends and combing towards the scalp so as to give body to a hairdo" is a kind of hybrid, "annoying" the normal flow of the hair, while "separating adhering fibers."

The dictionary's definition of "tickle" is gentler: "to touch or stroke lightly with fingers, a feather, etc., so as to excite a tingling sensation." "Tickling" is a favorite kind of "teasing." The *Random House College Dictionary* defines appetizer as "a portion of food or drink served before a meal to stimulate the desire to eat." Dorothy Grishaver taught her son a much simpler definition. In her words, "an appetizer is an 'appe-teaser'; it teases your appetite." That kind of teasing is much more like "exciting a tingling sensation," than "provoking with petty distractions."

The *Random House College Dictionary* contains no definition for *"Karpas,"* though we know it as the parsley which is dipped into salt water as the third step in the Seder. We are given no explanation of the action. With *Matzah* and *Maror* which follow, the *Haggadah* provides a deep historical context and expresses the acts as *mitzvot* via the *b'rakhot* recited. Here, no story is told, no context is given, and the *b'rakhah* is an everyday blessing recited over any act of eating vegetables. The *Karpas* seems to be merely a *forschpeiss.* Yet, from our childhood we have been trained to recognize that the dipping is weird.

As soon as we were old enough to remember, we were trained (in the second of four memorized questions) to consider "dipping" an act worthy of questioning. Even with an ordinary *b'rakhah,* something is puzzling about the *Karpas* step. We know instinctively that the act is meaningful, yet that meaning is not clear. This appetizer teases both our appetite and our curiousity. We have been invited to make meaning, to bring explanation to this unexplained action. It is as if we have been "ruffled, held at the ends and combed towards the scalp so as to give body..."

The word *midrash* is the essence of the rabbinic process. While it means "study" and is rooted in the notion of "investigation," it is much more. It is in reality a combination of "digging" and "stretching." *Midrash* is digging into a text or action to find its essence—its central meaning; and it is "stretching" an insight or concept to connect two or more passages or rituals together. It is isolating essences and making connections—and the distinction is not always clear. It is an intellectual "pulling apart or separating of adhering fibers." *Midrash* shaped the way the rabbis thought and formed the organizational core of the Seder.

The act of *Karpas* cries out for *midrash,* and a collection of explanations have been gathered around it. *Karpas* is the greens of springtime, the *mezuzah*-making dip of the hyssop plant into the blood of the paschal lamb, the salty taste of the tears of slavery, the salty taste of the Reed Sea, and more. When Mordy Karsch told us about his family Seder, he explained: "When we first start the Seder, my Dad will usually start out asking one of us—no, he'll start out with some of the first explanations—then he'll ask me or my brother or sister, and we'll give a whole bunch of explanations. Soon, the guests realize that that's the way we'll be doing it, and that there's so much to each part, and they'll add anything they know. Later on, they'll just say whatever they feel like saying." This is the perfect explanation of *Karpas*, an invitation to engage in the making of meaning.

The Seder indeed begins with an appetizer. While the Greeks began their feasts with the tickling of the palate, the Seder begins by gently stimulating the imagination, inviting all present to explore and explain and make meaning of this historic eve.

Not all definition comes from the dictionary.

CONCEPTS

DIPPING

In the days of the rabbis who composed the Seder, dipping food was serious business. In the Seder we have two instances of dipping food: *Karpas*—a vegetable into salt water, and *Maror*—a bitter herb into *Ḥaroset*. What's it all about?

First, dipping food was a sign of freedom. Slaves were not accustomed to dipping food or eating appetizers. Second, and much more intriguing, is the possibility that this dipping is a reminder of the actual paschal offering—the act which helped save the Israelites from the Angel of Death. Consider Exodus 12:21-24:

> Moses then summoned all the elders of Israel and said to them, "Go, pick out lambs for your families, and slaughter the *Pesaḥ* offering. Take a bunch of hyssop, dip it in the blood that is in the basin, and apply some of the blood that is in the basin to the lintel and to the two doorposts. None of you shall go outside the door of his house until morning. For when *Adonai* goes through to smite the Egyptians, He will see the blood on the lintel and the two doorposts, and *Adonai* will pass over the door and not let the Destroyer enter and smite your home. You shall observe this as an institution for all time, for you and for your descendants."

Hyssop is a green vegetable common to the Middle East. Could the ritual of *Karpas* be a reminder of this dipping?

After the destruction of the Temple when the actual paschal sacrifice could no longer be performed, blood was out of the question. But, the next best thing might have been salt, since salt was used extensively in the sacrificial ritual. Thus, the dipping of a green vegetable in salt water may harken back to this critical moment in the Exodus story.

PASSOVER AS *ḤAG HE-AVIV*

One of the names of Passover is *Ḥag he-Aviv*, the Festival of Spring. Passover occurs at the end of winter, a season which enslaves the vegetation of earth. The green vegetable of *Karpas* reminds us of the long winter of slavery endured by the Israelites and their liberation from bondage at the beginning of Spring.

KARPAS—APPETIZER

1. *Barukh attah Adonai*	1. Praised are You, *Adonai*,
2. *Eloheinu melekh ha-olam*	2. Our God, King of the universe,
3. *borei p'ri ha-adamah.*	3. who creates the fruit of the earth.

SALT WATER TEARS

The *Karpas* is to be dipped in either salt water or vinegar, both liquids which remind us of the bitterness of slavery. Just as tears are salt water, so the salt water we taste is a sharp reminder of the tears our ancestors shed during their long period of bondage.

APPETIZERS

The Seder was created in a context where the patterns of Greek and Roman banquets were part of the common culture. These banquets began with appetizers. Probably, in one way or another, the rabbis were influenced by these popular patterns. Regardless of the original influence, *Karpas* now functions as a culinary and spiritual appetizer in the service. In an evening when the meal had to be postponed until after the telling of the Exodus story, this appetizer serves both to spark the curiosity of the children (the dipping is one of the Four Questions) and to anticipate the meal ahead.

OBJECTS

Karpas is defined as a vegetable or "fruit of the earth." This is, after all, the blessing that is recited for *Karpas*. Depending on where Jews lived, the available vegetables for use as *Karpas* differed. For example, in Eastern Europe green vegetation was rare at Passover time, so boiled potatoes were used. The *Shulḥan Arukh* recommends: "Many are accustomed to take parsley, but it is best to take celery which also has a good taste when raw. And it is best of all to take radishes" (Chapter 118:2). Any of the above is fine.

The Talmud states that either salt water or vinegar can be the liquid into which the *Karpas* is dipped. However, salt water is nearly universally used today.

PRACTICE

In order to facilitate the eating of *Karpas*, either each participant should have a portion of the vegetable on his/her plate, or bowls of the vegetable should be passed. There should also be a bowl or small cup of salt water nearby. Then:

1. Dip the vegetable into the salt water.
2. Say the blessing for *Karpas*. (Remember, you need not say Amen.")
3. Eat the *Karpas* while reclining.

1. בָּרוּךְ אַתָּה יהוה
2. אֱלֹהֵינוּ מֶלֶךְ הָעוֹלָם
3. בּוֹרֵא פְּרִי הָאֲדָמָה.

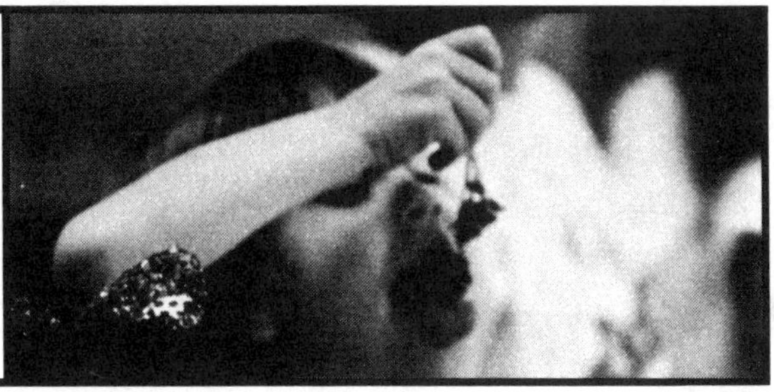

PRACTICAL QUESTIONS AND ANSWERS

Why do we recline when eating *Karpas?*

The rabbis differ over this point. Reclining is not absolutely required, yet most authorities agree that it is preferable to recline. A minority opinion holds that since the salt water is a symbol of bondage, it is inappropriate to recline.

How much *Karpas* must we eat?

The rabbis tell us to eat a piece of *Karpas* "*k'zayit*," about the size of an olive. Technically, to eat any more than that small amount would require the immediate recitation of a *b'rakhah aharonah*, a long concluding blessing.

The blessing formula used for the other acts of eating at the Seder is "*al akhilat*", "(commanded us) to eat..." This is not the form of the *b'rakhah* said over *Karpas*. Why is the blessing for *Karpas* "*borei p'ri ha-adamah*" and not "*al akhilat Karpas?*"

A very interesting question, indeed! After all, the blessings for *Matzah* and *Maror* follow the "*al akhilat*" formula. The reason is that *Karpas* is a *minhag*, a custom, and not a formal enactment of the rabbis. Unlike *Matzah* and *Maror* which are commanded in the Bible, *Karpas* is a much later custom and does not rate a "*v'tzivanu*" blessing.

INNOVATIONS

Karpas presents an opportunity for those who wish to have a leisurely first half of the Seder to placate those who cannot wait for dinner. Serve platefuls of *Karpas* appetizers—celery, carrots, parsley, radishes, broccoli—along with some dips—creamy Italian dressing, avocado guacamole—so those who are famished can eat something before the main meal. This is surely preferable to giving in to the inevitable pressure to skip or hurry through portions of the Seder service.

8

יַחַץ

YAḤATZ BREAK THE MIDDLE MATZAH

ACT 1, SCENE 4

YOUR AUTHOR:	Adina, what's your favorite part of the Seder.
ADINA WEBER:	It used to be the *afikomen.*
YOUR AUTHOR:	Why "used to be?"
ADINA WEBER:	Probably because we prayed for hours and we ate and then there was something fun to do.
YOUR AUTHOR:	It's not fun for you anymore? You said it "used to be."
ADINA WEBER:	Because now I am too old to do the *afikomen.* I can hide it, but I can't find it.
YOUR AUTHOR:	How does *afikomen* work at the Weber Seder?
ADINA WEBER:	Usually Dad hides the *afikomen.*
GAVI WEBER:	I don't know how they do it. They have it one minute, the next minute I don't know where it is.
ADINA WEBER:	I know.
GAVI WEBER:	They don't even get up! I keep my eyes on them. I would see if they stood up.
JERRY WEBER:	The Shadow knows.

The stage is dark and empty. A single white spot light defines a small area. A person dressed all in black emerges. The face is white—the hands are white, everything else is black in the white light. Every eye is focused. With a few gestures, a story is told. Nothing is said. Everyone understands, each in his/her own way. The art is called pantomime.

The table is filled with objects. All attention turns to three pieces of *matzah*. A hand takes the middle *matzah*. It is held high. Nothing is said. Every eye is focused. Everyone understands, each in his/her own way.

The eyes never leave the hands. The green pea is placed on the table top. It is covered with a shell. Three shells cycle in constant motion. Hands fly. The eyes never leave the hands. Then, everything stops. The shell is lifted. The pea is gone. The art is called prestidigition. Magic.

One half of the broken *matzah* is returned to the bag. One half of the broken *matzah* is wrapped in a napkin. For a while, it is in plain sight. The eyes never leave the hands. The Seder goes on. Suddenly, the *matzah* is gone.

Meanings will be made. Explanations will follow. The adventure begins.

CONCEPTS

YAḤATZ MEANS "BREAK"

The word "*Yaḥatz*" literally means to "break" or to "divide." It is basically a stage direction for the leader to break the middle *matzah* of the three ceremonial *matzot*. The larger half of this middle *matzah* becomes the "*afikomen*," the *matzah* which is hidden in the well-known ploy to keep the children awake.

The smaller part of the middle *matzah* is returned to its place as a symbol of "*leḥem oni*," the bread of affliction, which is discussed in the very next section of the *Haggadah*, the *Maggid* (the telling). It is entirely appropriate that the symbol of *leḥem oni* be an incomplete, broken piece of *matzah*.

AFIKOMEN FORESHADOWS REDEMPTION

Yaḥatz is a powerful symbol of redemption. Although the major theme of the *Haggadah* is the miraculous redemption of the Israelites from Egyptian slavery, the need for redemption is ever-present. It certainly was present when the *Haggadah* was compiled just after the destruction of the Holy Temple. The rabbis, reeling from this disaster which destroyed the very basis of Jewish ritual life, dreamed of a time when the Temple and the holy city of Jerusalem would be rebuilt and restored, when the Messiah would come to make whole again the broken people of Israel.

This may explain why the dominant themes of *Yaḥatz* are brokenness and hiding. The *matzah* is broken and part of it hidden away for the *afikomen*, the last piece of *matzah* eaten at the Seder and, as we will later learn, a symbol of the now-lost paschal sacrifice. In fact, the step of the Seder where the *afikomen* is found and redeemed is called *Tzafun*, literally "hidden." This is a "hiding" which will ultimately be discovered. This is a "hiding" which foreshadows the future. In the future, something now in hiding will make complete that which is now incomplete. This is a foreshadowing of the Messiah, establishing that we not only celebrate the Passover of the past, but the Passover of the future.

YAḤATZ HAS NO BLESSING

As pointed out earlier, among the four steps of the Seder which have no blessing attached to them are *Yaḥatz* and *Tzafun*—the breaking and hiding of the middle *matzah* and its discovery later. We have also said that this hiding is a hint of the redemption to come. But, why the silence? For such an important theme to be struck in the Seder and for there to be not one word spoken—well, the silence is deafening.

One theory explaining the silence again recalls the times in which the *Haggadah* was compiled, sometime around 100—200 C.E. The rabbis were living under the rule of Roman authorities who had just a few years earlier (70 C.E.) destroyed the very center of Jewish life, the Temple in Jerusalem. Although the idea of the Messiah had been part of Judaism from the days of the Prophets, long before Christianity, it gained urgency after this devastating blow to the Jewish people.

It was also a time of insurrection among the oppressed peoples of Palestine. After all, Jesus had been crucified and his disciples had already begun talking about him as the sacrificed Messiah. The Jewish idea of the Messiah was quite different, with no claims of being a son of God born of a virgin birth. For the rabbis, the Messiah would be a human being born of natural parents, a charismatic leader who would help restore the royal monarchy, the lineage of King David, and end the subservience of the Jews to a cruel occupation force.

Now, to dream of a Messiah such as this in a widely observed public ceremony would be like planning a revolution in the offices of the current government. The rabbis were quite concerned about this and created ways to keep the Messianic idea of redemption in the Seder, but "coded" these references in order not to raise the suspicions of the Roman authorities. The curious silence of *Yaḥatz* and *Tzafun* might be explained in this way. The rabbis and the people knew what the *afikomen* stood for; the Romans did not.

OBJECTS

There are three ceremonial *matzot* covered on the Seder table. The middle *matzah* is the object of *Yaḥatz*. You will also need a napkin in which to wrap the piece of *matzah* that is to be hidden, or there are special *afikomen* bags available just for this purpose.

PRACTICE

Here is how *Yaḥatz* is performed:

1. Take the middle *matzah* from its covering.
2. Break the *matzah* into two uneven pieces, one larger than the other.
3. Wrap the larger piece of *matzah* in a napkin or place it in a special *afikomen* bag. Set it aside as the *afikomen* to be found and eaten at the conclusion of the meal.
4. Replace the smaller piece of the middle *matzah* between the other two *matzot*.
5. When possible, hide the *afikomen* somewhere in the house for the children to find during the meal—or the children will "steal" the *afikomen* from the table or from underneath the leaning pillow, and you will have to ransom it later!

PRACTICAL QUESTIONS AND ANSWERS

Why is the middle *matzah* broken rather than the more obvious *matzah* on top?

The reason may have to do with the role assigned to this middle *matzah* later in the Seder. When we bless the *matzah* before the meal, two blessings are recited—*Motzi*, the all-purpose blessing over bread, and *Matzah*, a special blessing over the *matzah*. As we will learn, the *Motzi* blessing is recited over all three *matzot*, while the specific *Matzah* blessing is recited over the middle *matzah*, which we then eat from. It is entirely appropriate that the *matzah* reserved for this particular blessing be a broken piece of *matzah*, once again symbolic of *leḥem oni*, the bread of affliction.

Why are there three *matzot?*

There is a great debate among the commentators through the years about how many *matzot* are required for the Seder. Some say you only need two *matzot*, representing the *leḥem mishneh*, the two portions of bread required for Shabbat and Festivals. This is a reminder of the double portion of *manna* sent to the Israelites on Friday in the desert so they would not have to gather food on

Shabbat. Others argue that three *matzot* are required, two for *leḥem mishneh* and one to represent *leḥem oni*, the bread of affliction, the *matzah* broken at this point. Most authorities hold that the *matzah* broken for *Yaḥatz* cannot also be used for the *Motzi* since a full "loaf" of bread is required for that blessing. To satisfy everyone, the *halakhah* specified three *matzot*.

Why is the *afikomen* hidden under the pillow of the leader?

There seem to be three reasons: to protect it from being "stolen," to set it aside so it will not be mixed up with other *matzot*, and to prevent it from "embarrassment" until its moment in the limelight.

How can I hide the *afikomen* if I'm leading the Seder?

There are various strategies for hiding the *afikomen* without the children seeing you. This is no easy task, especially if you have alert kids who watch your every move. Barry Horwitz's strategy is to recruit an accomplice, to whom he passes the *afikomen* for hiding. Others simply wait until the break for the meal to quietly slip away from the table and hide the *afikomen*. The trick is to find a time when the attention of the children is diverted and when either you or another member of the family can successfully hide the *afikomen* without being detected.

Why in some families does the leader hide the *afikomen*, while in others, the children "steal" the *afikomen?*

Custom and tradition dictate the different approaches. From our research, it seems that the "stealing" approach was more prevalent among previous generations, but today, the children have a great deal of fun finding the hidden *afikomen*. Either way, the basic idea is to "redeem" the *afikomen* so it may be the last thing eaten at the Seder.

Why is the *afikomen* wrapped in a napkin?

This may be a reminder of the way in which the Israelites left Egypt, as detailed in Exodus 12:34: "And the people took their dough before it was leavened, their kneading utensils wrapped in their clothes upon their shoulders."

INNOVATIONS

Among the Sephardic Jews there is the custom of placing the wrapped *afikomen* in a bag, which is then thrown over the shoulder and carried around the Seder table in a reenactment of the Exodus as described above. (The Sabah family does this before *Avadim Hayinu*. See page 130.) The *Meḥilta*, a commentary, points out that the *mitzvah* of carrying the unleavened bread out of Egypt was too great to allow animals to do; thus, the people themselves took the *matzah* out on their own backs.

A tradition linked to the adherents of the *Kabbalah* is to break the middle *matzah* into the shape of a *dalet*, the fourth letter of the Hebrew alphabet, and a *vav*, equivalent to the number six, making a total of ten—the number of "*sefirot*" or levels of spheres of the universe in their cosmology.

Among Moroccan families, the middle *matzah* is broken into two pieces to resemble the Hebrew letter "*hei*," symbolic of God, while all assembled sing a song in Arabic which recalls God's miracle of splitting the Reed Sea. This "*hei*"-shaped *matzah* is then taken by each member of the family and held against the eyes as they recite "*Ha Laḥma Anya.*"

See *Tzafun* for other ideas regarding the *afikomen.*

9

הָא לַחְמָא עַנְיָא

HA LAḤMA ANYA
INVITATION
ACT 1, CURTAIN

When you eat *matzah* you can really taste the desert experience. I don't mean that you can taste the dust or anything, but when you crunch into it, history is there.

Paula Peck

You know, we really have to be very grateful to *matzah*. I mean, without *matzah*, none of us would ever make it through the Seder. *Matzah* is lots of fun. It keeps you busy through the second half of the Seder. You know, I always try to break my *matzah* right along the perforation, but I never can. Nobody can. With *matzah* there are always crumbs. I mean, every time you touch it... crumbs. You can make little piles out of them and then blow them all over the table. *Matzah* is great stuff.

David Coburn

Nothing is simpler than *matzah*. Take flour. Add water. Bake. That's it. *Matzah* is a way of life. It is the original fast food. Simple. Quick. Economical. *Matzah* is a spiritual commitment.

One very hot summer day, my friend Danny Rosen's mother picked us up in an old green Rambler. We were really sweating. Danny got in the car and rolled up his window. He ordered everyone to do the same thing. He had a simple explanation, "Everyone will think that we have air conditioning." At that moment, he had forgotten the message of *matzah*.

The Torah teaches with words. When you read it slowly, when you move your lips and listen, the echoes teach lessons. Consider these:

> Do not wrong a *stranger* and do not oppress him,
> for you were *strangers* in the land of Egypt.
>
> Exodus 22:20

> Do not oppress a *stranger*
> for you know the feelings of a *stranger*
> since you, yourselves, were *strangers* in the land of Egypt.
>
> Exodus 23:9

> Six days you shall labor
> and do all your work;
> but the seventh day is a Sabbath to the Lord your God;
> you should not do any kind of work,
> neither shall your son or daughter,
> neither shall your man-*slave* or woman-*slave*...
> that your man-*slave* and woman-*slave*
> may rest like you.
> And you shall remember
> that you were a *slave* in the Land of Egypt.
>
> Deuteronomy 5:13-15

> If your brother,
> a Hebrew man or woman
> is sold to you,
> s/he shall *slave* for you six years
> and in the seventh year you shall set him/her free.
> When you let him/her go free,
> you shall not let him/her go empty;
> you shall furnish him/her liberally
> out of your flock, out of your threshing-floor, out of your winepress...
> You shall remember that you were a *slave* in the land of Egypt,

> but the Lord your God redeemed you
> therefore I command this thing to you...
>
> Leviticus 25:35-42

The lesson here is as simple as *matzah*: Remembering slavery makes you a better person. Remembering how we were oppressed as *strangers* keeps us from oppressing *strangers*. Remembering the cruelty of slavery prevents us from being cruel masters. The words recycle the insight. In the story of the Exodus, we are told "The Egyptians enslaved the children of Israel *ruthlessly*... In every kind of work they worked them *ruthlessly* (Exodus 1:13-14). And, in the rules of treating our own servants we are told, "You shall not rule him *ruthlessly* (Leviticus 25:43). Over and over we remember our times as slaves. Over and over the message is reinforced: that which was done to you—should never be done to anyone.

Trevor Ferrell understands *matzah*. He is a teenager from Philadelphia, a good Christian, who since he was eleven has been devoting much of his effort to helping "his friends," the homeless living on the streets. His message is very simple. "When a person is hungry and cold, give food and clothing; when a person is sick or disturbed, arrange health care; when a person is homeless, give shelter; when a person needs to know someone cares, love them." That is exactly how this one teenager has faced the problem of the homeless. He has dealt with hunger one hamburger at a time (and a less-than-a-dollar fast-food hamburger will keep a person fed for a day) and faced the problems of the street one pillow and one blanket at a time. His commitment and his continual practice have inspired others; *Trevor's Campaign* has now become a national movement, teaching these simple lessons—and making a difference.

In the *Shulḥan Arukh* we find the same message: "If a person is hungry, the person should be fed. If the person needs clothes, the person should be given clothes. If the person has no household furniture or utensils, furniture and utensils should be provided... One who is used to warm bread should receive warm bread. One who is used to cold bread should receive cold bread. If one needs to be spoon-fed, the person must be spoon-fed." (*Yoreh Deah* 250:1) This is the lesson of *matzah*: "All who are hungry, let them enter and eat. All who are in need, let them celebrate *Pesaḥ*." This is the lesson learned from constantly renewed memory: "This is the bread of affliction."

In *matzah*, you find nothing extra. It is just flour and water—no yeast. Nothing rises, nothing expands, nothing is bloated or inflated. The *Ḥasidim* talked of *Pesaḥ* as a time to become a "*matzah*-person" to bring ourselves back to radical simplicity, to get rid of that which is bloated or inflated. The *matzah*-person is a person without leaven, a person who hasn't risen. S/he is a person who feels, perceives and understands human needs. S/he is a person without insulation.

It takes much effort to make something as simple as *matzah*—and a *matzah* bakery gives the impression of a "white-room" kind of scientific lab. Great care is taken to make sure that no water touches the flour until just the right moment. Much concern is given to keeping every surface constantly clean, lest some piece of dough be given a chance to ferment and become *ḥametz*. Baking *matzah* is a race. Everything must be done in eighteen minutes. Eighteen minutes after the first drop of water hits the flour, the *matzah* must be in the oven. Along the way, it must be kneaded, rolled, and punched full of little holes. Meanwhile, between every batch, the rollers must be sanded, the surfaces must be scoured, the perforator must be cleaned with steel wool.

But, making *matzah* is also a spiritual commitment. All through the process, in spite of the rush to beat the clock, you hear the words "*l'shem mitzvat matzah*," I am making this *matzah* so that Jews can fullfill the *mitzvah* of eating *matzah* (on *Pesaḥ*). In the mid-19th century, someone invented the first *matzah*-making machine. It caused a big stir. The rabbis argued over whether it could be used. In the end, the answer was both "yes" and "no." *Matzah* made by a machine isn't *matzah*. Only a person bound to follow the *mitzvot* can make real *matzah*. *Matzah* takes intention. However, a Jew can use a machine to do a *mitzvah*. So, as Rabbi Maurice Schwartz, the supervising religious authority at Manischewitz, explains, "The one who presses the button has the intent." Flour and water don't make *matzah*, intention makes *matzah*. For flour and water to become *matzah*, you have to want it to mean "All who are hungry, let them enter and eat." That's what makes it "the bread of affliction."

Once, when Danny Rosen and I were in Hebrew School, they took us out of class and asked us to help reset the social hall for the model Seder. There was a big time rush. Danny refused. He said to the teacher: "I ain't no slave. I don't have to do it." Our rabbi overheard and immediately sat the whole class down. That was when I first heard the true message of *matzah*. It is not easy to be a *matzah*-person.

It's natural to want our green Ramblers to have air conditioning.

02/26/2015

Item(s) Checked Out

TITLE 880-01 The Passover
BARCODE 33029069786093
DUE DATE 03-19-15

TITLE The origins of the seder :
BARCODE 3 3029 02311 7120
DUE DATE 03-19-15

Thank you for visiting the library!

Sacramento Public Library

www.saclibrary.org

Terminal # 6

CONCEPTS

THE BREAD OF AFFLICTION

Yaḥatz introduces the *matzah* as an important symbolic food of the ceremony to come. Now, it is defined as "*laḥma anya*" (Aramaic) or "*leḥem oni*" (Hebrew), the bread of affliction, the poor bread of slavery. In contrast, *matzah* is also a preeminent symbol of the Exodus, recalling the haste of the redemption which happened so fast that the Israelites could not wait for their bread to rise. How can one food represent two completely opposite ideas?

The *matzah* is a dialectic symbol which is literally transformed through the Seder experience from the bread of affliction of *Ha Laḥma Anya* into the bread of freedom of *Motzi/Matzah*. The dialectical nature of *matzah* is stated clearly in the Bible: "You shall eat no leavened bread with it (the paschal sacrifice); seven days shall you eat unleavened bread, the bread of affliction, for in haste did you come forth out of the land of Egypt." (Deuteronomy 16:3)

Why should the story be told over *matzah* and not the *z'roah*, the symbol of the *Pesaḥ* sacrifice, or the *maror*? Because the *Pesaḥ* sacrifice is no longer, and *maror* is not a symbol of both freedom and slavery. *Matzah* is the one symbol which applies in all generations.

HOSPITALITY

Ha Laḥma Anya contains within it the remarkable invitation "All who are hungry, let them enter and eat. All who are in need, let them come celebrate *Pesaḥ*." The notion of hospitality, *hakhnasat orḥim*, dates back to Abraham's welcoming the three guests who approached his tent. (By the way, this was also the first instance of *matzot* being baked, Sarah hurriedly preparing "*uggot*" which the rabbis interpreted as unleavened bread [Genesis 18:6].) Clearly, in the view of the rabbis, generosity to one's neighbors helps bring the redemption.

Yet, some questions are raised by the text. One would assume that the guests had been invited long before this point. One commentator suggests that this call is an attempt to make the poor at the table, who had come in response to an earlier invitation, feel comfortable and welcome. In some communities, however, the custom was to open the door and truly make a public invitation for anyone who still had no place for Seder.

There also appears to be a redundancy in the text. Why is it necessary to say "*kol dikhfin*" and "*kol ditzrikh*," two phrases which mean approximately the same thing—inviting people in need? One interpretation teaches that "*kol dikhfin*"—"those who are hungry"—refers to those who are actually physically hungry, while "*kol ditzrikh*"—"those who are in need"—refers to those who are not necessarily hungry, but are lonely and thus need the Seder for psychological reasons.

A note of universalism has also been sounded in connection with this text. The Talmud says you must feed the poor of the Gentiles together with the poor of the Jews. We are obligated to bury the dead of the Gentiles, as well as the dead of the Jews. We are told to visit the sick of the Gentiles, as well as the sick of the Jews.

Yet, a constant question at Passover time is "Can I invite a non-Jew to the Seder?" In Exodus, Chapter 12, the Exodus itself is described. "A mixed multitude" went out of Egypt with the Israelites, so the question must have come up even then, for the text stipulates that if you have a "stranger" (read: Gentile) who wants to join in the Passover service, he must be circumcised. Some people have interpreted this to mean that you may not invite non-Jews who are uncircumcised to the Seder.

But, this is simply untrue. Later we will learn that "*b'khol dor vador ḥayav adam lirot et atzmo k'ilu hu yatza mi'Mitzrayim,*" in every generation each individual, not just each Jew, should feel as though he or she had actually been redeemed from *Mitzrayim.* Thus, in our time at least, many families not only invite those Jews who need a place for Seder, but those who are non-Jews as well.

REDEMPTION

The preeminent theme of redemption appears once more early in the Seder text. A two-fold redemption is foretold: to be in Israel and to be free. The hope to return to Israel has been the dream of many centuries. In fact, the Seder begins and ends with this goal: "Next year in Jerusalem." (In Israel, the text reads "Next year in Jerusalem rebuilt!").

PRACTICE

The *matzot* are uncovered during the recitation of *Ha Laḥma Anya.* Many families raise the ceremonial *matzot* for all to see.

PRACTICAL QUESTIONS AND ANSWERS

In what language is *Ha Laḥma Anya* written?

The text is in Aramaic, the vernacular language during the time of the rabbis. It is clear that this text was written after the destruction of the Second Temple in 70 C.E. because of the strong theme of redemption. Some of the most famous of Jewish prayers are written in Aramaic, not Hebrew, including *Kaddish* and *Kol Nidre* just to mention two.

HA LAḤMA ANYA—INVITATION

1. *Ha laḥma anya*	1. This is the bread of affliction
2. *di a-khalu a-vahatana*	2. which our ancestors ate
3. *b'ar'a d'Mitzrayim.*	3. in the land of *Mitzrayim.*
4. *Kol dikhfin yei'tei v'yeikhul.*	4. All who are hungry, let them enter and eat.
5. *Kol ditzrikh yei'tei v'yifsaḥ.*	5. All who are in need, let them come celebrate *Pesaḥ.*
6. *Ha-shata hakha.*	6. Now we are here.
7. *Lashanah ha-ba'ah b'ar'a d'Yisrael.*	7. Next year in the land of Israel.
8. *Ha-shata av'dei.*	8. Now we are enslaved.
9. *Lashanah ha-ba'ah b'nei ḥorin.*	9. Next year we will be free.

Because *Ha Laḥma Anya* was considered very important, many commentators stress that it should be said in whatever the common language of the participants might be. It is therefore strongly recommended that the English translation of this text be read aloud at the Seder.

One final note: Legend has it that the angels do not understand Aramaic. So, why was *Ha Laḥma Anya* composed in Aramaic? To teach that where there is poverty, no one should rely on angels. It is up to each of us to feed the poor and shelter the homeless.

INNOVATIONS

Among some Sephardic families, a remarkable tradition takes place at this early point of the Seder. The Seder plate is lifted and passed over the heads of all assembled at the table, while all recite (in Hebrew): "We went out from Egypt: this is the bread of affliction…" In some communities, families visit each other on Seder night and the same procedure of passing the Seder plate over the heads of the visitors ensues before returning to the *Haggadah*.

Act I—The Beginning has come to a conclusion. We have set the scene, begun the ceremony, and invited the guests. Everything is in place for the all-important telling of the story of our slavery in Egypt and our miraculous redemption from bondage by God's mighty, outstretched arm. We are ready for **Act II—*Maggid*—The Tellings.**

1. הָא לַחְמָא עַנְיָא
2. דִּי אֲכַלוּ אַבְהָתַנָא
3. בְּאַרְעָא דְמִצְרָיִם.
4. כָּל דִּכְפִין יֵיתֵי וְיֵכֻל,
5. כָּל דִּצְרִיךְ יֵיתֵי וְיִפְסַח.
6. הַשַּׁתָּא הָכָא,
7. לַשָּׁנָה הַבָּאָה בְּאַרְעָא דְיִשְׂרָאֵל.
8. הַשַּׁתָּא עַבְדֵי,
9. לַשָּׁנָה הַבָּאָה בְּנֵי חוֹרִין.

ACT II—MAGGID
THE TELLINGS

SCENE 1: THE FIRST TELLING:
The Four Questions
SCENE 2: THE SECOND TELLING:
The Four Children

SCENE 3: THE THIRD TELLING:
Four Biblical Verses

SCENE 4: THE FOURTH TELLING:
Pesaḥ, Matzah, Maror, and Hallel

CURTAIN: KOS SHEINI
THE SECOND CUP OF WINE

Maggid takes a long, long time, but I guess it is worth sitting through, because at the end you get to drink the second glass of wine.

Matthew Gill

A Ḥasidic Teaching: All of us are asleep. By telling stories we are awakened.

A Ḥasidic Story: A student of the Baal Shem Tov was lame from birth. In his old age, he told a story about his famed teacher. He told of his recollection of how the Baal Shem Tov had prayed and his words of prayer led him to dance and jump around the room, skipping and hopping from corner to corner. While telling the story, the lame *Ḥasid* began to dance and move, acting out his tale. Telling the story cured the *Ḥasid* of his lifelong disability.

A business *Midrash*: A man wanted to know about the mind, not in nature, but in his large computer. He asked it, "Do you compute that you will ever think like a human being?" The machine set to work to analyze its own computational habits. Finally the machine printed the answer on a piece of paper, as such machines do. The man ran to get the answer and found, neatly typed, the words: THAT REMINDS ME OF A STORY... (from Gregory Bateson, *Mind and Nature: A Necessary Unity*)

Recently, the world of business has discovered something the Jewish tradition has long known—the power and importance of stories. Tom Peters and Nancy Austin, the authors of *A Passion for Excellence*, explain: "Stories are memorable...Remember Ray Kroc's visit to a McDonald's franchise in Winnipeg? He finds a single fly. Even one fly doesn fit with QSC&V (Quality, Service, Cleanliness and Value). Two weeks later the Winnipeg franchisee loses his franchise. You'd better believe that after this story made the rounds, a whole lot of McDonald's people found nearly mystical ways to eliminate flies—every fly—from their shops. Is the story apocryphal? It doesn't really matter. Mr. Kroc *did* do things *like* that." (Thomas J. Peters and Nancy K. Austin, *A Passion for Excellence, The Leadership Difference*)

They are not the only ones who have noticed. In *Corporate Cultures*, Terrence Deal and Allan Kennedy come to the same conclusion: "People tell stories to gain power and influence—and because they enjoy doing it. Storytellers are in a power position because they can change reality... Storytellers preserve institutions and their values by imparting legends of the company to new employees. They also carry stories about the visionary heroes or the latent outlaw over in the manufacturing plant." (Terrence E. Deal and Allan Kennedy, *Corporate Cultures: The Rites and Rituals of Corporate Life*). They also tell this story:

> Thomas Watson Jr., son of IBM's founder, often told a story about a nature lover who liked watching the wild ducks fly south in vast flocks each October. Out of charity, he took to putting feed for them in a nearby pond. After a while, some of the ducks no longer bothered to fly south; they wintered in the pond on what he fed them. In time they flew less and less. After three or four years, they grew so fat and lazy that they found it difficult to fly at all...He always ended the story with the point that you can make wild ducks tame, but you can never make tame ducks wild again. Watson would further add that "the duck who is tamed will never go anywhere anymore. We are convinced that business needs its wild ducks. And at IBM we try not to tame them."

Peters and Austin conclude: "Care about the stories you hear and treat them as the crucial… heartbeats they are. In fact, the drift of stories over time is arguably the single best measure of corporate vitality."

American corporations have now learned that stories are the key to their culture, and that preserving their culture is the key to their prosperity and survival. It is interesting that as Jews, we can come to relearn one of our own most important lessons from the world of commerce.

Peninnah Schram is the dean of North American Jewish storytellers. In her most recent book, *Jewish Stories One Generation Tells Another*, she explains her love of storytelling:

> Once I asked my own master, "I understand why the *mitzvot*, the laws, were so scrupulously transmitted from generation to generation, but why the *aggadot*? Why the legends?" And my master answered, "They are important because they stress the importance of the listener."

Reading or telling a child a story is a personal experience. Any parent who has ever shared his or her love for a child by reading or telling a story understands this insight. The act of reading together is a shared experience, and something transpires that no tape recording could accomplish. The reading is dynamic. It invites questions and answers. It contains intonations and touches. It is shared laughter and reflection. It is high-level communication. Both the listener and the teller effect the tale.

On Seder night, we experience the primal Jewish read-aloud experience. It is the event which has classically bound child to parent, as well as to the Jewish people. It is a connection forged by the act of telling stories.

Jim Trelease is the author of the *Read Aloud Handbook*, the work which refocused attention on the act of parents reading to children. He explains why reading together is important: "The initial reasons are the same reasons you talk to a child: to reassure, to entertain, to inform or explain, to arouse curiousity, and to inspire—and to do it all personally, not impersonally with a machine." Seder personifies these goals. It is a night on which stories are both told and made.

Elie Wiesel is one of our greatest writers. His life has been dedicated to the writing, telling, retelling and reading of stories. In *Souls on Fire*, he explains that his love of stories is interwoven with his family relations:

> My father, an enlightened spirit, believed in man.
> My grandfather, a fervent *Ḥasid*, believed in God.
> The one taught me to speak, the other to sing.
> Both loved stories.
> And when I tell mine, I hear their voices.
> Whispering from beyond the silent storm.
> They are what links the survivor to their memory.
> God created man because He loved stories.

Pesaḥ is our time to tell stories.

CONCEPTS

THE TELLING

The central commandment of the Seder is to tell the story of the Exodus from Egypt. "*V'higad'ta l'vinkha*"—"You shall tell your child on that day saying: 'This is because of what *Adonai* did for me when I came out of Egypt'" (Exodus 13:8). The word "*higad'ta*"—"you shall tell"—comes from the root "*l'hagid*"—"to tell." The words "*Haggadah*" and "*Maggid*" derive from the very same root—meaning, "the telling."

Why is the commandment "to tell" and not "to remember?" Rav Chaim of Brisk teaches that while we remember the Exodus from Egypt all year long in the liturgy, the *mitzvah* of telling the story of the Exodus is unique to *Pesaḥ*. There are, after all, differences between remembering and telling. Remembering is a *mitzvah* performed individually; telling is the act of relating the entire story to at least one other person. Remembering is a process of thinking about the general nature of an event; telling involves the development of the story. Moreover, telling involves reading and speaking out loud, one of the most powerful ways to create memories.

Maggid, then, is the long section of the *Haggadah* which tells the story of the Exodus from Egypt. Regrettably, this most important part of the Seder is the section often given the least attention, probably because it appears to be so intimidating and repetitious. As a matter of fact, *Maggid* can be viewed as a carefully constructed series of texts and experiences which tells the Exodus story through a variety of teaching styles tailored to the different types of learners at your Seder table.

Educators know that everyone has a preferred learning style. Some people learn best from experiences which employ visuals and manipulatives, actual objects which visually symbolize concepts. Other people learn best from didactic approaches based on the ability to hear and synthesize verbal information which is often analytical in nature. The rabbis who formulated the Seder, superb innate educators all, knew this about people and provided a variety of learning experiences in the *Haggadah* so that, whatever one's learning style, the message of the evening is taught.

This is especially true in the *Maggid*, which is composed of four separate tellings of the Exodus story, each one following the same lesson plan, but with learning experiences geared to different learning styles. Why four tellings? We are told in the *Haggadah* itself: "*v'khol ha-marbeh l'saper b'tziat Mitzrayim, harei zeh meshubaḥ*:" "anyone who elaborates on the telling of the Exodus story is praiseworthy." We put forward the thesis that the reason for these four tellings is not only to elaborate, but to offer four different approaches to telling the story, hoping that at least one of them will reach and teach each person at the Seder.

Each of the four tellings in *Maggid* follows the same lesson plan. The telling begins with a QUESTION, followed by an ANSWER, followed by PRAISE for God, the Hero of our story. This paradigm sets the methodology for the evening—to ask questions, to tell stories, and to sing songs of praise to *Adonai*, the God who liberated us from Egyptian bondage.

Let's look at each of the four tellings, first for the general structure as it appears in the *Haggadah*.

SCENE 1: THE FIRST TELLING

QUESTION: *Mah Nishtanah* (Four Questions)

The *Maggid*'s First Telling begins with the famous Four Questions. They ask (or state) how different this night is from all other nights of the year. More specifically, they ask why we eat *matzah*, why we eat bitter herbs, why we dip food twice, and why we recline at the table.

ANSWER: *Avadim Hayinu* (We Were Slaves)

The *Haggadah* answers these questions by initiating the telling of the story of the Exodus, beginning with the fact that once we were slaves to Pharoah in Egypt.

PRAISE: *Barukh ha-Makom* (Praised Be He)

After two brief tangents which illustrate the importance of elaborating the story, the *Haggadah* pauses to praise God with the four-part statement: "Praised be He who is everywhere. Praised be He. Praised be He who gave the Torah to His people Israel. Praised be He." Note that the word "*barukh*" (praised) appears four times, foreshadowing the Four Children's questions which begin the Second Telling.

SCENE 2: THE SECOND TELLING

QUESTION: *Arba'ah Banim* (Four Children)

The Four Children represent the four archetypes of Jewish learners, each with his/her own questions about *Pesaḥ* and, indeed, Jewish belief and practice.

ANSWER: *Miteḥilah Ovdei Avodah Zarah* (We Were Idol-Worshippers)

The *Haggadah* begins to tell the Exodus story again, this time beginning with our ancestral origins as idol-worshippers.

PRAISE: *Barukh Shomer/V'hi She'amda* (Praised Be He Who Keeps His Promise to Israel)

Adonai is praised as the God who keeps His promises to His people. He kept His promise to Abraham and made Israel a great nation, and in each generation, He saves us from those who seek our destruction.

SCENE 3: THE THIRD TELLING

QUESTION: *Tzei u-L'mad* (Consider These Verses)

The *Haggadah* begins the Third Telling with the instruction "Consider these verses!," or, "Go and learn!"—a call to ask questions about the four verses from Deuteronomy which provide a summary of the Exodus story.

ANSWER: *Arami Oved Avi* (My Father Was A Wandering Aramean)/ *Eser Makot* (Ten Plagues)

The answer to the question of what these verses mean is provided through the process of *midrash*, elaborating the simple meaning of these texts by analyzing the single words and phrases which tell the story of the Exodus. The last phrase of this version of the story, "signs and wonders," leads to a recitation of the Ten Plagues which eventually convinced Pharoah to let the Israelites go from Egypt.

PRAISE: *Dayyenu* (Enough!) The *Haggadah* cannot continue after this dramatic retelling of the Plagues without praising God who has done more than enough for the Jewish people.

SCENE 4: THE FOURTH TELLING

QUESTION: *Rabban Gamliel Hayah Omer (Pesaḥ, Matzah, Maror)*
The Fourth Telling of the story parallels the First Telling, beginning with specific questions about the ritual items on the table—the *Pesaḥ*, the *Matzah*, and the *Maror.*

ANSWER: *B'khol Dor va-Dor* (You Yourself Were Redeemed)
The specific answers about *Pesaḥ*, *Matzah* and *Maror* are given directly after the question is posed. But, the more important reason that we explain these three objects is that each and every one of us should consider her/himself as if s/he had been redeemed from Egypt.

PRAISE: *L'fikhakh* (Therefore, We Praise God) *Halleluyah* (Halleluyah!) *Ga'al Yisrael* (Praised Is The Redeemer of Israel)
Therefore, we praise God who took us from slavery to freedom, we sing a new song to Him, and we praise the Redeemer of Israel.

Upon closer examination, we see an unusual sensitivity to the needs of different types of learners. In the First Telling, the questions ask about specific practices—*Matzah, Maror*, dipping, reclining—and the answer focuses on the personal stake the learner has in the Exodus story: "If *Adonai* had not taken our ancestors out of Egypt, we would still be slaves to Pharoah." The Second Telling takes a different approach. The questions of the Four Children run the gamut from asking about specific laws to ideological confrontation and the answer centers on God who makes and keeps promises. The Third Telling is an exercise in pure *midrash*, designed for those with analytical, probing minds. And, the Fourth Telling returns us to the practical, asking questions about particular ritual symbols that lie before us which are answered by pointing to them, proof positive that the Seder is truly a "hands-on" learning experience, a kind of grand simulation exercise designed to make each participant feel as if he or she were actually redeemed from Egypt.

The finale of Act II is the Second Cup of Wine, celebrating God's promise to deliver us which, of course, He did.

Let us now look at each of the Four Tellings in more specific detail.

10

THE FIRST TELLING

THE QUESTION: MAH NISHTANAH—FOUR QUESTIONS
THE ANSWER: AVADIM HAYINU—WE WERE SLAVES
THE PRAISE: BARUKH HA-MAKOM—PRAISED BE HE WHO IS EVERYWHERE

ACT II, SCENE 1

When I was either five or six years old, I was supposed to do the Four Questions at my family's Seder and I said the Four Questions from underneath the table. I'm not even sure why, whether it was shyness or what....

Jerry Weber

What do I think of the Four Questions? Well, when you first get to ask the Four Questions, you think it is the coolest thing you can do, and then for the next couple of years it is still okay. But six or seven years later it's just no fun to still be the youngest. I'll probably have to say the Four Questions until I have my own kids.

David Coburn

I still remember when my Bubbie taught me to say the "*Fier Kashes*" (Four Questions). I must have been 2 or 3 years old and I learned them in Yiddish and I can remember some of it. I do remember standing up on a chair and saying them for my Grandfather. Sometimes I think I would like to teach them to my youngest child in Yiddish. She does them in Hebrew each year. I know that my father would just blow his mind if he saw it, but I can't find anyone who can teach them to me so I can teach them to my daughter in Yiddish.

Abby Kantor

THE QUESTION: MAH NISHTANAH

CONCEPTS

THE IMPORTANCE OF QUESTIONS

Questions are central to the Seder experience. In fact, questions are central to the Jewish view of religion. Judaism is not a dogmatic, static list of catechisms. Rather, Jewish law and thought have always allowed--even welcomed--questions, for in the process of questioning, new knowledge and new understandings emerge.

Questioning is also a sign of freedom. Slaves don't ask questions. To ask a question is to demonstrate one's freedom to explore, to analyze, to investigate, indeed, to question the symbols, rituals, and philosophies of the Seder experience.

This is an all-important point. For Jewish ritual, including the ritual of the Seder, is really Jewish philosophy. The ritual comes to teach the philosophy. That is why we avoid orthopraxis—the doing of ritual for the sake of the ritual, and instead concentrate on understanding the meaning of the ritual act—the underlying philosophy the act comes to represent. That is why the question is critical, for without it, we would be reduced to a behavioristic religion, devoid of meaningful substance and belief.

IN EACH GENERATION, THE QUESTIONS CAN CHANGE

The Four Questions in our *Haggadah* today are *not* the same questions prescribed in the *Mishnah*, the compilation of the Oral Law which forms the basis for the Talmud. There, they are not even the Four Questions! The Three Questions found in the earliest texts of the Mishnah are:

> Why is this night different from all other nights?
> 1. For on all other nights we dip once, but on this night we dip twice.
> 2. For on all other nights we eat leavened and unleavened bread, whereas on this night we eat only unleavened bread.
> 3. For on all other nights we eat meat roasted, stewed or boiled; on this night, roasted only.
>
> *Pesaḥim* 116a.

By the time the Talmud was redacted, a fourth question had been added:

> 4. For on all other nights we eat all kinds of herbs, on this night bitter herbs.

In view of the destruction of the Temple and the end of the actual practice of sacrificing the paschal lamb, the question about roasted meat was eliminated. In its place, a question about "reclining" was added. And, once the standard practice of dipping foods at meals was no longer in vogue, that question was reformulated to "we do not usually dip vegetables even once; why, on this night, do we dip twice?"

The point is, of course, obvious. The questions changed over time to reflect current practice so they can do the job they are intended to do—to stimulate the *answers*.

The notion of asking questions is so important that the Talmud specifies that even if you find yourself alone on Seder night, you should ask yourself the questions! Even two scholars who know all the laws of Passover are to ask one another. Incredibly, there is also a view that we are not obliged to tell the *Haggadah* unless a question is asked. Can there be a doubt as to the importance of questions at the Seder?

CHILDREN AND THE FOUR QUESTIONS

It is a very old custom for the youngest child to ask the Four Questions. The reason goes back to the biblical account of the Exodus itself. Four times the text says "When your child asks... you shall say... 'We were slaves in Egypt and *Adonai* brought us out...'" Naturally, it is difficult for a child to learn unless he or she has a question in mind. The genius of the Seder is to involve the youngest generation by putting the questions in their mouths. Moreover, the very continuity of the Jewish family and the people Israel depends in large measure upon the ability of the children to participate in and maintain the religious rituals, to ask and answer the questions of their ancestors.

Of course, asking the Four Questions has become one of the earliest Jewish rites of passage. *Mah Nishtanah* is one of the first Jewish texts that children learn in religious school, and proud is the parent whose youngest progeny stands before all assembled to chant these ancient verses. Indeed, as more children join the family and the youngest suddenly becomes the oldest, a new, younger generation takes on the responsibility of asking the questions while the growing children proudly "graduate" from this status.

QUESTIONS AS PRETEXT

One might ask, "How can we ask questions about eating *Matzah* and *Maror* when no *Matzah* or *Maror* has as yet been eaten?" Clearly, it would make a great deal more sense for the questions to be asked *after* having seen the ritual take place. In fact, originally the meal was eaten first, stimulating questions about the ritual surrounding it (*Matzah*, *Maror*, dipping, and reclining), and then the story was told. But, because the children often could not stay up late enough to hear the story, the rabbis reversed the order of the Seder so that the story came first and the meal later. The questions were retained near the beginning of the Seder in order to stimulate the children's curiosity about what was going to happen.

PRACTICE

Traditionally, the *Mah Nishtanah* is recited or chanted by the youngest child in attendance at the Seder. In some families, there are two recitations: one in Hebrew and one in English, with children in the family participating according to their language skills. At some larger family *Sedarim*, there are a number of "youngest" children who join together in chanting the Four Questions. It is a good idea to identify who among those children attending are prepared to do what and then decide how to handle this sometimes emotional issue.

Before *Mah Nishtanah* is recited, the *matzot* are covered and we fill the Second Cup of Wine. This is designed to stimulate further curiosity among the children. The remainder of the *Maggid* is recited over this Second Cup.

MAH NISHTANAH—FOUR QUESTIONS

1. *Mah nishtanah ha-lilah ha-zeh*	1. How different this night is
2. *mikol ha-leilot!*	2. from all other nights!
3. *Sheh-b'khol ha-leilot anu okhlin*	3. On all other nights we eat
4. *ḥametz u'matzah.*	4. either *ḥametz* or *matzah.*
5. *Ha-lilah ha-zeh kulo matzah?*	5. Why, on this night, do we eat only *matzah?*
6. *Sheh-b'khol ha-leilot anu okhlin*	6. On all other nights, we eat
7. *sh'ar y'rakot.*	7. all kinds of vegetables.
8. *Ha-lilah ha-zeh maror?*	8. Why, on this night, must we eat bitter herbs?
9. *Sheh-b'khol ha-leilot*	9. On all other nights
10. *ein anu mat'bilin*	10. we do not usually dip (vegetables)
11. *afilu pa'am eḥat.*	11. even once.
12. *Ha-lilah ha-zeh sh'tei f'amim?*	12. Why, on this night, do we dip twice?
13. *Sheh-b'khol ha-leilot*	13. On all other nights
14. *anu okhlin bain yoshvin*	14. we eat either sitting upright
15. *u-vain m'subin.*	15. or reclining.
16. *Ha-lilah ha-zeh kulanu m'subin?*	16. Why, on this night, do we eat reclining?

PRACTICAL QUESTIONS AND ANSWERS

Why is the translation "How different this night is from all other nights!"? I always remember it as a question, "Why is this night different from all other nights?"
Actually, the translation of the Hebrew indicates more of a declarative statement than a question here. The questions follow the observation that the night (read: the meal) is so very different from the usual.

What vegetables do we dip twice?
The two dippings refer to the *Karpas* vegetable dipped in salt water and the *Maror*, bitter herbs, dipped in *Ḥaroset* just before the meal.

1. מַה נִּשְׁתַּנָּה הַלַּיְלָה הַזֶּה
2. מִכָּל הַלֵּילוֹת.
3. שֶׁבְּכָל הַלֵּילוֹת אָנוּ אוֹכְלִין
4. חָמֵץ וּמַצָּה,
5. הַלַּיְלָה הַזֶּה כֻּלּוֹ מַצָּה?
6. שֶׁבְּכָל הַלֵּילוֹת אָנוּ אוֹכְלִין
7. שְׁאָר יְרָקוֹת,
8. הַלַּיְלָה הַזֶּה מָרוֹר?
9. שֶׁבְּכָל הַלֵּילוֹת
10. אֵין אָנוּ מַטְבִּילִין
11. אֲפִילוּ פַּעַם אֶחָת,
12. הַלַּיְלָה הַזֶּה שְׁתֵּי פְעָמִים?
13. שֶׁבְּכָל הַלֵּילוֹת
14. אָנוּ אוֹכְלִין בֵּין יוֹשְׁבִין
15. וּבֵין מְסֻבִּין.
16. הַלַּיְלָה הַזֶּה כֻּלָּנוּ מְסֻבִּין?

INNOVATIONS

The Talmud talks of distributing nuts to the children following *Mah Nishtanah*, perhaps as a way to keep them occupied during the *Maggid* story to come.

Many families ask additional sets of Four Questions with a more modern ring to them: for example, "Why must the arms race continue?," "Why is there homelessness when society is so wealthy?"

In some families, the practice is to remove the Seder plate from the table altogether or to place it at the end of the table just before *Mah Nishtanah* and return it at *Rabban Gamliel Hayah Omer*. Once again, this is designed to stimulate the curiosity of the children.

THE ANSWER: AVADIM HAYINU
CONCEPTS

AN ANSWER WITH TWO BEGINNINGS

The Mishnah that records the *Mah Nishtanah* questions also suggests the basic principle which is to structure the answer: "Begin with degradation and end with glory" (*Pesaḥim* 116a). The Talmud then presents a debate between Rav and Shmuel concerning what this "degradation" refers to. For Shmuel, this means the slavery of Egypt, and so our *Haggadah* begins the answer to the Four Questions with "*Avadim Hayinu*," "We were slaves to Pharoah in *Mitzrayim*..." Rav, however, equates degradation with the idolatry of Abraham's father, "*Miteḥilah ovdei avodah zarah*," "In the beginning our ancestors served idols...," tracing the very roots of the Exodus back to Abraham who rejected his father's gods. In good Talmudic style, the compilers of the *Haggadah* included both "beginnings" in our text.

Rabbi Harold Schulweis tells a story which illustrates the importance of this point. He was once invited to speak at a meeting of a black church congregation during the week before Passover. He used as his text "*Avadim Hayinu*"—"Once we were slaves, but the Lord brought us out with a mighty hand and an outstretched arm." After he finished, a black leader of the church commented: "We would never say that in our church. We never remind our people about slavery." Rabbi Schulweis asked, "Why?" "Because it is demeaning to us," was the reply. It was then that the rabbi understood the power of this paragraph of the *Haggadah*. We emphasize our lowly state because, for the Jew, what is important is not only what you were, but what you have become.

WE WERE SLAVES

This single paragraph provides a concise answer to the children's questions: "We celebrate *Pesaḥ* because once we were slaves to Pharoah in Egypt, but *Adonai* brought us forth with a mighty hand and an outstretched arm. If He hadn't, we would still be enslaved to Pharoah. And our duty is to tell the story. In fact, the more we elaborate upon it, the more we will be praised."

That's it. There need be no other reason to do the Passover ritual than to recall the fact that God redeemed us from slavery. If the children should fall asleep or tune out at this point, the essence would have been stated. All the rest is commentary.

GOD REDEEMED US

This is the essential point of the *Haggadah* and Seder ritual. It is made ultimately clear in this first part of the answer that it was God who brought us out of slavery—not Moses, not Pharoah, not angels—but God and God alone. This becomes abundantly clear as the story continues to be told without as much as a single mention of Moses. (His name is cited once, but only within the context of a biblical quotation). Moses was simply God's messenger. Nothing more, nothing less. God Himself redeemed us, without an intermediary. By liberating us from our bondage, *Adonai* created a people belonging to Him. Therefore, He singularly deserves our praise and our devotion.

WHAT IF?

The *Haggadah* asks itself and those reading it a question: "What if *Adonai* had not redeemed us?" The answer given is quite interesting: "*M'shubadim hayinu*"—"We would have remained enslaved." The text does not say we would have remained "*slaves*," rather "*enslaved*." If not to Pharoah in his time, then to someone else. We would have remained enslaved to the things that Pharoah and Egypt stood for.

WHOEVER ELABORATES THE STORY DESERVES PRAISE

The *Haggadah* tells us that there is great merit in elaborating the basic answer given in *Avadim Hayinu*. And, in fact, the rest of the *Haggadah* does just that—it elaborates the story of the Exodus from Egypt with three additional tellings. This statement is not simply a motivational device to get us to continue with the rest of the narrative. Even those who have acquired the three qualities of wisdom as defined in the *Kabbalah* and enumerated here—*de'ah*, knowledge; *binah*, understanding; and *ḥokhmah*, wisdom—have a duty to tell the story of the Exodus. The point: There is no way to exhaust the depth of meaning the Exodus story has for us.

FIVE RABBIS MEETING IN THE NIGHT

In the Talmud, one idea stimulates the next. The *Haggadah* often demonstrates this "train-of-thought" technique. *Avadim Hayinu* ends with the suggestion that "whoever elaborates upon the story of the Exodus deserves praise." Immediately, the *Haggadah* brings a proof text, the interesting story of five rabbis gathered at B'nei B'rak who discussed the Exodus from *Mitzrayim* all through the night. What could they have been discussing all night? Professor Louis Finkelstein hypothesized that these five elders were, in fact, planning the ill-fated Bar Kokhba rebellion against the Romans of 132-135 C.E. It is known that Rabbi Akiva, at whose Seder this summit meeting took place, was a prominent supporter of Bar Kokhba. Thus, this could be a "coded" text, included in the *Haggadah* as a kind of message-within-a-message about freedom and its price. Ultimately, Rabbi Akiva was tortured and killed for his support of Bar Kokhba's unsuccessful attempt to restore religious freedom to the Jews of his time.

RECALL THE EXODUS EVERY NIGHT

Talmudic style continues with the text picking up on the mention in the previous paragraph that the rabbis' students had to alert them that their all-night discussion had taken them to the time for saying the "*Shema*." For the editor of the *Haggadah*, that recalls a problem Rabbi Elazar ben Azariah had in convincing his colleagues that the Exodus was so important that the paragraph of the *Shema* which mentions it, the "*Tzitzit*" section, should be recited at night, even though *tzitzit*, the fringed *tallit* (prayer shawl), is not worn then. His friend, Ben Zoma, helped the cause by interpreting the word "all" in the phrase "all the days of your life," a seemingly superfluous word in the verse from Deuteronomy 16:3, to mean that the nights are included in the days. Although not directly tied to the line of inquiry about discussing the Exodus at night, it is obvious that if we are to mention the Exodus every night of the year, how much more so should we elaborate the story on this, the anniversary night of the Exodus itself.

AVADIM HAYINU—WE WERE SLAVES

1. *Avadim hayinu l'Pharaoh b'Mitzrayim*	1. We were slaves to Pharoah in *Mitzrayim*
2. *va-yotzi'einu Adonai Eloheinu mishahm*	2. but *Adonai* our God brought us forth
3. *b'yad ḥazakah*	3. with a mighty hand
4. *u-viz'roa n'tuyah.*	4. and with an outstretched arm.
5. *V'ilu lo hotzi ha-kadosh barukh hu et avoteinu*	5. And if the Holy One, praised be He, had not taken our ancestors out
6. *mi'Mitzrayim,*	6. of *Mitzrayim,*
7. *harei anu u-vaneinu,*	7. then we, and our children,
8. *u-v'nei vaneinu,*	8. and our children's children,
9. *m'shubadim ha'yinu l'Pharoh*	9. would still be enslaved to Pharoah
10. *b'Mitzrayim.*	10. in *Mitzrayim.*
11. *Va-afilu kulanu ḥakhamim,*	11. Now even if all of us were scholars,
12. *kulanu n'vonim,*	12. even if all of us were sages,
13. *kulanu z'keinim,*	13. even if all of us were elders,
14. *kulanu yodim et ha-Torah,*	14. even if all of us were learned in the Torah,
15. *mitzvah aleinu l'saper*	15. it would still be our duty to tell the story
16. *bi'tzi'at Mitzrayim.*	16. of the Exodus from *Mitzrayim.*
17. *V'khol ha-marbeh l'saper*	17. Moreover, whoever elaborates upon the story
18. *bi'tzi'at Mitzrayim,*	18. of the Exodus
19. *harei zeh m'shubaḥ.*	19. deserves praise.

1. עֲבָדִים הָיִינוּ לְפַרְעֹה בְּמִצְרָיִם
2. וַיּוֹצִיאֵנוּ יהוה אֱלֹהֵינוּ מִשָּׁם
3. בְּיָד חֲזָקָה
4. וּבִזְרוֹעַ נְטוּיָה.
5. וְאִלּוּ לֹא הוֹצִיא הַקָּדוֹשׁ בָּרוּךְ הוּא
   אֶת אֲבוֹתֵינוּ
6. מִמִּצְרַיִם,
7. הֲרֵי אָנוּ וּבָנֵינוּ
8. וּבְנֵי בָנֵינוּ
9. מְשֻׁעְבָּדִים הָיִינוּ לְפַרְעֹה
10. בְּמִצְרָיִם.
11. וַאֲפִילוּ כֻּלָּנוּ חֲכָמִים,
12. כֻּלָּנוּ נְבוֹנִים,
13. כֻּלָּנוּ זְקֵנִים,
14. כֻּלָּנוּ יוֹדְעִים אֶת הַתּוֹרָה,
15. מִצְוָה עָלֵינוּ לְסַפֵּר
16. בִּיצִיאַת מִצְרָיִם.
17. וְכָל הַמַּרְבֶּה
    לְסַפֵּר
18. בִּיצִיאַת מִצְרָיִם
19. הֲרֵי זֶה מְשֻׁבָּח.

PRACTICE

A basic principle of practice is to uncover the ceremonial *matzot* during the recitation of the *Maggid*, except when the wine cup is raised. Then, we cover the *matzot* for the reasons alluded to earlier, mainly so as not to "shame" the *matzot* while they are ignored in favor of the wine. Before beginning *Avadim Hayinu*, the *matzot* are uncovered. If the Seder plate has been moved to the end or off the table, it is returned to its original place.

INNOVATIONS

Rica Sabah recalls an ancient tradition in her family which has its counterpart in many Sephardic communities. It is the custom for the leader or one of the participants to leave the room after the Four Questions and before *Avadim Hayinu*, only to return a few moments later with the napkin containing the *afikomen* slung over his/her shoulder. Everyone at the table would then ask in Hebrew: "Who are you?" The answer from the person acting out the drama of the Exodus: "A Jew." "Where do you come from?," the dialogue continues. "From Egypt." "What did you do there?" "I was a slave." "How many years did it take you to come here?" "Forty years." "Why did you come?" "To be free."

In some variations of this custom, the "actor" would then tell the story of the Exodus, referring to several biblical quotations and the *afikomen*. The participants would repeat these key phrases in a kind of refrain, until the last statement: "*V'khol ha-marbeh l'saper b'tziat Mitzrayim, harei ze meshubaḥ*," the concluding phrase of *Avadim Hayinu*.

Bukharian Jews have a similar custom at this point in the Seder. The leader stands up and walks around the Seder table in a bent-over position, as if he or she were, in fact, a slave.

BARUKH HA-MAKOM—PRAISED BE HE

1. *Barukh ha-Makom*	1. Praised be He who is everywhere,
2. *Barukh Hu.*	2. Praised be He.
3. *Barukh shenatan Torah*	3. Praised be He who gave the Torah
4. *l'amo Yisrael.*	4. to His people Israel.
5. *Barukh Hu.*	5. Praised be He.

THE PRAISE: BARUKH HA-MAKOM
CONCEPTS

PRAISE FOR GOD

The *Haggadah* pauses at the end of each of the Four Tellings to praise God, the Hero of the Exodus story. In this, the First Telling, the praise comes in the form of a four-phrase formula of praise: "*Barukh ha-Makom, Barukh Hu, Barukh shenatan Torah l'amo Yisrael, Barukh Hu*--" "Praised be He who is everywhere, Praised be He, Praised be He who gave the Torah to His people Israel, Praised be He."

This fourfold statement of praise is both the conclusion to the First Telling and a transition to the Second Telling. The number four, as we have already seen, is crucial to the *Haggadah*'s structure. The word "*barukh*," "praise," is the key term of blessing in Jewish liturgy. The reference to God who gave the Torah to Israel foreshadows the four biblical verses which are about to be cited as answers to the questions of the Four Children.

It could be argued that "*Barukh ha-Makom*" is really the introduction of the Four Children. But a medieval Jewish commentator, Abravanel, and a modern Israeli scholar, Kasher, both point out in their commentaries that, while there could be a notion of transition in these statements of praise, the Four Children is clearly a new section of the *Haggadah*, the beginning of the Second Telling.

1. בָּרוּךְ הַמָּקוֹם.
2. בָּרוּךְ הוּא.
3. בָּרוּךְ שֶׁנָּתַן תּוֹרָה
4. לְעַמּוֹ יִשְׂרָאֵל.
5. בָּרוּךְ הוּא.

11

THE SECOND TELLING

THE QUESTION: ARBA'AH BANIM—THE FOUR CHILDREN
THE ANSWER: MITEḤILAH OVDEI AVODAH ZARAH—WE WERE IDOL-WORSHIPPERS
THE PRAISE: BARUKH SHOMER/V'HI SHE'AMDAH—PRAISED BE THE GUARDIAN WHO KEEPS HIS PROMISE

ACT II, SCENE 2

In our Seder I always try to be the wise son and we see to it that Uncle Sidney comes out the wicked son.

David Coburn

You want to know my first thoughts when I hear the Four Sons? Why no daughters? But then, I wouldn't change the text. It's been around too long.

Paula Peck

THE QUESTION: ARBA'AH BANIM
CONCEPTS

TEACH EACH CHILD ACCORDING TO HIS/HER WAY (Proverbs 22:6)

The passages dealing with the Four Children could be among the first parental advice columns ever written. The *Haggadah* suggests that the parents of biblical times had the same troubles parents have today: how to talk to your children so they will listen and learn. No less than four times the Bible warns that there will come a time when your children will ask about the meaning of their parents' religious observances.

The text of the "Four Children" is deduced from these four verses and provides the rabbis with an opportunity to suggest that religious instruction must be geared to each child individually. Let us examine each child's question and the answer suggested by the *Haggadah*.

THE WISE CHILD

The question: "What are the statutes, the laws and the ordinances which *Adonai* our God has commanded us?" (Deuteronomy 6:20) . The question itself indicates that this child is already a knowledgeable and mature learner. The three references to various commandments indicates that the child understands that *eidut* (statutes) refer to laws that testify to historical events, such as God's interventions in history; that *ḥukim* (laws) refer to laws whose reasons are not given directly in the Torah or whose meaning is not easily understood, such as the prohibition against breaking the bones of the paschal sacrifice; and that *mishpatim* (ordinances) are rules for improving relationships among human beings, such as the invitation to all who are hungry to join the Passover celebration.

Note also that the wise child includes him/herself in the community of those who are to follow these laws. Some texts, including ours, change the biblical quotation slightly to say "*otanu*" (us) instead of "*etkhem*" (you [plural]) for purposes of clarity and distinction between the wise and wicked child, who, as we shall soon see, separates him/herself from the community.

The answer: "You should inform this child of all the laws of *Pesaḥ*, including the ruling that nothing should be eaten after the *afikomen*."

Actually, the Torah directly answers the wise child in the verses of Deuteronomy 6:21-25 with the by-now familiar refrain "We were slaves to Pharoah in Egypt and *Adonai* brought us out with a mighty hand... and *Adonai* commanded us to do all these statutes..." Why doesn't the *Haggadah* give this same answer?

There are several possibilities. First, the essence of the Bible's answer is given in *Avadim Hayinu* which we just read in the *Haggadah*. Second, the wise child's question indicates s/he already knows the basic answers and is now looking for the details. So, the *Haggadah* suggests that the way to handle this child is to teach him/her the myriad Passover laws, down to the last one specified in the Mishnah: "Nothing should be eaten after the *afikomen*."

THE WICKED CHILD

The question: "What does this ritual mean to *you*?" (Exodus 12:26).

This question really upset the rabbis. What is "wicked" about the "wicked" child? The fact that s/he removes her/himself from the community. The question is phrased as "What does this ritual mean to *you*?" not "What does this ritual mean to *us* or to *me*?" A better understanding of the *rasha* might be "the impious child."

The answer: Again, the Torah provides an answer to this question: "You shall say, 'It is the sacrifice of *Adonai*'s passover, for He passed over the houses of the children of Israel in Egypt. . . (Exodus 12:27)." This can be interpreted to mean that the *Pesaḥ* sacrifice can only be shared by those who accept God, and clearly, the wicked child does not.

But, the rabbis of the *Haggadah* are more concerned with the kind of question asked by the wicked child than with the so-called "correct" answer. For them, the task with this child is to bring him/her back within the fold. And, thus, the *Haggadah*'s answer is quite blunt. First, shake the child up! If not with a physical blow (the literal translation of "*ha-k'heih et shinnav*" is "set his teeth on edge"), then certainly this child needs a direct instruction. The rabbis pick Exodus 13:8: "This is done because of what *Adonai* did for me when I went out of *Mitzrayim*." They point out to the wicked child that the verse says "to *me*," not even "to him." In other words, unless you see yourself as having been liberated from Egypt, unless you include yourself as part of this community, then you cannot be a part of this people at all. As if to drive the point home, the rabbis really let the wicked child have it by suggesting that if s/he *had been* on hand at the moment of Exodus, s/he would *not* have been redeemed.

Pretty drastic, this. Yet, it is asked "Why does the wicked child's question come second, before the simple child and the child who does not know how to ask?" Because at least this child is asking questions, and as long as the child asks questions, there is a chance of reaching him/her. After all, in the end, the *Haggadah* tries to answer the *rasha* rather than turn away.

THE SIMPLE CHILD

The question: "What is this all about?" (Exodus 13:14). An innocent question, the question of the untrained, unsophisticated child who takes it all on face value.

The answer: This time the *Haggadah* gives the same answer as the Torah. Tell the simple child: "It was with a mighty hand that *Adonai* took us out of *Mitzrayim*, out of the house of bondage" (Exodus 13:14).

THE CHILD WHO DOES NOT KNOW HOW TO ASK

The question: There is no question, because the child does not even know how to ask it. (Exodus 13:8 begins "And you shall tell your child on that day. . . "—an instruction without the prompt of a specific question from the child.)

The answer: As any good teacher knows, you can't get anyone to learn unless they can ask the question. The rabbis here suggest that the approach to the child who does not know how to ask is to help him/her learn how to ask, to "open the discussion," to stimulate the questions. Begin with "It is because of what *Adonai* did for me when I went free out of *Mitzrayim*" (Exodus 13:8), the essential answer to the basic question "Why do we celebrate *Pesaḥ*?"

CHILDREN OR ALL OF US?

There are at least two ways to interpret the meaning of the *Arba'ah Banim* passage in the *Haggadah.* Since we just had children asking the prescribed Four Questions, the opportunity to consider how to instruct children as to the meaning of the Passover is timely and appropriate. Another way to view this passage is, of course, as a paradigm for all of us.

The four types of children can be seen as the four types of people who approach religious life. There are those of us who have already studied a great deal and are anxious to know the laws and

ARBA'AH BANIM—FOUR CHILDREN

1. *K'neged arba'ah banim dibrah Torah:*	1. The Torah alludes to four types of children:
2. *Eḥad ḥakham,*	2. one who is wise,
3. *V'eḥad rasha,*	3. and one who is wicked,
4. *V'eḥad tam,*	4. and one who is simple,
5. *V'eh.ad she'ayno yodei'a lishol.*	5. and one who does not know how to ask.
6. *Ḥakham mah hu omer?*	6. What does the wise child ask?
7. *Mah ha-eidot v'ha-ḥukkim*	7. "What are the statutes, the laws
8. *v'ha-mishpatim asher tzivah Adonai Eloheinu otanu?*	8. and the ordinances which *Adonai* our God has commanded us?"
9. *V'af attah emor lo*	9. You should inform this child
10. *k'hilkhot ha-Pesaḥ ahd:*	10. of all the laws of *Pesaḥ* including (the ruling that):
11. *Ayn maftirin ba'okhel aḥar*	11. nothing should be eaten after
12. *ha-afikoman.*	12. the *afikomen.*

understandings of Judaism down to the last detail. There are those of us who have a simple knowledge of Jewish practice, but very little understanding of its true meaning. There are those of us who hardly know how to ask a religious question. And, there are those of us who set ourselves apart from the community and ask "What does it all mean to you?"

At your Seder, you may have people representing all four types. The genius of the *Haggadah* is that it gives you specific guidance on how to deal with each during the course of your Seder experience. It's up to you to take it!

PRACTICE

The *matzot* remain uncovered.

1. כְּנֶגֶד אַרְבָּעָה בָנִים דִּבְּרָה תוֹרָה.
2. אֶחָד חָכָם
3. וְאֶחָד רָשָׁע
4. וְאֶחָד תָּם
5. וְאֶחָד שֶׁאֵינוֹ יוֹדֵעַ לִשְׁאוֹל.

6. חָכָם מַה הוּא אוֹמֵר?
7. מָה הָעֵדֹת וְהַחֻקִּים
8. וְהַמִּשְׁפָּטִים אֲשֶׁר צִוָּה יהוה אֱלֹהֵינוּ אוֹתָנוּ?
9. וְאַף אַתָּה אֱמָר לוֹ
10. כְּהִלְכוֹת הַפֶּסַח עַד:

11. אֵין מַפְטִירִין בָּאֹכֶל אַחַר
12. הָאֲפִיקוֹמָן.

1. *Rasha mah hu omer?*	1. What does the wicked child ask?
2. *Mah ha-avodah ha-zot lakhem?*	2. "What does this ritual mean to *you?*"
3. *Lakhem v'lo lo.*	3. To "you" and not to "him."
4. *U-l'fi she-hotzi et atzmo*	4. Since he removes himself
5. *min ha-klal*	5. from the community
6. *kafar ba-ikkar.*	6. by denying God's role in the Exodus,
7. *V'af attah ha-k'heih et shinnav*	7. shake him (lit. "set his teeth on edge")
8. *v'emor lo:*	8. by replying:
9. *Ba-avur zeh*	9. "This is done because of what
10. *asah Adonai li*	10. *Adonai* did for me
11. *b'tzeiti mi'Mitzrayim.*	11. when I went out of *Mitzrayim.*"
12. *Li v'lo lo.*	12. "For me." Not for him.
13. *Ilu hayah sham,*	13. Had he been there,
14. *lo hayah nig'al.*	14. he would not have been redeemed.

15. *Tam mah hu omer?*	15. What does the simple child ask?
16. *Mah zot?*	16. "What is this all about?"
17. *V'amarta eilav:*	17. You should tell him:
18. *B'ḥozek yad*	18. "It was with a mighy hand
19. *hotzi'anu Adonai mi'Mitzrayim*	19. that *Adonai* took us out of *Mitzrayim,*
20. *mi'beit avadim.*	20. out of the house of bondage.

1. רָשָׁע מַה הוּא אוֹמֵר?
2. מָה הָעֲבֹדָה הַזֹּאת לָכֶם?
3. לָכֶם וְלֹא לוֹ.
4. וּלְפִי שֶׁהוֹצִיא אֶת עַצְמוֹ
5. מִן הַכְּלָל
6. כָּפַר בָּעִקָּר.
7. וְאַף אַתָּה הַקְהֵה אֶת שִׁנָּיו
8. וֶאֱמָר לוֹ:
9. בַּעֲבוּר זֶה
10. עָשָׂה יהוה לִי
11. בְּצֵאתִי מִמִּצְרָיִם.
12. לִי וְלֹא לוֹ.
13. אִלּוּ הָיָה שָׁם,
14. לֹא הָיָה נִגְאָל.

15. תָּם מַה הוּא אוֹמֵר?
16. מַה זֹּאת?
17. וְאָמַרְתָּ אֵלָיו:
18. בְּחֹזֶק יָד
19. הוֹצִיאָנוּ יהוה מִמִּצְרַיִם
20 מִבֵּית עֲבָדִים.

1. *V'she-ayno yodei'a lishol,*	1. As for the child who does not know how to ask,
2. *At p'taḥ lo,*	2. you should open the discussion for him,
3. *she'ne-emar:*	3. as it is written:
4. *V'higad'ta l'vinkha*	4. "And you shall explain to your child
5. *ba-yom ha-hu leimor,*	5. on that day (saying),
6. *ba-avur zeh asah Adonai li*	6. "It is because of what *Adonai* did for me
7. *b'tzeiti mi'Mitzrayim.*	7. when I went free out of *Mitzrayim.*"

THE ANSWER: MITEḤILAH OVDEI AVODAH ZARAH

CONCEPTS

IN THE BEGINNING WE SERVED IDOLS

The answer to the questions raised by the Four Children is the second beginning of the *Maggid* as advocated by Rav, tracing our initial degradation back to our pagan roots. The paragraph essentially tells the history of the Israelites from before Abraham's time, to Isaac, and then to Jacob and his children who went down to *Mitzrayim.* The text is quoted from the Book of Joshua 24:22-4.

THE *HAGGADAH* AS A MIRROR OF JEWISH HISTORY

The texts and traditions handed down throughout the generations were sometimes changed as a reflection of the political realities of a particular moment of Jewish history. In the story of Ḥanukkah, for example, the Maccabees were fighting not only the Syrian-Greek rulers, but also their own fellow Jews who advocated Hellenization.

It is also true that those who maintained the oral traditions were influenced by whoever the ruling parties were in Palestine at the time. For instance, in the third century B.C.E., before the time of the Maccabees, the Hebrews were ruled, off and on, by either the Ptolemies of Egypt or the Seleucids of Syria (also known as Aram), each other's mortal enemies and both wishing to lay claim to the Hebrews. It suited the Ptolemies of Egypt to recall the Egyptian origins of the Hebrews, while the Seleucids of Syria preferred to view the Hebrews as descended from the ancestors who lived "beyond the River Euphrates," a place known to historians as Aram Naharayim. In fact, Professor Louis Finkelstein argues that when the Seleucids took control of Palestine, the priests deleted references in the *Haggadah* to the Egyptian origins of the Israelites (the entire text of *Avadim Hayinu*). Yet, the people continued to recite both *Avadim Hayinu* and *Miteḥilah Ovdei Avodah Zarah* which helps explain why our *Haggadah* still contains these two beginnings to the *Maggid* section.

1. וְשֶׁאֵינוֹ יוֹדֵעַ לִשְׁאוֹל,
2. אַתְּ פְּתַח לוֹ,
3. שֶׁנֶּאֱמַר:
4. וְהִגַּדְתָּ לְבִנְךָ
5. בַּיּוֹם הַהוּא לֵאמֹר,
6. בַּעֲבוּר זֶה עָשָׂה יהוה לִי
7. בְּצֵאתִי מִמִּצְרָיִם.

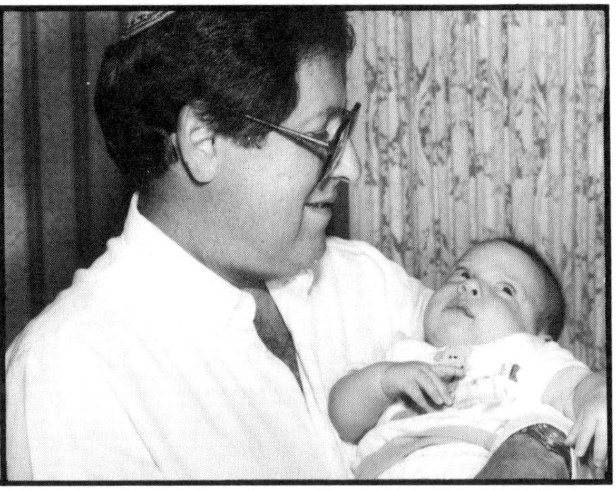

THE PRAISE: BARUKH SHOMER/V'HI SHE'AMDAH

CONCEPTS

GOD KEEPS HIS PROMISES

These two paragraphs complete the Second Telling. They praise God for keeping the promise of His covenant with Abraham. This is probably a post-Talmudic addition which was included to emphasize the three-fold promise of deliverance: 1)the promise to deliver Abraham from idol-worship to the Covenant with the One God, 2) the promise to deliver the Israelites from Egyptian slavery, and 3) the promise to deliver the Israelites to the Promised Land as God's nation.

GOD'S PROMISE SUSTAINS US TODAY

"*V'hi She'amdah*" is a remarkable statement of belief in God's promise to watch over the Jewish people. It contemporizes the Seder, connecting the ancient promise of the Covenant with Jews in every generation. Just as everyone is to see him/herself as having been liberated from Egypt, so too, all Jews in every generation should remember that we are bound to God in a sacred Covenant through which God promises to sustain us and save us.

PRACTICE

V'hi She'amdah is such a powerful reminder of God's Covenant with us that the *matzot* are covered and the wine cup is raised while we recite or chant the paragraph, almost as if in a toast to this promise. The cup is replaced and the *matzot* uncovered upon conclusion of the prayer.

From the beginning of the *Maggid* section, the *matzot* have been uncovered, serving as a visual prompt for the tellings. Each and every time we use the *Kiddush* cup, they will be covered as a sign

V'HI SHE'AMDAH—THE PROMISE

1. *V'hi she-amdah*	1. It is this promise that has sustained
2. *la-avoteinu v'lanu,*	2. our ancestors and us,
3. *she-lo eḥad bilvad*	3. for not just one (enemy)
4. *amad aleinu l'khalloteinu;*	4. has arisen to destroy us;
5. *ella sh-b'khol dor va-dor*	5. rather in every generation
6. *omdim aleinu l'khalloteinu,*	6. there are those who seek our destruction,
7. *v'ha-kadosh barukh hu*	7. but the Holy One, praised be He,
8. *matzileinu mi-yadam.*	8. saves us from their hands.

of respect. Why? The pedagogic designers of the Seder want us to give our full attention to the object being used. This same notion is also reflected on Shabbat when we cover the *Ḥallah* during *Kiddush*, and in the sanctuary when the *Sefer Torah* scroll is covered except during its actual reading. As we have reviewed earlier, there is also a *midrash* of "not embarrassing" the object not under consideration.

1. וְהִיא שֶׁעָמְדָה
2. לַאֲבוֹתֵינוּ וְלָנוּ,
3. שֶׁלֹּא אֶחָד בִּלְבָד
4. עָמַד עָלֵינוּ לְכַלּוֹתֵנוּ
5. אֶלָּא שֶׁבְּכָל דּוֹר וָדוֹר
6. עוֹמְדִים עָלֵינוּ לְכַלּוֹתֵנוּ,
7. וְהַקָּדוֹשׁ בָּרוּךְ הוּא
8. מַצִּילֵנוּ מִיָּדָם.

12

THE THIRD TELLING

THE QUESTION: TZEI U-L'MAD—GO AND LEARN
THE ANSWER: ARAMI OVED AVI—MY FATHER WAS A WANDERING ARAMEAN
ESER MAKOT—THE TEN PLAGUES
THE PRAISE: DAYYENU—STEPS OF KINDNESS

ACT II, SCENE 3

How can I see myself in Egypt? Well, I could see myself as a simple bricklayer. I'd work all day in the hot sun molding bricks from the mud. I could feel the heat of the sun, the flies all over my body and the mud caking all over. That was Egypt. Heat, flies, and mud.

David Domroy, from *My Exodus*

He is dirtier than vines or pigs from treading under his mud. His clothes are stiff with clay; his leather belt is going to ruin. Entering into the wind, he is miserable... his sides ache, since he must be outside in a treacherous wind... his arms are destroyed with technical work... what he eats is the bread of his fingers, and he washes himself only once a season. He is simply wretched through and through.

From *A Satire on Trades*
an ancient Egyptian manuscript,
circa 1400 B.C.E

Midrash is the ultimate Jewish art form. In fact, it is more than an art form; it is a way of viewing reality. *Midrash* is a rabbinic way of seeing connections and associations—it is a way of seeing meaning. Technically, *midrash*, which means "investigation," is a way of studying biblical texts. It involves perceiving patterns and problems in the text, and then using other pieces of the biblical experience, personal experience, and logic to explain their meaning, or to resolve their difficulty. In reality, it is more.

The text of the *Pesaḥ* Seder is very much a creation of *midrash*. It is a non-linear array of texts, rituals and activities, woven together by *midrashic* association. To understand the Seder (and particularly to understand the third section of *Maggid* which is itself a formal *midrashic* text), one needs to understand the world-view inherent in the process of *midrash*. One has to learn to read texts with "rabbinic eyes." In order to attain this understanding, one has to know something about the way the Torah tells its stories and teaches its lessons. *Midrash* is more than an original act of creation; it is a response, the manifestation of the patterns of association suggested by the biblical narrative.

Learning Torah means relearning how to slow down and move our lips when we read. To work its magic, the Torah needs to be heard and its words need to echo and linger in our ears.

The Torah works through meiosis and mitosis. Its word-clusters fill our consciousness as we read. Like DNA, the words combine and connect with other text fragments, as well as linking with pieces of our own experience. We learn through harmonics and resonances. Over and over again, meanings are built and connected in a constant re-configuration of understanding. The word-images divide, connect, combine—weaving a whole effervescent fabric of meaning.

The biblical text is a multilayered, complex document. It demands that a reader process and reprocess its words. Slowly, over time, its message reveals itself. Let's follow the process. In Genesis 15, God makes a promise and a prediction to Abraham:

> Know for a fact
> that your future-family will be **strangers**
> in a land which is not theirs.
> They shall be slaves and suffer for 400 years.
> But I will punish the nation they serve,
> and after that, they will exit with riches.

We already know these echoes. From the beginning of the story of the Jewish people, the Torah directs us towards the Exodus. The Egypt experience is definitional. In this one verse, we are connected to three key word-themes, "stranger," "slave," and "suffering." This is but one of many foreshadowings. Another "secret" way of revealing this is found in the last word of each of the five books of the Torah. When we look them up, we find "Egypt" at the end of Genesis, "their wanderings" at the end of Exodus, "Sinai" at the end of Leviticus, "Jericho" at the end of Numbers, and "Israel" at the end of Deuteronomy. The hidden message is the story of the Exodus: ***The Jewish*** *people left* **Egypt**, **their wanderings** *took them to Mt.* **Sinai**, *then across the river to* **Jericho** *and finally to* **Israel**. As we know (from the verse we traced in the introduction to *Ha laḥma anya*) the word "stranger" continues to echo through the Torah, connecting the experience of being a slave in Egypt to the ethics of human responsibility, one for the other. That echo continues in the story of Moses. When Moses has a son, we see this statement (Exodus 1:25):

> He named his son GERSHOM (meaning the ***stranger***).
> He said: I have been a **stranger** in a **strange** land.

Likewise, the constant clues to the meaning, importance and significance of the Exodus are embedded in the story of Joseph. Twice in that story, we witness Joseph rise from slavery to success. First he is thrown in the pit and sold into servitude in Potiphar's house. The Torah tells us:

> **The Lord was with Joseph**...
> Everything placed in Joseph's hands *succeeded.*
> Joseph found *favor in his eyes.*
> *Joseph personally served him.*
> *Everything that was his, he put in Joseph's hands.*
> The Lord blessed this Egyptian's house
> because of JOSEPH.

Within a few verses, Joseph is back in trouble—thrown into jail. There, in a passage rich in echoes, we learn what happens to him:

> Even in the dungeon
> the Lord was with Joseph.
> *Joseph found favor in the eyes of the dungeon-master.*
> The dungeon-master *put in Joseph's hands all the prisoners,*
> and all that was done there.
> The dungeon-master didn't need to check on anything
> Joseph did, because the Lord was with him
> Everything he did, the Lord made *succeed.*

Later in the story, when Joseph interprets Pharaoh's dreams, we learn the reason for this repetition. He tells Pharoah, "Pharaoh had two dreams because this thing is true. It came from God, and God will quickly do it." With this kind of overlapping, the Torah tells its story, each cycle revealing more about the Exodus to come. In it all, we learn that there is nothing to fear as long as God is with us. Our story of liberation will be like Joseph's multiple liberations. In turn, that idea goes all the way back to Jacob's first trip out of the land of Israel. There God promises him, "I am with you. I will keep you in all your goings and I will return you to this soil because I will not leave you until I have done all that I promised you." The trip to Egypt to visit Joseph is his second trip out of Israel. The cycle continues. There are more and more connections; more and more insights awaiting discovery.

If we have read carefully and closely, we are well prepared for the experience of the Exodus story. Not only do we know that it is coming, but we have been trained and sensitized by the language used to interpret its meaning through a series of key word-themes, "stranger," "slave," "suffering" on the negative side, "God being with us" on the positive side. Each of the lessons we will learn from that narrative has been prepared and directed in earlier narratives. This is more than foreshadowing, it is episodic instruction.

As the rabbis read and reread the Torah text, this intertwining word-web began to reveal itself to them. The more they studied, the more the Torah led them into evolving a form of study—a form of study they called *midrash.* They learned that every word must be taken seriously, that every phrase reveals meaning, that nothing is extra. For them, every repetition, every redundancy, was a clue to look for an insight. If two passages or two clauses seemed to reveal the same message, the rabbis knew that each must reveal its own purposeful insight. "*Lashon Yiteira*" means "extra language." It is a technical term coined by the rabbis to describe one pattern of biblical interpretation. The Torah frequently lists a series of descriptive phrases. God tells Abram, "*Take yourself* (1) from your land, (2) from your birthplace, (3) from your father's house, to the land: there I will let you see." (Genesis 12:1) Likewise, later in the Torah God tells Abram (now named Abraham), "Please take (1) your son, (2) your only one, (3) the one you love, (4) Isaac, and *take yourself* to the land of Moriah (meaning "seeing")... (Genesis 22:2). It is made clear both by word-echo and by rhythm that these two passages are interconnected. *Midrashic* reading makes them the first and the tenth test given to Abram by God, the epochs in his spiritual odyssey. It is equally clear that both passages share the problem of *lashon yiteira.* In the first, God could have just told him "take yourself from your father's house and go..." In the second, God could have just ordered him, "Take Isaac and go..." The extra phrases demand interpretation; they mandate the making of *midrash.*

The *Tzei u'l'mad* passage in the *Haggadah* is made up of four biblical verses (Deuteronomy 26:5-8) and accompanying *midrashic* passages. Each of these verses is rich in the overlapping phrases which mandate explanation. By providing us with one traditional interpretation, the rabbis are providing an invitation to all at the Seder to join them in making meaning from these verses. *Midrash* is an interactive art form.

One of these verses reads: "The Egyptians (1) dealt harshly with us, (2) and oppressed us, and (3) they imposed hard labor upon us." The problem is obvious: We must find the difference between "harsh dealings," "oppression," and "hard labor." Each must teach us something different. Here is where the *Midrash* begins.

> *What is the meaning of* **The Egyptians dealt harshly with us?**
> *One explanation:* They were ungrateful, for they paid back with evil the kindness that Joseph had done for them. The proof for this explanation can be found in Exodus 1:8, where it is written, "A new king arose over *Mitzrayim* who did not know Joseph." *This means that* he acted as if he did not know Joseph.
>
> Another interpretation of **The Egyptians dealt harshly with us.** They made us appear to be the ones who were bad. We can find proof for this in Exodus 1:9-10. There it is written, "Behold, the Israelites are too many and too mighty for us. Come, let us deal cunningly with them..."

And so, the pattern continues. When you read through the entire *midrashic* passage you discover that **harsh dealings** can be either ignoring an old obligation or destroying our self-image,

oppression is regulating our hard work by imposing outside bosses (taskmasters), and **hard labor** is explained: "They would impose a difficult task upon the weak and an easy task upon the strong... the Egyptians wanted not only to enslave them but also to break their spirits." In the world of *midrash*, these three descriptors become the opportunity to create three different snapshots of the Egypt experience. But this is more than an exercise in visualizing slave life. Embedded in these descriptions are two other important lessons.

First, there is a process lesson—all biblical verses are interconnected. To learn of the Exodus, we must gather biblical clues. The second is an ethical lesson—self-image, self-worth, a sense of accomplishment, a sense of independence are important elements of freedom. The enslavement of dignity is the worst form of punishment. To make sure that we will never be like the Egyptians, we must be concerned with the dignity of those who work for us.

But even these explanations are only a beginning. The words of Torah are a kind of spiritual "LEGO set." The challenge of *midrash* is to use these phrase-clauses and these insights to fabricate new constructions, to constantly reexpress our sense of what is important and valuable. *Midrash* is an ongoing process. Each retelling and each rereading is a new opportunity to find connection and express significance. In telling the story of *Pesaḥ*, we are required to personalize and interpret. *Maggid* is not an act of rote recitation; rather it is a recital—the setting for personal and collective artistic expression.

THE QUESTION: TZEI U-L'MAD—GO AND LEARN

CONCEPTS

The Third Telling begins with a call to further elaborate the story of the Exodus: "*Tzei u-l'mad*," literally "Go and learn." This is a shorthand expression indicating that we are about to learn a *midrash*, a rabbinic interpretation of biblical verses. An alternative translation of "*Tzei u-l'mad*" is "Consider these verses," a directive which in its essence leads us to a deeper understanding of the story told between the lines and words of the biblical text.

"*Tzei u-l'mad*" poses the question of the Third Telling. The question is inferred, but it is there nonetheless. The question is: "What is the real story told in these verses?" By analyzing meanings and suggesting reasons for the use of certain words and phrases, the *Haggadah* seeks to embellish the story by filling in what it assumes are the details behind the outline.

The question "*Tzei u-L'mad*" includes a statement of the verses to be considered. Thus, the way to read this part of the *Haggadah* is: "Consider what the following verses mean: 'My father was a wandering Aramean...."

THE ANSWER: ARAMI OVED AVI
CONCEPTS

MY FATHER WAS A WANDERING ARAMEAN—or—
(LABAN) THE ARAMEAN TRIED TO DESTROY MY FATHER

We have now come to the core of the *Haggadah.* We are about to engage in the process of *midrash,* the attempt to uncover meanings in the biblical text according to different readings of the words.

The biblical verses brought by the *Haggadah* are Deuteronomy 26:5-8 and contain a succinct summary of the Exodus story. In order to expand and fill in the details and teachings inherent in these texts, the *midrashic* process isolates phrases and words and holds them up for inspection and sometimes alternative interpretation. In fact, the first three words of the first verse themselves are the subject of controversy.

Most *Haggadot* begin this section with the verses:

> *Tze u-l'mad: Mah bikesh Lavan ha-Arami la'asot l'Ya'akov avinu, shePar0 lo gazar ela al ha-z'kharim, v'lavan bikesh la'akor et ha-kol, shene'emar 'Arami oved avi…'*

"Look at what Laban the Aramean (Syrian) tried to do to our father Jacob! For Pharoah ordered the destruction of the male children only, while Laban intended to uproot all! As it is said: 'An Aramean would have destroyed my father…"

This reading of the verse is achieved by understanding the adjective "*oved*" (wandering) as the verb "*ibbed*" (would have destroyed).

Look up the verse in the Torah and you will find a completely different understanding. There, the verse is read "My father was a wandering Aramean…" Who is the wandering Aramean? From the context of the quotation in the Bible, it is not Laban, but Jacob who traveled to Egypt to live with his son Joseph when a great famine came upon Canaan. Why, then, did the *Haggadah* change the clear meaning of the Torah text to something entirely different?

This question bothered Professor Louis Finkelstein. In a landmark piece of scholarship, Finkelstein sought to explain this obvious discrepancy by pointing out that in *midrashic* literature, Laban is portrayed as a dishonest man by transposing the letters *aleph, resh, mem, yud* (*arami*—Aramean) to *resh, mem, aleph, yud* (*ra-ma-i*— dishonest). The reason the *Haggadah* wants to read the verse this way is to portray Laban as a Syrian, a dishonest man who was even worse than Pharoah. But, the question remains, why?

Finkelstein suggested that this entire section of the *Haggadah* was written in pre-Maccabean Palestine which, as we learned before, was under the control of the Ptolemies of Egypt. It would hardly sit well with these rulers for the Hebrews to assemble in a huge celebration such as *Pesaḥ* and declare that they were descended from a man of Syria, since Syria was the arch-rival of Ptolemaic Egypt. So, the Palestinian authorities turned the verse into an anti-Syrian polemic, interpreting the biblical words as a reference to Laban, who was most definitely not the father of the Jewish people and not a worse oppressor than the Egyptian Pharoah (an ancestor of the Ptolemies who doesn't fare too well in the rest of the *Haggadah*).

Another explanation of the anagram "ra-ma-i" is " Roman," a coded word linking Laban to the dreaded occupation force during the time of the rabbis.

The Rabbinical Assembly *Haggadah* eliminates all references to Laban and the polemical text, for it certainly does not have any meaning for us today. What does have meaning is the original text from the Torah : "My father (Jacob) was a wandering Aramean, and with just a few people he went down to *Mitzrayim* and sojourned there." This establishes the historical conection between our ancestors and their journey into Egypt which becomes the substance of the *midrashic* text analysis to follow.

MIDRASH

The remainder of this section presents the verses of Deuteronomy 26:5-8 with *midrashic* interpretations of each phrase. This does two things: first, it tells the story of the Exodus with embellishment, and second, it enables the rabbis to make points about the situation in the time of the Exodus that could have meaning for Jews in every generation.

One of the most interesting of these observations is the comment on the phrase "and there he became a great nation," referring to the fact that Jacob came to Egypt with only a few family members, but over the years, his progeny became numerous and important.

The rabbis found in this phrase, "a great nation," the idea that the Israelites retained their identity as Jews in *Mitzrayim*. The rabbis infer that the Israelites became easily identifiable there, a unique and distinctive nation, through their observance of the *mitzvot*. They did not change their names, nor did they change their language. One can imagine that the temptation to take on aspects of the ruling culture would be enormous, even though the Israelites were an enslaved people. The rabbis insist they did not. And if the Hebrew slaves maintained their identity as Jews, shouldn't we liberated Jews fight the forces of assimilation as well?

PRACTICE

This section of the *Maggid* is read straight through as an exercise in text analysis. The *matzot* remain uncovered.

INNOVATIONS

To enhance the understanding of the participants at the Seder, prepare a chart with each of the four verses from Deuteronomy 26:5-8. Refer to the words of each verse as the narrative is read.

Some families choose to substitute a more direct story of the Exodus at this point. Others have introduced dramatic plays, improvised discussion, even reenactments of the story featuring Seder participants in costume. A number of creative suggestions can be found in the companion Workbook to this volume.

ARAMI OVED AVI—MY FATHER WAS A WANDERING ARAMEAN

These are the four biblical texts upon which the *Midrash* is based:

1. *Arami oved avi*	1. My father was a wandering Aramean,
2. *vayeired mi'Mitzraimah,*	2. and he went down to *Mitzrayim*
3. *va-yagar sham bimtay m'at.*	3. and sojourned there with the few people (he brought with him).
4. *Va-y'hi sham l'goy gadol*	4. And there he became a great nation,
5. *atzum va-rav.*	5. mighty and numerous.
6. *Va-yarei'u otanu ha-Mitzrim*	6. And the Egyptians dealt harshly with us
7. *va-y'anunu*	7. and oppressed us;
8. *va-yitnu aleinu avodah kashah.*	8. and they imposed hard labor upon us.
9. *Va-nitzak el Adonai,*	9. We cried out to *Adonai,*
10. *Elohei avoteinu;*	10. the God of our ancestors;
11. *va-yishma Adonai et koleinu*	11. and *Adonai* heard our plea
12. *va-ya'ar et an'yeinu,*	12. and saw our affliction,
13. *v'et amaleinu,*	13. our misery,
14. *v'et laḥatzeinu.*	14. and our oppression.
15. *Va-yotzi'ainu Adonai mi'Mitzrayim*	15. Then *Adonai* took us out of *Mitzrayim*
16. *b'yad ḥazakah*	16. with a mighty hand
17. *u-viz'roah n'tuyah*	17. and an outstretched arm,
18. *u-v'mora gadol*	18. with awesome power,
19. *u-v'otot u-v'moftim.*	19. with signs and wonders.

1. אֲרַמִּי אֹבֵד אָבִי
2. וַיֵּרֶד מִצְרַיְמָה,
3. וַיָּגָר שָׁם בִּמְתֵי מְעָט.

4. וַיְהִי שָׁם לְגוֹי גָּדוֹל,
5. עָצוּם וָרָב.

6. וַיָּרֵעוּ אֹתָנוּ הַמִּצְרִים
7. וַיְעַנּוּנוּ.
8. וַיִּתְּנוּ עָלֵינוּ עֲבֹדָה קָשָׁה.

9. וַנִּצְעַק אֶל יהוה
10. אֱלֹהֵי אֲבֹתֵינוּ,
11. וַיִּשְׁמַע יהוה אֶת קֹלֵנוּ,
12. וַיַּרְא אֶת עָנְיֵנוּ
13. וְאֶת עֲמָלֵנוּ
14. וְאֶת לַחֲצֵנוּ.

15. וַיּוֹצִאֵנוּ יהוה מִמִּצְרַיִם
16. בְּיָד חֲזָקָה
17. וּבִזְרֹעַ נְטוּיָה
18. וּבְמֹרָא גָּדֹל
19. וּבְאֹתוֹת וּבְמֹפְתִים.

THE ANSWER (CONTINUED): ESER MAKOT—THE TEN PLAGUES

CONCEPTS

GOD'S WONDERS

The last verse to be examined in the long *midrashic* exposition reads: "Then *Adonai* took us out of *Mitzrayim* with a mighty hand and outstretched arm, with awesome power, with signs and wonders" (Deuteronomy 26:8). "Wonders," according to the *Haggadah*, refers to the plagues, the terrible Ten Plagues which God brought upon Egypt in an effort to demonstrate the true power of the Israelite deity.

This leads directly to the recitation of the Ten Plagues. Interestingly, there is no elaboration of the plagues, no lengthy, phrase-by-phrase analysis as in the previous section of the story. Just a simple list of what they were: Blood, Frogs, Vermin, Beasts, Cattle Plague, Boils, Hail, Locusts, Darkness, and the Death of the Firstborn. We will suggest below why this is the case.

It was up to generations of commentators to fill in the meaning of these plagues to the Exodus story. Some point out that the plagues were actually opportunities for Pharoah to repent and let the people go. But, in the grand scheme of things, God would be the force to liberate the Israelites, not Pharoah, demonstrating the ultimate power of God as the Hero of this story. Others believe that the plagues exacted punishment on the Egyptians as "*midah k'neged midah*," measure for measure—each plague a response for the wrongs the Egyptians perpetrated on the Israelites. Some commentators speculate on the specific details of what these plagues were, how long they lasted, their effect on the populace, and so on. Still others interpret the plagues as a kind of cosmic battle between the gods of Egypt and the God of the children of Israel, with the winner never in doubt.

COMPASSION FOR THE ENEMY

As evil as Pharoah and the Egyptians were, when it came to their destruction at the hands of God through the plagues (particularly the death of the firstborn) and at the Sea of Reeds, the rabbis went to great lengths to temper our joy. A famous *midrash* in the Talmud makes the point:

> When the Egyptians were drowning in the Sea of Reeds, the ministering angels began to sing God's praises. But God silenced them, saying: "How can you sing while my children perish?"
>
> (*Megillah* 10b)

We may rejoice in our liberation, but we may not celebrate the death of our foes.

To underscore the point and reinforce the value, the rabbis instructed that ten drops of wine be spilled from our cups, diminishing the joy of our celebration, as a reminder of those who perished in the course of our liberation. It is said that this is also the reason why a portion of the *Hallel* (the great songs of praise) is omitted on the last six days of Passover. And perhaps it is this notion of compassion for one's enemies that caused the editors of the *Haggadah* to simply list the Ten Plagues rather than dwell on them at any length whatsoever.

D'TZAKH, ADASH, B'AḤAV

This mnemonic device, created by Rabbi Judah out of the initials of each of the plagues, has stimulated commentators to look for other messages in this part of the story. Some point out that within the three groups of plagues, the first two of each triad were preceded by warnings to Pharoah, but the third came without warning. Samson Raphael Hirsch, a great rabbi of the 19th century, suggested that the first plague in each group (blood, beasts, hail) reduced the Egyptians to strangers in their own land (*gerut*); the second plague (frogs, cattle plague, locusts) robbed the Egyptians of their pride and sense of superiority (*avdut*); and the third plague in each triad (vermin, boils, and darkness) imposed actual physical suffering on the people of Egypt (*enui*). The tenth plague (the death of the firstborn, including Pharoah's own son) was, of course, the final blow which led to the capitulation of Pharoah.

OBJECTS

You will need your filled wine cup, a spoon (optional), and a saucer or plate.

PRACTICE

The Ten Plagues are generally recited by all in a rather dirge-like chant. As each plague is called out, we spill out a drop of wine from our cups and onto a saucer or plate, a total of ten drops. This may be done with either a spoon or by dipping your finger into the cup. Some also spill out three additional drops of wine when the three-part acrostic of Rabbi Judah is read. We do *not* refill the wine cups.

PRACTICAL QUESTIONS AND ANSWERS

Why do some use a finger to spill out the wine?

When the magicians of Pharoah could not replicate the plague of vermin, they said to Pharoah: "This is the finger of *Adonai*" (Exodus 8:15). Using the finger is a reminder that it was the "finger of God" which brought the plagues upon Egypt. Some use the pinky finger, while others use the index finger.

Why do we need to mention the plagues at all?

Mordecai M. Kaplan, the founder of the Reconstructionist Movement, asked the same question. In his controversial "*New American Haggadah*" published in 1942, Kaplan eliminated any mention of the plagues in favor of a more elaborate telling of the general Exodus story. As we have tried to point out, the traditional text of the *Haggadah* does not dwell on the plagues, and, in fact, the rabbis go to great lengths to be sensitive to the plight of the Egyptians. Our recommendation is to use the plagues as an opportunity to teach the important value of compassion for one's enemies while at the same time recognizing their meaning in the Bible, i.e. that it is only God who could have accomplished the redemption.

ESER MAKOT—THE TEN PLAGUES

1. *Eser makkot*	1. These are the ten plagues
2. *heivi ha-kadosh barukh hu*	2. which the Holy One praised be He brought
3. *al ha-Mitzrim b'Mitzrayim*	3. upon the Egyptians in *Mitzrayim,*
4. *v'eilu hein:*	4. and they are:
5. *Dahm, tzefardei'a, kinnim,*	5. Blood, Frogs, Vermin,
6. *arov, dever, sh'ḥin,*	6. Beasts, Cattle Plague, Boils,
7. *barad, arbeh, ḥoshekh,*	7. Hail, Locusts, Darkness,
8. *makkat b'khorot.*	8. Death of the Firstborn.

INNOVATIONS

Ask participants to list ten plagues which "plague" us today. Are there any from which you think only God can redeem us? Why?

THE PRAISE: *DAYYENU*—STEPS OF KINDNESS

CONCEPTS

Dayyenu is one of the most famous songs of the Seder. We joyfully sing its repetitive refrain, familiar to many. It is, in fact, a song of praise to *Adonai,* the God whose great miracles led to our liberation. We praise God who not only brought us out of slavery, but who continues His kindnesses to us throughout history.

If we look carefully at the content of the verses of *Dayyenu,* we will find a continuation of our story—an account of the successive "*ma-alot tovot,*" steps of kindness, which God bestowed upon the Jewish people since the Exodus. The word "*ma-alot*" may be familiar to you in the context of "*Shir ha-Ma-alot,*" the Song of Ascending (Psalm 126) which begins the *Birkat ha-Mazon,* the Blessings after Food. *Dayyenu* is, in fact, a step-by-step accounting of the creation of the Jewish nation from the Exodus to the establishment of the Temple in Jerusalem.

The traditional text lists fifteen steps. The Rabbinical Assembly *Haggadah* edits out four of the fifteen steps: the death of the firstborn Egyptians, the giving of Egyptian wealth to the Israelites, the drowning of the Egyptians in the sea, and the sustenance of the Israelites in the desert for forty years. Three of these deal with the defeat of the Egyptians and, in the spirit of the compassion for our enemies noted in our discussion of the Ten Plagues, they have been edited from our text. The

1. עֶשֶׂר מַכּוֹת
2. הֵבִיא הַקָּדוֹשׁ בָּרוּךְ הוּא
3. עַל הַמִּצְרִים בְּמִצְרַיִם
4. וְאֵלּוּ הֵן:
5. דָּם, צְפַרְדֵּעַ, כִּנִּים,
6. עָרוֹב, דֶּבֶר, שְׁחִין,
7. בָּרָד, אַרְבֶּה, חשֶׁךְ,
8. מַכַּת בְּכוֹרוֹת

fourth, sustaining for forty years in the desert, is somewhat redundant with the step of *manna*, the vehicle for sustaining the people Israel in the desert.

The rabbis enjoyed recounting the many parallels to the 15 steps in *Dayyenu:*

1. The letters of a name of God, "*yud-hey*," equals the number 15.
2. There were 15 generations from Abraham to King Solomon.
3. There were 15 types of materials contributed by the people to the building of the sanctuary.
4. There were 15 steps from the forecourt to the inner court of the Temple in Jerusalem.
5. King David wrote 15 Songs of Ascent, "*shirei ma-alot.*"
6. There are 15 steps in this Seder service.

IT WOULD HAVE BEEN ENOUGH

The theology of this prayer is that any one of the steps would have been sufficient for us. The fact that *Adonai* saw to it that we progressed from slavery to the Promised Land and the establishment of the Holy Temple is evidence of His promise fulfilled. The genius of *Dayyenu* is both to fill in the gaps of the rest of the story from Exodus to the Temple while simultaneously summarizing the directive "Begin with degradation and end with glory."

PRACTICE

The singing of *Dayyenu* is one of the highlights of the Seder, for many know its catchy refrain. Enjoy the singing, but don't forget to examine the progression of favors listed in *Dayyenu* as well.

We present only two of the eleven verses of *Dayyenu* included in the Rabbinical Assembly *Haggadah*.

INNOVATIONS

Rabbi Gilbert Rosenthal tells a story about a congregant who brought him a German/Hebrew *Haggadah* published in Germany around 1920. Like most bilingual *Haggadot*, this *Haggadah* had Hebrew text on the right-hand page and a German translation on the left-hand page. As Rabbi Rosenthal browsed through the text, he noticed an asterisk next to the word "*Dayyenu*" in the

DAYYENU—IT WOULD HAVE BEEN ENOUGH

1. *Ilu natan lanu et ha-Shabbat*	1. Had He given us Shabbat
2. *v'lo kairvanu lifnei har Sinai*	2. without bringing us to Mount Sinai,
3. *Dayyenu.*	3. *Dayyenu.*
4. *Ilu natan lanu et ha-Torah,*	4. Had He given us the Torah
5. *v'lo hikh'nisanu l'eretz Yisrael,*	5. without leading us to the Land of Israel,
6. *Dayyenu.*	6. *Dayyenu.*

German translation. His eye went to the bottom of the page where, typeset in German, was the following directive (which we have liberally paraphrased): "*To the hausfrau: Dos is dine time to plop the kneidlach in der boiling vasser.*"

There is a unique custom practiced in some Sephardic communities at *Dayyenu.* Seder participants pick up bunches of green onions, scallions, or leeks and literally beat each other on the back and shoulders. Of course, this "beating" is done half-heartedly, but nevertheless provides a remarkable simulation of the whippings endured by the Israelite slaves in Egypt.

1. אִלּוּ נָתַן לָנוּ אֶת הַשַּׁבָּת
2. וְלֹא קֵרְבָנוּ לִפְנֵי הַר סִינַי
3. דַּיֵּנוּ

4. אִלּוּ נָתַן לָנוּ אֶת הַתּוֹרָה
5. וְלֹא הִכְנִיסָנוּ לְאֶרֶץ יִשְׂרָאֵל
6. דַּיֵּנוּ

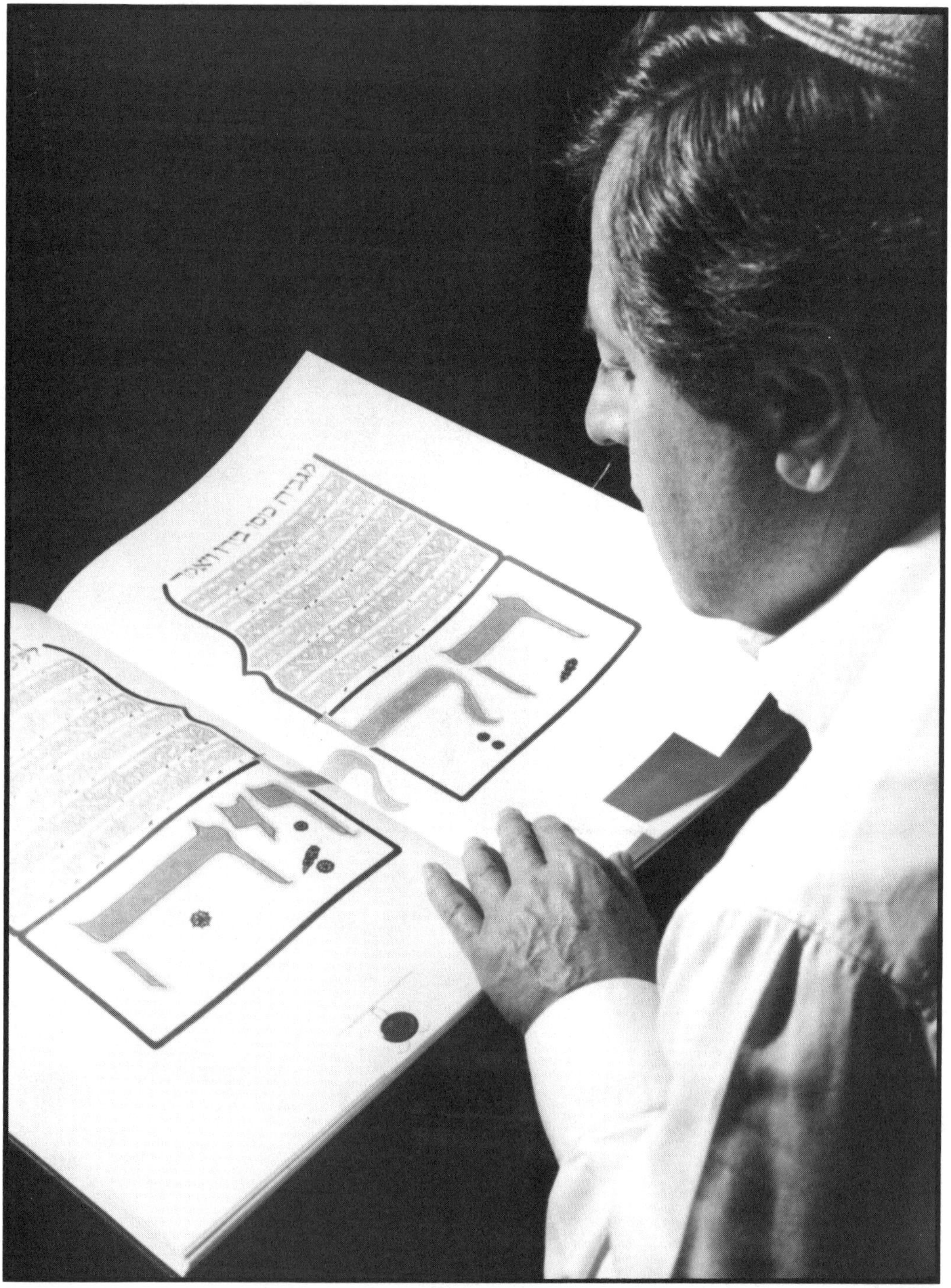

13

THE FOURTH TELLING

THE QUESTION: RABBAN GAMLIEL HAYAH OMER—RABBAN GAMLIEL'S SEDER
THE ANSWER: B'KHOL DOR VA-DOR—IN EVERY GENERATION
THE PRAISE: L'FIKHAKH—THEREFORE.... HALLELUYAH—HALLELUYAH

ACT II, SCENE 4

The synagogue cannot substitute for a Jewish home, and if you think about the Seder, maybe some synagogues perform a Seder, but all the feeling and the Jewish identity that emerges from the experience of *Pesaḥ* has to be done in the family. It has to come from the family; it can't come from anywhere else.

Carol Karsch

Speak to the whole assembly of Israel and say that on the tenth of this month, each of them shall take a lamb to a family, a lamb to a household... They shall eat the flesh that same night; they shall eat it roasted over the fire, with unleavened bread and with bitter herbs.

Exodus 12:8

THE QUESTION: RABBAN GAMLIEL HAYAH OMER: PESAḤ, MATZAH, MAROR

CONCEPTS

RABBAN GAMLIEL HAYAH OMER: PESAḤ, MATZAH, MAROR

Dayyenu has taken us through history, from the the time of the Exodus to the building of the Temple. Next, we find ourselves in Jerusalem, just after the destruction of the Temple, at the Passover Seder of Rabban Gamliel, one of the greatest scholars of the Talmud.

The *Haggadah* quotes from Talmud *Pesaḥim* 116a/b in which Rabban Gamliel states that those who have not explained three things during the Seder have not fulfilled their obligation. These three things are: the *Pesaḥ* offering, *Matzah*, and *Maror*, three of the central symbols of the Passover ritual.

The importance of this section of the *Haggadah* cannot be overestimated. In fact, some commentators point out that while the Seder participants *should* be present at the table for all of the ritual, they are *obligated* to be present for the explanation of *Pesaḥ*, *Matzah*, and *Maror*. Why? In the wake of the very destruction of the religious center of the people, the rabbis knew that they had to raise the level of meaning of these symbols if they were to replace the very powerful paschal sacrifice itself.

So, the question is asked: "Do we simply 'tell about' these symbols or do we actually 'eat' them?" The answer is: Our objective is to recreate the experience of the Exodus from Egypt, and thus, we will both explain the symbolism of these foods and eat them (except for the *Z'roah* representing the *Pesaḥ* offering) in our attempt to feel as if each of us had actually been redeemed from *Mitzrayim*.

Thus, the Fourth Telling begins with a series of three questions about these three important Passover symbols.

PESAḤ

The question: Why did our ancestors eat the *Pesaḥ* offering at their Seder?

The answer: As a reminder that the Holy One passed over the Israelite dwellings in *Mitzrayim* during the terrible night of the Exodus when he struck the Egyptians and spared our homes.

(Exodus 12:27)

It is important to understand that, until 70 C.E. when the Second Temple was destroyed, our ancestors' religion was based on a sacrificial cult. They believed that by offering a physical sacrifice in the Temple, they were bringing God closer to them. In fact, the Hebrew word for "sacrifice" is "*korban*," from the root word "*karov*," "to bring close." "*Karov*" also means "to relate;" the word for "relative" is "*karov*." Thus, to engage in a "*korban*" is to relate to God, to become a relative in God's family. Of course, the great innovation in the sacrificial ritual introduced by the Jews was to substitute a lamb for a human being.

Nevertheless, there is no escaping the fact that we were a sacrificial people. And to some extent, the Passover table becomes a substitute altar on Seder night. The "*Z'roah*," the roasted shankbone on the Seder plate, is a reminder of the *korban Pesaḥ*, the sacrificial lamb slaughtered by each family on that fateful night which began the Exodus from *Mitzrayim*.

MATZAH

The question: Why do we eat it?

The answer: To remind ourselves that even before the dough had time to rise, the Holy One, Praised be He, redeemed them from Egypt. (Exodus 12:39)

The first *matzah* we ate in Egypt was *leḥem oni*, the bread of poverty, the bread of slavery, the bread of humility. The *Haggadah* tells us that, overnight, the bread of affliction became the bread of freedom. The Exodus came so fast, that even though the Jews had been instructed to prepare food for the journey, there was no time to let the bread rise. In fact, they fled Egypt with the dough on their backs. What began as *leḥem oni*, a symbol of our degradation at the beginning of the Seder, has now become the *matzah* of freedom, a reminder of the glory of our redemption.

MAROR

The question: Why do we eat it?

The answer: To remind ourselves that the Egyptians embittered the lives of our ancestors with the hard labor of slavery. (Exodus 1:14)

Maror is a taste of slavery. It is the bitter, pungent symbol of degradation, a reminder of the bondage in *Mitzrayim*. Tragically, the Jewish people throughout the centuries have tasted the bitterness of *maror* in countless oppressions, enslavements, and pogroms.

1. *Rabban Gamliel hayah omer:*	1. Rabban Gamliel would say:
2. *Kol sh'lo amar*	2. "Those who have not explained
3. *shloshah d'varim eilu ba-Pesaḥ*	3. three things during the Seder
4. *lo yatzah y'dei ḥovato.*	4. have not fulfilled their obligation.
5. *V'eilu hein:*	5. These (three) things are:
6. *Pesaḥ, Matzah, u-Maror.*	6. the *Pesaḥ* offering, *Matzah*, and *Maror*.

7. *Pesaḥ, she'hayu avoteinu okhlim*	7. *Pesaḥ*: Why did our ancestors eat
8. *biz'man she-beit ha-mikdash hayah kayam,*	8. (the *Pesaḥ* offering) at the time of the Holy Temple?
9. *al shum mah?*	9. What's the reason?
10. *Al shum she-pasaḥ ha-kadosh barukh hu*	10. As a reminder that the Holy One praised be He passed over
11. *al batei avoteinu b'Mitzrayim,*	11. the Israelite dwellings in *Mitzrayim*,
12. *she-ne'emar:*	12. as it is written:
13. *Va-amartem*	13. "You shall say,
14. *zevaḥ Pesaḥ hu l'Adonai,*	14. 'It is the *Pesaḥ* offering to *Adonai*,
15. *asher pasaḥ al batei*	15. because He passed over the houses of
16. *v'nei Yisrael b'Mitzrayim,*	16. the Israelites in *Mitzrayim*,
17. *b-nag'po et Mitzrayim,*	17. when He smote the Egyptians
18. *v'et bateinu hitzil.*	18. and spared our homes."

1. רַבָּן גַּמְלִיאֵל הָיָה אוֹמֵר:
2. כָּל שֶׁלֹּא אָמַר
3. שְׁלֹשָׁה דְבָרִים אֵלּוּ בַּפֶּסַח
4. לֹא יָצָא יְדֵי חוֹבָתוֹ.
5. וְאֵלּוּ הֵן:
6. פֶּסַח, מַצָּה, וּמָרוֹר.

7. פֶּסַח, שֶׁהָיוּ אֲבוֹתֵינוּ אוֹכְלִים
8. בִּזְמַן שֶׁבֵּית הַמִּקְדָּשׁ הָיָה קַיָּם
9. עַל שׁוּם מָה?
10. עַל שׁוּם שֶׁפָּסַח הַקָּדוֹשׁ בָּרוּךְ הוּא
11. עַל בָּתֵּי אֲבוֹתֵינוּ בְּמִצְרַיִם,
12. שֶׁנֶּאֱמַר:
13. וַאֲמַרְתֶּם
14. זֶבַח פֶּסַח הוּא לַיהוה,
15. אֲשֶׁר פָּסַח עַל בָּתֵּי
16. בְנֵי יִשְׂרָאֵל בְּמִצְרַיִם,
17. בְּנָגְפּוֹ אֶת מִצְרַיִם,
18. וְאֶת בָּתֵּינוּ הִצִּיל

1. *Matzah zo she-anu okhlim, al shum mah?*	1. *Matzah*: Why do we eat it?
2. *Al shum she-lo his'pik b'tzeikam shel avoteinu*	2. To remind ourselves that even before the dough of our ancestors
3. *l'ha-ḥamitz,*	3. had time to rise,
4. *ad she-niglah aleihem melekh mal'khei ham'lakhim*	4. the supreme King of kings revealed Himself
5. *ha-kadosh barukh hu*	5. the Holy One, praised be He,
6. *u-g'alam, she-ne'emar:*	6. and redeemed them, as it is written:
7. *Va-yofu et ha-batzek*	7. "And they baked the dough
8. *asher hotzi'anu mi'Mitzrayim*	8. which they had brought from *Mitzrayim*
9. *ugot matzot,*	9. into unleavened cakes,
10. *ki lo ḥametz ki gor'shu*	10. it did not rise since they hurried out
11. *mi'Mitzrayim*	11. of *Mitzrayim*,
12. *v'lo yakhlu l'hit'mah'mei'ah,*	12. and they could not delay,
13. *v'gam tzeidah lo asu la-hem.*	13. nor had they prepared other provisions for themselves."

1. מַצָּה זוֹ שֶׁאָנוּ אוֹכְלִים, עַל שׁוּם מָה?
2. עַל שׁוּם שֶׁלֹּא הִסְפִּיק בְּצֵקָם שֶׁל אֲבוֹתֵינוּ
3. לְהַחֲמִיץ,
4. עַד שֶׁנִּגְלָה עֲלֵיהֶם מֶלֶךְ מַלְכֵי הַמְּלָכִים
5. הַקָּדוֹשׁ בָּרוּךְ הוּא
6. וּגְאָלָם, שֶׁנֶּאֱמַר:
7. וַיֹּאפוּ אֶת הַבָּצֵק
8. אֲשֶׁר הוֹצִיאָנוּ מִמִּצְרַיִם
9. עֻגֹת מַצּוֹת,
10. כִּי לֹא חָמֵץ, כִּי גֹרְשׁוּ
11. מִמִּצְרַיִם
12. וְלֹא יָכְלוּ לְהִתְמַהְמֵהַּ,
13. וְגַם צֵדָה לֹא עָשׂוּ לָהֶם.

1. *Maror zeh she-anu okhlim, al shum mah?*	1. *Maror*. Why do we eat it?
2. *Al shum she-mer'ru ha-Mitzrim*	2. To remind ourselves that the Egyptians embittered
3. *et ḥayei avoteinu b'Mitzrayim*	3. the lives of our ancestors in *Mitzrayim*
4. *she-ne'emar:*	4. as it is written:
5. *Va-y'mar'ru et ḥayei'hem*	5. "And they embittered their lives
6. *ba-avodah kashah,*	6. with hard labor,
7. *b'ḥomer u-vil'veinim,*	7. in mortar and in brick,
8. *u-v'khol avodah*	8. and in every manner of drudgery
9. *ba-sadeh,*	9. in the field;
10. *eit kol avodatam asher avdu vahem b'forekh.*	10. and worked them ruthlessly in all their labor."

PRACTICE

1. When the section on the *Pesaḥ* is read, do **not** point to the *Z'roah*. The reason is that one should not think that we can restore the Passover sacrifice now that the Temple is lost. We are also not permitted to eat the *Z'roah* at the Seder, nor to break its bones, boil its meat nor save it to eat later. These latter points are all reminders of the instructions given to the people with regard to the paschal sacrifice on the night of the Exodus.
2. Before reading the paragraph on *Matzah*, lift the ceremonial *matzot*.
3. Before reading the paragraph on *Maror*, lift the *maror* from the Seder plate.

PRACTICAL QUESTIONS AND ANSWERS

Was the Last Supper actually a Seder?

While there are differences of opinion among scholars, it is clear that the disciples of Jesus who wrote the Gospels knew Jewish ritual practice. Jesus was, of course, Jewish, and it is possible that the Last Supper was a Passover Seder. However, what is perhaps more revealing about the differ-

1. מָרוֹר זֶה שֶׁאָנוּ אוֹכְלִים, עַל שׁוּם מָה?
2. עַל שׁוּם שֶׁמֵּרְרוּ הַמִּצְרִים
3. אֶת חַיֵּי אֲבוֹתֵינוּ בְּמִצְרַיִם,
4. שֶׁנֶּאֱמַר:
5. וַיְמָרְרוּ אֶת חַיֵּיהֶם
6. בַּעֲבֹדָה קָשָׁה,
7. בְּחֹמֶר וּבִלְבֵנִים
8. וּבְכָל עֲבֹדָה
9. בַּשָּׂדֶה,
10. אֵת כָּל עֲבֹדָתָם אֲשֶׁר עָבְדוּ בָהֶם בְּפָרֶךְ.

ences between Judaism and Christianity is the account of Jesus' crucifixion. When Jesus was crucified, the Gospel of John records that those attending were to dip hyssop into a bowl of vinegar and then place it in the mouth of Jesus (an echo of the hyssop dipped in the sacrificial blood on the night of Passover). Even more interesting is the account that the Romans who crucified Jesus broke the legs of the two men alongside Jesus, but they did not break his legs. This is critical to Christian theology, for Jesus is the new sacrifice to God, and it must be whole, just as the paschal sacrifice had to be whole.

THE ANSWER: B'KHOL DOR VA-DOR— IN EVERY GENERATION

CONCEPTS

YOU WERE LIBERATED FROM *MITZRAYIM*

The true answer to the question of the meaning of the three ritual symbols is this remarkable assertion: "In each generation, every individual should feel as though he or she had actually been redeemed from *Mitzrayim*." This is the key to our personal involvement with the Passover Seder.

B'KHOL DOR VA-DOR—IN EVERY GENERATION

1. *B'khol dor va-dor*	1. In each generation
2. *ḥayav adam*	2. every individual
3. *lirot et atzmo*	3. should feel as though he or she
4. *k'ilu hu yatza*	4. had actually been redeemed
5. *mi'Mitzrayim,*	5. from *Mitzrayim,*
6. *she-ne'emar:*	6. as it is said:
7. *V'higad'ta l'vinkha bayom ha-hu*	7. "You shall tell your children on that day,
8. *laymor,*	8. saying,
9. *Ba'avur zeh asah Adonai li*	9. "It is because of what *Adonai* did for me
10. *b'tzeiti mi'Mitzrayim.*	10. when I went free out of *Mitzrayim.*"
11. *Lo et avoteinu bilvad*	11. Not only our ancestors alone
12. *ga'al ha-kadosh barukh hu,*	12. did the Holy One, praised be He, redeem;
13. *ella af otanu ga'al imahem,*	13. He redeemed us with them,
14. *she-ne'emar:*	14. as it is said:
15. *V'otanu hotzi mi'sham*	15. "He brought us out of there,
16. *l'ma'an havi otanu latet lanu*	16. so that He might bring us
17. *et ha-aretz asher nishba la'avoteinu.*	17. to the land He promised our ancestors."

The proof text is Exodus 13:8, the instruction to the people to tell their children when they ask the meaning of the Passover: "It is because of what *Adonai* did for **me** when I went free out of *Mitzrayim.*" The rabbis see in this a tremendous opportunity to invest each generation of Jews in the process of redemption.

For the rabbis, all of us were at *Mitzrayim*, all of us were redeemed, all of us stood at Sinai, all of us received the Law. Rabbinic Judaism is inclusive Judaism, and the Seder ritual is an attempt to re-create the moment of liberation for each Jew in every generation. Certainly, the *Haggadah* is an historical document. Certainly, the Seder is an ancient ritual. But, the power of this holiday is that we all long to be redeemed from our personal *Mitzrayims*, we all hope and work and pray for Messianic times, we all strive to retain our identification as free people and as Jews. This makes the Passover Seder a living expression of a living people.

1. בְּכָל דּוֹר וָדוֹר
2. חַיָּב אָדָם
3. לִרְאוֹת אֶת עַצְמוֹ
4. כְּאִלּוּ הוּא יָצָא
5. מִמִּצְרַיִם,
6. שֶׁנֶּאֱמַר:
7. וְהִגַּדְתָּ לְבִנְךָ בַּיּוֹם הַהוּא
8. לֵאמֹר:
9. בַּעֲבוּר זֶה עָשָׂה יהוה לִי
10. בְּצֵאתִי מִמִּצְרָיִם.
11. לֹא אֶת אֲבוֹתֵינוּ בִּלְבַד
12. גָּאַל הַקָּדוֹשׁ בָּרוּךְ הוּא,
13. אֶלָּא אַף אוֹתָנוּ גָּאַל עִמָּהֶם,
14. שֶׁנֶּאֱמַר:
15. וְאוֹתָנוּ הוֹצִיא מִשָּׁם
16. לְמַעַן הָבִיא אֹתָנוּ לָתֶת לָנוּ
17. אֶת הָאָרֶץ אֲשֶׁר נִשְׁבַּע לַאֲבֹתֵינוּ.

INNOVATIONS

The Portuguese Jews also share the tradition of someone throwing the ***afikomen*** over the shoulder and pretending to be a refugee from Egypt. Their play-acting of this tradition comes at *B'khol dor va-dor.*

THE PRAISE: L'FIKHAKH—THEREFORE....

CONCEPTS

WE GIVE THANKS TO GOD

The Exodus story has now been thoroughly told (four times) and the *Haggadah* again turns to praising God who made it all happen. The "*L'fikhakh*" paragraph uses nine different verbs of praise to describe what we therefore must do to glorify God who performed all these miracles for our ancestors and for us: thank, praise, laud, glorify, exalt, honor, bless, extol, and give respect. These terms, along with the phrase "let us sing a new song, Halleluyah," may represent the ten "*sefirot*" (emanations) of the *Kabbalah* according to the mystical tradition. The Vilna Gaon sees a parallel between the nine terms of praise and the nine plagues, with "*v'nomar l'fanav,*" the verse that introduces the *Hallel* to come, said in response to the final deliverance, the result of the tenth plague.

FIVE STAGES OF REDEMPTION

The text continues by identifying five stages of deliverance which some commentators think illustrate the five exiles of the Jewish people:

1. From slavery to freedom = slavery of Egypt to the freedom of the Exodus
2. From despair to joy = despair of the Babylonian exile to the joy of rebuilding the Second Temple
3. From mourning to celebration = mourning under Persians to celebration of *Purim*
4. From darkness to light = darkness of Greek rule to light of Ḥanukkah
5. From enslavement to redemption = enslavement of present exile to the redemption of the future.

The Four Cups of Wine correspond to the first four of these redemptions, while the Fifth Cup of Elijah represents the redemption to come.

V'NOMAR L'FANAV—SING A NEW SONG

1. *V'nomar l'fanav shira ḥadashah:*	1. And we sing before Him a new song:
2. *Halleluyah.*	2. Halleluyah.

V'NOMAR L'FANAV

This well-known verse is the introduction of the psalms of praise called the *Hallel.* Of course, the last word of the verse—*Halleluyah*—sounds the theme for what is to come. *L'fikhakh* tells us that we must praise God for the miracles He has performed by saving the Jewish people, and for this, we sing a new song—*Halleluyah,* the *Hallel.*

PRACTICE

As the introduction to the *Hallel,* we raise the wine cup (and thus cover the *matzot*) as we recite *L'fikhakh.* This practice was probably instituted to call everyone's attention to the important songs of praise about to be recited. Replace the cup and uncover the *matzot* upon concluding "*V'nomar l'fanav.*"

THE PRAISE: HALLELUYAH

CONCEPTS

CONCLUDE WITH PRAISE

Recall that the *modus operandi* of the *Maggid* is to tell the story of the Exodus, beginning with our degradation and concluding with glory. The *Maggid* is now completed and we begin to sing the praises of *Adonai* in the *Hallel,* one of the oldest texts of the *Haggadah.* The "Egyptian *Hallel,*" consisting of Psalms 113 through 118, was undoubtedly sung by the Levites in the Temple during the *Pesaḥ* ritual. The *Hallel* is recited on the special Holy Days and Festivals of the Jewish people. However, there are a number of differences that characterize this special recitation of *Hallel* at the Seder:

1. The *Hallel* is never said at night, except at the Seder. The reason given is that we can see God's works during daylight. But, the events of the night of Passover, a night of vigil, certainly deserve our praise.
2. This *Hallel* is divided into two parts: Psalms 113 and 114 are said before the meal and the rest are recited after *Birkat ha-Mazon.* Why? Some commentators view the first two Psalms as referring to the Exodus from Egypt. Psalm 113 speaks of the people as "servants of *Adonai,*" a pointed difference from our previous status as "servants of Pharaoh." Psalm 114 directly refers to the Exodus experience. Thus, both properly belong to this first part of the Seder. Psalms 115-118 look ahead to Messianic times, a major theme of the second half of the Seder experience.

1. וְנֹאמַר לְפָנָיו שִׁירָה חֲדָשָׁה.
2. הַלְלוּיָהּ.

jor theme of the second half of the Seder experience.

3. There is no blessing "*likro et ha-Hallel*" normally said before reciting the *Hallel.* Several reasons are offered: this *Hallel* is said at night, it is divided into two parts, it is not commanded to be read as in the daytime on Holy Days and Festivals. Some suggest that the preceding paragraph "*L'fikhakh*" is a kind of introductory blessing, substituting for the normal introduction.
4. Normally we stand for the *Hallel*; here we sit as a sign of our freedom.

GA'AL YISRAEL

The *Maggid* now officially draws to a close with a summary paragraph, composed, in part, by Rabbi Akiva himself. God is praised for redeeming us and our ancestors from *Mitzrayim* and for bringing us to this night when we eat *Matzah* and *Maror.* We pray for God to enable us to celebrate in peace other Holy Days and Festivals. And significantly for us, and certainly for a bold Rabbi Akiva, who wrote these words under the rule of Rome, we hope for the rebuilding of Jerusalem and Your service. (In some *Haggadah* texts, "Your service" includes Rabbi Akiba's hope of restoring the actual paschal sacrifice which cannot now happen). The *ḥatimah*, the concluding benediction, reveals the theme: "Praised are You, *Adonai*, Redeemer of the people Israel.

GA'AL YISRAEL—
REDEEMER OF ISRAEL

1. *Barukh attah Adonai*	1. Praised are You, *Adonai*,
2. *ga'al Yisrael.*	2. redeemer of the people Israel.

KOS SHEINI—
THE SECOND CUP

3. *Barukh attah Adonai*	3. Praised are You, *Adonai*,
4. *Eloheinu melekh ha-olam*	4. our God, King of the universe,
5. *borei p'ri ha-gafen.*	5. Creator of the fruit of the vine.

THE CURTAIN: KOS SHEINI—THE SECOND CUP

CONCEPTS

The *Maggid* is formally concluded with the blessing of the Second Cup of Wine. This cup is a reminder of the second promise of redemption: "I will deliver you." (Exodus 6:6)

PRACTICE

The concluding paragraph of the *Maggid* is said as we lift the cup of wine. Upon reciting *borei p'ri ha-gafen*, we drink the Second Cup of Wine while reclining.

1. בָּרוּךְ אַתָּה יהוה
2. גָּאַל יִשְׂרָאֵל.

3. בָּרוּךְ אַתָּה יהוה
4. אֱלֹהֵינוּ מֶלֶךְ הָעוֹלָם
5. בּוֹרֵא פְּרִי הַגָּפֶן.

ACT III—THE FEAST

SCENE 1: PREPARE TO EAT
ROḤTZAH
MOTZI/MATZAH
MAROR
KOREKH
SCENE 2: SHULḤAN OREKH (SET THE TABLE)
SCENE 3: TZAFUN (DESSERT)
SCENE 4: BAREKH (BLESSINGS AFTER FOOD)
CURTAIN: KOS SH'LISHI (THE THIRD CUP OF WINE)

14

PREPARING TO EAT:

ROḤTZAH, MOTZI/MATZAH, MAROR, KOREKH

ACT III, SCENE 1

Matzah is not something we eat in my house only on *Pesaḥ*. We do have it in the house all year round and the kids will put peanut butter on it or I will fry it for breakfast, but it never tastes quite the same as it does when you break into that first piece of *matzah* at Seder time. You know that when you eat *matzah* at Seder that the holiday has really begun, and the Seder, all of it, just becomes alive for us all.

Abby Kantor

Now let's face it, eating *maror* is a Jewish test of manhood. There is the red stuff for woosies and wimps, and then the white for real men. Of course everyone jokes about the sinuses and the hair on your chest. I mean, there's a lot of talking but that is all a part of the ritual. My pappa always claims that Chicago *ḥ'rein* is the best. You know, the stuff that makes your eyebrows fall out, but everyone knows that you become a man when you can eat a man-size portion.

David Coburn

Don't tell anyone, but when I eat the *maror*, I really cry. Just a little bit but I do cry. Not because I can't handle the horseradish or anything, but because it really does make me think of all the sad things there are.

Matthew Gill

High on a closet shelf is a box of memories which is ritually reviewed each and every time my sister and I make our requisite pilgrimages back to the suburb of our origins. We return home, stand on the chair, and bring the box down from the shelf—spreading the contents on the bed. Some memories are yellowing, the chemicals fading with age. Others are cracked, the emulsion breaking away from the surface. Most are smeared with fingerprints. Many are curling, their images rolling in on themselves. Every family has its own collection. Ours goes back three generations, each storing its posed persona, its candid insights, its critical gatherings in silver-nitrate perpetuity.

Among the images is one of me, all of three or four years old, dressed for combat. I am wearing a western holster with two cap six-shooters, a plastic battle helmet, and a pair of goggles. I know the image well, I have looked at it for years. While I have no memory of the event, the helmet or the goggles, I remember the image. It has become a memory, though the actual event it records has drifted back into obscurity. I suppose most people have this kind of secondhand recall. I know the faces of relatives I've never seen. I feel at home in rooms I've never entered. All are part of my family legacy.

The Exodus wasn't recorded on film. There are no polaroids of the family roasting their paschal lamb. But, the experience of the event was carefully stored for secondhand recall. The feelings of Egypt, the feelings of freedom, have been contained in *matzah*, *maror* and *ḥaroset*. They are waiting for our annual trip home. They present themselves to us, as both first- and secondhand memories. They let the past live in us.

The story has been told and we have been redeemed. Now, it is time to enjoy the feast. There are four preliminary steps before the meal can be eaten: *Roḥtzah* (Wash Hands), *Motzi/Matzah* (Blessings for Sustenance and *Matzah*), *Maror* (Bitter Herbs), and *Korekh* (Binding the *Matzah* and the *Maror*—Hillel's Sandwich). Let's examine each of these four important steps.

ROḤTZAH

CONCEPTS

Once the Temple was destroyed, each family's home became a *mikdash m'at*, a miniature Temple, with the dinner table its altar. Just as the priests prepared for the sacrifices brought to the Temple by a ritual washing of the hands, so too observant Jews wash hands before breaking bread at every meal. As celebrants of the Passover meal, we wash our hands before breaking the *matzah* bread.

Recall that this is the second washing of the hands at the Seder. But, this time there is a blessing—"*al netilat yadayim.*" Curiously, the blessing itself uses the word *netilat* instead of a form of the word *roḥtzah* (wash). *Netilat* literally means "take" or "lift up." The use of this term indicates that the hands are in fact "lifted up" to a higher level by this symbolic cleansing, elevating the animal act of eating into a ritual filled with meaning.

OBJECTS

A large cup or pitcher and, if the handwashing is performed at the table itself, a basin are required for *Roḥtzah* (also known as "*Netilat Yadayim*"). Special pitchers with dual handles have been developed for this purpose. Some families have such pitchers for use during the rest of the year. Depending on the kind of material it is made of, it could be *kashered*, or, you may wish to buy a special pitcher for use at the Seder. Any glass and basin or sink will do. You will also need a towel for drying the hands.

PRACTICE

1. Remove any jewelry from your fingers. As in other ritual cleansings, nothing should come between your hands and the water.
2. Fill a cup or pitcher with water, take the cup in the left hand, and pour some of the water over the right hand, letting the water cover the hand from the wrist down. Turn your hand under the water so it gets completely wet.
3. Switch the cup into the right hand and pour water over the left hand. Some repeat this procedure three times.
4. Lift up your hands and begin reciting the blessing. Dry your hands after completing the blessing.
5. Do not talk from the time you finish the blessing until you have recited *Motzi/Matzah* and you have eaten a piece of *matzah*. Since the handwashing is done in order to eat the *matzah*, *Roḥtzah* and *Motzi/Matzah* are considered one act. A ritual is not completed until both the blessing is recited and the act is done. These moments of silence can be absolutely golden, a real challenge to the young people in your group.

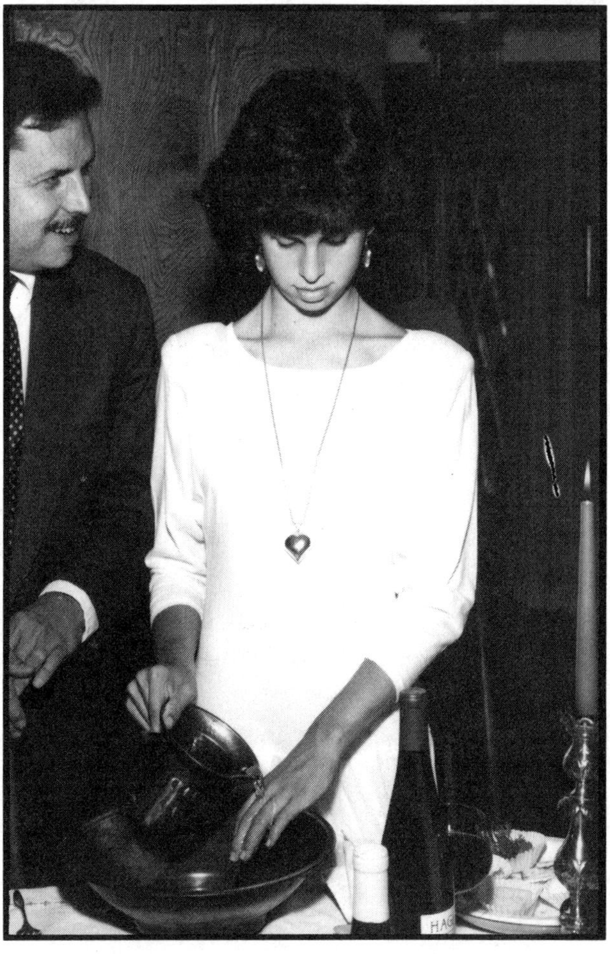

Please note that because of this rule against talking between *Roḥtzah* and *Motzi/Matzah*, any explanations you wish to make about any of these three blessings should be made before washing the hands or after eating the *matzah*.

ROḤTZAH—WASH HANDS

1. *Barukh attah Adonai*	1. Praised are You, *Adonai,*
2. *Eloheinu melekh ha-olam*	2. our God, King of the universe,
3. *asher kidshanu*	3. who has sanctified our lives
4. *b'mitzvotav*	4. through His commandments
5. *v'tzivanu*	5. and commanded us
6. *al netilat yadayim.*	6. to perform the ritual washing of our hands.

PRACTICAL QUESTIONS AND ANSWERS

Does everyone have to wash hands?

Yes, everyone should wash hands. At a Seder with many participants, having everyone wash hands can be a challenge. Getting everyone up from the table can seem either crazy (especially if quarters are tight) or a wonderful idea after sitting through the first half of the Seder. You might want to have several handwashing stations convenient to all. The kitchen is probably not a good idea for one, since there is very likely a good deal of activity going on in preparation for serving the meal. Set up pitchers and basins on separate card tables in a nearby room, or, if the party is small, pass a pitcher and basin around the table. Some families assign two people to actually carry the pitcher, basin, and towel around the table to each participant. Do whatever seems comfortable in your situation, but encourage everyone to participate.

Who washes first?

There is no particular order. Of course, whoever washes first has the longest period of silence before the *matzah* is eaten!

What if I can't get my rings off?

Go ahead and wash. If you do take off valuable jewelry, be careful where you put it. We know of more than one person who has lost a ring down a drain during handwashing!

Why is the first washing called *Urḥatz* and the second washing called *Roḥtzah*?

The names of these steps were created to fit the rhyme of the mnemonic *Kadesh, Urḥatz.* Both "*urḥatz*" and "*roḥtzah*" are forms of the Hebrew word "*raḥatz*," to wash oneself. Their slight difference also makes it easier to differentiate between the two handwashings.

1. בָּרוּךְ אַתָּה יהוה
2. אֱלֹהֵינוּ מֶלֶךְ הָעוֹלָם
3. אֲשֶׁר קִדְּשָׁנוּ
4. בְּמִצְוֹתָיו
5. וְצִוָּנוּ
6. עַל נְטִילַת יָדָיִם.

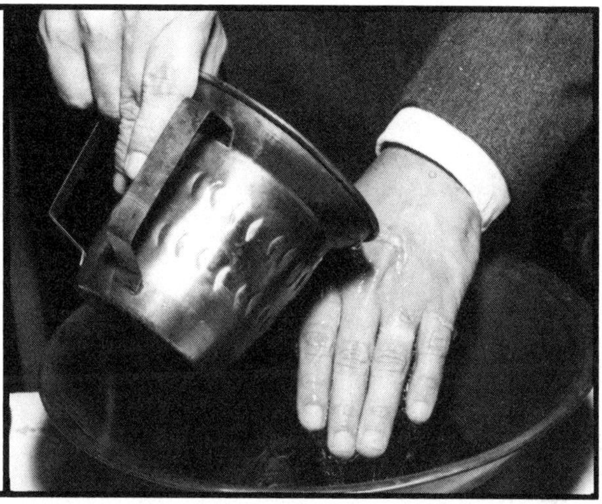

MOTZI/MATZAH

CONCEPTS

RITUAL BREAD

Contrary to popular belief, the bagel is not the bread of the Jewish people. Neither is pita the bread of Israeli Jews. No, there are only two forms of bread which are accorded ritual status in Judaism—the *ḥallah* of Shabbat and *Yom Tov* and the *matzah* of *Pesaḥ*.

On Shabbat and Holy Days, *ḥallah* serves as a reminder of the *manna* which God provided the Israelites during the forty years of wandering in the desert, a clear symbol of the Exodus theme. It also symbolizes the bounty God provides us through nature, focusing on bread, the "staff of life."

On Passover, the ritual bread is *Matzah*, the dialectical symbol of the Seder, at one and the same time the "bread of affliction" and the "bread of freedom." As we have already seen, three *matzot* are set aside for our ritual, each one with its own purpose, each one with its own symbolism.

The top two *matzot*, including the broken middle *matzah* left over from *Yaḥatz*, stand for *leḥem mishneh*, the double portion of *manna* brought by God to the Israelites on the day before Shabbat so they would not have to gather food on the day of rest (see Exodus 16:22-30). The middle *matzah* is also symbolic of the *leḥem oni*, the bread of affliction, with which we began our story. The bottom *matzah* is reserved for *Korekh*, the so-called Hillel sandwich which will be discussed below. It is also a reminder of the *Pesaḥ* wheat offering in the Temple. Later, commentators interpreted the three *matzot* to represent the three classes of Jews: *Kohanim* (High Priests), *Levi'im* (Priests), and *Yisraelim* (Israelites—commoners)

The origin of *Matzah*, the unleavened bread eaten on Passover, can be traced *midrashically* in the Bible all the way back to Abraham and Sarah. When the three strangers visit Abraham in his tent, Sarah runs to bake unleavened cakes for them called "*uggot matzot*"—*matzah* cakes (Genesis 18:6). The word "*uggah*" indicates a round-shaped cake which explains why, until the advent of *matzah*-making machines, *matzot* were always round in shape. Later in the Bible, King Saul is served *matzah* by a woman at En-Dor (Samuel I 28:24.)

TWO BLESSINGS

Two blessings are recited over *matzah*. The first, the familiar "*ha-motzi leḥem min ha-aretz*" is a general blessing recited over all breads when eaten. It praises God who brings forth bread from the earth. Although we want to differentiate between *leḥem* (leavened bread) and *matzah* (unleavened bread) in our attempt to follow the rules prohibiting the eating of *ḥametz* bread during Passover, remember that *matzah* is bread. It may not look like bread, but it is. It is a special kind of bread, created from flour and water kneaded and baked within 18 minutes. Therefore, the rabbis decided that the blessing for *leḥem* should be recited over *matzah* bread.

The second blessing is a specially-constructed *b'rakhah* for just this occasion. Notice that the form of the blessing for *matzah*—"*al akhilat matzah*" is different from the blessing for bread. The *matzah* blessing uses the formula "*asher kidshanu b'mitzvotav v'tzivanu*," a very specific formulation for ritual acts commanded by God, whereas the simpler "*ha-motzi leḥem min ha-aretz*" formula is more of a statement of praise and fact. In the first *Motzi* blessing we praise God who brings forth bread from the earth, while in the second *Matzah* blessing we praise God who sanctifies us through His commandments and *commands* us to partake of *Matzah*.

Why is the "*Motzi*" said first, before the "*Matzah*" blessing? The Talmud states: "What is usual precedes that which is not usual" (*B'rakhot* 51b). Thus, "*Motzi*," which is said over all bread, takes precedence over the special blessing of "*Matzah*" which is specific to *Pesaḥ*. The value inherent in this principle is that the rabbis considered the regular, repeated evidence of God's love for humanity as demonstrated in daily life even greater than miracles.

MOTZI

1. *Barukh attah Adonai*	1. Praised are You, *Adonai*,
2. *Eloheinu melekh ha-olam*	2. our God, King of the universe,
3. *ha-motzi leḥem*	3. who brings forth bread
4. *min ha-aretz.*	4. from the earth.

MATZAH

5. *Barukh attah Adonai*	5. Praised are You, *Adonai*,
6. *Eloheinu melekh ha-olam*	6. our God, King of the universe,
7. *asher kidshanu b'mitzvotav*	7. who has sanctified us through His commandments
8. *v'tzivanu*	8. and commanded us
9. *al akhilat matzah.*	9. to partake of *matzah*.

OBJECTS

The objects required for *Motzi/Matzah* are the three *matzot* described earlier in *Yaḥatz*, the *matzot* bag or napkin, and extra *matzot* to supplement the ceremonial pieces.

PRACTICE

The two blessings for *Motzi* and *Matzah* are to be said together, the *Motzi* first, immediately followed by the *Matzah*, without interruption.

There is some disagreement about whether all three *matzot* are lifted for both blessings. The debate is over whether the broken middle *matzah* can count for *leḥem mishneh*, since normally two whole loaves are required for the *Motzi* blessing. The decision:

1. Lift up all three *matzot* (within which are two whole *matzot*) and recite the *Motzi*.
2. Then, put the bottom *matzah* back in its place and recite the *Matzah* blessing while holding up the top and middle *matzot*.
3. Distribute and eat small portions of both the top and middle *matzah* while reclining. Do not salt the *matzah*.

1. בָּרוּךְ אַתָּה יהוה
2. אֱלֹהֵינוּ מֶלֶךְ הָעוֹלָם
3. הַמּוֹצִיא לֶחֶם
4. מִן הָאָרֶץ.

5. בָּרוּךְ אַתָּה יהוה
6. אֱלֹהֵינוּ מֶלֶךְ הָעוֹלָם
7. אֲשֶׁר קִדְּשָׁנוּ בְּמִצְוֹתָיו
8. וְצִוָּנוּ
9. עַל אֲכִילַת מַצָּה.

PRACTICAL QUESTIONS AND ANSWERS

Why can't we distribute the bottom *matzah*?

This *matzah* is reserved for *Korekh*, the Hillel sandwich. The *Motzi/Matzah* blessings are performed over the top and middle *matzot.*

Why do we eat portions of both the top and middle *matzah*?

There is some disagreement over whether the *Matzah* blessing is said over the broken middle *matzah* or the unbroken top *matzah.* To be sure the blessing is not said in vain, the decision was reached to eat pieces of both.

How much *matzah* must we eat?

The rabbis require each person to eat a "*k'zayit*"*-size piece of matzah.* What's an olive-sized piece of *matzah*? Some authorities hold that a *k'zayit* is half the size of an egg. One authority holds that in order to eat a *k'zayit*-sized piece of *matzah* from both the top and middle *matzot*, the amount is equivalent to an area 7 x 6 and 1/4 inches.

What if there are not enough *matzah* pieces from the ceremonial *matzot* to go around?

Distribute small pieces of the top and middle *matzot* and supplement with extra *matzah* on the table. Just as we eat a small portion of the *ḥallah* over which we said the blessing at the Shabbat table, here too everyone should have at least a small piece of both the top and middle *matzot.*

Why don't we use salt on the *matzah*?

Unlike Shabbat, we do not sprinkle salt on the ritual bread. The use of salt on the *ḥallah* of Shabbat is a reminder of the Temple sacrifice. At the Passover Seder, we have an abundance of reminders of the sacrificial rite in the Temple. Moreover, we have already used salt in the water for *Karpas* as a reminder of the condition of slavery; we certainly don't need it on *matzah* which is already known as the bread of affliction. The salt is also said to interfere with the pure taste of the *matzah.* On the other hand, some authorities do require the use of salt on *matzah.*

MAROR—BITTER HERBS

1. *Barukh attah Adonai*	1. Praised are You, *Adonai,*
2. *Eloheinu melekh ha-olam*	2. our God, King of the universe,
3. *asher kidshanu*	3. who has sanctified our lives
4. *b'mitzvotav*	4. through His Commandments
5. *v'tzivanu*	5. commanding us
6. *al akhilat maror.*	6. to eat *maror.*

Can we use egg *matzah* for these blessings?

No. Egg *matzah* is considered *matzah ashira*, enriched *matzah*. For the purposes of the Seder ceremony, only plain *matzah* or *matzah shmura*, specially guarded *matzah*, should be used. However, if for medical reasons, one cannot eat regular *matzah*, egg *matzah* may be substituted.

Must we eat *matzah* during the rest of *Pesaḥ*?

No, only at the *Sedarim*. The commandment to eat *matzah* applies only to the Seder itself, not the rest of the week. So, if *matzah* does not agree with you, the only obligation is to eat it the three times required at each of the *Sedarim*: 1) for *Motzi/Matzah*, 2) as part of the *Korekh* sandwich, and 3) the *afikomen* to complete the meal. We may not, of course, eat leavened bread for the full eight days of Passover, but the obligation to eat *matzah* only applies to the *Sedarim*.

MAROR

CONCEPTS

THE BITTERNESS OF SLAVERY

Maror is the preeminent symbol of the bitterness of the bondage in Egypt. As with *matzah*, the eating of *Maror* is a biblically commanded ritual act based on the prescription for the Passover celebration detailed in Exodus 12:8.

ḤAROSET

Clearly, *maror* is the bitterness of slavery. But, the rabbis decided to temper this symbol of bitterness somewhat by dipping the *maror* into *ḥaroset*, the sweet mixture of apples, nuts, cinnamon, and wine. As with *matzah*, *ḥaroset* is a dialectical symbol, sending two different messages simultaneously. On the one hand, *ḥaroset* symbolizes the mortar with which our ancestors were forced to bake bricks in the grueling heat of the Egyptian sun. On the other hand, *ḥaroset* is sweet, dulling the sharpness of the *maror*, hinting at optimism in the midst of degradation.

1. בָּרוּךְ אַתָּה יהוה
2. אֱלֹהֵינוּ מֶלֶךְ הָעוֹלָם
3. אֲשֶׁר קִדְּשָׁנוּ
4. בְּמִצְוֹתָיו
5. וְצִוָּנוּ
6. עַל אֲכִילַת מָרוֹר.

Perhaps the *ḥaroset* is the theological opposite of the breaking of the glass at the moment of marriage when, at the instant of ultimate joy, we recall with sadness the tragedy of the Temple's destruction. Here, we vividly recall the bitterness of our enslavement to Pharoah, and yet, we continue to hope that God's promise of liberation and national fulfillment will be realized.

By the way, the dipping of *maror* into *ḥaroset* is the second dipping referred to in the Four Questions. The first dipping was the *Karpas* in salt water.

OBJECTS

A variety of vegetables qualify as bitter herbs. Among the most common foods used are horseradish root and the stalks of romaine lettuce. Horseradish root in its natural state is quite bitter. Pure grated horseradish is extremely sharp in taste, which is why much of the prepared horseradish found in supermarkets has beets added to it to subdue some of its pungency. If you prefer, you can prepare slivers of horseradish root instead of grating it. An alternative, romaine lettuce, was a favorite of many of the rabbis. Its bitterness mounts gradually, much like slavery which at first can feel secure, even comfortable, but which quickly becomes bitter to the mind, spirit and body!

Ḥaroset is a mixture of apples, nuts, wine, cinnamon, and, in some traditions, dates, raisins, figs, honey, etc. Clearly the favorite symbolic dish of children (and many adults!), *ḥaroset* is used as the food into which the *maror* is dipped.

Quantities of *maror* and *ḥaroset* should be available to all participants at the table.

PRACTICE

Here is how to perform the *Maror* ceremony:

1. Dip some *maror* into the *ḥaroset*, shaking off any excess so that the bitterness of the *maror* can be tasted.

KOREKH—HILLEL'S SANDWICH

1. *Zekher l'mikdash*	1. This is a reminder of the Temple
2. *k'Hillel.*	2. and a reminder of the practice of Hillel.
3. *Ken asah Hillel*	3. This is what Hillel would do
4. *biz'man she-beit ha-mikdash*	4. when the Temple
5. *hayah kayam.*	5. was in existence.
6. *Hayah korekh matzah u'maror*	6. He would make a sandwich of (the *Pesaḥ* offering) *matzah* and *maror*
7. *v'okhel b'yaḥad,*	7. and he would eat them together
8. *l'ka'yem mah she-ne'emar:*	8. in fulfillment of the verse,
9. *al matzot u-m'rorim yokh'luhu.*	9. "with *matzot* and *maror* they shall eat it."

2. Recite the blessing "*al akhilat maror.*"
3. Then eat the *maror* without reclining.

PRACTICAL QUESTIONS AND ANSWERS

Why is there no blessing for *ḥaroset*?

According to the rabbis, *ḥaroset* is to be considered an integral part of the *maror.* There is also a dispute in the Mishnah as to whether *ḥaroset* is a *mitzvah* or not.

Why do we not recline while eating maror?

Maror is a symbol of slavery and slaves do not recline while eating. The contrast between eating the *maror* of bondage should be quite stark compared to the eating of most of the other symbolic foods.

KOREKH

CONCEPTS

RABBI HILLEL'S SANDWICH

The Bible records God's instructions to the people to celebrate the Passover night by "eating the flesh (of the paschal lamb) in that night, roasted with fire, and unleavened bread, with bitter herbs." (Exodus 12:8). Again, in Numbers 9:11, God commands this recipe for eating the results of the paschal sacrifice. Hillel, one of the greatest rabbis in Jewish history, created a reminder of this by eating a sandwich consisting of the roast of the *Pesaḥ* offering and *maror* between pieces of *matzah.*

1. זֵכֶר לְמִקְדָּשׁ
2. כְּהִלֵּל.
3. כֵּן עָשָׂה הִלֵּל
4. בִּזְמַן שֶׁבֵּית הַמִּקְדָּשׁ
5. הָיָה קַיָּם.
6. הָיָה כּוֹרֵךְ מַצָּה וּמָרוֹר
7. וְאוֹכֵל בְּיַחַד,
8. לְקַיֵּם מַה שֶּׁנֶּאֱמַר:
9. עַל מַצּוֹת וּמְרֹרִים יֹאכְלֻהוּ.

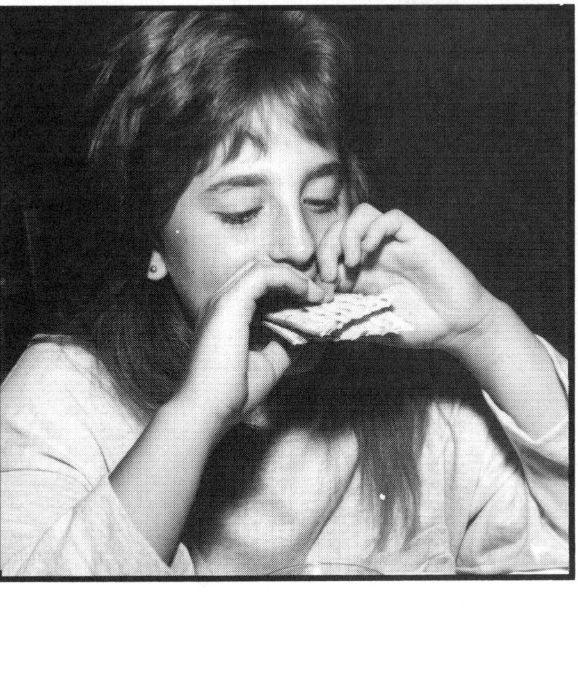

This sandwich, of course, could only have been made while the Temple still stood and sacrifices were still performed on Passover. Once the Temple was destroyed, one of the three ingredients of Hillel's sandwich, the roasted meat, was no longer available. So, although our *Korekh*—which literally means "bind together"—is vegetarian, this ritual serves as another reminder of the original Passover meal and one rabbi's attempt to re-create the experience for himself.

Korekh is the third step of the *Pesaḥ* Seder which does not require a *b'rakhah*. Our only text is a paragraph describing Hillel's custom which has become a required part of our Seder experience.

PRACTICE

Here's the recipe for making a Hillel sandwich:

1. The leader distributes pieces of the bottom ceremonial *matzah*. If more *matzah* is necessary to create the sandwich, take from the supplementary stocks of *matzot* on the table.
2. Sandwich some *maror* between two pieces of the bottom *matzah* and recite the paragraph of text. Some dip the *maror* into *ḥaroset* before making the sandwich. Others use the *ḥazeret* for the *maror* of *Korekh*.
3. Eat the sandwich while reclining.

PRACTICAL QUESTIONS AND ANSWERS

Should the sandwich include *ḥaroset*, too?

There are different opinions on this point. Some authorities hold that since *ḥaroset* is a part of *maror*, it is perfectly acceptable to dip the *maror* into *ḥaroset* before creating the sandwich. Others feel that to fulfill the biblical idea of eating *matzah* and *maror* (*ḥaroset* was a later rabbinic notion), we should eat unadulterated *maror* in the *Korekh* sandwich. Follow your own custom.

What is *Ḥazeret?*

Another name for *maror*. *Ḥazeret* comes from the root word *laḥzor*—to return. It is not directly mentioned in the *Haggadah* text, but the rabbis deduce its name from the phrase "*ha-Kadosh Barukh Hu he-ḥe'ziranu la-avodato*," "the Holy One Blessed Be He brought us back to His service". A place for *Ḥazeret* is sometimes found on Seder plates. It is generally grated horseradish or romaine lettuce which can be used as the *maror* in *Korekh*.

Why doesn't the word "*Pesaḥ*" appear in the Hebrew text?

Some *Haggadot* include the mention of the *Pesaḥ* sacrifice; others do not. Clearly, Hillel included the meat of the *Pesaḥ* in his sandwich; we cannot.

15

שֻׁלְחָן עוֹרֵךְ:

SHULḤAN OREKH
THE FEAST

ACT III, SCENE 2

We have the gefilte fish, Chris's mother-in-law's fish, which is done in the Sephardic tradition. It is served cold or at a room temperature, and it's done with tomatoes, and it's covered with parsley.

Rica Sabah

This is Bubbie's *kugel*. Essentially I learned it from my mother-in-law, and she still does come and prepare it every year. She warns me around March that she is too tired to make nut cake and *kugel*, but she comes and she does. I always put her to work. She makes this *kugel* with apricots, prunes, and apples, and it's a *matzah*-meal base, and it's very light because you whip it up. The important thing is that we do not make it during the year, and I know that's a very strong Jewish *minhag* (custom) that time and place have religious meaning...

Carol Karsch

It tastes like *kugel*, except there's a lot more to it. I mean you can't even tell it's on Passover that you're eating it.

Benjy Karsch

Yeah, it doesn't taste like it's *matzah* or anything. It's full of fruit, is mainly what it is, and it's very good.

Mordy Karsch

CONCEPTS

SEUDAT MITZVAH

It is time for the festive meal, usually a multi-course culinary extravaganza, but it too is carefully structured as an integral part of the Seder ritual. Food is very important in Jewish celebration and the rabbis tried to merge the performance of significant *mitzvot* with a festive meal. This they called a "*seudat mitzvah,*" literally, a *mitzvah* meal.

The *seudat mitzvah* of Passover is a reminder of the first *Pesaḥ* meal as recorded in the Bible with, of course, one major difference. In the Torah account, and for centuries thereafter, the menu consisted of the roasted meat of the paschal sacrifice together with *matzah* and *maror.* Once the Temple was destroyed, sacrifices could no longer be brought. As we have learned, there was a specific prohibition against eating any roasted meat on Passover night to prevent even the slightest suspicion that sacrifices could be done once again.

Yet, the meal took on other symbolic and traditional foods. A hard-cooked egg dipped in salt water became the opening course. Why? Many reasons are given: the egg represents birth, springtime, circularity of life, fertility, and the ever-turning cycle of history. For some, the absence of the paschal sacrifice provokes a sense of loss. The egg is the first food offered mourners upon returning from a funeral, a symbol of mourning.

The menu ideas for Passover are numerous and we have suggested a few below. Suffice it to say, whatever the menu, the Passover dinner is perhaps the most elaborate meal served during the Jewish festival cycle.

SET THE TABLE

The literal translation of "*Shulḥan Orekh*" is "set the table." Why is this term used to describe the meal? In olden days, the small tables used for eating were removed from the dining room at the beginning of the Seder. Now, the tables are returned and "set" so the meal can be served.

OBJECTS

Traditional foods for the Passover meal vary depending on the country and cultural backgrounds people come from. Among the Ashkenazim, traditional foods include gefilte fish (stuffed fish), chicken soup with *kneidlakh* (*matzah* balls), beet *borscht* (a soup), carrot *tzimmes* (a kind of carrot stew), rhubarb sauce, asparagus, and a variety of *Pesaḥdik* desserts. Among the Sephardim, whose tradition allows the eating of *kitniot,* rice is a popular side dish, along with a kind of meat casserole called "*meyina*" or "*megina*". In almost all traditions, dessert includes fruit compote, heavy with prunes, an important aid to *matzah*-afflicted diners.

A number of excellent Passover cookbooks are available offering many creative suggestions for holiday cookery. In an ironic sort of way, the prohibition against *ḥametz* has stimulated the creativity of generations of cooks who try to discover what can be made with *matzah* flour. As you can imagine, there is no end to the suggestions. We have annotated some of the better *Pesaḥ* cookbooks in the Selected Bibliography.

PRACTICE

Most people are famished by the time the meal is served and there is inevitable pressure to serve quickly. Then, everyone eats hurriedly until stuffed to the point they can hardly move.

Ideally, the meal should proceed at a more leisurely pace, allowing everyone, including the people responsible for the kitchen, a chance to sit and enjoy the results of the tremendous preparation that goes into producing these culinary delights. I recall that my Bubbie would never sit down during the meal to eat; she was always running from table to kitchen, clearing one course while preparing to serve the next. Even though there is more of the *Haggadah* to read, try to take your time with the dinner.

Dessert is served before eating the *afikomen* and the continuation of the *Haggadah* reading. Unlike Shabbat, the singing of *Z'mirot*, table songs, is not generally done during the meal. They are reserved for the end of the Seder.

PRACTICAL QUESTIONS AND ANSWERS

What is "gebrukht?"

The practice of eating hard-cooked eggs mixed with salt water is known as "*gebrukht*," a Yiddish word meaning "broken." Many families break up these hard eggs into bowls of salt water and eat it as a first course.

16

צָפוּן

TZAFUN

FINDING THE HIDDEN

ACT III, SCENE 3

It always amazes me how the Seder works. On any other night you can't get the kids to sit at the table. As soon as they are through eating, it is up and gone, but during the Seder they sit through an hour-long service—and boy is it long—and as soon as dinner is over, they are right back at the table with the *afikomen* in hand, ready to go right back at it again. I guess the rabbis really knew how to plan a family event.

Abby Kantor

Last year, $7.50 was the most that anyone made on the *afikomen.* That was Avi, but I think I got the best prize. I got $5.00 and I got to go out to lunch with my Zaida.

Yonina Dorph

We always used to fight over the *afikomen.* The *afikomen* at our Seder traditionally would be stolen six, seven times. The *afikomen* would be taken originally from the leader from the head of the Seder. The initial steal was very easy, but after that we would steal it from each other. It would go from one hiding place to another.

Benjy Karsch

"Hide and Go Seek" is a big part of the Jewish experience. Usually, God does the hiding and we do the seeking.

> In ancient times, man captured knowledge by playing out magic rituals, telling myths, and by competing in games. In contemporary life, man, like his ancestors, will continue to need the playing out of cultural meaning. For man is destined to play with the ideas and skills of civilization before he can inherit them. As long as civilization incorporates playfulness within its culture, its supporting knowledge and practices will continue to develop. (Mary Reilly, *Play as Exploratory Learning*)

> What a great wonder that man should be able to draw so near to God in prayer. How many walls there are between man and God! Even though God fills all the world, God is very hidden! Yet a single word of prayer can topple all the walls and bring you close to God. (*Likkutim Yekarim* 2b)

There are certain Passover stories that every family can tell. Everyone has their own version of "The Great Wine Spill," of "Guess What Happened When We Opened the Door for Elijah," and of "The Big Battle for the *Afikomen*". These are all as integral to the Seder experience as are the jokes about the strength of the horseradish, the reactions over who is chosen to be "the wicked child" and the "simple child," and the unofficial licking of the wine off the finger just used to dip out the Ten Plagues. While Seder is a formal, regimented ritual,it is also a folk experience, enriched by the spontaneity of human interaction.

> One day little Yeḥiel was playing hide-and-seek with his friend. Having hidden himself well, he waited to be found. But, a long time passed and his friend did not come near him. Then Yeḥiel realized that his friend had not so much as begun to look for him. He burst into tears and ran to his grandfather, crying: "Grandfather, Grandfather, he didn't even try to find me!" Then the tears brimmed in the grandfather's eyes, too, as he answered, "God says the same thing: 'I hide, but no one wants to seek me.'"

> Games are a form of poetry. Like poetry, they offer the artist's view of the world interpreted through his own feelings and experiences... a game is a cultural reservoir; it continually captures more and more life as it is played. (Bob Parnes, quoted in *Design And Sell Toys, Games and Crafts*)

Afikomen is one of the great kid moments in the Seder. They plan and plot, anticipate hiding places and strategize the negotiations for the finder's fee. Likewise, parents and grandparents go into training. Rewards are considered, maneuvers are worked out, and sometimes even an espionage ring is created. *Afikomen* is "Spy vs. Spy," sleight-of-hand, a well-placed "pick," and sometimes even an end run from a "slot-t" with a halfback in motion. *Afikomen* is fun.

Religion is all about "finding." It is finding God, finding truth, finding faith, finding the way. Most religions center on finding, because the things that are worthwhile seem to be hidden. If it was easy to know what is right, if there were good answers to questions like "Why do people die?", "Why do good people suffer?", and "What is the meaning of life?"—then religion would simply be a matter of saying "Thank You" to the Creator. But, life is puzzles and being religious is a quest.

Judaism has its own versions of "hide and seek." *Midrashim* and *Ḥasidic* literature center on the image of a "hiding" God whom people must find. The celebration of Ḥanukkah centers on finding light (and the oil) when the world is darkness, the story of the Book of Esther (*Purim*) is also a series of "hidings:" Esther is in hiding, her name means hidden, and God, whose presence is felt in the story, is never mentioned. Reading the *Megillah* is learning to find God in the best of human actions. So, too, with *Pesaḥ*. The story of the Exodus is the story of waiting 400 years for a hidden God to fulfill promises made long before. It was a matter of waiting and searching for signs that the Covenant would be fulfilled. In our modern age, we too know of waiting and seeking.

At the end of the meal, those assembled are re-gathered through a contest—*afikomen*. It is a contest which brings joy and excitement to those assembled. It is one of the Seder's high points.

QUESTION: Is *afikomen* a children's game or a symbolically significant experience?
ANSWER: It depends on whether anyone is seeking.

CONCEPTS

KORBAN PESAḤ

We have learned that we cannot perform sacrifices nor eat of roasted meat after the destruction of the Temple. The Talmud records this curious direction: "Nothing is to be eaten after *afikomen*" (*Pesaḥim* 119b). The rabbis understood the *afikomen* to be a symbol of the *korban Pesaḥ*, the actual paschal sacrifice. We eat the *afikomen*, the special piece of *matzah* broken off and hidden earlier in the Seder, as the last food of the meal, a substitute for the sacrifice we can no longer eat.

The Greek word for *afikomen* is "epikomoi" and is generally thought to either mean "dessert" or refer to the revelry that often took place after Roman banquets. Thus, the meaning of the Mishnah's directive is either "don't eat anything else after you eat the *afikomen*," or "don't engage in revelry after the meal is completed." The rabbis thought both of these to be good ideas and prohibited partying after the Seder ceremony (as if anyone had the energy to do so!) and stipulated the *afikomen* as the final act of eating.

AFIKOMEN AS REDEMPTION

Recall our discussion of *Yaḥatz* as a silent ritual with overtones of the redemption theme. The *afikomen* signals the beginning of the second part of the Seder whose theme is redemption. We have told the story of how we rose from degradation to glory and we have begun the songs of praise due God for His act of redemption. Now, we look to further redemption as we hope for Messianic times.

The eating of the *afikomen* completes the eating of the broken middle *matzah*, which began as *leḥem oni*—the bread of affliction—and has become the bread of redemption. We eat the *afikomen* last because the key to a future redemption may be found in keeping the taste of the *matzah* in our mouths, in continuing to remember the experience of the Exodus from Egypt.

THE HIDDEN

Now, we may understand the name of this ritual: "*Tzafun*"—hidden. What is hidden? Redemption. The Exodus from Egypt was a redemption, but not the final redemption. That is still hidden from us. We search to reveal it, to complete it. Not only we, but every generation must work to bring the Messianic Age.

There is no text for *Tzafun*, the fourth ritual of the Seder with no blessing.

PRACTICE

At some point during the meal, the children will anxiously await the signal which allows them to begin their search for the *afikomen*. Or, if your tradition is that the children hide it for ransom, you will need to negotiate for its redemption. Either way, this is an eagerly awaited moment for the children.

In our home, the signal to start the search unleashed a mad dash of exploration of every inch of the house. Usually an older child in the family would find it, much to the disappointment of the younger children. As we talked to families, we discovered situations where the *afikomen* search ended in disaster, with crying kids and hurt feelings. Here are some hints at how to have a successful *afikomen* search:

1. State the rules. It is very important to spell out the guidelines of the search. Limit the search to several rooms. Decide if the *afikomen* can be hidden away completely out of sight, or if some portion of the napkin or cover must be visible. Give additional parameters such as, "It's not above eye level," etc.
2. Decide who can participate. Some families establish a cut-off age for participation in *afikomen* hunts. In others, everyone is eligible.
3. Announce that everyone will get a prize. This will discourage cutthroat searching. You might also suggest creating teams of kids instead of each person for him/herself. The idea is that all of the kids together try to find it and each should take pride that one of their number does come up with the *afikomen*.

When the *afikomen* is found and the scream "I found it!" reverberates in the house, congratulate the finder, but make more of a commotion over the rest of the kids. Invite all of them to receive an *afikomen* gift, a small token of your appreciation that the *afikomen* was found so the dinner can be completed and the Seder continued.

My Zadie loved this part of the Seder because he got to give his nine grandchildren a present. For him, the giving of presents was one of his greatest joys. His *afikomen* gift was always money. Of course, I later learned that the handling of money on *Yom Tov* was prohibited by Jewish law. I doubt whether Zadie ever knew that and, I must admit, those twenty dollar bills were a pretty spectacular *afikomen* present thirty years ago! Nevertheless, today observant families give books, records, stickers, games—a whole variety of things that make wonderful *afikomen* presents, or promise a gift of money to be made after *Yom Tov*.

Once the presents are distributed, pass out pieces of the *afikomen* to every participant. The *afikomen* is eaten while reclining, but without a blessing.

PRACTICAL QUESTIONS AND ANSWERS

Does the *afikomen* have to be eaten by a certain time?

Yes. The rabbis determined that the *afikomen* should be eaten before midnight, just as the paschal sacrifice was eaten before that hour. Believe it or not, there are families who conduct a long Seder where this can be a problem!

What if the *afikomen* cannot be found?

This, too, is no idle question. There are times when the leader forgets where the *afikomen* was hidden. More likely, when children steal the *afikomen* to hold for ransom, they hide it somewhere and then forget its location.

The problem is, of course, that the Seder cannot continue without the *afikomen*. That's its value as an object for ransom. But, the rabbis anticipated this situation and stipulated that if the original *afikomen* cannot be found, a substitute piece of *matzah* can be used.

I once saw a piece of *matzah* hanging on a wall. What's that?

In some families, a tradition arose to keep a part of the *afikomen* from year to year in the house, a kind of symbol of continuity between the Passover past and the Passover of the future. Some families actually poke a hole in the *matzah* and string it up on the wall as an ornamental decoration.

INNOVATIONS

There are many creative *afikomen* hunt ideas. We've included some in the Workbook that accompanies this text.

17

בָּרֵךְ

BAREKH
BLESSINGS AFTER FOOD

ACT III, SCENE 4

With my friends, it's easy to reconvene the Seder after the meal. The great percentage of them would want to *bensch* anyway and go on to finish the Seder. With family what tends to happen is, the few who feel either a necessity or want to continue do, while the rest of the family sits at the table and chit-chats.

Miriam Prum

CONCEPTS

BIRKAT HA-MAZON

With the meal completed, it is time to praise God of whose bounty we have just eaten. Unlike the "grace" of other religions which thanks God for the food about to be eaten, *Birkat ha-Mazon* is recited after the fact as a culmination. The rabbis rooted the placement of blessings after food in a verse from Deuteronomy (8:10) which says, in essence, first "eat and be satisfied," then "bless *Adonai* your God for the good land."

Thus, *Birkat ha-Mazon* has evolved into a series of *b'rakhot* that lead us through the entire Jewish experience, review our total relationship with God, and direct us towards a full sense of Jewish mission. These themes are expressed in four major blessings which constitute *Birkat ha-Mazon* (literally, "the blessing for the sustenance"):

1. **The Blessing for Food.** Closing with the line, "*Barukh attah Adonai, hazan et ha-kol,*" "provides food for all," this blessing acknowledges God as the Great Provider.
2. **The Blessing for the Land.** Culminating with the phrase, "*Barukh attah Adonai, al ha-aretz ve'al ha-mazon,*" "Praised are You, Adonai, for the Land and for the sustenance," this blessing fulfills the biblical command to bless God for "the good land which God has given you." We link ourselves to the experience of entering the Promised Land, the ultimate destination of the Jewish people.
3. **The Blessing for Jerusalem.** Originally, the *Birkat ha-Mazon* contained a prayer of thanks for Jerusalem and the Temple. After the Temple was destroyed, the wording was changed to emphasize the rebuilding of the holy city. The signature is "*Barukh attah Adonai, boneh v'raḥamav Yerushalayim, Amen,*" "Praised are You, *Adonai,* who in compassion rebuilds Jerusalem, Amen," highlights this aspiration to national soverienty. (By the way, this is one of the few times "Amen" is a required part of a blessing you yourself say.)
4. **The Blessing of Goodness.** Shortly after the destruction of the Temple, the rabbis added this blessing to *Birkat ha-Mazon*: "*Barukh attah Adonai, Eloheinu melekh ha-olam, ha-melekh ha-tov v'hameitiv la-kol,*" "Praised are You, *Adonai,* our God, Ruler of the universe, the Ruler who is good and does good for all." The unending belief that God is good and will continue to show kindness and mercy to His people now and in the future is the theme of this *b'rakhah.*

These four blessings are said after every meal throughout the year. On Passover (and also on Shabbat and other Festivals), a paragraph and a line ("*Ya'aleh v'yavo*" and the special "*Ha-Raḥaman*") are added regarding the special occasion.

These texts form a "salvation-history" of the Jewish people. Beginning with a universalistic appreciation of God's role in nature, we follow the Jewish people into the land of Israel, through the destruction of the Temple, and stand waiting for the redemption. Our final expectation is: "*Oseh shalom bimromov, hu ya'aseh shalom aleinu,*" "The One who makes peace in the heavens above will make peace for all of us." We end affirming our belief and involvement in the positive outcome of history—the final redemption.

PRACTICE

Birkat ha-Mazon is recited over the Third Cup of Wine which will conclude Act III of the Seder talk-feast. There is an old tradition of saying these prayers over a cup of wine, lending it special importance. The procedure then is:

1. Fill the Third Cup of Wine.
2. Recite *Birkat ha-Mazon*. (You will need to choose to recite the full *Birkat ha-Mazon* or the shortened version).
3. Then immedieately recite the *b'rakhah* over the Third Cup of Wine.

The anatomy of *Birkat ha-mazon* is:

a. *Shir ha-Ma-alot*—A Song of Ascending. Psalm 126 serves as the introduction to *Birkat ha-Mazon*. It speaks of a dream-like joy that will be experienced when *Adonai* returns us to Zion, an appropriate introduction to the redemption theme of the second part of the Seder. The famous line "those who sow in tears will reap with joyous song" reverberates with the symbolism of the salt water tears of slavery turned into the psalms of praise in *Hallel* which immediately follows *Barekh*.

b. *Zimmun*—Invitation to Bless. Judaism is partial to communal prayer. "When three have eaten together without speaking words of Torah, it's as if they had worshipped idols." The *Zimmun* is an invitation to those assembled to join in praising God, sung as a responsive chanting. With a *minyan*, a quorum of ten adults, the word *Eloheinu*, our God, is added to the *Zimmun* formula.

c. *Hazan et ha-Kol*. The Blessing for Food. This is the first of the four core *b'rakhot* thanking God for providing sustenance to all living things.

d. *Al Ha-aretz V'Al ha-Mazon*. The Blessing for the Land. The second of the four core *b'rakhot* thanks God for the gift of *Eretz Yisrael*.

e. *R'tzei*. When Passover is celebrated on Shabbat, this paragraph is added. It asks God to help us to observe the commandments, especially the *mitzvah* of Shabbat as a "day of rest, free from trouble, sorrow, or sighing."

f. *Ya'aleh V'Yavo*. On *Yom Tov*, this paragraph is added to the *Birkat ha-Mazon*. It summarizes many of the ideas of the entire prayer, asking God's blessings of life, well-being, lovingkindness and peace, and it reminds God to remember His promise of mercy and redemption.

g. *U-v'ney Yerushalayim.* The Blessing for Jerusalem. This is the third of the core *b'rakhot,* which asks God to speedily rebuild Jerusalem.

h. *Hu Heitiv, Hu Meitiv.* The Blessing of Goodness. The fourth core *b'rakhah* affirms God's goodness.

i. The *Ha-Raḥaman* Prayers. These are a series of short petitions recited by the leader to which the table-group responds "Amen." They ask God, among other things, to give us an honorable livelihood, to lead us in dignity to the land, to send blessings to the household, and to bless all who are gathered together. Specific petitions are added for Shabbat and *Yom Tov.*

j. *Migdol.* The Prayer for Redemption. The final paragraph wishes for future salvation, peace and prosperity.

A complete text for *Birkat Ha-mazon* can be found in most traditional *Haggadot* or in *The Art of Jewish Living: The Shabbat Seder.*

18

כּוֹס שְׁלִישִׁי

KOS SH'LISHI
THE THIRD CUP

ACT III, CURTAIN

Lou Miller:	The other problem we have is that our wine goblets are too big.
Judy Miller:	We have to get new wine goblets.
Lou Miller:	See, I insist everyone drink the entire *kos* (cup) each time we say *Kiddush*. All four times. None of this little sip of wine stuff. You gotta go for it all.
Judy Miller:	It's totally ridiculous.
Lou Miller:	I have to buy a lot of wine for this.
Judy Miller:	The problem is it's a water goblet, not a wine goblet. We have to get rid of those. Just remind me, I have to buy some regular-sized wine glasses.

CONCEPTS

As in Act II, the third act of the Seder—The Festive Meal—concludes with a cup of wine. The Third Cup of Wine recalls the third promise of redemption offered by God in the Torah, "I will redeem you," a statement of the theme of Act IV to come: Redemption.

TEXT

See *borei pri ha-gafen* in *Kadesh.*

PRACTICE

Say *borei p'ri ha-gafen* for the Third Cup of Wine immediately after the conclusion of *Birkat ha-Mazon.* Drink the wine while reclining.

ACT IV—REDEMPTION

SCENE 1: SHFOKH ḤAMATKHA
("POUR OUT YOUR ANGER")
ELIYAHU HA-NAVI (ELIJAH THE PROPHET)
SCENE 2: HALLEL (SONGS OF PRAISE)
SCENE 3: Z'MIROT (SONGS)
SCENE 4: SEFIRAT HA-OMER (COUNTING OF THE OMER)
CURTAIN: KOS R'VI'I (THE FOURTH CUP OF WINE)
NIRTZAH (ACCEPTANCE)

19

שְׁפֹךְ חֲמָתְךָ/אֵלִיָּהוּ הַנָּבִיא

SHFOKH ḤAMATKHA— "POUR OUT YOUR ANGER"/ ELIYAHU HA-NAVI— ELIJAH THE PROPHET

ACT IV, SCENE 1

LOU MILLER: I told my grandson Joey to watch Elijah's glass. He was really watching, and after a while he says, "It's going down."

JUDY MILLER: I don't remember my own children being that taken with it.

MARLENE HORWITZ: Now, we've adopted the tradition of starting with an empty cup for Elijah and we pass it around, and everyone pours a little from his or her cup into Elijah's. It's like we all have to contribute if we're going to bring the *Mashiaḥ*.

SALLY WEBER: We had a funny thing at my uncle's Seder when I was young. He would put Elijah's cup outside the front door, close the door, and when we opened the door again, the wine would be gone from the cup. It was very mysterious. We noticed my uncle Carl was a little drunker after that, but we never knew why until many years later.

CONCEPTS

WE REMEMBER OUR ENEMIES

On balance, Judaism is not a religion of revenge. As persecuted as the Jews have been throughout the millenia, it is relatively rare to find as explicit a call for Divine retribution as in the *Shfokh Ḥamatkha* paragraph.

It is a difficult part of the Seder ritual. Not difficult to understand, but difficult to do. It is entirely understandable that generations of Jews who lived under the rule of oppressive foreign governments would want to vent their feelings. But why on Passover?

The evening is about remembering, and *Shfokh Ḥamatkha* reminds us of those times in Jewish history which cannot be forgotten. For earlier generations, it was the destruction of the Temple and the subsequent exiles from our homeland, or the Crusades of Christian Europe, or the Inquisition of Spain, or the pogroms of Czarist Russia. For us, it is the painful, recent memory of the Holocaust. On this festive night when we remember our initial deliverance from tyranny, and at the very moment we pray for the coming of the Messiah, we remember our enemies.

We open the door and recite *Shfokh Ḥamatkha*. How curious! One would imagine that it would be much more prudent to keep the door closed while lambasting our foes. Yet, the rabbis saw in this act of defiance a note of courage. We are not afraid of our enemies, for we expect and await deliverance.

Somehow the idea of opening the door during the Seder more appropriately belongs at the beginning of the evening, perhaps at *Ha Laḥma Anya* when the poor and needy are invited to join in the celebration. Some scholars believe that was the case, until it became common for hostile authorities to watch the Seder ceremony carefully, particularly at the beginning of the evening. In fact, it actually became dangerous for Jews to let strangers into the house. As the ceremony proceeded late into the night, it was less and less likely that the authorities would be around to hear what was being said. So, *Shfokh Ḥamatkha* was placed near the end of the Seder, and the opening of the door was delayed and later associated with the singing of *Eliyahu ha-Navi*.

THE NIGHT OF VIGIL

The dramatic account describing the night of the Exodus in the Torah is summarized with the following: "That was for the Lord a night of vigil to bring them out of the land of Egypt; that same night is the Lord's, one of vigil for all the children of Israel throughout the ages" (Exodus 12:42). And what a night it was, with a hurried sacrifice and a fast-food meal, eaten with sandals on and staff in hand; with blood-stained doorposts to ward off the Destroyer sent by God to inflict the terrible tenth and final plague—the death of the firstborn Egyptians; with the moment's-notice departure east into the desert. All this in the dead of night, a night of watching, a night of vigil.

This is why the Seder is held at night. This is why Passover night is a different night. It is a night to stay up late, embellishing and retelling the amazing story of our liberation from Egypt. In fact, for our children, staying up late on Passover is the Jewish equivalent to staying up until midnight on New Year's Eve.

In Jewish folklore, the night was not the kindest of times. Before retiring to sleep, a prayer is recited asking the angels to protect us, for the night is full of danger. But on the night of vigil, on Passover night, this prayer was not recited. We are not to be fearful of the night, we are to break out of our slave mentality during the night of watching.

HOLOCAUST

The Seder represents a remarkable opportunity for Jews to be together. As such, it is a time for reflection, not just upon the actual Exodus from Egypt, but upon the centuries of oppression and slavery our ancestors have endured. Thus, a number of *Haggadot* suggest supplementary readings which deal with this disaster which afflicted the Jewish people in our own time.

There can be no doubt that the shadow of the Holocaust falls upon our generation and will likely fall upon generations to come. The Seder is a time to tell and to remember, and therefore it is fitting that the tragedy which befell European Jewry be recalled in some way at the Seder.

ELIJAH—SYMBOL OF REDEMPTION

The theme of redemption is climaxed by the prayer for *Eliyahu ha-Navi*, the prophet, to come speedily in our day. Historically, Elijah was a prophet from Gilead who was the outstanding religious leader of his time. The Bible records that he did not die, but was carried to heaven in a chariot pulled by horses of fire (Kings II 2:1-11). A later prophet, Malachi, built onto this legend with his prophecy that Elijah would be sent by God "before the coming of the great and terrible days of the Lord..." (Malachi 3:23). Thus began the connection between Elijah and the promise of the Messianic age.

For centuries, the legends and folklore surrounding Elijah have firmly established him as the forerunner of the Messiah. He is not considered to be the actual Messiah; rather, he will herald the future redemption of Israel. We remember Elijah daily (in the *Birkat ha-Mazon* where he is portrayed as bringing good news) and weekly (especially at *Havdalah*).

The popular legend of Elijah quickly became associated with the Passover Seder and its theme of redemption. Stories of Elijah visiting the homes of every Jewish family on *Pesaḥ* probably stem from another popular view of Elijah as a kind of heavenly emissary sent to earth to combat injustice. On Passover eve, he is said to punish misers and provide necessities for the Seder to the poor. His appearance at the Seder is to announce the coming of the Redeemer.

Today, we can integrate the Elijah legends into our understanding of the great hope for redemption which characterizes this second part of the Seder service. Coming on the heels of *Shfokh Ḥamatkha*, the messianic dream of a time when Jews, and indeed all peoples, will no longer suffer oppression and will enjoy the fruits of freedom, seems entirely appropriate. So, we sing *Eliyahu ha-Navi* in honor of redemptions past and in hope of future redemption.

THE FIFTH CUP

Another role ascribed to Elijah is that of the supreme scholar who will solve any legal disputes which have been left unresolved in the Talmud. We have learned that the Four Cups of Wine represent the fourfold promise of redemption given in Exodus 6:6-8. But, there is a fifth promise in the verse—"I will bring you to your land"—which led some rabbis to suggest that there should be a corresponding Fifth Cup of Wine. The ensuing dispute ended in an unusual ritual compromise: the fifth cup is poured, but we do not drink it. We leave it for Elijah who, when he comes, will resolve the dispute.

OBJECTS

The cup of Elijah is traditionally the most beautiful wine cup on the Seder table, even more elaborate than the *Kiddush* cup. Actually, any cup will do. You will also need a door, preferably one to the outdoors, and someone to open it.

PRACTICE

With the confluence of two prayers and a ritual action, the procedure for this section of the Seder is as follows:

1. Fill the Fourth Cup of Wine.
2. Pour the cup of Elijah. There are several options for filling Elijah's cup:
   a. The cup is filled before the Seder begins.
   b. The leader fills the cup at this point in the Seder.
   c. Pass the goblet around the table, each participant adding some wine from his or her cup. This was the custom of Rabbi Naftali of Ropshitz as a demonstration that we must all work together to bring the Messianic time.
3. Open the door (use a door to the outside of the house when possible). Generally, this privilege is awarded to a young child (or all the children in attendance).
4. Stand and recite *Shfokh Ḥamatkha* and/or alternative readings.
5. Sing "*Eliyahu ha-Navi.*"
6. Close the door and be seated.

ELIYAHU HA-NAVI—ELIJAH THE PROPHET

1. *Eliyahu ha-navi,*	1. Elijah the Prophet,
2. *Eliyahu ha-Tishbi,*	2. Elijah the Tishbite,
3. *Eliyahu (3) ha-Giladi,*	3. Elijah the Gileadite,
4. *bimheirah b'yameinu*	4. soon, in our day,
5. *yavo eileinu,*	5. come to us,
6. *im mashiaḥ ben David.(2)*	6. bringing the Messiah.

PRACTICAL QUESTIONS AND ANSWERS

Do we lift Elijah's cup from the table while singing *Eliyahu ha-Navi*?

No, this cup is not to be used during the Seder. We do not lift it after it is filled, and we do not drink from it.

Why do we open the door for Elijah?

Actually, in former times, the door of the house was first opened at the very beginning of the Seder when the invitation "All who are hungry come and eat" was declared. It was then left open during the remainder of the Seder. In the 18th and 19th centuries, this practice became dangerous as unfriendly authorities would carefully watch the conduct of the Seder to try to detect evidence of the infamous blood libel. As the evening wore on, these authorities would leave and it became safe to open the door, ever so briefly, to welcome Elijah into the home. This also explains the positioning of the *Shfokh Ḥamatkha* reading—late in the Seder, although bravely recited when the door is open.

Is it true that Elijah supposedly comes to each house, and while we are not looking, drinks from the cup?

I remember as a child carefully examining the Elijah's Cup for signs that some of the wine was drunk by the invisible visitor. One year, I was certain he had come! (I think my father kicked the table or took a little sip while we were opening the door!) In all seriousness, there is a bit of a (you should excuse the expression) "Santa Claus" mystique to the idea that Elijah visits each and every Jewish home on Seder night. However, unlike our Christian friend, Elijah does not leave gifts, nor does he appear in shopping malls before Passover. (Although see *Innovations* for some interesting ideas for *Eliyahu*). On a more serious note, Elijah does not reward us for our past actions as much as he goads us to work for a better future.

What about setting an extra place for Elijah?

Another vivid memory of my childhood was of setting a full place setting at the table along with an empty chair for Elijah. I am not certain I understood the symbolism of an empty chair as an expression of hope for the day when Elijah would come, but I was impressed that the table was

1. אֵלִיָּהוּ הַנָּבִיא,
2. אֵלִיָּהוּ הַתִּשְׁבִּי,
3. אֵלִיָּהוּ, אֵלִיָּהוּ, אֵלִיָּהוּ הַגִּלְעָדִי,
4. בִּמְהֵרָה בְיָמֵינוּ
5. יָבֹא אֵלֵינוּ
6. עִם מָשִׁיחַ בֶּן דָּוִד.

incomplete, that an important guest was missing. As I recall, even the chair itself we placed at Elijah's setting was among the finest chairs in the house. This custom has fallen somewhat out of favor, perhaps because many families simply cannot afford the space at the table.

We cannot bring ourselves to say "*Shfokh Ḥamatkha.*" What are the options?

Many *Haggadot* now offer alternative readings at this point in the Seder. This is how the *Haggadah* has changed over a long history. A particular section no longer holds deep meaning for moderns, or they find it offensive, and so alternatives are formulated and traditions change. Many families read selections about the Holocaust or the continuing enslavement of the Jews of the Soviet Union, Syria, and other oppressive nations. This is an excellent opportunity to express your creativity and sensitivity by choosing readings that resonate with messages you wish to convey.

I was at a Seder where a Fifth Cup of Wine was actually drunk in honor of the State of Israel. Is that okay?

Not at this point in the Seder. According to a strict interpretation of Jewish law, no wine should be drunk between the Third and Fourth Cups. Some *Haggadot* suggest that the Fifth Cup be dedicated to the establishment of the State of Israel, which many regard as a sign of redemption. This should not be Elijah's Cup of Wine; rather a separate cup is dedicated. Our suggestion: insert a Fifth Cup after the Fourth Cup or simply insert a reading about the State of Israel at this point.

I have also seen a fourth *matzah* dedicated at a Seder as "The *Matzah* of Hope." What about this?

This is another recent addition to the Seder celebration. Beginning in the 1970's, readings which dedicated a *Matzah* of Hope to the plight of Soviet Jews gained widespread acceptance at *Sedarim* across North America and in Israel. Many families have made this a permanent part of their Seder celebration by setting aside a single *matzah* and reciting the following prayer, written by Chief Rabbi Untermann of Israel:

THE *MATZAH* OF HOPE

THIS IS THE "*MATZAH* OF HOPE"

Master of the universe, on this night of vigil of the Passover festival, we gratefully praise Your great and holy Name in a joyful and fervent mood, for having delivered our ancestors in Egypt from slavery to freedom, from bondage to liberation.

As we welcome the *Pesaḥ* holiday this evening, we voice our deepest concern for the bitter lot of our fellow Jews who are languishing under the yoke of evil decrees and persecution in the Arab Diaspora and in the Soviet Union. They are denied the opportunity of observing our festivals and celebrating the Feast of Unleavened Bread, in accordance with our tradition.

May it be Your will, O Rock of Israel and its Redeemer, as You have brought our ancestors out of slavery in Egypt, so may Your mercy encompass our brethren in the Arab lands and in the Soviet Union. Redeem them, gather the dispersed families of our people and bring them back to the soil of our ancient land.

May we be worthy to enjoy the *Pesaḥ* holiday together with the whole house of Israel, in freedom and unity. Amen.

INNOVATIONS

The Karsch family has taken an old custom of setting an empty place for Elijah at the table and expanded it to demonstrate their remembrance of the Jews of oppressed lands where the celebration of Passover is difficult, if not impossible. They set up a card table in the center of a U-shaped Seder table, complete with chair and place setting for Elijah. It is also a stark and constant reminder to all participants that many Jews in the world are still not free to celebrate *Pesaḥ* unharrassed.

On a more humorous note, one year, the Weber family invited us to talk about Elijah the Prophet at their very beautiful and stimulating Seder. When the children came to open the door, and as the singing of *Eliyahu ha-Navi* began, I walked in, dressed in a black robe, sandals, a *tallit,* a fake beard, with a large *kipah* (skullcap) on my head. I introduced myself as "*Eliyahu ha-Navi*" with the explanation "I stopped by when I heard you singing my song." I then told the children and adults that I, Elijah, was supposed to be able to answer difficult questions about Jewish law and practice and that I was prepared to answer such questions. Since it was the second Seder, someone asked me "Where were you last night?" "Last night," I replied, "I did a Seder in Beverly Hills!" For about five minutes, "Eliyahu" fielded serious and not-so-serious questions about the Seder ritual. Before leaving, Eliyahu made it clear that this was a one-time visit, encouraging everyone to work hard toward bringing the real thing.

Another family we know refuses to just open doors for *Eliyahu.* They rise from their chairs, leave the room where the Seder is being held, and march through the neighborhood on a kind of "*Eliyahu* walk." Besides offering some much-needed exercise after the big meal, the point they wish to make is that we must not wait for the Messiah to come, but go out and work to bring Him/Her, speedily and in our own day.

20

הַלֵּל

HALLEL
SONGS OF PRAISE

ACT IV, SCENE 2

Hallel is saying a bunch of psalms which praise God. I like the one by Shlomo Carlebach. Well, he wrote the tune to it.

Mordy Karsch

CONCEPTS

WE PRAISE ADONAI

The *Hallel*, which actually began before the meal with the recitation of Psalms 113 and 114, continues here with Psalms 115—118. These songs of praise are directed toward the Redeemer, the God of Israel. Each Psalm builds in momentum until the final verses of Psalm 118 which, by tradition, are repeated twice: "Deliver us, *Adonai*, we implore You. Prosper us, *Adonai*, we implore You." The *ḥatimah* recalls the theme: "Praised are You, *Adonai*, King acclaimed with songs of praise."

The last part of the *Hallel* is actually an added-on passage from the morning synagogue service of Shabbat and *Yom Tov*, the *Nishmat*. In soaring prose, the prayer recalls God's beneficence, His rescuing us from *Mitzrayim*, and our duty to praise His glorious name. The section concludes with "*Yishtabaḥ shimkha*," "Your name shall always be praised," a fitting conclusion to this series of songs of praise.

HALLEL—SONGS OF PRAISE

1. *Hodu l'Adonai*	1. Give thanks to *Adonai*
2. *ki tov,*	2. for He is good,
3. *Ki l'olam ḥasdo.*	3. His love endures forever.
4. *Yomar na Yisrael:*	4. Let the house of Israel declare:
5. *Ki l'olam ḥasdo.*	5. His love endures forever.
6. *Yomru na veit Aharon:*	6. Let the House of Aaron declare:
7. *Ki l'olam ḥasdo.*	7. His love endures forever.
8. *Yomru na yirei Adonai:*	8. Let those who revere *Adonai* declare:
9. *Ki l'olam ḥasdo.*	9. His love endures forever.

PRACTICE

Some of the songs of the *Hallel* may be familiar to you from the synagogue service. Among those most likely to be sung are: Psalm 115:12—18, "*Y'varekh et bet Yisrael*...," Psalm 116:12—19, "*Mah ashiv l'Adonai kol tagmulohi alai*...," Psalm 118: 1—4, "*Hodu l'Adonai ki tov, ki l'olam ḥasdo*," Psalm 118:14, "*Azi v'zimrat yah vayhi li lishuah*," Psalm 118:15, "*Kol rina vishuah*...," Psalm 118:19, "*Pitḥu li sha'arei tzedek*...," and Psalm 118:25-26, "*Ana Adonai hoshi'ah na*..." Those who are familiar with tunes for these parts of the *Hallel* can join in singing. Otherwise, choose selections to read.

An interesting point about this recitation of *Hallel* is the fact that we sit rather than stand for it. In the synagogue, the *Hallel* is always said while standing, but at the Seder, as we have already seen, virtually all the texts are said while reclining.

1. הוֹדוּ לַיהוה
2. כִּי טוֹב
3. כִּי לְעוֹלָם חַסְדּוֹ.
4. יֹאמַר נָא יִשְׂרָאֵל
5. כִּי לְעוֹלָם חַסְדּוֹ.
6. יֹאמְרוּ נָא בֵית אַהֲרֹן
7. כִּי לְעוֹלָם חַסְדּוֹ.
8. יֹאמְרוּ נָא יִרְאֵי יהוה
9. כִּי לְעוֹלָם חַסְדּוֹ.

21

זְמִרוֹת

Z'MIROT
SONGS

ACT IV, SCENE 3

At our Seder, nothing like that would happen. When we were kids, if we would giggle, my father would just look at us. All he had to do was look at you. He didn't have to say anything. We'd do the whole Seder in Hebrew and we didn't understand a thing. But, we would sing the songs.

Eve Clapick

My favorite part of the Seder is the beginning part. Actually, it's the end with all the songs. They're fun.

Gavi Weber

At the Seder, I sing *Mah Nishtanah*, La La, and "Frogs on Your Bed".

Ari Fife

You mean: "One morning, when Pharoah awoke in his bed, there were frogs in his bed. There were frogs on his head..." Is that the song?

Your Author

CONCEPTS

The singing of table songs, *Z'mirot*, is a favorite activity at Jewish ceremonial meals. Every week on Shabbat, *Z'mirot* are sung at the Friday night Shabbat Seder, at lunch, and at *Seudah Shelishit*, the third meal. This opportunity to sing increases our enjoyment of the Seder, summarizes important lessons learned, and provides great fun for all after what may have been a long evening.

The songs of the Passover Seder are a combination of poems, acrostics, rhymes, and jingles which were basically included to keep the children awake. In traditional *Haggadah* texts, six songs are found:

1. "*U-v'khein vay'hi ba-ḥatzi ha-lailah*"—"It Happened at Midnight." This *piyyut* (a liturgical poem), was written by Yannai, a great poet of Israel who probably lived in the 4th or 5th century C.E. An alphabetical acrostic, it lists the miracles that occurred and saved the Jewish people at night. It ends with the anticipation of future redemption. By tradition, it is said only on the first night of Passover. It is not even included in the Rabbinical Assembly *Haggadah*.

2. "*U-v'hein va-amartem zevaḥ Pesaḥ*"—"And You Shall Say, 'It is the Passover Sacrifice.'" This *piyyut* was written in the 5th or 6th century C.E. by Rabbi Elazar Kalir, another great poet of Israel. Arranged in alphabetical order, the verses detail in chronological order the various events which occurred through history on Passover. It is generally said on the second night of *Pesaḥ*. This song is also not found in the Rabbinical Assembly *Haggadah*.

3. "*Ki lo na-eh, Ki lo ya-eh*"—"For to Him Praise is Proper, For to Him Praise is Due." This alphabetical song lists the many reasons God deserves our praise. Of unknown authorship, this *piyyut* began to appear in *Haggadot* during the Middle Ages. The structure of each verse is quite interesting: the first two phrases refer to *Adonai*—"*Adir bimlukha, baḥur ka-halakhah*," "Mighty in His kingdom, chosen as of right;" then the third phrase refers to those who praise Him—"*g'dudov yomru lo*," "the host of angels say to Him."

4. "*Adir Hu*"—"Mighty is He." An all-time favorite of Seder night, *Adir Hu* is another ancient alphabetical song that has been known for many generations, although the author is unknown. The theme is the building of the Temple, together with the prayer that it be rebuilt soon, another reference to the hoped for Messianic age.

5. "*Eḥad Mi Yodei'a*"—"Who Knows One?" This is a medieval counting song associating numbers with the merits of the Jewish people which qualify it for redemption. *Eḥad Mi Yodei'a* is one of the songs that is the most fun to sing. It is sung along the same lines as (you should again excuse the expression) "Twelve Days of Christmas." Ask for volunteers to take a number. When the entire group asks "*Eḥad Mi Yodei'a?*," the person who has number 1 answers: "*Eḥad, Ani Yodei-a!*" Then all join in "*Eḥad Eloheinu sheh-ba'shamayim u-va'aretz*." Then, the group asks "*Shnayim Mi Yodei-a?*" And the person who will be number 2 answers: "*Shnayim, Ani Yodei-a!*

Shnai luḥot ha-brit," which is immediately followed by person number 1 singing "*Eḥad Elo-heinu sheh-ba'shamayim u-va'aretz.*" The group continues to ask the numbers and individuals answer in turn, each one singing his/her number as it is repeated throughout the song.

6. "*Ḥad Gadya*"—"One Kid, Just One Kid." Undoubtedly the most famous Passover song, *Ḥad Gadya* is the Jewish version of "I knew an old lady who swallowed a fly." Clearly an entertaining and popular song, especially for children, *Ḥad Gadya* has nevertheless been interpreted as an allegory describing the trials and tribulations of Israel's journey through history. In this theory, each object symbolizes one of Israel's enemies through the years. Israel (the only kid) is purchased by the father (*Adonai*), for two *zuzim* (the two tablets of the Law) and is subjected to peoples who supplant each other as Israel's foes: Assyria (the cat), Babylon (the dog), Persia (the stick), Greece (the fire), Rome (the water), the Saracens (the ox), the Crusaders (the *shoḥet*), and the Ottomans (the angel of death). But, in the end, the Holy One, Praised be He, saves the Jewish people.

Ḥad Gadya was probably composed in the Middle Ages by an unknown author. Written in tongue-twisting Aramaic, it is tremendously fun to sing, with a number of approaches in current use. As in *Eḥad Mi Yodei'a,* individuals can take the various parts and sing them when their turns come up. Or, our favorite, the Onomatopoeia *Ḥad Gadya,* taught to us by Jerry and Sally Weber who learned it from Rabbi Dov Gartenberg. In this singing, people take a character or object in the song, for example "cat," but instead of singing "*va-ata shunra,*" or "then came a cat," the person makes up a sound which sounds like the object they are portraying—"cat" may elicit a "meeeow." The entire group then sings the song, and everytime a "*shunra*" is mentioned, the person acting the part says the sound. So, the singing goes like this:

Everyone: "*V'ata khalba*" Person 4: "woof,woof" "*V'nashakh l'shunra*" Person 3: "meeow" "*D'akhal l'gadya*" Person 2: "ba-a-a-a" "*Dizvan Aba bitrei zuzei*" Person 1: "clink" Everyone: "*Ḥad Gadya, Ḥad Gadya.*"

Another favorite challenge for those who have drunk four full cups of wine is to sing the entire *Ḥad Gadya* in one breath. No easy task, this, but it is great fun to see grown people try!

PRACTICE

Traditionally, the singing of songs comes after the *Nirtzah,* the formal conclusion of the Seder. However, the Rabbinical Assembly *Haggadah* suggests that the songs be sung immediately following *Hallel,* reserving *Nirtzah* and its climactic "Next Year in Jerusalem!" for the very end of the Seder. This reminds us of the common practice at the conclusion of *Yom Kippur* to save the seven-fold saying of the *Shema* and the final *shofar* blasts until after the recitation of the *Maariv* service for that evening. Of course, you can make your own choice about this, although the rearrangement does seem to make a great deal of sense.

22

סְפִירַת הָעוֹמֶר
SEFIRAT HA-OMER
COUNTING THE OMER

ACT IV, SCENE 4

I'm not really sure what an *omer* is. I think it is like a bushel or something. Anyway, we count one *omer* each night until *Shavuot.*

Gavi Weber

CONCEPTS

COUNTING

Counting marks time. We count the days leading up to major events in our lives. We count the days until school lets out, the days until vacation, the days until a birthday or anniversary, the days until a big event such as a *Bar/Bat Mitzvah*, the days until Ḥanukkah.

Sefirat ha-Omer, the Counting of the *Omer*, is a counting of the days between one major festival, Passover, and the next major festival, *Shavuot*. *Pesaḥ* and *Shavuot* are unequivocally tied to each other. Passover celebrates the Exodus from Egypt and the beginning of the wanderings of our ancestors in the desert, while *Shavuot* celebrates the culmination of this Exodus with the Revelation at Sinai, the giving of the Torah, the constitution of the Jewish nation.

The *Omer* (literally "sheaf") is an ancient measure of grain (equal to about a half-gallon) which was brought to the Temple on the sixteenth of *Nisan*, the eve of the second day of *Pesaḥ*. Each day of 49 days between *Pesaḥ* and *Shavuot*, another measure was brought, each one counted daily. This is the "*Sefirat ha-Omer*."

The Jews of ancient Israel were an agricultural people. Passover was also a festival of the first spring crops and the seven weeks until *Shavuot* was a time of harvesting. Thus, the Counting of the *Omer* also reminds us of our tie to the land and our gratitude for the yearly harvest.

SEFIRAT HA-OMER—COUNTING THE OMER

1. *Barukh attah Adonai*	1. Praised are You, *Adonai*,
2. *Eloheinu melekh ha-olam*	2. our God, King of the universe,
3. *asher kidshanu*	3. who sanctifies us
4. *b'mitzvotav*	4. through His commandments
5. *v'tzivanu*	5. by commanding us
6. *al sefirat ha-omer.*	6. to count the *Omer*.
7. *Ha-yom yom eḥad la-omer.*	7. Today is the first day of the *Omer*.

PRACTICE

The Counting of the *Omer* takes place at the second Seder. We rise and say the *b'rakhah* for Counting the *Omer* and then announce "Today is the first day of the *Omer*." This action will be repeated every night until *Shavuot* during the evening prayers. If you happened to have gone to synagogue before Seder on the second night, you will have counted the *Omer* during the evening service and need not repeat it at the Seder.

INNOVATIONS

Some families create *Omer* counting charts which can be used during the next seven weeks.

1. בָּרוּךְ אַתָּה יהוה
2. אֱלֹהֵינוּ מֶלֶךְ הָעוֹלָם
3. אֲשֶׁר קִדְּשָׁנוּ
4. בְּמִצְוֹתָיו
5. וְצִוָּנוּ
6. עַל סְפִירַת הָעוֹמֶר
7. הַיּוֹם יוֹם אֶחָד לָעֹמֶר.

הגדה
Passover Haggadah
The Feast of Freedom

23

כּוֹס רְבִיעִי/נִרְצָה

KOS R'VI'I/NIRTZAH THE FOURTH CUP/ ACCEPTANCE

ACT IV, CURTAIN

LOU MILLER: The second half of the Seder gets a little more difficult.

JUDY MILLER: I remember the first time we finished a Seder, this must have been 10 or 12 years ago. We completed the Seder and everyone was very restless. And afterwards, when everyone was leaving, my father came over to Lou and said, "I want to congratulate you." He thought it was terrific that he finished it because, I mean, he really finished it against a lot of odds.

CONCEPTS

THE FOURTH CUP OF WINE

The Seder now draws to a close, signified by a concluding Fourth Cup of Wine. This cup is a reminder of God's promise of redemption, "I will take you to be My people and I will be your God" (Exodus 6:7). A summation paragraph, a kind of mini-*Birkat ha-Mazon*, follows the "*borei p'ri ha-gafen*" which praises God for the land and its produce, asks God to fully restore Jerusalem and to grant us joy on this *Pesaḥ*, and thanks God for His goodness, the land, and the fruit of the vine.

ACCEPTANCE

The Seder ends with a poem, *Ḥasal Siddur Pesaḥ*, the last verses of a *piyyut* written by Rabbi Joseph Tov Elem (Bonfils). The entire poem summarizes the laws of *Pesaḥ* and was intended to be read in the synagogue on *Shabbat ha-Gadol*, the Shabbat before *Pesaḥ*, when it was customary to review the requirements for Passover celebration.

NIRTZAH—ACCEPTANCE

1. *Ḥasal siddur Pesaḥ*	1. The order of the Passover has been completed
2. *k'hilkhato,*	2. according to its precepts,
3. *k'khal mishpato v'ḥukato,*	3. with all its customs and ordinances.
4. *ka'asher zakhinu l'sader oto,*	4. Just as it has been granted us to order it now,
5. *ken nizkeh la'asoto.*	5. so may we be worthy to fulfull it in the future.
6. *Zakh shokhein m'onah,*	6. Pure One, dwelling on high,
7. *komeim k'hal adat*	7. raise up to Yourself a congregation
8. *mi manah.*	8. without number.
9. *B'karov naheil nitei khana,*	9. Bring us back soon, the plants of Your vineyard.
10. *P'duyim l'tzion b'rinah.*	10. Redeemed into Zion with joyful song.
11. *Lashanah ha-ba'ah b'Yirushalayim.*	11. Next year in Jerusalem!

This passage states that we have completed the order of the *Pesaḥ* service and prays that it be found worthy of acceptance. We then look to the future with the prayer that God restore us, redeemed, to Zion. And the Seder ends with the Messianic dream of Jews throughout the centuries: "Next Year in Jerusalem!" In a beautiful example of symmetry, recall that this same sentiment ended Act I—The Beginning. Now, it brings the Seder experience to a triumphant, hopeful close.

PRACTICE

As mentioned above, some *Haggadot* place the Fourth Cup of Wine and the *Nirtzah* directly after the conclusion of the *Hallel* and *Nishmat.* Then, with the formal Seder service completed, the *Z'mirot* are sung. The Rabbinical Assembly *Haggadah* moves the *Nirtzah* to the very end of the *Haggadah*, a somewhat untraditional, but nevertheless more appropriate conclusion to the Seder.

INNOVATIONS

Many families have adopted the custom of singing "*Hatikvah*", the national anthem of the state of Israel, at the conclusion of the Seder. Some even recite selections from *Shir ha-Shirim*, the Song of Songs, the book of the Bible read in the synagogue on the Shabbat of *Pesaḥ*. This poetic, lyrical book sings of springtime and our eternal love for God, Redeemer of His beloved people Israel.

1. חֲסַל סִדּוּר פֶּסַח
2. כְּהִלְכָתוֹ,
3. כְּכָל מִשְׁפָּטוֹ וְחֻקָּתוֹ.
4. כַּאֲשֶׁר זָכִינוּ לְסַדֵּר אוֹתוֹ,
5. כֵּן נִזְכֶּה לַעֲשׂוֹתוֹ.
6. זָךְ שׁוֹכֵן מְעוֹנָה,
7. קוֹמֵם קְהַל עֲדַת
8. מִי מָנָה.
9. בְּקָרוֹב נַהֵל נִטְעֵי כַנָּה,
10. פְּדוּיִם לְצִיּוֹן בְּרִנָּה.
11. לַשָּׁנָה הַבָּאָה בִּירוּשָׁלָיִם

PART TWO: PREPARING FOR PESAḤ

LEARNING TO MAKE PESAḤ
ORGANIZING THE SEDER SERVICE
ON BECOMING KOSHER FOR PASSOVER
THE PASSOVER CHANGEOVER
THE RITUALS OF PESAḤ PREPARATION
PREPARING THE SEDER TABLE
AFTER PESAḤ

24

LEARNING TO MAKE PESAḤ

We started celebrating Shabbat and *Pesaḥ* as soon as we were married, 28 years ago, in our first little apartment. Vic said, "What's the matter? Are you trying to make a Jew out of me?"

Rica Sabah

We always did Shabbat, but then it came time to make our first *Pesaḥ*. We went to a class Rabbi Zeldin gave on how to conduct a Seder; I still have the notes.

Vic Sabah

THE SABAH FAMILY

Rica Sabah: I think the first year we did the Seder, it was like, you jump in and you do it. You do the best you can, and every year, your own traditions grow. I can't say that we're doing today what we did twenty years ago. You really develop your own traditions and create memories for your children. They may be quite different from the memories that you had as a child. I would like my kids to have my memories, but they can't, so they're going to have what we gave them.

The first year that Vic did the Seder, he picked a *Haggadah* that he was comfortable with and he marked the pages, and he said: "This is what I'm going to do." And I have *Haggadahs* where we've written people's names in and then crossed them out. Every year somebody else reads different parts and they get all marked up. It's harder to conduct a Seder when your book is brand new, but when it has a few stains of wine and *matzah* crumbs and all that, then it's like an old sock or an old shoe. It's really more comfortable.

Vic Sabah: Then, we start. We go right through the book. I pretty much know everyone's capabilities—whether they can read in English or Hebrew. Sometimes, I will have called up one of the kids and asked if they can do one of the Four Questions this year. When they do those questions, everyone just loves it and makes a really big thing out of it.

Some of the adults are shy; some of them can't read too well. So, maybe I'll ask them to lead us as everyone reads a paragraph. We go counterclockwise around the table.

Rica Sabah: After the meal, there's a rush to end the service. The kids are tired, it's late…Besides, the impact is already there. Why make it a torturous thing after that?

THE HORWITZ FAMILY

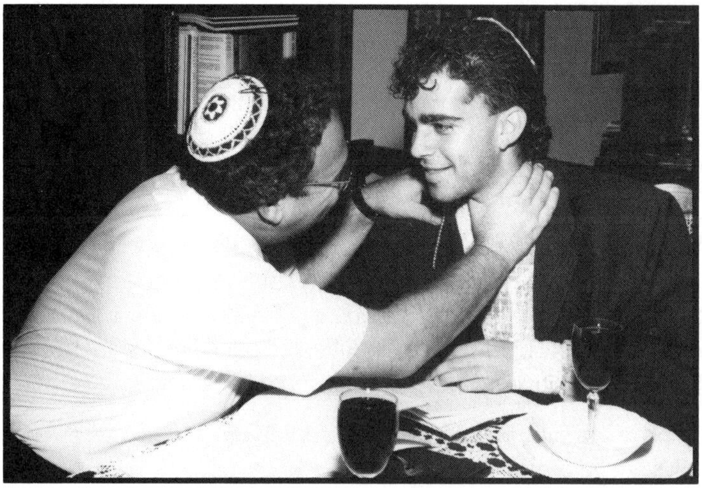

Barry Horwitz: First, we decide what *Haggadah* we're going to use. This year Brad came up to my office a couple of days before the Seder, and we ran through the whole Seder, picking out the prayers and the things we wanted to say. And we assigned people's names to the particular parts. I have a written outline of the whole Seder. Sometimes I change it, but most of the time we follow it.

Mark Horwitz: There are some really good things about having non-Jews at the Seder. You have to talk to people who really don't know what it's all about. You want to show them how beautiful it is, what beautiful traditions we have, which makes us more conscious of what we're doing instead of just goofing around.

I think it's better when you don't understand. We use all this English, but it's not as special as when you don't understand. It's a mystery to you. You use English and it is demystified, making it not as special as it was back in 1910 or whenever they were doing it.

Marlene Horwitz: I disagree. I enjoy the Seders much more now because I understand what I'm saying or reading...

Barry Horwitz: When I was Mark's age, I never kept kosher for Passover the whole week. It wasn't important to me. Now, I keep Passover all week. We have a kosher home all year, but I have to admit, I eat *treif* out. But not on Passover. I really make an effort to keep completely kosher. We don't go to restaurants; we don't go to anyone's house who isn't kosher for Passover. I guess it's easier to do for just 8 days. Besides, you spend all this time getting your house ready, changing the dishes, preparing the house, the Seder. Why spoil it by not keeping kosher 100% of the way?

THE KARSCH FAMILY

Carol Karsch: Every year, my in-laws call from Philadelphia before they come to Tucson, assuming that we're really in the *midbar* (desert), and they say, "Tell us what you're going to need." But, we usually find that everything is available here.

Sometimes the supermarkets are unpredictable. One year, they have mayonnaise; the next, they don't. So, if I really want something, I have to order it. It's not like being in a city where you can go to one of a dozen places and they're all competing for your Passover business.

Benjy Karsch: Keeping *Pesaḥ* at school is no problem. Actually, a lot of people who don't usually keep kosher keep kosher for *Pesaḥ*. In fact, they were commenting at Hillel at Penn that they just totally fill up for *kosher l'Pesaḥ* meals...A lot of my peers like the idea of *kashrut*, but they find it difficult. For eight days a year they can handle it. I'm pretty positive about that. I tell them "That's great!"

Dan Karsch: When we're through, it's usually pretty late—11:30, midnight. But, we always talk about the Seder. It's not an official type evaluation. It's sort of like if you go to the symphony, afterwards you're going to talk about the symphony. So, before we go to bed, we usually talk about how things went.

Carol Karsch: I do a post-mortem on food at the end of *Pesaḥ*. I sit down and make a notation of every single item of food—how much we bought and then how much we used. Then I make some notes about what I should get next year. We always have a couple of boxes of *matzah* meal left over, we can't help it, and somewhere around *Sukkot*, it gets tossed.

I think it would be helpful for husband and wife, assuming it's a family like that, to sit down with somebody ahead of time and identify the sequence: that they prepare well in advance so they can purchase the proper items, that they commit to a few hours of reading through a *Haggadah* which is very explicit and written in laypeople's language so they don't feel overwhelmed. Then, they can pick out eight or ten segments that appeal to them and that seem symbolic and concentrate on them. They should not attempt to do more than they're comfortable with the first year, because you can assume that they will grow in their knowledge and ability. And finally, the one concept to communicate to them is that it's a "no fail" situation, because from the very outset, if you're making a Seder, you're fulfilling a *mitzvah*. And, as long as everyone participates, you fulfill the *mitzvah*. As long as you make the attempt, you're successful and next year, you can do more.

THE MILLER FAMILY

Judy Miller: Over the years, I have found that we have a much nicer Seder if we have 12 or 14 people, but it's getting harder and harder to do that. Somebody always calls up and says "Can we bring so-and-so," and you can't say "no," especially on *Pesaḥ*.

My mother was a wonderful cook, and she loved to cook for people, and there were a lot of things she made that I would never even attempt. First of all, when she was alive, she would make them and bring them to Seder; but there were a lot of things I wouldn't try because I knew they would never taste like my mother's. But, I made a *tzimmes* for the first time maybe about eight or nine years ago for *Pesaḥ*, and the greatest thing I ever heard was when my father said to me: "That's a good *tzimmes*, that tastes almost like Mama's." After that, I always make *tzimmes* because that was a wonderful thing to hear.

Lou Miller: Yeah, but what about the first time you made *matzah* balls?

Judy Miller: I was terrified, but they came out good.

Lou Miller: My mother showed you how to do that.

Judy Miller: I read it on the Manischewitz *matzah* meal box.

Lou Miller: At any rate, she makes *matzah* balls as well as my mother, and my Mom makes the best.

Well, it's a Super Seder because everybody there knows something about what's going on. Sometimes Philip prepares something... We encourage a lot of discussion. They know there's going to be a lot of discussion. I may bring in different *midrashim*. I always look for new material to use... We went through three different *Haggadahs*... We tried the Rabbinical Assembly *Haggadah*, the Silverman *Haggadah*...

Judy Miller: We started with the Maxwell House *Haggadah*. We used to get them free at the market.

Lou Miller: It's a big decision—which *Haggadah* to use. You've got to find one that is in order, that you can do the service in Hebrew or English, and then you have to invest in 20 or 30 copies.

THE WEBER FAMILY

Jerry Weber: I once heard someone say that even though the proper greeting for Passover is "*Ḥag sameaḥ v'kasher*" ("a happy and kosher Passover"), it's not "*sameaḥ*", because of the amount of work, particularly for women. I asked a spouse of a distinguished colleague of mine what he did to prepare for Passover. The answer was that he cleans his study, but since he never eats there, he never cleans it. He does get the wine and he does run the Seder.

Sally Weber: When the kids were toddlers, their job was to stay out of the way. I mean, they did peel the eggs, we always had eggs with little fingernail holes in them... Last year, they got to set the table. I liked that.

Jerry Weber: I make the horseradish. I also do almost all the marketing for Passover.

Sally Weber: He loves shopping. Jerry loves finding the most unbelievable things for Passover. The first *kosher l'Pesaḥ* potato chip on the market, Jerry was there to catch it.

Jerry Weber: The real story is that when Sally went back to work, we had to divide up the responsibilities. It was something I more or less enjoy doing. Besides, I can do it at 11, 12 at night. Saturday night, we came home from a party, and I was at Hughes Market shopping for *Pesaḥ* at 12:30 in the morning. I also go early in the morning, the produce is always fresher. Two weeks before Passover, we've done most of the shopping.

Sally Weber: We sit together and go over the questions we've asked in the past. We recycle some and add others that occur to us. We don't send everyone who's coming a question, and we try to tailor the questions to the people, depending on their backgrounds, what they're likely to come up with, whatever.

Jerry Weber: People sometimes come up with brilliant responses to the questions. Two of the most creative responses have been about *afikomen*. We always ask about the significance of the number four.

MIRIAM PRUM

Miriam Prum: I have the Seder because there are some people that I really want to spend Seder with and the only way to really have that grouping of people is to have it myself.

Actually, I think if it were up to my family's logic, I would be the last one to be chosen to carry on the leadership of the Seder. I'm a woman. I'm the only one who's not married. I'm the youngest in my family. And, I come from a very European, traditional family. To have me be the person who took over doing the Seder in this generation has really been a big issue. I think it happened because I'm the one in my family who cares the most about it. It's not that my father or brother could not lead a Seder—they could. But, I'm afraid it would be the kind of Seder that I grew up with, which was you do the whole thing in Hebrew as quickly as you can. It was not a meaningful Seder for me and it was not the kind of Seder that I wanted to expose my nieces and nephews to.

I guess I learned how to do this from a variety of sources. I've been keeping kosher for a long time, I started in college, so I know a lot about it generally. Then, I was lucky to have a very close friend, David Berner, who was the Hillel rabbi at UCLA, who I kept going to with a myriad of questions. Now, I might ask somebody at the UJ (University of Judaism) about something, but usually I'll ask friends.

THE GOLDBERG FAMILY

Keren Goldberg: The shopping seemed endless. Back and forth between the market and the house. I had to take everything down from the shelves. Washing the china, polishing the silver. And then, the setting of the table takes an enormous amount of time. There are three or four layers of plates at every setting...I think it was probably at least about three full days working on the Seder. And besides John, I really didn't have much help. Next time, I would definitely get more help.

Actually, for that first Seder, I had to borrow a Seder plate. Now, I have one that my friend Melinda gave me. She is the person I went to for *Pesaḥ* all the years since my divorce, until I gave the Seder myself. She's wonderful. She brought over the *Haggadahs*, too.

One year, I was invited to Jerry and Sally Weber's Seder. I got this letter and it said, you know, "You're coming to our Seder, and we're very happy to have you, and it would be a great pleasure for us if you would prepare a 2-3 minute comment on the following question. Everyone's going to have something, and it would be part of our service, and if you have any questions, call us up." I really liked that. I thought it was a great idea. I did all this research. I took some notes. When I was called on, it felt a little like being on stage. But, once I got started, I sort of felt more relaxed. I enjoyed it. It was as if everybody played sort of a teacher and student simultaneously.

THE FIFE FAMILY

Linda Fife: It used to be that Lorin and I shared the preparation for Passover 50-50. Lately, he is so busy with taxes and work at this time of year, that I *kasher* my kitchen, I change the dishes, I cover my counters.

Lorin Fife: I carry the boxes in and out of the house.

Linda Fife: Actually, he also cleaned behind the washer and dryer.

Lorin Fife: I did most of the vacuuming, as a matter of fact.

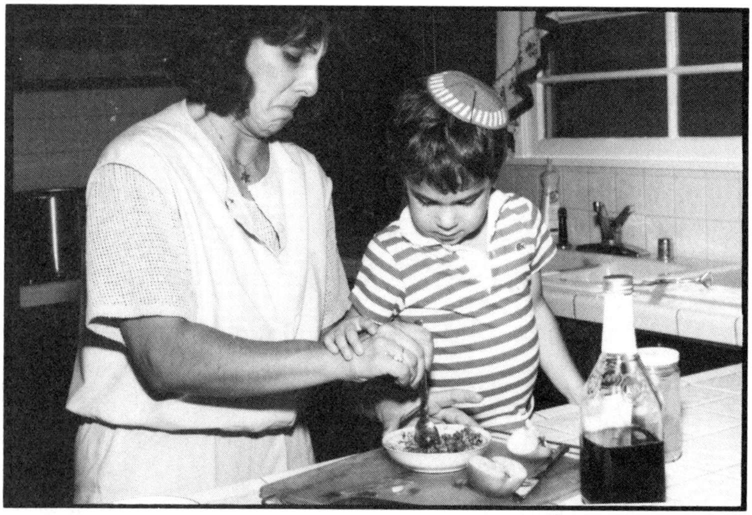

Linda Fife: He just used to do a lot more. It's a sore spot.

Last year, the first Seder was on Monday night. I started cleaning Saturday night and finished the changeover of the kitchen on Sunday morning. As far as I was concerned, the kitchen was closed until the Seder. So, we went out Saturday night for dinner, Sunday morning breakfast, Sunday lunch, Sunday dinner, and Monday breakfast.

A couple of years ago, we made the decision with my parents that we would spend one night with them and the other night they would be with their friends and we would be with ours. My mother has a difficult time sitting through a more extensive Seder. My father enjoys it. But, we each have our own friends that we also want to share *Pesaḥ* with, so it has worked out well.

Lorin Fife: I would tell someone who had just converted to Judaism to try and sample as many Seders as they can, to try to get as broad an experience as possible before they did their own. You can go to a group which is maybe more observant to see what happens there. Then go to a less knowledgeable group; actually, what they do might be a little more comfortable to begin with at first. It takes time to develop an expertise in this.

Linda Fife: The whole Seder is the most complicated home ritual we have and it really takes some effort to learn to do it. People are afraid of not doing it right, or making a fool of themselves, or not knowing what they're doing. But, if you take the time to go through it, to learn the structure of the *Haggadah* and some of the basic rituals, anyone can make a decent first Seder.

25

ORGANIZING THE SEDER SERVICE

Putting together a Seder is kind of like producing a play. There is a script and props and actors, and your job as a director is to keep the action going. It takes some planning, but when it all comes together, it's great.

Barry Horwitz

WHO LEADS THE SEDER?

Anyone capable of leading a Seder can do so, male or female. Until recently, the father or head of the household usually led the Seder. Sometimes, another male of the family, perhaps one better-versed in the Seder ritual, would lead the ceremony. More recently, women have asserted their rights to Seder leadership. Whatever the case might be, there is almost inevitably one person who acts as the leader of the ritual.

There is good reason for a leader to take charge of the conducting of the Seder. As we have seen, the Seder is a multi-faceted ritual, combining aspects of a banquet with choral reading and a dramatic play with many parts. Just as a play needs a director, a choir a conductor, a dance a choreographer, and a class a teacher, so too the experience of the Seder is enhanced when a capable leader is directing the flow of the evening. This is not to say that the leadership cannot be shared; only that there is a clear leadership role that someone or some group of people must fill.

What are the characteristics of a great Seder conductor? Here are a few:

1. **A great Seder leader is prepared.** This person knows the structure of the Seder experience, has studied the content of the *Haggadah*, and has given some thought to the goals of the evening.

2. **A great Seder leader encourages all guests to participate in the celebration.** S/he delegates parts of the *Haggadah* to read, in Hebrew or English, assigns people to lead various ritual acts, and generally orchestrates the flow of the evening.

3. **A great Seder leader sets a tone that makes the guests feel comfortable and want to participate.** Although most Seders tend to be rather formal, this does not preclude a relaxed, warm atmosphere at the table. This is accomplished by much more than exchanging pleasantries. Creating such an environment depends primarily on how the leader models the behavior s/he wants to predominate during the ritual. For example, if people are to feel comfortable enough to ask their own questions, the leader should not only say that this is permissible, but s/he should actually stop and initiate such spontaneous questions. If the leader wants to create a Seder characterized by dialogue among the participants, s/he should be willing to stop the action, step back and engage people in discussion and debate. To free the guests to relate to the *Haggadah* requires the ability to free oneself as the leader to improvise extemporaneously from the script, to follow promising tangents, to ask the questions that elaborate the tellings, the *Haggadah*, and the Seder experience.

4. **A great Seder leader keeps the action moving.** This requires a good sense of timing. A good leader knows when a subject has been exhausted and it's time to move on. A good leader also knows how to tactfully cut off a person who is rambling. A good leader watches the reactions of the guests in order to gauge their interest level. Keeping things moving keeps people's attention, and the great Seder leader is a master at the transitions from one step of the Seder to the next.

5. **A great Seder leader has a sense of humor.** While the Seder is certainly serious business, this is, after all, a very festive evening. Lighten up and enjoy what should and can be a stimulating, enlightening, and fun evening.

CHOOSING A HAGGADAH

The *Haggadah* contains the basic script for the Passover Seder. As such, the style and substance of your Seder will be determined, in part, by your choice of a *Haggadah* text. And what a choice you have! More versions of the *Haggadah* have been published than any other Jewish text. The great library of the Jewish Theological Seminary of America has catalogued more than 2,000 editions of the *Haggadah*, while one bibliographer has annotated well over 3,000 *Haggadot*.

Today, dozens of *Haggadah* editions are available for use at the Seder. They range in simplicity and expense from the once ubiquitous (and once free) Maxwell House *Haggadah* to the magnificent, limited edition work of art by San Francisco artisan David Moss, *The Moss Haggadah*. Embossed in gold, with detailed illuminations and paper cuts created by laser beams, flowing in inventive calligraphy and micrography and valued at thousands of dollars each, one of these would be an investment in a family heirloom rather than a utilitarian text for the Seder. (You certainly wouldn't suffer wine stains on this incredible, modern illuminated *Haggadah*!)

Because the *Haggadah* is the basic script of the Seder drama in which everyone participates, it is highly desirable for every person at the table to have his or her own text. Yes, it is possible for two people to share a book, but it is far more comfortable and expedient for everyone to have a copy of the *Haggadah*. Moreover, we recommend that everyone at the Seder have a copy of exactly the same *Haggadah*. This facilitates the smooth flow of the ceremony more than any other single thing you can do. (The exception being a Seder where all the participants are highly fluent in the texts of the *Haggadah*, and can bring to the discussion commentaries and resources from their own volumes.) Although having an assortment of *Haggadot* at the table could be interesting, you end up with the infamous Fifth Question: "What page are we on?" Our suggestion (gleaned from the Weber family): Invite guests to bring copies of their favorite *Haggadot* and display them on a table for sharing while people arrive for the Seder and during the meal. But for the ceremony itself, invest in a full complement of uniform *Haggadot*. You won't be sorry.

Unless, of course, you choose the wrong *Haggadah*. Since there are so many choices, you will need to spend some time previewing and analyzing several *Haggadah* texts well before the Seder in order to make your decision. What are the factors to look at in choosing a *Haggadah* for your Seder celebration? Here are a few guidelines:

1. **Who will use the *Haggadah*?** The first thing to consider in making this choice is the group of family and friends likely to be at your Seder. If you have many young children, you may want to choose an abridged version of the traditional text. Families with older children may want an annotated edition featuring commentaries which embellish the text. Look closely at the following points, keeping in mind those likely to use the *Haggadah*.

2. **Content.** How much of the traditional text is included in the *Haggadah*? Has the traditional order of the Seder been retained or has it been altered? Are any commentaries included which help you understand the texts and the order of the ritual? Are there alternative readings from which to choose to expand your Seder experience?

3. **Language.** Nearly all *Haggadot* contain the Hebrew texts. But, what about the English language used? Is it "medieval English," with the formal "Thee, Thou, Hast, and Shalt" sort of words, or is it rendered in modern usage? Do the translations seem literal or poetic? Are there English transliterations of the major blessings and songs so those who cannot read the original texts can participate?

4. **Ideology.** The editing of a *Haggadah* text can be done to reflect particular ideologies of Judaism. Mordecai M. Kaplan's *New American Haggadah* reflected his philosophy of Jewish life. There are *Haggadot* which embrace any number of causes (vegetarianism, women's liberation, antinuclear activism) and any number of religious or non-religious orientations (Conservative, Reform, Orthodox, Reconstructionist, Secularist, Zionist). Beware: There are even *Haggadot* published by so-called Jewish Christians which look like the traditional *Haggadah*, but have been laden with Christological references and interpretations.

5. **Aesthetic Presentation.** Is the *Haggadah* illustrated? If so, is the art appropriate and meaningful to the text? Are the graphics attractive and the typography clear and readable? Some *Haggadot* are set in type so small that they virtually require a magnifying glass to read!

6. **Organization.** Are the fifteen steps of the Seder clearly marked in the text? Are the page layouts consistent with the text, allowing for a smooth flow in the recitation of the *Haggadah*? Are the pages numbered to facilitate finding the place of particular sections of the *Haggadah*? (Some recent editions even feature numbered lines on each page, further facilitating participation as in: "Uncle Harry, would you please read beginning with line 4 on page 32?") Are there instructions for performing the various rituals?

7. **Durability.** *Haggadot* should be durable enough for use at many *Sedarim* through the years. Does the binding of the book seem strong enough to take the wear and tear of constant bending? Is the cover material of sufficient weight to protect the inside pages of the book?

8. **Cost.** If you follow our recommendation to purchase enough uniform *Haggadot* for everyone at your Seder to have a copy, this could mean buying as many as two dozen books or more. Cost can certainly be a factor in your choice. When you are ready to invest in a large number of uniform *Haggadot*, be certain that you feel the edition will serve your needs for a considerable length of time.

In addition to your own investigation, ask friends and relatives who own sets of *Haggadot* for their opinions. You might ask a knowledgeable librarian of Jewish books, a Jewish bookseller, or your rabbi for recommendations.

Of course, we are partial to the source of the texts used in this book, *Passover Haggadah: The Feast of Freedom*, the Rabbinical Assembly *Haggadah*, edited by Rachel Anne Rabinowicz and illustrated by Dan Reisinger. Hailed by liberal Jewish scholars and rabbis (two leading Reform rabbis, Herbert Bronstein and Jacob Petuchowski, both wrote rave reviews) as a *Haggadah* which embodies the traditional text while reflecting Conservative ideology, this *Haggadah* is an excellent choice for Seder use and is quite beautiful in presentation. The strengths of *The Feast of Freedom* include its marvelous selection of commentaries, positioned as sidebars to the text, its lucid and poetic English translations, and its superb organization and layout. A major drawback for some will be the virtual absence of any transliteration of the Hebrew texts, with the exception of the concluding songs. Using the transliterations provided in this book can alleviate this situation. Nevertheless, we highly recommend the use of *The Feast of Freedom* at your Seder.

There are certainly other *Haggadot* worthy of your consideration. We have annotated some of the better, most widely available editions in the Selected Bibliography.

Last, but certainly not the least, of the possibilities is to create your own *Haggadah*. The Fife family has done this for a number of years and we know of other families (Jacob Lish of Washington, D.C. is one) who have pulled together texts and commentaries from a variety of sources in order to compile a *Haggadah* which is meaningful and usable in their particular situations. Sometimes families begin with "homemade" *Haggadot* created by the children at religious school. This requires a good deal of research and knowledge, not to mention hard work and a good copy machine or instant printer. But, for many families, creating a "family *Haggadah*" can be an exciting and wonderful experience, both in its creation and use.

TRANSLATIONS

The importance of the *Haggadah* to the Seder experience cannot be overestimated. This unusual compilation of prayers, *midrashim*, songs, and ritual instructions is our script for the evening, the text which is the vehicle for fulfilling the basic goal of the ceremony—to tell the story of the Exodus from Egypt.

Contrary to the impression many people have, the *mitzvah* of *Maggid* is not simply saying the words, but understanding them as well. There is an unusual concern among the commentators on the proper way to conduct a Seder so that all in attendance will truly comprehend the meaning of the ritual, so that each person will feel as if s/he was liberated from Egypt. Thus, many commentators do not only suggest, but *require* the translation of key parts of the *Haggadah* into the common language of the time.

Unfortunately, we live in an era when many Jews do not understand the Hebrew language. It is highly likely that a majority of your guests at the Seder table will not be able to either read or comprehend the Hebrew and Aramaic of the *Haggadah*. Thus, you will need to employ the translations offered in your *Haggadah* text for many passages. By giving these people the opportunity to read English parts, they too will feel part of the Seder experience.

On the other hand, there are a number of steps in the ritual which should be performed in the original language. Among them are the major blessings: *Hadlakat Nerot, Kiddush, Karpas, Roḥtzah, Motzi, Matzah, Maror, Sefirat ha-Omer and Birkat ha-Mazon*. Other sections which are somewhat more well-known in Hebrew or Aramaic are: *Ha Laḥma Anya, Mah Nishtanah, Avadim Hayinu, V'hi She'amda, Eser Makot, Dayyenu,* selections from the *Hallel, Korekh,* and the Songs. We encourage the use of the original texts. But, remember the goal of the Seder, and use translations and explanations liberally to ensure the greatest level of understanding possible.

EDITING YOUR *HAGGADAH* TEXT

To the beginning Seder conductor, the traditional *Haggadah* text can seem quite imposing. It is not unusual for a family that celebrates every step of the ritual to take 1—2 hours to complete the reading of the *Haggadah* and the performance of the attendant rituals—before the meal begins!

Yet, this need not be the case. If you are just beginning the process of giving *Sedarim*, you might consider shaping a Seder experience that will be appropriate for you and your guests by "editing" the *Haggadah*. By selecting the most important texts and the minimal ritual actions, it is possible to plan a Seder ceremony that "tells the story" of the Exodus in a meaningful way.

This editing process begins by studying the *Haggadah* in order to understand its structure and content. The first part of this book is designed to do help you accomplish this task. By using the "talk-feast" structure of the *Haggadah* script, it is now possible to choose representative texts and rituals from each segment of the ceremony.

The question is often asked: "What is the minimum amount of the *Haggadah* we should do at the Seder?" Following the suggestions of the Talmud, *Shulḥan Arukh*, and many commentators, we propose the following sections of the *Haggadah* as essentials for a basic traditional Seder, as found in the outline presented in *The Art of Jewish Living*.

Act I: The Beginning

Prologue: Preparation, Candle Lighting
Scene 1: *Kadesh* (First Cup of Wine)
Scene 2: *Urḥatz* (Leader Washes Hands)
Scene 3: *Karpas* (Appetizer)
Scene 4: *Yaḥatz* (Break Middle *Matzah*)
Curtain: *Ha Laḥma Anya* (Invitation)

Act II: *Maggid*—The Tellings

Although there are four separate tellings of the Exodus story in the *Maggid*, here are the most popular segments of the *Maggid:*
Mah Nishtanah (Four Questions)
Avadim Hayinu (We Were Slaves)
Arba'ah Banim (Four Children)
Eser Makot (Ten Plagues)
Dayyenu (Enough!)
Rabban Gamliel Haya Omer: Pesaḥ, Matzah, Maror,
B'khol Dor va-Dor (You Were Redeemed)
L'fikhakh/Halleluyah (Therefore, We Praise God)
Ga'al Yisrael (Praised Is The Redeemer of Israel)
Kos Sheini (Second Cup of Wine)

Act III—The Feast

Scene 1: Prepare To Eat.
Roḥtzah (Wash Hands)
Motzi/Matzah (Sustenance/*Matzah*)
Maror (Bitter Herbs)
Korekh (Bind *Matzah* And *Maror*)
Scene 2: *Shulḥan Orekh* (The Meal)
Scene 3: *Tzafun* (*Afikomen*)
Scene 4: *Barekh* (*Birkat ha-Mazon*—Short Version)
Curtain: *Kos Sh'lishi* (The Third Cup Of Wine)

Act IV—Redemption

Scene 1: *Eliyahu ha-Navi* (Elijah The Prophet)
Scene 2: *Hallel* (Songs Of Praise)—[Pick one song]
Scene 3: *Z'mirot* (Songs)—[Pick one or two songs]
Scene 4: *Sefirat ha-Omer* (Count The Omer)—[Second Seder only]
Curtain: *Kos R'vi'i* (The Fourth Cup Of Wine)
Nirtzah (Acceptance)

Including these steps will result in a fairly traditional Seder. Of course, you may decide to further edit the *Haggadah* which will result in a more abbreviated ceremony.

In the Workbook which accompanies this text, we have provided a worksheet on which you can construct your own outline of the Seder ceremony you will conduct. If the Workbook is unavailable, simply transcribe the outline above onto a sheet of paper. Next to each item mark the page number(s) where each step that you plan to use at the table is found in the *Haggadah*. If you have supplementary readings you wish to include, write them in at the point of the Seder you intend to add them. This outline now becomes your basic script for the ceremony.

The next step in the editing/planning process is to think about how you will assign parts. You might even want to write in the name of the person at your Seder you will ask to read or do the particular step. Or, many Seder conductors just follow the outline, assigning parts as they come up. A favorite technique to handle the *Maggid* section is to simply go around the table, asking each person to read a paragraph in Hebrew or English.

A wonderful new tool for Seder editors is the versatile little stick-on "Post-It" notes. Use them for marking the various steps in the *Haggadah* and/or as reminders to you about your plans for the ceremony. They can easily be moved around the text and changed from year to year.

Finally, the best laid plans of Seder leaders must be treated as the plans they are. Great Seder leaders are very flexible when guiding the flow of the Seder. Many are those who have "edited" the *Haggadah* text on the spot. But, with careful planning, you won't end up editing out the most important parts of the Seder.

SOURCES FOR SUPPLEMENTARY READINGS

One of the wonderful things about the Seder is that it virtually begs for additional material. The central pedagogic strategy of asking questions opens up the ceremony to discussion, interpretation, and supplementary texts.

During the past twenty years, a great deal of material has emerged which can be added to the traditional *Haggadah* texts in an effort to contemporize the experience. These readings can be found in the wide variety of *Haggadot* which have been published and in source books on Passover. Many families add readings sent home from the synagogue or religious school or included in congregational bulletins. Favorite readings, like favorite recipes, are handed down and shared from family to family.

Two of the most popular recent additions to the Seder are readings which dedicate a Fifth Cup of Wine for the State of Israel and a Fourth "*Matzah* of Hope" for oppressed Jews around the world.

Consider creating a special file of Seder readings in which you can collect the material you especially like. Keep it with your "leader's" *Haggadah* so you will have it from year to year. If you decide to include the reading as part of your Seder, make copies for each of your guests. This facilitates sharing at the Seder and they can then add the reading to their own collection of Seder material.

GUESTS

First, who will they be? The art of inviting guests to the Seder is to find just the right mixture of those people who resonate to your idea of a Seder. Or, if you have some guests who must be invited, think about how they can be integrated into a meaningful experience of the Seder.

Let's begin with family. Family members will probably be the basis of any list of invitees. Some families try to have one gigantic Seder with all members of the extended family in attendance. Other families split off and organize smaller groups of family members. As children marry, they often must spend one Seder with the in-laws. Clearly, this is an area where family politics might dictate who goes to which Seder.

Friends are the next target for your list. Sometimes friends are unavailable for one or the other Seder because of their own family obligations. Other times, friends who live far from their own extended families welcome the opportunity to celebrate Seder with close friends. These associations often last for many years.

Then, there are the tagalongs. For example, the Webers invite the Wolfsons for second Seder. But, the Wolfsons feel obligated to have their only relative living in Los Angeles, Uncle George, for Seder. So, they ask the Webers if it is okay to bring along Uncle George. This "bringing along" can add a number of people to the party.

Then there is the issue of those who have no Seder to go to. Many families look forward to having guests at the Seder who otherwise would be alone. They search out college students and Jewish servicepeople to invite to their *Sedarim*. Call your local synagogue which usually keeps a list of requests from folks looking for invitations. Other places to inquire would be Hillel Foundations on local college campuses, Jewish Federations, Jewish Family Service agencies, and local armed forces bases. These guests often enlivened our Seders beyond the routine and had an amazing calming effect on the children. Best of all, it felt especially good when we recited *Ha Laḥma Anya* to have a guest at our table.

Our friend, Danny Siegel, has written eloquently of guests at his father's Seder:

MY FATHER'S PERSONAL PASSOVER RITUAL

Passover in my father's household has always been a celebration of freedom and equality. Two nights a year, twenty to thirty people would sit around our table and join my father in the recitation of the tale of the Jews leaving their bondage in the Land of Egypt.

From the first Seder-nights I can recall, our guests were our closest friends, plus soldiers (there was World War II, and Korea, and they were far away from home), and students at universities in the area who could not afford to go back to Missouri or Illinois or California for the holiday... and a special element, as if Chagall or Dali or Kafka designed the scenery and script: a month before the onset of Passover, my mother would call local institutions for brain-damaged children. She would ask to come down to acquaint herself with six or seven of the children, to talk with them, to bring them things, and to tell them Passover was coming. And then, the afternoon before the first Seder, my brother and sister and I would set the tables as my parents took both cars to the institutions, to bring the children back in preparation for the evening in our home. Besides the regular guests, there were always some new faces—a rotation of doctors, a new patient of my father's who had not seen a Seder-ritual in years, perhaps the parents of a child my father had delivered in their home long ago. My grandfather was there, of course, and my grandmother, until she died while I was still a teenager, an aunt and some cousins, a friend or two of mine, and the six or seven children.

You will say their noises disturbed the recitations. That is true. You will say my mother was burdened enough cleaning house and cooking the week through for fifty or sixty people. That is true.

You will say the children needed watching every minute: they would spill things, they would throw up, they might start to shout, and that, too, is true.

But next to each member of my family and in between other couples was one of these children, and each of us was charged with caring for the child, watching over all of them and treating them as best as Moses might have treated them among the masses being taken from Pharoah's slavery—for we must assume that there were palsied and polioed children three or four thousand years ago, too. Each of us was to bring the message, however dimly perceived, to these children.

And when it came time to eat the meal itself, my father would rise in his white robe, having tasted of the food as prescribed by Jewish law, and would go from seat to seat, cutting the lamb or roast beef and spoonfeeding whoever needed to be fed in such fashion, and joking with each.

The meals would last long past midnight. The mishaps were many, and the fulfillment of the dictum "He who is hungry shall come in to eat" went slowly, for each had his own needs and peculiarities. Yet each was to be fed with the utmost care.

In our house on Passover nights, everyone felt at home, everyone was comfortable. No one winced, no one sat in silence while my father's personal ritual was performed, no one ignored or paid extra attention to what was taking place. Our guests-of-many-years knew what was to happen, and the newcomers soon learned, became momentarily uneasy, then leaned back against their pillows (as free men must have pillows on Passover night), and partook of the wonders of freedom.

The following afternoon each disease was explained to me. The names were impressive in their Latin and Greek configurations, but the symptoms and the sufferings were a terror to conceive, a travesty of creation. Nevertheless, at our table they were an integral part of our People, of our Greater Family, no more or less normal for their chromosomal defects and their birth-traumas, the disorders of their nervous systems and their Mongoloid features, than the doctor who fed them, their Father.

Those nights, the feeding done, the thanks recited, the singing would begin. It was a dissonant chorus resembling in my early imagination a choir of Heavenly Host, but with flesh and blood instead of halos, twisted words and sounds of human beings in place of the perfect harmonies of angels who need neither food nor drink, nor the affection of my father.

That is why it is better to be a human being than an angel.

From *Unlocked Doors*, Danny Siegel, The Town House Press, Spring Valley, New York, 1983, pp. 3-4. Reprinted with permission.

ON THE TREATMENT OF GUESTS

An important aspect of creating a wonderful Seder is how guests experience the evening. For many, the Seder and the *Haggadah* are quite intimidating. For others, their expectations range from boredom to anticipation. There are steps you can take before and during the Seder which will make the experience a successful one for those attending your Seder.

First, **let your guests know what kind of a Seder you are planning**. If you are expecting a rather complete reading of the *Haggadah*, let them know, especially if they have young children. Then, they can feed the kids something before the Seder to hold them over until the meal. There are many good suggestions about assigning families parts in the Seder, but you can only do this with those families who will be receptive. You do not want to burden these people to the point where they are not looking forward to coming.

Second, you might also want to **tell them what they can bring**. If your guests *kasher* their home for Passover, then ask them to prepare desserts or even part of the meal. If they don't keep kosher for Passover, then suggest they bring *kosher l'Pesaḥ* wine or candy. My parents always asked if they could send the floral arrangement for the Seder table, checking on the size of the table, the color scheme, etc.

Third, once they are in your home, **treat them nicely**. This may sound like a ridiculous suggestion, but many are those who remember the Seder disintegrating into a cacophony of family squabbles among the adults and fights under the table among the kids. We're not sure how this can be altogether avoided except perhaps by creating a warm, relaxed climate where best behavior is modelled and expected.

Fourth, **make important decisions before you begin the ceremony**, such as who is going to sing *Mah Nishtanah*? Many families avoid this problem by asking all children under a certain age to join together in the singing. There is already enough tension among the kids at a Seder without adding to it by waiting until the moment has arrived to make this decision.

Fifth, **include your guests in the ceremony** as much as possible. Many leaders approach the reading of the *Haggadah* as if conducting an open reading of a play, each person taking a part as the ceremony proceeds. Look up from the text. Feel free to invite comments and, especially questions. There is no need to know the answers. Speculate, discuss, try out ideas—that is what the *Haggadah* tries to get us to do.

Sixth, **do not force anyone to do anything**: no nudging, no barbs, no sarcasm, no contests, no put-downs, and no "hurry ups." If people do not wish to participate, including your own children, do not insist or you are inviting disaster.

Seventh, **do not embarrass your guests or family members** if they bumble through a reading. Ignore a slip-up or quietly whisper the correct pronunciation.

Eighth, **decide how guests can help in the kitchen**. Some Kitchen Directors love to have people help. Others feel that a constant stream of well-meaning helpers into the kitchen is about the worst thing that can happen. There is an enormous amount of serving and cleaning in these Seder extravaganzas, so decide what kind of help you want and then don't be bashful about asking for it or insisting that people sit down. Helpful hint: Ask those who are eager to help during the meal to stay a few minutes after the conclusion of the Seder to help with the cleanup and teardown of the Seder tables. That's when you're really going to need some help!

A UNIQUE INVITATION TO SEDER

Sally and Jerry Weber have an unusual and very effective method of inviting Seder guests. They call prospective invitees at least three weeks before the Seder date, ensuring that the people they want to come are available. Once their list is nearly complete, they send the following letter to each family or person, confirming the date and time, and giving an assignment to prepare for sharing at the Seder table:

> Shalom!
>
> We're pleased that you'll be joining us at our Seder on Thursday evening, April 14. Please plan to arrive by 7:00 P.M. A few minutes earlier is okay, too!
>
> In keeping with a long-standing Weber Seder tradition, we are asking you to share some of your talent, ideas, and creativity with us. (Don't knock it... it's easier than cooking!) Please come prepared to discuss the following issue: (the question changes in each letter)
>
> The Seder table is replete with symbols—*matzah*, *Pesaḥ*, Bitter Herbs. What are they and what do they mean? How do symbols work? Do the *Pesaḥ* symbols still work? Do they work the same for us today as they did for our ancestors?
>
> We will be using the Rabbinical Assembly *Haggadah* (1982) and recommend it as a resource. In addition, we refer you to the Lehmann *Haggadah*, the Baskin *Haggadah* (CCAR) and *A Feast of History* (Chaim Raphael). Please feel free to bring any *Haggadot* to share or refer to. Personal ideas and *bubbemeisses* are also accepted!
>
> We look forward to seeing you on the 14th! Call if you have any questions.
>
> Sally and Jerry

With thirty or so people in attendance at the Weber Seder, you can imagine the kind of "talk-feast" it is! Actually, different families and individuals approach this assigment in a variety of ways. Over the years, the Webers tell us that they have had everything from serious dissertations by friends who have spent several hours studying the subject of their question to family skits, complete with costumes. They never know what comments people will bring to their Seder, but it is usually stimulating.

It is important to note that not everyone is sent a question. Sometimes the whole family receives a question, sometimes one or the other or both parents get one, and occasionally older children have a chance to answer a query, custom-tailored to their level of knowledge. But, the effect of this novel idea is to encourage people to think about the Seder and its meaning before getting to the table. And, once at the table, the usually brief commentaries (no more than five minutes) are delivered intermittently between the ritual actions and reading of the *Haggadah*. It is truly a wonderfully participatory Seder experience.

WEBER SEDER QUESTIONS

1. *Mitzrayim* is the symbol of oppression, yet is in a way necessary. Without *Mitzrayim*, there would be no way to experience divine redemption. Was it worth it? Can we or should we believe in that kind of Divine intervention? Where is the arena of human action?
2. *Afikomen*: A curious conclusion! Is it dessert? The coming of the Messiah? An end to revelry? Enlighten us!
3. Passover involves drudgery, scouring, and more to remove all the *Ḥametz*. Why all the fuss? Can you speak at the Seder about the significance of *Ḥametz*? Why do we get rid of all of it?
4. 10 plagues—blood, frogs, vermin, wild beasts, pestilence, boils, hail, locusts, darkness, smiting of the firstborn. Why do we clutter up this joyous meal with references to the hopes of vengence and the remembrance of our grievous misfortunes? What are 10 plagues that threaten us today?
5. We currently have four questions that are traditionally asked at every Seder. Please develop four other questions which you would like to share with the group.
6. Four sons, four cups of wine, four questions. What is it about the number "four" that is significant?
7. Passover bids us to welcome the stranger. Some have interpreted it as "to welcome the Jew—the Israelite." Others have proposed that this extends to all people. What do you believe? How should we express what you propose?

8. Of the three Pilgrimage festivals, only *Pesaḥ* continues to be observed with some degree of uniformity among the Jewish people. What is a Pilgrimage festival? How do you explain this phenomenon? Is there a special message or appeal that *Pesaḥ* conveys that the other festivals do not?

9. "Just as there is the totality—the people of Israel—so there is the particular—the individual human being. And before one prays for the general Redemption, one has to pray for the redemption of one's own soul..." (from the Baal Shem Tov). How do you interpret that?

10. Is the *matzah* a bread of freedom? Or a bread of affliction? Comment. How do you see it?

11. The first two stages of redemption are "being taken out from the burdens imposed by the Egyptians" and "being rescued from enslavement." Do you think they are the same? If they are different, comment. How?

MAKING MIDRASH

As we have seen in the long section about *Maggid*, much of the *Haggadah* text contains *midrash*, interpretations of biblical texts. The process of making a *midrash* is not a super secret of the ancient rabbis. As a matter of fact, should you be asked to prepare some comments on a particular part of the *Haggadah* to share at a Seder, you may very well be engaged in making *midrash* (sometimes called simply a "*drash*.")

Here's an example of Marlene Horwitz's *drash* on the three ceremonial *matzot*:

> Traditionally, each *matzah* represents one of the tribal statuses of Jews (Kohen, Levi, Israelite), but these divisions are not appropos to me in modern times. As suggested by Art Waskow (in *The Freedom Haggadah*), what about the unfree, the free who don't care, and the free who care? Put the apathetic free on the bottom, the unfree in the middle. When we break the middle *matzah*, we can hope for the breaking out of the as yet unfree. The retrieval of half of this *matzah* as the *afikomen* can symbolize the future redemption of the unfree by us, the committed free, resting on top of the *matzah* stack, unfettered and ready to act.
>
> If one of the three *matzot* signifies our liberation from Egypt, and the second the messianic redemption yet to come, the middle *matzah* stands for our present situation in between. We break off a piece and hide it, as redemption is still hidden from us—though, because of the Exodus, we know that it is there—and at the end of the meal, our children find the piece we have hidden, so that we can all eat of it and taste the redemption yet to come. We are forbidden to eat anything after that *afikomen*, so that we leave the Seder with the taste of redemption on our lips.

See pages 146-149 for excellent directions on how to make a *midrash*.

INVOLVING CHILDREN AT THE SEDER

For many children, their earliest, most powerful memories of Jewish life in the home are those of Passover *Sedarim*. This is hardly surprising given the rabbi's initial conception of the Seder evening as a multi-sensory simulation of the Exodus, designed especially to fulfill the injunction "to tell your child on that day that it is because of what *Adonai* did for me that I went free from *Mitzrayim*."

It is always amazing how much even the youngest children get from the Seder. Children love to play-act at being adults, and if the adults in their surroundings are celebrating Jewish rituals, they naturally imitate and thereby learn the rudiments of Jewish practice.

Susie and I had an experience with our son Michael which illustrates the point. A few weeks after *Pesaḥ* when Michael was two years old, we went out to dinner at a very fancy restaurant. We were seated at a formally set table, complete with fine china, silverware, and crystal water glasses which were filled with ice water. When our main courses were served, each plate was garnished with a sprig of parsley. The instant Michael saw the parsley on his plate, he picked it up and promptly dipped it into the ice water before him and ate it! We were absolutely amazed at the time, but upon reflection, not surprised. Since we generally do not garnish our meals at home with parsley, the only experience Michael had had with parsley was at the Passover Seder. He had learned that parsley is a food to be dipped in water before eating. And he learned this little fact of Jewish ritual life long before he would be able to articulate its meaning. Perhaps most important is not what he learned, but *where* he learned. He learned about Jewish ceremonies in his home from his family.

On the other hand, for some children, Passover is a problematic time of the year. To begin to understand how jarring *Pesaḥ* is to children, it is important to look at what Passover does to the family from the child's point of view. Children feel safe in an environment which is familiar and does not change much. Along comes Passover and we take great pains to change the environment significantly. Familiar dishes are packed away and new ones brought out of storage. The house undergoes an extraordinary cleaning. New clothes are purchased. Favorite foods are in short supply and soon altogether unavailable. A gigantic party is planned and days of preparation precede it. Finally, the house is filled with friends, family and strangers, among them other little kids to compete for attention. In short, *Pesaḥ* has the potential to be a life-disturbing event in the experience of a small child.

Of course, we want *Pesaḥ* to be just the opposite—a wonderfully different, exciting time of year, full of anticipation for the changes to come. Involving the children in preparation for the Seder is an important step towards their acceptance of the Passover experience in the home. Depending on their ages, children can certainly help unpack dishes, set tables, and clean their own rooms. Making favorite Passover foods, especially *ḥaroset*, can become an anticipated event. The *Bedikat/Bi'ur Ḥametz* ritual, with its "treasure hunt" qualities, is a favorite pre-*Pesaḥ* time in the house. Of course, if you include any Passover ritual objects made by the children in school—*matzah* covers, wine cups, etc.--they will be especially excited to see their handiwork on the beautiful Seder table.

Once everyone is at the table, the biggest challenge to conducting a great Seder with young children present is keeping them involved in the ceremonial activities preceding the meal. Here are a number of ideas for improving your chances of keeping the little ones interested:

1. **Location.** Ask yourself if it is absolutely necessary to hold the first part of the Seder at the formal table. Sitting at attention for an hour or two is hardly a natural thing for anyone, certainly not for young people. Consider conducting the first part of the Seder in the comfort of the living room. Place the Seder plate on a central table and have guests seated on your living room furniture, or even on the floor bolstered by pillows. In this more informal setting, children can stretch out, engage in alternative activities, or come and go as they please. It is also a much more comfortable environment for the adults as well.

   A couple in our *ḥavurah*, David and Shira Milgrom-Elcott, took this idea and made it an unforgettable Passover experience. One year, they constructed a huge Bedouin-type tent in their living room, under which the Seder ritual was conducted. They draped a couple of large bedsheets from the walls and ceiling to create the tent, and decorated it with pillows for reclining and a table for the Seder plate. All the guests sat on the floor around the table which became the centerpiece of the ceremony. Later, the guests adjourned to the dining room to sit at the formal table for dinner.

2. **Activities.** Ask yourself what parts of the Seder ceremony you have planned will interest the children. Certainly, the Four Questions are a highlight, but what else? The rabbis included a number of things in the Seder to involve children: eating *Ḥaroset*, dipping *Karpas* in salt water, making the *Korekh*, the Hillel sandwich, eating dinner, finding the *afikomen*, opening the door for Elijah, and singing songs.

   Consider alternative ways to tell the *Maggid* story—we've seen puppet shows, magic shows, short dramalogues, even plays. There are many good *Pesaḥ* stories which can be read out loud at the Seder, both for fun and educational purposes. One of our favorites is *Only Nine Chairs* by Deborah Uchill Miller, the first Jewish "Dr. Seuss" book. Find ways to involve the children in the actual celebration of the Seder ritual. Depending on their ages, they may be able to read parts of the text in Hebrew or English, sing familiar songs, or even offer their own commentaries. Ask the children or the parents of the children in advance of Seder night to provide you with copies of Passover songs they may have learned at Jewish schools. Some of the more popular are: The Ballad of the Four Sons; Go Down, Moses; One Day When Pharoah Awoke in His Bed; Let the Hammer Blow; etc.

Another question to ask is: What roles do the children perform at the Seder beyond the Four Questions? Do the children have the opportunity to participate in some specific ways? Do they pass the symbolic foods around the table? Can they help with the serving of the meal? Have they already helped in the preparation of the Passover foods? The more "ownership" they feel about your Seder, the greater the likelihood that they will enjoy participating in it.

3. **Materials.** One year, Susie prepared a Seder "goodie-bag" for the children at our table. In a clear plastic bag, she collected scratch-'n-sniff stickers of smells common to the Seder experience (grape for wine, apple for *Ḥaroset*, etc.), frog stickers, a bookmark, and fresh-wipes!

   The most ambitious project Susie ever undertook was the creation of a *Haggadah* just for the children. Modeled after the popular baby book *Pat The Bunny*, the *Haggadah* was compiled of sheets of songs and stories brought home from nursery school, embellished by tactile materials. For example, Susie attached a cotton ball to a picture of a goat, a piece of sandpaper to a picture of the clay of slavery, etc. She also created paper cut-out puppets of Moses and his staff and a paper wheel of the Ten Plagues. Needless to say, the *Haggadot* were the hit of the Seder, and together with a slightly abbreviated ritual, proved to engage the attention of the children throughout the evening.

4. **Time-Out.** Some families create an alternative play area for the children to retreat to if sitting becomes too difficult. The play area is generally nearby to facilitate easy access to and from the Seder table. The area is equipped with storybooks, toys, puzzles, and a variety of activities which neither make noise nor require adult supervision. An announcement is made by the Seder leader that this area is available to children during the Seder and that they may come and go from the table as long as they do not disturb the proceedings.

5. **Sitters.** The ultimate solution may be to hire a babysitter to supervise the children who cannot sit through the Seder. The sitter should have an activity area available to the children and might even be encouraged to tell a simplified Exodus story to the kids.

One final thought: If you know that you will have a number of young children as guests at your Seder, you have a fundamental decision to make: Will you gear the Seder to the children or the adults? Some families choose to conduct a Seder that is clearly child-centered. The advantage of this approach is that the children will more likely be involved and attentive if the proceedings are geared to their level. The disadvantage, of course, is that many of the adults may come away unsatisfied with this inevitably elementary Seder experience. If you decide to do a child-centered Seder, you should notify your adult guests of this fact.

The alternative view is to conduct an adult-oriented Seder to which the children will, over time, become accustomed. This approach risks the problems inherent in squirmy and bored children, but amazingly enough, many families report that, year by year, the socialization process works on the young people so that as their education about Seder increases, so too does their participation and understanding of the traditional ritual.

Of course, the best approach may be a combination of the two. Experiment with some of the ideas listed above and you too will find an effective approach to involving children in your Seder experience.

HOW TO KEEP THEM AT THE TABLE AFTER THEY'VE HAD DESSERT

If there is one complaint we heard from family after family, it is the difficulty faced in getting the guests to resume the *Haggadah* reading after the meal is concluded. This is quite unfortunate, since some of the most interesting and fun parts of the Seder come after dessert, including two more cups of wine, the appearance of Elijah the Prophet, the beauty of the *Hallel*, the counting of the Omer (at the second Seder), and the great fun of the concluding songs.

A basic step to take in order to avoid the collapse of your ceremony after the meal is to make it very clear to your family and guests that the Seder consists of four acts—the Beginning, the Tellings, the Meal, and the Redemption—and you plan to do all four. Invest a few minutes at the beginning of the ceremony to outline the evening's program. When people know what to expect, it helps.

As for the children, the ransoming of the *afikomen*, opening the door to welcome Elijah and a spirited songfest can help bring them back to the table.

Nevertheless, there may be some guests who just cannot stay past ten (or midnight!) and they may excuse themselves before the Seder is completed. A number of families we know expect this to happen, but they do not let it shorten their own experience of the Seder. They simply pause for a moment to wish their guests well, and then return to the singing and talking which animate the last steps of the ceremony.

TZEDAKAH OPPORTUNITIES

It is customary to give *Tzedakah* (charitable) contributions before every Jewish holiday. The act of *Tzedakah* benefits both the receiver and, perhaps more importantly, the giver. There are a number of ways to give *Tzedakah* which are unique to the Passover season:

1. ***Maot Ḥittim* Funds.** There is an ancient custom to make special *Tzedakah* contributions before Passover to a fund known as "*Maot Ḥittim*," literally "wheat fund." In olden days, the head of the family purchased a supply of wheat suitable for Passover which was brought to a mill to be ground into flour from which the family *matzot* were baked. For those too poor to purchase this wheat, monies were collected to ensure that every family could have its *Pesaḥ* supply of flour. When this practice was discontinued, there were nevertheless needy families in the community that could not afford the basic necessities to celebrate a joyous Passover Seder, and the funds collected to help them do so kept the name "*Maot Ḥittim*." Many congregations and communal agencies sponsor *Maot Ḥittim* funds and take collections beginning on *Purim*.

2. **Mazon**. Another idea for a *Pesaḥ Tzedakah* contribution is to donate a portion of the cost of your Seder to Mazon: A Jewish Response to Hunger, an organization dedicated to feeding the poor and homeless of the community. Each year, Mazon conducts a *Pesaḥ* appeal, suggesting the donation of 3% of the cost of your Seder to its program. They will even provide you with a table card which informs your guests about your donation and may encourage them to do the same whenever they are celebrating a *simḥa*. Contact Mazon at 2940 Westwood Boulevard, Suite #7, Los Angeles, California, 90064.

3. ***Ḥametz* or *Pesaḥ* Baskets**. A more personal form of *Tzedakah* involves putting together a food basket for distribution to various needy folks. Remaining *ḥametz* products can be made into a basket for non-Jewish needy and kosher for *Pesaḥ* products can be purchased for those Jewish individuals or families who may have difficulty buying necessities. *Ḥametz* baskets can be given to local food banks, while *Pesaḥ* baskets can be offered to Jewish family service agencies.

4. **Passover Foods Abroad.** In an effort to get Passover supplies to Jews in countries where they are in short supply, some people have tried to send boxes of Passover food to families in the Soviet Union, Syria, etc. There is no guarantee that these packages arrive, but there is a lesson to be learned in the effort itself.

5. ***Kol Dikhfin* Invitations.** The *Ha Laḥma Anya* states that our doors are open to all who are hungry. Unless we actually invite people in need of a Seder before we recite these words, the likelihood that someone will respond is not high. Contact local armed services bases, college campuses, Hillel Foundations, and synagogues to invite students and servicepeople who are away from home to your Seder.

6. ***Mekhirat Ḥametz*.** When you sell your *ḥametz*, it is customary to make a *Tzedakah* donation as a gesture of thanks to whomever is acting as your agent for the sale. No specific amount is required, but many people give "*Ḥai*," $18.

PARODIES

The Seder, while serious in nature, seems especially suited to the unique wit of the Jewish people. Through the years, numerous parodies of the Passover script have been suggested by those who seek to inject some humor and fun into the Seder proceedings.

Here are some of the top songs of the Seder which present wonderful opportunities for parody. We've suggested the title—you write the song:

Singin' in the *Ḥ'rein*.
Afikomen 'round the Mountain.
Ḥad Gadya Under My Skin.
Haggadah Wash That Man Right Out of My Hair.
Shanks for the Memories.

Additional parody ideas, including the popular *Ballad of the Four Sons*, can be found in the Workbook accompanying this volume.

BEGINNING

We end this chapter with our summary suggestions, **15 Steps to a Great Seder**:

1. START. You can begin to observe a Seder with a number of small steps. You can also begin your observance of Passover by refraining from eating *ḥametz*, attending a Seder, going to Passover services in the synagogue.
2. TRY your own Seder with your immediate family on a small scale before inviting large numbers of guests.
3. INVITE GUESTS well in advance of the Seder. Decide what they can bring.
4. PLAN AHEAD for the meal.
5. GET HELP—paid or volunteer.
6. GAUGE how much your guests are likely to participate in the Seder. ENCOURAGE them to come prepared to contribute in some way (read or sing Hebrew or English, lead discussion, ask questions).
7. DECIDE IN ADVANCE who will say the Four Questions and who will be eligible to search for the *Afikomen*.
8. FEED the children something before the Seder begins. Alert your adult guests that dinner will be served late and that they should give their children something to eat, too.
9. DECIDE how much of the Seder will be geared to the children. What parts will they have? DISCOVER what children can contribute to the Seder from their studies at religious school.
10. SELECT a *Haggadah* that fits your family's needs. READ and select those sections which are most meaningful to you. OUTLINE your choices and assign parts.
11. PROVIDE for young children by offering opportunities for participating with songs they know or by allowing quiet reading or play at or near the table.
12. DO NOT PRESSURE children to perform, or for that matter, do not force any guest to participate.
13. IMPROVISE during the reading of the *Haggadah*. Do not be a slave to the text. Encourage questions and discussion.
14. EVALUATE your Seder the next day. Review your practice each year as the family matures and needs change.
15. CONTINUE your study of the *Haggadah* and bring new insights to your ceremony each year.

26

KOSHER FOR PESAḤ

Sally Weber: I started getting real compulsive a couple of years ago, so I have a notebook that lists menus from every year: quantities, things that I doubled, tripled. I have a whole page with all of my desserts listed and a column for how many cups of nuts you need and how many eggs you need and how much chocolate you need, so I can just sit down with the list and figure out that we need 12 dozen eggs or whatever. Things that we don't open we save from year to year, and I have a list of things like that we already have. If we have too many things leftover, I'll say: "Don't buy this, don't buy that."

Your Author: You're sure they stay good from year to year?

Sally Weber: Well, I write down on the box the year it's from because one year, we had an overload of cake mixes going back to like 1961. No, I'm just kidding… So, I have the produce list, the dairy list, the dry goods list. Jerry gets all these lists, and then he has in his head the pickles-olives-potato chips-ice cream list.

Jerry Weber: You've got to do this early, or the markets run out of things. Last year, it was brown sugar. Now, some of my colleagues wouldn't ask about brown sugar, others ask about tuna in water. There are always discussions and questions about whether such-and-such needs to be *kosher l'Pesaḥ*.

ḤAMETZ

Ḥametz is defined as food containing any amount of leavened product derived from five types of grain: wheat, barley, oats, spelt and rye. What is "leavened?" Leavened refers to the process of fermentation which results when flour from these grains is mixed with water and allowed to sit 18 minutes or longer. Why 18 minutes? Just as water has a boiling point, flour has a fermentation point—18 minutes. After 18 minutes, the dough created by the mixture of flour and water begins to ferment and rise, creating "leavened bread." "Unleavened bread" (i.e., *matzah*) is bread made with flour ground from these same grains (usually wheat) which has been kept absolutely dry until mixed with water and then baked *before* this 18-minute point of fermentation or leavening. This flour, when baked, becomes a flat cake of *matzah* bread because the dough was not allowed to rise. The hurried nature of baking *matzah* before the 18-minute point is what reminds us of the hurried flight of the Israelites from Egypt during the Exodus.

The prohibition of eating leavened bread is stated by the Torah: "Seven days shall you eat unleavened bread, thus, the first day you shall put leaven out of your houses." (Exodus 12:15) But the rabbis interpreted *ḥametz* as much more than leavened bread. For them, the restriction against *ḥametz* was so powerful that *any* food product containing *any amount* of fermented grain product was considered unfit for *Pesaḥ* use. This restriction is, in fact, more stringent than normal rules of *kashrut*. Generally, if a non-kosher food particle falls into a kosher food in a ratio of one part or less non-kosher to sixty parts kosher, the law is "*batel b'shishim*"—"annulled as 1/60th," and the resulting food is considered kosher. But, on Passover, even the minutest amount of *ḥametz* ingredients is not permitted for Passover use.

Another set of restricted foods is called *kitniot*—legumes. Ashkenazic Jews of Eastern European origin do not eat vegetables such as beans, rice, corn, and peas because they can be ground into a kind of flour and made into foodstuffs which might *appear* to be *ḥametz*. So, to guard against the possibility of confusion, legumes were forbidden. Sephardic, Yemenite, and Oriental Jews generally permit these foods for Passover.

This explains the extraordinary restrictions placed on the use of any processed food which contains the slightest amount of flour, grain, or legume product. Unless the product has been prepared under the supervision of rabbinic authority, we cannot be sure if the flour or grain used reached the fermentation point. The approval of the rabbinic authority is called a *"hekhsher"* (from the word "*kasher*" or "kosher"), literally a certification that a particular product is suitable or "kosher" for Passover.

These are the basic rules of *kashrut* for Passover. In addition, of course, are the general rules of *kashrut*: no mixing of milk and meat products, no shellfish, no beef from an animal that does not chew its cud, etc. Naturally, there are many, many food products on the market and therefore many, many questions about what is considered kosher for Passover and what is not.

Herein lies part of the artistry of *Pesaḥ* observance. To fully observe this part of Passover, you need to learn which food products are kosher for Passover without rabbinic certification, which items are kosher for Passover with rabbinic certification, and which items are not permitted under any circumstances.

One might think that the safest bet for finding out if a particular food, say processed cheese, is kosher for *Pesaḥ*—with or without a *hekhsher*— is to ask a rabbi. But, for some items, ask two rabbis and you will get at least two opinions. Why? Rabbis interpret the laws differently, depending on their own level of observance and the customs with which they grew up.

We have compiled a list of foods which cover these various categories based on the decisions of the Law Committee of the Rabbinical Assembly of America. The Law Committee functions as a rabbinic court, hearing questions of Jewish law and offering legal opinions based on the interpretation of various sources. The Law Committee of the Rabbinical Assembly sets standards for ritual observance for members of the Conservative Movement, although individual rabbis may accept or reject the decisions of this committee in their own practice and in what they advise others. Nevertheless, as of this writing, these lists are as comprehensive as possible. If a specific type of food does not appear, ask your rabbi.

PERMITTED FOODS

A. The following foods **do not require** *kosher l'Pesaḥ* certification at any time:
Fresh fruit
Fresh vegetables (with the exception of *kitniot*: rice, peas, corn, beans--lima, kidney, baked, garbanzos)
Green beans
Eggs
Fresh fish
Fresh meat and poultry
Raw peanuts

B. The following foods **do not require** *kosher l'Pesaḥ* certification if purchased **before** *Pesaḥ* in unopened packages or containers (because of the law of *batel b'shishim* which does apply to *ḥametz* in products if purchased **before *Pesaḥ***):
Frozen uncooked vegetables (except *kitniot*)
Pure tea
Pure coffee (with no cereal additives)
Sugar
Salt
Pepper
Natural spices
Honey
Pure fruit juices (with no additives—bottled, canned or frozen)
Milk
Butter
Cottage cheese
Cream cheese
Ripened cheeses, such as cheddar (hard), Muenster (semi-soft), and Camembert (soft)

Tuna in water (no oil added)
Frozen (uncooked) fruit (with no additives)
Baking soda

C. The following foods **require** a *kosher l'Pesaḥ* label if purchased **before or during** *Pesaḥ*:
Sodas
Baked goods (*matzah, matza* flour, farfel)
Condiments (ketchup, mayonnaise)
Canned goods
Grape juice
Wine
Vinegar
Liquor
Oils
Dried fruits
Candy
Chocolate-flavored milk
Ice cream
Yogurt
Egg noodles

D. The following foods **require** *kosher l'Pesaḥ* certification if purchased **during** *Pesaḥ*:
Processed foods (canned, frozen, or bottled):
Milk
Juices
Dairy products
Spices
Coffee
Tea
Fish
All foods listed in Category C. above.

E. The following commonly used foods all require certification for *Pesaḥ* use:
Ketchup
Oils (except linseed and cottonseed oils which never require certification; vegetable oils do not require certification if purchased before *Pesaḥ*)
Margarine
Potato chips
Soda
Pickles

KITNIOT (LEGUMES)

Most Ashkenazic authorities forbid the use of *kitniot* (legumes) on Passover. These include rice, corn, millet, and legumes—beans and peas. Green beans are permitted because the kernel in them has not yet grown. Peanuts and peanut oil have been found permissable. Some Ashkenazic authorities permit, while others forbid, the use of legumes in a form other than their natural state, for example, corn sweeteners, corn oil, soybean oil. In fact, some disallow many canned fruits because they use corn sweetners. Sephardic authorities permit the use of all of the above. Consult your rabbi for guidance in the use of these products.

TOTALLY PROHIBITED FOODS

Leavened bread, rolls, bagels, muffins, biscuits, croissants, doughnuts, crackers
Cakes
Cereals
Coffee with cereal additives
Wheat, barley, oats, spelt, rye
All liquids containing ingredients or flavors made from grain alcohol.

DETERGENTS

If permitted during the year, powdered and liquid detergents **do not require** a *kosher l'Pesaḥ* certification.

MEDICINES

Many pills use *ḥametz* binders so the following guidelines apply:

1. If the medicine is required for life-sustaining therapy, it may be used on *Pesaḥ*.
2. If the medicine is not for life-sustaining therapy, some authorities permit, while others prohibit. Consult your rabbi.
3. In all cases, capsules generally do not use these *ḥametz* binders and are therefore preferable.

BABY FOOD

Believe it or not, there is kosher for Passover baby food. However, it seems just as simple to prepare food for the baby using fresh fruits and vegetables, with a little help from a food processor.

CHILDREN'S FOOD

I can recall that as a child, it was difficult to give up cereal for breakfast during Passover. As much as she tried to convince me I could do without my precious cereal, my mother could not and so kept a box of cereal, together with a year-round bowl and spoon in a corner of the kitchen. I would eat my cereal far away from the kitchen. In our own time as parents, we have solved this problem by creating "Passover cereal" out of broken *matzah*, raisins, and plenty of sugar.

There is little doubt that children will complain about "nothing to eat" in the house during Passover. The "nothing" turns out to be candy bars, bread, cereal, pizza, and a variety of junk food that they probably shouldn't be eating anyway. It seems to us good practice for children to learn to deal with this at an early age. There is plenty of good food to eat on *Pesaḥ*, including specialties like fried *matza brei* that are only served on Passover which can substitute for the "regular" food children seem to miss. Another favorite is "*matzah* pizza," made by putting tomato paste and cheese on *matzah* and heating.

WHEN ASHKENAZI MARRIES SEPHARDI

An interesting problem arises when someone of Ashkenazic origins marries someone from the Sephardic tradition. Since the Sephardim eat *kitniot*, rice, beans, and other legumes are permitted for them on *Pesaḥ*, while Ashkenazim are not accustomed to eating these foods on Passover. Couples we spoke to in this situation have differing solutions to the problem. Most avoid using *kitniot*, at least for the Seder, in deference to members of the Ashkenazic side of the family. In fact, among the Spanish Portuguese Sephardim it was common practice to avoid using legumes in order to be able to invite those who follow this restriction to attend the Seder. This seems to be prudent practice, although in other couples the Ashkenazic partners alter their tradition and eat rice at *Pesaḥ*.

CHANGING TRADITIONS

Actually, this points out the inordinate strength certain traditions have in the celebration of Jewish festivals. Even though peanuts have been allowed by the Conservative rabbinate, the overwhelming number of people we interviewed reported they would feel very uncomfortable eating peanuts on *Pesaḥ*. The force of tradition sometimes overwhelms even the most rational and informed approaches to Jewish practice. On the other hand, given our previous discussion about children and *Pesaḥ* food, peanut butter and jelly *matzah* sandwiches may quickly become a traditional part of your family's fare on Passover!

WHAT IF I STILL HAVE QUESTIONS?

If you have a question about a particular item, consult your rabbi. That's what most guidebooks say. But, many people feel they don't want to "waste" the rabbi's time with what they may consider to be silly questions. First, there is no "silly" question when it comes to Jewish observance. Second, most rabbis are happy to answer these questions. Nevertheless, if you want to know, but the rabbi is not your source for an answer, there are places to turn.

To begin with, try your friends who you know are observant of Passover *kashrut*. Call a kosher butcher. Find the people at the synagogue who are active in kitchen affairs. The folks at congregation Adat Ari El in North Hollywood, California, solved this problem by creating a group of people known as "Jewish Resource Persons," knowledgeable laypeople who are available to answer questions about Jewish observance. Get a copy of *The Kosher Directory*, a manual listing all kosher for Passover foods certified by the Union of Orthodox Jewish Congregations of America (order from UOJCA, 45 West 36th Street, New York, NY 10018).

CAUTION

Not every label that says "kosher for Passover" can be relied on as sufficient certification. Some unscrupulous manufacturers will print a "K" of "KP" on a package with no further indication that it is kosher. In some cases, a separate document attesting to the *kashrut* of the product will be posted on the display (sodas are often displayed like this). But, generally, any label should have the supervising rabbi's signature as well as the "kosher for Passover" or *"kosher l'Pesaḥ"* statement. The best known and one of the most reliable indications that a product is kosher for *Pesaḥ* is the Ⓤ P *hekhsher* from the Union of Orthodox Jewish Congregations of America's *kashrut* division. ® does **not** indicate rabbinical supervision; it stands for "Registered Trademark."

Also, beware of products which state in Hebrew "*l'okhlim kitniot*." This means that the product is kosher for Passover, but contains *kitniot* derivatives which are generally eaten only by Sephardic Jews.

Finally, avoid so-called "kosher for Passover" baked goods for sale in bakeries which are also selling leavened bread products. Unless the entire bakery is made kosher for *Pesaḥ*, the products being sold as "kosher for Passover" are products made from *matzah* flour using *ḥametz* utensils, thereby rendering them *ḥametzdik*. A truly kosher for Passover bakery will have done a thorough cleaning under rabbinic supervision, use only kosher for Passover ingredients, and post a statement in which the supervising rabbinic authority attests to these facts.

PASSOVER SHOPPING

Once you know what foods are required to have certification and which are not, you can begin to construct a shopping list for foodstuffs. One important criterion is to buy those items which require no certification if purchased before *Pesaḥ*. Items in this category include: fresh fruit and vegetables (these need no certification during *Pesaḥ* either), cream cheese, cheeses, cottage cheese, milk, tea, coffee, canned or frozen juices with no additives. Those foods which might have spoil problems should be purchased as close to the beginning of the holiday as possible. The last thing we buy before *Pesaḥ* is several gallons of milk, enough to last us the eight days. Buying enough milk is especially important because, if you run out, you must buy certified kosher milk at much higher prices, if you can find any towards the end of the holiday!

Smart shoppers also shop the *Pesaḥ* displays at local markets *early*. The stores are putting out displays earlier than ever, as much as eight weeks before *Pesaḥ* begins. Obviously, the best selection is available as soon as the displays are put out. Moreover, as the holiday approaches, the displays get a distinct "picked over" feeling and the more popular items (ketchup, mayonnaise, salad dressings) may be long gone.

If you are fortunate enough to live in a Jewish population center with well-stocked kosher butcher shops and stores, you may be able to flirt with last-minute shopping. On the other hand, these same kosher butchers and merchants often close shop for the entire week of Passover, leaving you to beg and borrow from neighbors during the week, a time-honored process which tests the depths of friendship, as in "Susie, do you have an extra bottle of *Pesaḥdik* ketchup I can borrow?"--as if you'll ever see it again!

In a word, shop early and buy plenty. Tracking your use of products from one year to the next can help tremendously in gauging how much to buy. But, better to have more than to run out. After all, many Passover products can be saved for use the following year if you overbuy.

Place your order with the kosher butcher early. Remember, the closer to *Pesaḥ*, the higher the prices. And don't forget to ask for a shank bone—you'll find them in short supply the week before the holiday.

SELECTING MATZAH FOR PESAḤ

Matzah is the preeminent symbol of *Pesaḥ*. Even though we are obliged to eat *matzah* only at the Seder, most Jews eat substantial amounts of *matzah* during the eight days of the holiday. As a matter of fact, people who may normally eat very little bread seem to eat lots of *matzah* during Passover.

With so many people eating so much *matzah* in such a short period of time, the making and supplying of *matzah* has become big business. In the month before *Pesaḥ*, supermarkets are loaded with huge displays of Passover *matzah* from the large *matzah* manufacturers: Manischewitz, Horowitz-Margareten, and Streits in the United States and Yehuda and Aviv in Israel. Manischewitz alone produces well over 200 million "*matzos*," as they are called on their package, each year. About twenty percent of *matzot* sold in the United States and Canada is imported from Israel, for undoubtedly there is something thrilling about saying "Next Year in Jerusalem" over *matzah* made in Israel.

There also seems to be a resurgence of interest in baking one's own *matzah*. Some groups operate "*matzah* factories" before *Pesaḥ*. It is very interesting to watch the *matzah* being made and even more meaningful to take home *matzah* you helped bake for use at the Seder. Before the advent of *matzah*-making machines in the mid-19th century, all *matzot* were made by hand. Going to the local *matzah* bakery before *Pesaḥ* to choose your bundle of *matzah* was an anticipated rite of Passover preparation.

Even though all plain *matzah* consists of just flour and water, different brands of *matzah* can taste better to you than others. Some have a crunchy taste, others smooth. Some are baked longer and are a bit more burnt than others. What tastes like cardboard to one is marvelous *matzah* to another. So, before buying large quantities of *matzah*, you may want to conduct your own family "*Matzah* Taste Test" to find the *matzah* you like best.

Matzah companies know that most families will consume a large amount of *matzah* during Passover week. They package their product in large, shrink-wrapped bundles containing five one-pound boxes of *matzah*. Of course, you can buy single one-pound boxes of *matzah* as well. Each box contains about 15 sheets of *matzah*.

There are several kinds of *matzah* available for Passover use:

1. **Machine-Made Plain *Matzah***. This is the most common type of *matzah* available in markets. Made from *Pesaḥdik* flour and water, these are square-shaped sheets of *matzah*, perforated with small holes that prevent blistering during the quick baking process, and often have a slightly burnt taste.

2. ***Matzah Shmurah***. Sometimes called *shmurah matzah*, this special *matzah* is made from flour of grain that is actually watched or guarded (*shmurah*) from the time the grain is cut at harvest through its grinding into flour and final baking. Most *matzah shmurah* is hand-baked, although some companies make machine-baked *matzah shmurah*. The hand-baked variety is round in shape and probably resembles what *matzah* actually looked like at the time of the Exodus. Those who have eaten *matzah shmurah* truly understand the meaning of "bread of affliction." Yet, the Torah says "*Ushmartem*," "*you shall observe" (the festival of Matzot)*, so many families use *matzah shmurah* at least for the three ceremonial *matzot*. If you have two *Sedarim*, this means you need a minimum of six pieces of *matzah shmurah*. This *matzah* is invariably more expensive than regular *matzah*. It can be ordered from synagogues, kosher grocery stores, or other religious organizations.

3. **Egg *Matzah***. This *matzah* is made with *Pesaḥdik* flour, but with apple cider instead of water. The resulting *matzah* is more flavorful and not as crunchy or coarse as plain *matzah*. Known as "*matzah ashira*" (enriched *matzah*), egg *matzot* may not be used to fulfill the

obligation of eating ***matzah*** at the Seder, nor may they be used as the ceremonial ***matzot.*** However, because the commandment to eat ***matzah*** is only applicable to the *Sedarim* themselves, it is permissible to eat egg ***matzah*** during the remainder of the week of Passover. Some Ashkenazim nevertheless refrain from eating egg ***matzah*** altogether.

4. **Whole Wheat *Matzah*.** This is ***matzah*** made from whole wheat and water. While darker in color than regular ***matzah***, it nevertheless qualifies as ***matzah*** to be used at the Seder or during the week.

27

THE PASSOVER CHANGEOVER

My goal in life is to have a house where I can have a set of shelves just for *Pesaḥ* stuff and I can open it up the morning of *Pesaḥ* and there it is, just waiting for me.

Linda Fife

Sally Weber: We keep all the *Pesaḥdik* stuff in a bunch of cupboards in our bedroom which are closed all year. When we bring down those boxes, it's a really special feeling. Every time we open the boxes, it's like finding old friends. We find all the beautiful things the kids have made over the years in school. We have this wonderful little jar that says "Passover Goodies" that our friends gave us. The only problem this year was I couldn't find the salt shaker.

Carol Karsch: I plan how I'm going to change the kitchen very carefully. When we started making *Pesaḥ* 21 years ago, we had very few *Pesaḥdik* dishes. Now, we've collected just about everything we need, so we hardly ever have to *kasher* anything. The Sunday before the Seder, the kids and staff are signed up to help. The "staff" are college kids I hire to help with getting ready. We happen to live in a university town, so I put an ad in the college newspaper and I always get these energetic kids to help out. It's very well-planned. We know which day we evacuate the kitchen, which day we *kasher* the appliances, which day we replace everything...

Sally Weber: I start thinking about Passover in June. In June, I start worrying if I'm going to start preparing early enough. In September, around *Sukkot*, I start panicking that I'm really not going to allow myself enough time, that Jerry's probably going to invite too many people. In January, I start looking at the calendar to start working backward to figure out when I have to start thinking about menus and purchases and changing the kitchen. In March, I start feeling really relieved that I started worrying so early because all that worry does is relieve me of an enormous amount of anxiety. One year, I didn't start worrying in June. What happened was that a whole eight months' worth of worrying had to go on between March and April and I was a basket case.

Jerry Weber: I start thinking about Seder sometime in February. A couple of years ago, a friend of mine called at my office in January to plan the Seders. I said: "What business do you have calling me on January 17 to plan a Seder for April 20? He said: "Well, last year we goofed up and we couldn't trade Seders, so I didn't want that to happen again." I said: "Call back in three weeks. I'm not ready to think about this yet..."

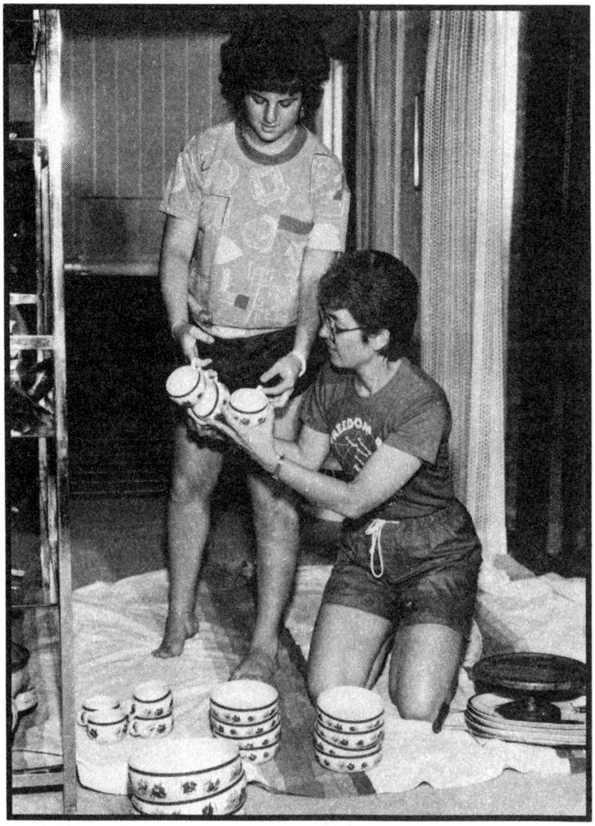

Marlene Horwitz: I start thinking about next Passover right after this one is over with.

Barry Horwitz: I think about Passover when it's tax season... because it is usually the week before April 15 or on April 15, so I never have any time to prepare properly.

Brad Horwitz: I think about Passover when the cabinets start getting empty. My mother raids the food cabinets and takes everything out and we starve for a few weeks.

Mark Horwitz: Yeah, and we'd all pretend we were some kind of famished savages on some island. Mom would leave nothing and we would complain all day. She would say, "There's plenty to eat," but there would really be nothing.

Judy Miller: When I first start thinking about *Pesaḥ*, I start hyperventilating, I stop sleeping, and I start making lists.

Here's a quick overview of the Passover changeover:

1. **Make lists.** Most of the families we interviewed told us that this is one of the first tasks for Passover. Here is a list of the lists you'll need:

   a. Food shopping list
   b. Kosher butcher list
   c. Guest list
   d. Seder menu list
   e. Cleaning list
   f. Special order list
   g. Task list

   Sometimes these lists have lists. Check off each item as it is taken care of. Keep your lists from year to year, so you need not reinvent the wheel each *Pesaḥ*.

HAMETZ –
Busters
Were Here!

2. **Use up your *ḥametz*.** Plan meals that gradually use up the *ḥametz* in your house during the week or two before *Pesaḥ*. You'll want to especially try to use refrigerated items such as condiments (ketchup, mustard, mayonnaise), salad dressings, dairy products, beverages, etc. It's fairly easy to lock up a can of corn; it's impossible to lock up an open container of mustard (unless you have a sealable second refrigerator or freezer). (See "The Kitchen Changeover" for why we lock-up food.) "Pure" *ḥametz* products, such as bread, cereals, flours, pastas, beans, barley, etc. should also be used up, if possible.

3. **Have a *ḥametz party*.** We know of people who bring leftover *ḥametz* to someone's home on an evening two or three days before *Pesaḥ* for a *Ḥametz*-Eating Party. Definitely a high-carbohydrate affair, this can be a fun way to get rid of your *ḥametz*! Some *ḥavurot* (groups of friends) get together on the night before *Pesaḥ* and cap the evening with a *Bedikat Ḥametz* search. Another possibility in this vein is to collect the *ḥametz* in your *ḥavurah*, synagogue, or school and donate it to the local food bank. This can be a wonderful *Tzedakah* project.

4. **Cleaning.** While many people consider *Pesaḥ* the ideal time for a thorough spring cleaning of the house, it does not have to be so. The basic requirement is to rid the house of *ḥametz*. Nevertheless, there seem to be those families who clean the house top to bottom; I recall my mother

used to have all the drapes in the house cleaned before *Pesaḥ* every year. Other families do a more superficial cleaning. But, if you are into *Pesaḥ* time as spring cleaning time, here are some helpful hints:

a. **Plan your cleaning schedule**. Attack the house beginning with the rooms farthest away from the kitchen; it will be last, unless you plan to do a lot of *Pesaḥ* cooking ahead of time (See *The Kitchen Changeover* below). Usually the bedrooms have the least chance of harboring *ḥametz*, unless, of course, you have teenagers. Don't forget closets, drawers, toy chests, bookshelves, under the bed—you will not believe where kids can put food. One year, we found a birthday favor bag filled with six-month-old leftover candy hidden under a pile of toys in the kids' closet. Tackle one room at a time. When one room is cleaned, post a sign on the door that reads:

KOSHER L'PESAḤ

READY FOR *PESAḤ*

NO *ḤAMETZ*

or our personal favorite:

ḤAMETZBUSTERS WERE HERE!

Your creative geniuses may come up with something even better. This sign indicates no eating or transporting of food in the marked space. As the signs sprout up around the house, you and your family can sense that what looked like an insurmountable task is on its way to completion.

b) **Get help.** If at all possible, get cleaning help. The chore of cleaning and changing over the house is a formidable task. First, enlist every family member to do specific jobs tailored to their abilities. You might want to create a checklist for all to see with a listing of tasks and who is responsible for getting each one done. Second, if you can afford paid cleaning help, by all means, now is the time to arrange it. Professional cleaning services that clean carpeting, wax floors, wash window, etc., can be life savers. Be sure to contact them well in advance of your needs; a lot of other folks are also into spring cleaning at this time of year. If you have once-a-week cleaning help, create a work plan for the weeks leading up to Passover and try to schedule the help for additional time on the day or days you change your kitchen over. The Karsch family certainly has the right idea with their "staff" of college students who help out.

5. **Service your appliances.** The horror stories we have heard about ovens and refrigerators breaking down precisely on *Erev Pesaḥ* are enough to send shudders down anyone's spine! It happened to us just last year. Our twenty-year-old electric stove top died three days before Passover. It was a miracle that we were able to replace it in time for the Seder. The month before Passover is a great time to have regular annual maintenance or check-ups done on your major appliances.

28

THE KITCHEN CHANGEOVER

I'm in charge of *kashering* the pots. We put on a giant pot of boiling water. You have to boil it so the water just rolls over the top, and you *kasher* your stuff with that. Certain things you need a blowtorch for, so I go to the synagogue for that. I don't have a blowtorch.

Lou Miller

Sally Weber:	I also know *Pesaḥ* is coming because we always clean out the kids' bookcases, giving away the books they've outgrown. And we get some new books and toys at Passover time.
Judy Miller:	I start by emptying out the drawers and cupboards that I'm going to use for *Pesaḥdik* stuff. I put the year-round things in one corner of the kitchen and then clean out the cupboards really well. Then, I start unpacking the stuff I'm going to need for *Pesaḥ* cooking. I clean a couple of burners on the stove and start with my soup. Later, I complete the cleaning. If the house can be *Pesaḥdik* early, I have one little corner for *ḥametz.*
Your Author:	How do you ***kasher*** your oven?
Linda Fife:	Well, I take my stove apart, scrub it all up, and then I heat my kitchen to 1000 degrees.
Your Author:	How long do you keep the oven at 1000 degrees?
Linda Fife:	I don't know. You know what I do? Every year I take out Blu Greenberg's book and I look it up and I say: "Oh yeah, that's what I'm supposed to do."
Miriam Prum:	I ***kasher*** the stove by cleaning it real well and then putting it on for 20 minutes to a half hour. The trick is not to put all the burners and the top and bottom of the oven on at the same time or you can really have everything melt. I have heard stories of people who did that and the tile melted off the sides of the kitchen!
Your Author:	I suppose you could blow a fuse.
Miriam Prum:	Blow a fuse! That's minor compared to burning down your house for *Pesaḥ*. I can hear it now: "Well, we ***kashered*** the whole house for *Pesaḥ* this year!"

Changing over your kitchen from its normal state to kosher for Passover is one of the most challenging steps in preparing the home for *Pesaḥ*. Here is a suggested game plan, based on our interviews with families:

1. **Store your *Pesaḥ supplies*.** If you take our suggestion to do your Passover shopping early, you will have bags of *Pesaḥdik* food well before you have made space in the kitchen for them. Many families keep the food in the bags and store them in the garage, a basement, an extra closet, or even a corner of a den or bedroom. To help identify and keep separate the *Pesaḥdik* food from *ḥametzdik* food, mark the bags with the word "*Pesaḥ*." One supermarket chain in Los Angeles actually provides special white grocery sacks printed with a Passover message.
2. **Clean the kitchen cupboards.** If you must move year-round dishes or utensils from their cupboards for storage during *Pesaḥ*, you will need some boxes to store and transport the objects. Many families actually take these boxes of *ḥametzdik* utensils outside to the garage, or to the basement or attic, physically removing them from the main part of the house. The emptied cabinet can then be washed out thoroughly and lined with fresh liner paper or aluminum foil. Food cabinets cleaned in this manner can then be filled with the *Pesaḥ* food stored in the other part of the house. Once prepared for *Pesaḥ*, identify the cupboard with a sign ("kosher for *Pesaḥ*" or some variation).

   The Horwitz family avoids the closet-cleaning chore completely by simply not using their regular cabinets for storing *Pesaḥ* dishes and utensils. Instead, they lock up and seal their cabinets containing *ḥametzdik* items and put their Passover utensils on movable tea carts. When the holiday is over, they store the *Pesaḥ* items and tea carts away and simply reopen their *ḥametzdik* cabinets.

   If you are able to simply close off cupboards with *ḥametzdik* dishes or foods during the week of *Pesaḥ*, seal the doors closed with a strip of masking tape, or tie a piece of colored yarn, or twist a rubber band around the doorknobs and label "*Ḥametz*." Make sure that everyone in the family realizes that these cabinets are off-limits until *Pesaḥ* is over. Taping cabinets shut may sound a bit drastic, but do not underestimate how deeply ingrained our "reaching for a glass" behavior can be!
3. ***Kasher* the Sink.** Once your cabinets are cleaned and prepared to receive the stored Passover utensils, it's time to *kasher* at least one basin of the kitchen sink. (See directions on *kashering* below). Also *kasher* at least one counter top so you have some *Pesaḥdik* work space. Once *kashered*, many families cover the counter surfaces with aluminum foil or liners. If you can do without your dishwasher between this point and the beginning of *Pesaḥ, kasher* it as well.
4. **Bring the boxes of *Pesaḥ dishes into the kitchen from your storage areas*.** Wash them in the sink or dishwasher and place in *Pesaḥ* cabinets. If you haven't done so already, you can store any remaining Passover dry goods in the *Pesaḥ* pantry.
5. ***Kasher* the stove top and oven.** Once it is clean, use small toaster oven (if available) to cook *ḥametz* meals. Better yet, announce that the kitchen is closed until *Pesaḥ* and go out to dinner!
6. ***Kasher* any pots, pans, silverware, glassware or other utensils.**
7. ***Kasher* the refrigerator and freezer.** Or, if you have the luxury of luxuries—two refrigerators—*kasher* one for *Pesaḥ* and store leftover *ḥametz* needing refrigeration in the second refrigerator, seal and identify as "*Ḥametz*."

8. **Creeping *Pesaḥ*.** As you get into the changeover, you will find the areas of the kitchen which are exposed to *ḥametz* are dwindling in size. This is a process known as "creeping *Pesaḥ*." But, you will need to create a small corner of a counter and perhaps one shelf of the refrigerator to keep whatever *ḥametz* dishes and/or food stuffs you need before the final cleaning is done. Cover these areas with foil or liner which can be disposed of at the moment of the final changeover. This co-existence of *Pesaḥdik* and year-round items is a tricky business and you must be very careful not to mix things up. Some families use a small table covered with a disposable tablecloth to store this last-minute *ḥametz*. Once you have *kashered* the kitchen table, you will need to transfer the serving of *ḥametz* meals to another room of the house. It's a good idea to use paper plates and cups for these meals. I vividly remember eating breakfast on the morning before the first Seder on a card table set up in the living room. Some families serve these last *ḥametz* meals on a sun porch, in a den, even outside (weather permitting)!
9. **Preparing *Pesaḥ* food.** At this point, it is possible to begin to prepare food for *Pesaḥ*. Some cooks like to do holiday baking up to a week in advance, freezing the prepared foods in the ready-for-*Pesaḥ* freezer. Other cooks need to have the kitchen *kashered*, at least in part, several days in advance of the Seder to allow time to prepare the Seder feast.
10. **The final morning.** By the morning of the Seder, the entire changeover should be completed. You will only have a tiny area left where the *ḥametz* for that morning's breakfast has been kept. Any remaining *ḥametz* after breakfast should be destroyed along with the *ḥametz* collected the night before during *Bedikat Ḥametz*. Then you can *kasher* the last remaining area. Now, the entire kitchen is completely prepared for *Pesaḥ*.

KASHERING UTENSILS FOR PASSOVER

No objects that have been used for *ḥametz* cooking may be used for *Pesaḥ* without first purging them of any lingering *ḥametz*.

How can a pot contain *ḥametz*? In the cooking process, the vessels absorb the taste of the food. Because the rabbis were so careful to prevent any contact with *ḥametz*, they insisted that any pot, appliance, utensil, or glass that has been used during the year must be specially prepared for use on Passover, or it may not be used.

So, there are two alternatives to creating a set of kitchen and tableware for Passover:

1. Have a complete set of utensils *exclusively* for Passover use; or,
2. "*Kasher*" your regular utensils for Passover use.

To be quite honest, it is far easier to have a complete set of separate dishes, pots, pans, broilers, glasses, silverware, etc. just for *Pesaḥ*. But, when you consider that not only one set of *Pesaḥ* dishes is required, but two sets—one set for meat (*fleishig*) and one set for dairy (*milḥig*)—suddenly the economics, not to mention the physical space restrictions, come into play.

Thus, an elaborate set of rules developed for *kashering*—making kosher or fit—utensils for Passover use. They are based on the following factors:

1. The kind of material the utensil is made from;
2. The construction of the utensil;
3. How the utensil is used.

The basic principle which guides the *kashering* process is: "*K'volo kakh polto*"—"as the vessel absorbs, so does it rid itself of what is absorbed" (*Pesaḥim* 30a).

This principle, in turn, is based on *kashering* procedures recorded in the Torah after the Israelites had conquered the Midianites. Elazar the priest instructs the soldiers how to prepare the captured utensils:

> "This is the ritual law that the Lord has enjoined upon Moses: Gold and silver, copper, iron, tin, and lead—any article that can withstand fire—these you shall pass through fire and they shall be clean... and anything that cannot withstand fire, you must pass through water." (Numbers 31:21-24)

Specifically, there are four methods of *kashering* utensils:

1. *Hagalah*—immersion in boiling water
2. *Libun*—fire
3. *Irui*—pouring boiling water over a surface
4. *Milui v'irui*—soaking in cold water

Let's examine how to do each method and then list some of the kitchen items that can be *kashered* using each procedure.

1. **Hagalah**. To begin with, it goes without saying that the first step in *kashering* any object using any of these methods is to thoroughly clean the utensil. Many of the utensils can simply be run through a dishwasher; others will require heavy scrubbing with scouring pads to remove baked on oil or food residue. This general cleaning should be done at least twenty-four hours before the *kashering* process begins. To do this requires some careful planning or lots of eating out.

Now, you are ready to *kasher* most of your pots, pans and silverware through the process of *hagalah*. First, you will need to *kasher* the largest pot in your collection. This pot will then become the "host" pot in which you can *kasher* smaller pots and utensils. We use a gigantic soup pot. Fill it with water to within an inch of the top and bring the water to a bubbling boil. Some then add a red-hot stone or piece of metal (a metal hammer with a long padded handle works well) to the water which causes the boiling water to overflow the sides of the pot, thus, "immersing" the entire pot in boiling water. Be sure you prepare for the inevitable mess that follows by placing towels around the circumference of the burner. If you don't want to use the stone in the pot, put the pot on your *Pesaḥdik* liners in the sink and pour boiling water over the outside of the pot. Once this pot is *kashered*, you now have a kosher for *Pesaḥ* pot that can be used to *kasher* smaller items.

TIP: Buy a huge, new pot to be used only for Passover. This can automatically become your "*kashering*" pot for the smaller items.

You are now ready to immerse smaller pots and utensils into the boiling water of the larger *kashering* pot. If the item is too big, put half in at a time, rotating it with an already-*kashered* pair of metal tongs. Be sure to change the spot where the tongs hold the object, so all surfaces touch the water. Smaller objects, such as silverware, can be placed in a perforated basket, colander, or net. These items need only be immersed for an instant.

QUESTION: Is there a blessing for *kashering*?

ANSWER: No, because this is not an obligated act. You could avoid this *kashering* by purchasing new utensils.

2. **LIBUN**. Utensils that acquire *ḥametz* through direct contact with a source of heat, such as baking utensils, oven interiors, stove burners, etc., are *kashered* by means of the heat of a flame—either their own or a blowtorch. A blowtorch is a small cylinder of butane gas with a nozzle that can be lit, creating a torch of flame. This flame is passed over (no pun intended) every inch of the surface of the utensil until it is heated to a glow. In many cases, the heat of the heating utensil itself can be used. Items to be *kashered* by *libun* need not sit idle for 24 hours before *kashering* as in *hagalah*. They can be *kashered* immediately after use with *ḥametz*.
   Here is the way to *kasher* heating appliances:

   a. Gas burners should be thoroughly cleaned and then *kashered* by turning the gas jets on full-blast until the grates glow red-hot. Or, the grates can be blowtorched. Since enamel cannot be *kashered*, cover any enamel cooktops with aluminum foil.

   b. Electric stove tops should be cleaned thoroughly and the burners turned on maximum heat for 5-10 minutes or until they glow red-hot. Line the pans with fresh aluminum liners.

   c. Ovens should be cleaned thoroughly with a chemical oven cleaner and then *kashered* either by the heat of their own elements or by blowtorch. If you use the appliance's own elements, turn it on to maximum heat (including the broiler) for at least as long as the time of its maximum use. Usually an hour is enough. The oven racks can be left in and thereby *kashered*, but broiler pans should be replaced or blowtorched. Many families use disposable aluminum broiler pans during *Pesaḥ*. Some authorities hold that after the oven is cleaned thoroughly, the insides can be completely lined with aluminum liners which renders the oven usable for *Pesaḥ*.

   d. Self-cleaning ovens, truly a gift to *Pesaḥ*-makers everywhere, can be *kashered* by simply setting the oven on the self-clean cycle, wiping out the residue ash, and leaving it idle for 24 hours.

   e. Microwave ovens are cleaned by an adaptation of the *irui* process known as autoclaving. Clean the oven thoroughly and do not use it for 24 hours before *kashering*. Then, place a bowl of water inside and heat the oven until the water boils, creating a dense steam which cleans the entire oven. Unfortunately, browning elements cannot be *kashered* for *Pesaḥ*.

   f. Barbecue grills can be blowtorched or heated by means of charcoal or other fuel until sparks fly or the grill becomes red-hot.

   g. Convection ovens are *kashered* in the same manner as electrical ovens. A combination convection/microwave oven should be *kashered* as if it were an electrical oven.

   h. Toasters and toaster ovens used for *ḥametz* during the year cannot be *kashered* for *Pesaḥ*.

3. **IRUI.** *Irui* is *kashering* by pouring boiling water over surfaces. Metal kitchen sinks are *kashered* through this process. First, wash the sink out well. Do not use it with hot water for 24 hours. Wash it out again and then pour boiling water over the entire surface area, including faucets. Porcelain sinks cannot be *kashered*, so they must be lined with plastic or wooden sink liners used only during *Pesaḥ*.

   Tables and countertops made of Formica or wood are washed and then covered with plastic liners or aluminum foil.

   Dishwashers are also *kashered* by a type of *irui*. Most authorities hold that the stainless steel interiors of dishwashers can be *kashered* through their own autoclaving. However, there is a question whether the rubber or plastic racks can be *kashered*. Strict authorities require that new racks be purchased for *Pesaḥ*. The Conservative Movement allows dishwashers to be used if they sit idle for 24 hours and then run through a full cycle with detergent. If your dishwasher has a porcelain interior, it may not be *kashered*.

   By the way, since the same rules apply for *kashering* during the rest of the year, you might take this into account the next time you buy an oven (get a self-cleaning one!) or a dishwasher (get one with metal insides!), or remodel your house (put in new metal sinks!).

   Food processors can be *kashered* by dismantling and *kashering* as follows: pyrex bowls through *hagalah*, metal parts through *libun*, the blade through *libun* or *hagalah*, and the motor base washed thoroughly. Dough mixing attachments cannot be *kashered* for use on *Pesaḥ*. Many families purchase extra bowls and blades to be used just for *Pesaḥ*. Then, it is a simple matter to wash the base clean and attach the *Pesaḥdik* parts.

   Coffee makers can be *kashered* through *hagalah*.

4. **MILUI V'IRUI.** *Milui v'irui* is *kashering* by soaking in cold water. It is mainly employed for *kashering* glassware which is used for cold food or drink. Take a large, clean vessel or basin which is not used for 24 hours. Fill with cold water. Submerge glassware completely. After 24 hours, drain and refill. Again after 24 hours, drain and refill. When the third 24 hour soak is completed, the glasses are kosher for *Pesaḥ* use. Some authorities hold that glasses may simply be run through the dishwasher cycle.
5. **Other points.** Earthenware and porcelain cannot be *kashered* because they are porous and therefore cannot be competely purged. Fine china is also considered earthenware, but some authorities hold china can be considered kosher for *Pesaḥ* if it has gone unused during the previous twelve months.

   Pyrex dishes are classified by some as earthenware, by others as glass. Most consider it strong enough to withstand the heat of *kashering*, and thus it may be *kashered*.

   Metal pots and pans glazed with Teflon or Silverstone are also controversial. Most within the Conservative Movement follow the ruling of Rabbi Isaac Klein who holds that these linings are not made of a porous substance (not a substance damaged by boiling) so they may be *kashered*. Some consider such utensils un*kasherable*.

   Knives, forks and spoons are *kashered* in the same way as any metal utensil. But, if the handles are made of wood or other material attached to the blade, *kashering* is not effective because *ḥametz* particles can be caught in these cracks and crevices. If the material is welded to the blade and is *kasherable* itself, then it may be *kashered*.

   Tables, closets and cupboards can be *kashered* by cleaning and then covering the surface areas with plastic liners or aluminum foil.

Don't forget to *kasher* the covers of the pots and pans by immersing them in your large pot of boiling water or by pouring boiling water over them.

THE EASIEST SOLUTION

After all this, the easiest solution again is to acquire complete sets of utensils for *Pesaḥ*. It may take several years, but it is worth the effort and expense. Actually, it may sound more expensive than it actually is. Attractive and inexpensive plastic dishes can be bought in large numbers for Passover. Even if they are not the finest dishware, the novelty involved in using these dishes only on *Pesaḥ* will make them special and well worth the savings in effort. (TIP: More than one family has relied on paper plates while beginning to collect Passover china!)

If you have a complete set of *Pesaḥ* dishes, unpack them after *kashering* and covering the kitchen surfaces, and after *kashering* the ovens, cooktops, dishwasher, etc. Then run the dishes in the dishwasher and place in lined cabinets reserved for *Pesaḥ* dishes.

PURCHASING NEW SUPPLIES

Pesaḥ is a great time to buy a new appliance, pots, dishes, silverware, utensils, wine glasses, etc. These new items do not need *kashering*, and, after *Pesaḥ*, they can either be saved along with your Passover collection or integrated into your regular *ḥametz* dishes.

I always got a big kick out of how the hotels in the Catskill Mountain region manage to make *Pesaḥ* for thousands of people. The answer: tons of beef, thousands of pounds of *matzah*, and cases of new silver, china, and glassware. This is their yearly replenishment cycle for broken utensils.

COST OF PESAḤ

Let no one be misled. It costs a considerable amount of money to observe Passover. There are extra sets of dishes, tableware, linens, utensils, and pots and pans. There are special foods requiring rabbinic certification. There are large dinner parties to mount. There are many people to feed. There is the complete replenishment of a freezer, refrigerator and pantry. There is lots of wine. There is kosher meat, and on and on.

Nevertheless, here are some practical hints on how to cut down on this expense:

1. Buy ahead of time and freeze whatever you can. Prices go up the closer it gets to the holiday. This is especially true for kosher meat and fish. Kosher meat does not need any special *Pesaḥdik* certification if purchased before Passover, so buy ahead and save.

2. Many kosher food items are kosher year-round. For example, most domestic kosher wines and all Israeli kosher wines are always kosher for Passover because the wineries where they are made are kept *ḥametz*-free all the time. So, you may find you can purchase your supply of wine at cheaper prices before the holiday rush begins. On the other hand, some markets run special sales on *Pesaḥ* products to get you into their stores. Shop carefully.

3. There is almost no need for canned foods on Passover. Buy fresh fruit and produce instead of the usually more expensive canned or frozen foods.

4. Be sure to buy foods **before** the holiday that do not require Passover certification if purchased before *Pesaḥ*, but do require it if purchased during *Pesaḥ*. These include milk, frozen fruit juices, tea, sugar, and club soda.

5. Don't overbuy. Stick to your shopping list and estimates.

6. As wonderful as Passover potato chips can be, can't you get along without the more exotic and very expensive Passover novelty items?

When we were kids growing up, there were foods we missed having during Passover, just as there were Passover goodies we only had during that week. Somehow, the change in our eating habits and available foods made the Passover week truly different. Now, with virtually every conceivable food product available in kosher-for-Passover form, this special feeling seems harder to achieve.

29

THE RITUALS OF PESAḤ PREPARATION

Ari Fife:	My Mom usually hides it in the living room.
Your Author:	Hides what? What does she hide?
Ari Fife:	The Fritos.
Linda Fife:	It was all I had left. Actually, they don't leave crumbs. I thought it was very innovative.
Ari Fife:	Then we take a feather and a spoon and a candle, and it's all dark, and we look for the Fritos. Then in the morning we burn them... in the barbecue.

Miriam Prum: For *Bedikat Ḥametz*, I usually invite some people who I think would enjoy seeing this very bizarre ceremony. It's actually more fun when you have other people and can make a game out of it. I mean, to hide bread crumbs and go around searching for them all by yourself... I put the crumbs in a coffee can with holes punched in the bottom—that brings in the air and helps burn the crumbs.

I sell my *ḥametz* every year. Usually I give *ḥai*, $18. I also like to contribute to the *Maot Ḥittim* fund when the letter comes around from Federation.

Dan Karsch: I came from an observant home, but we really didn't do the little rituals like search for *ḥametz* and burn the *ḥametz*. But, we do it in our home. And as I listen to the kids talk, it's something they have grown up with and hopefully it has become part of them. Sure, they make fun of it and fun of me sometimes, but I think they've really enjoyed it. I hope they've enjoyed it half as much as I have. I think my grandparents and great grandparents probably did these things in their home. We didn't in my home when I was a child. Now, we're doing them again. That's very exciting to me.

Mordy Karsch: One year, we were searching for *ḥametz* and there was one piece we couldn't find. I mean, we looked everywhere. Dad always hides it. He's walking around, laughing, because we can't find that last piece of *ḥametz*. You know where he put it? Behind his ear. The last piece of *ḥametz* was behind his ear!

BEDIKAT ḤAMETZ
CONCEPTS

REMOVING *ḤAMETZ*

A central law of Passover observance is the requirement to remove all traces of *ḥametz* from our homes and our lives. The tremendous care with which we are told to clean our homes for *Pesaḥ* is directly tied to this attempt to rid ourselves of *ḥametz*. The quite stringent laws of *kashrut* for Passover, more exacting than the dietary restrictions during the rest of the year, are designed to eliminate even the slightest possibility that a product containing the minutest trace of *ḥametz* would be used during Passover.

All of this precaution must indicate that the removal of *ḥametz* is a serious ritual action, replete with symbolism and meaning. The rabbis understood *ḥametz* as a symbol of the "*yetzer ha-ra*," the evil inclination. In the Talmud we learn:

> "...and the *yetzer ha-ra* was called *ḥametz* (the leaven) that is in the dough. So, Rabbi Alexander would add the following after his daily prayers: 'Master of the Universe, it is revealed to You that it is our duty to do Your will, but what prevents us? The *ḥametz* in the dough, the *yetzer ha-ra*.'" (*B'rakhot* 17a)

What is this "*yetzer ha-ra*?" The word "evil" does not fully convey the meaning of this concept. The rabbis understood that everyone, even the most pious person, has within him or her the capacity for the negative. It is a condition of being human that we will at times be boastful, arrogant, enslaving, unjust, revengeful—inclined toward evil. *Ḥametz* is the embodiment of this side of our personalities.

By removing *ḥametz* from our lives for one week, we hope to remove these negative inclinations from within us as well. We cannot always do this; we eat *ḥametz* 51 weeks of the year. But, for these eight days, we will do our best to find, remove, burn, and nullify that which is evil in our lives.

Removing *ḥametz* is also a lesson in slavery and freedom. Who among those who have ever experienced the hard work of a Passover cleaning and changeover would not agree that this intense period is a taste of slavery? Yes, but the result of this effort is our freedom from *ḥametz*.

There are four steps in the overall process known as *Bedikat Ḥametz:*

1. *Bedikat Ḥametz*—The Search for *Ḥametz*
2. *Bittul Ḥametz*—Nullifying *Ḥametz*
3. *Bi'ur Ḥametz*—Burning *Ḥametz*
4. *Mekhirat Ḥametz*—Selling *Ḥametz*

BEDIKAT ḤAMETZ—THE SEARCH FOR *ḤAMETZ*

Although the house has been thoroughly cleaned, a final search for traces of *ḥametz* is conducted, complete with the symbolic collection of the last pieces of *ḥametz*. This search itself is symbolic of the innermost searching of our hearts to rid ourselves of the *yetzer ha-ra*, the evil inclination. A candle is used because "the soul of a human is a lamp of the Lord, searching all the innermost parts" (Proverbs 20:27). We search for and remove this *ḥametz*, freeing us to fully celebrate our freedom.

BITTUL *ḤAMETZ*—NULLIFYING *ḤAMETZ*

Immediately following the search for *ḥametz*, a formula is recited which effectively nullifies any *ḥametz* which may not have been found during the search. This is a kind of insurance policy which ensures that any *ḥametz* that inadvertently escaped detection is considered "as dust of the earth."

OBJECTS

You will need ten pieces of *ḥametz* (bread crusts, broken pieces of bread, or bagel), a candle, a match, a feather, a wooden spoon, and a paper plate or container (e.g., an empty coffee can).

PRACTICE

Here's how to conduct a *Bedikat Ḥametz* search:

1. On the night before *Pesaḥ*, immediately after sundown, someone hides ten pieces of *ḥametz* around the house. The "searchers" should not see where the pieces are hidden.
2. A candle is lit.
3. Recite the "*Bedikat Ḥametz*" blessing, "*al bi'ur ḥametz.*"
4. Conduct the search, using the candle to illuminate areas. When a piece of *ḥametz* is found, sweep it onto the wooden spoon using the feather, and then deposit it into the container or on a paper plate.

BEDIKAT ḤAMETZ—THE SEARCH FOR *ḤAMETZ*

1. *Barukh attah Adonai*	1. Praised are You, *Adonai*,
2. *Eloheinu melekh ha-olam*	2. our God, King of the universe,
3. *asher kidshanu*	3. who has sanctified us
4. *b'mitzvotav*	4. through His commandments,
5. *v'tzivanu*	5. commanding us
6. *al bi'ur ḥametz.*	6. to remove all *ḥametz*.

5. Be sure you collect all the pieces of *ḥametz* that were hidden.
6. After the search is concluded, recite the *Bittul Ḥametz*—nullification formula, "*Kol ḥamira.*" It is to be said out loud and in a language one understands, on the theory that if you are unaware of what you are saying or doing, the formula is ineffective. So, recite "*Kol ḥamira*" in the ancient Aramaic and/or the English translation.
7. Secure all the *ḥametz* in the container or in a small area of the kitchen where *ḥametz* for the morning of *Erev Pesaḥ* is kept.

PRACTICAL QUESTIONS AND ANSWERS

Why is a candle used?
The search is conducted at night when the candle's illumination is more effective. The candle is considered the best tool for illuminating the search because it can be used in crevices, nooks and crannies.

Wouldn't a flashlight work better?
Perhaps. Actually, some authorities allow the use of a flashlight, indeed prefer its use in places where a candle would be dangerous. But, the tradition of using a candle seems more authentic.

What kind of candle should be used?
Use a standard utility candle, not a *Havdalah* candle which is considered a torch. Besides, the *Havdalah* candle is unwieldly and could burn something.

Why use a wooden spoon?
A wooden spoon was probably used because it too can be burned with the *ḥametz.*

1. בָּרוּךְ אַתָּה יהוה
2. אֱלֹהֵינוּ מֶלֶךְ הָעוֹלָם
3. אֲשֶׁר קִדְּשָׁנוּ
4. בְּמִצְוֹתָיו
5. וְצִוָּנוּ
6. עַל בִּעוּר חָמֵץ.

BITTUL ḤAMETZ—NULLIFYING *ḤAMETZ*

1. *Kol ḥamira va-ḥami'a d'ika vir'shuti,*	1. All *ḥametz* in my posssession
2. *d'la ḥamitei u-d'la va-aritei,*	2. which I have not seen or removed,
3. *u-d'la yadana lei,*	3. or of which I am unaware,
4. *liv'til v-le'hevei hefker*	4. is hereby nullified and ownerless
5. *k'afra d'ara.*	5. as the dust of the earth.

Why use a feather?

Whisk brooms were often made of feathers, so this one feather for *Bedikat Ḥametz* acted as a miniature whisk broom.

Must we use a feather and spoon?

No. This is a custom. The law requires the searching for and removal of the *ḥametz*. What tools you use to accomplish this are strictly matters of custom and tradition.

Why are ten pieces of *ḥametz* used?

Actually, any number of pieces can be hidden. The reason that any pieces of *ḥametz* are hidden is to be sure that at least some *ḥametz* is indeed found. Otherwise, the whole ritual, including the blessing for the ritual act, would be considered a "***b'rakhah u-l'vatola***," a blessing offered in vain. Moreover, if you put out a random number, you may forget how much *ḥametz* you actually distributed, creating a problem. So, it became traditional to put out ten pieces.

What happens when *Pesaḥ* begins on Saturday night? Can we search for *ḥametz* on Shabbat?

No. If *Erev Pesaḥ* occurs on Shabbat, we conduct the search for *ḥametz* on Thursday night, with *Mekhirat Ḥametz* and *Bi'ur Ḥametz* following on Friday morning.

I am leaving my home on a trip before *Pesaḥ*. Do I search for *ḥametz* before I leave?

It depends. If you are departing on a trip during the 30 days before *Pesaḥ* and do not plan to return by *Pesaḥ*, perform *Bedikat Ḥametz* without a blessing before leaving. If you are leaving more than 30 days before *Pesaḥ*, no *Bedikat Ḥametz* is necessary. Wherever one is, one should recite the *Bittul Ḥametz* formula before *Pesaḥ*. If you plan to return to your home just before *Pesaḥ*, you should perform *Bedikat Ḥametz* before you leave in case you return too late to do it then. If you are going away for the entire period of *Pesaḥ*, you should sell your *ḥametz* (see *Mekhirat Ḥametz*) and lock up the house.

1. כָּל חֲמִירָא וַחֲמִיעָא דְּאִכָּא בִרְשׁוּתִי
2. דְּלָא חֲמִיתֵּהּ וּדְלָא בִעַרְתֵּהּ,
3. וּדְלָא יָדַעְנָא לֵהּ
4. לִבְטִיל וְלֶהֱוֵי הֶפְקֵר
5. כְּעַפְרָא דְאַרְעָא.

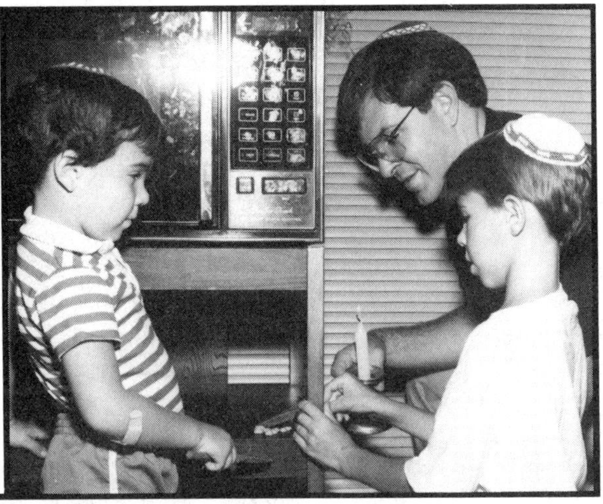

INNOVATIONS

The kind of *ḥametz* used for the search can vary from pieces of bread to virtually any kind of *ḥametz*. We know one family that uses Cherrios, claiming the cereal stays intact and avoids the problem of falling crumbs. The Fife family uses Fritos.

Speaking of crumbs, some families wrap each piece of *ḥametz* in cellophane wrap to eliminate the chance that crumbs will fall in unwanted places.

Some families save the *aravot* (willows) of the *lulav* of *Sukkot* to use as a tool for sweeping the *ḥametz* instead of a feather. This is a lovely way to tie two important Festivals together.

The *Bedikat Ḥametz* ritual is a favorite among children given its similarity to "Hide and Seek" games. You may find your kids asking to repeat the search several times. Why not? It's great fun. (But only recite one *b'rakhah*!)

MEKHIRAT ḤAMETZ

CONCEPTS

POSSESSION

The great lengths to which the rabbis were prepared to go to remove *ḥametz* from our lives went far beyond prohibiting the eating of *ḥametz* and the retention of *ḥametz* in the house. We are not allowed to own any *ḥametz* during *Pesaḥ*! This means that it is not sufficient to lock up your *ḥametz* in a closet for the week. We must actually sell our *ḥametz* to a non-Jew who retains ownership of it until we can purchase it back after *Pesaḥ*. How do we explain this? Sometimes our possessions own us; witness what some of us do to acquire the most expensive cars or homes (the expression "house-poor" says it all!). *Pesaḥ* teaches us that we must be freed from things which possess us.

OWNERSHIP OF *ḤAMETZ*

In olden days, when *Pesaḥ* came around, people simply used up whatever *ḥametz* was in their possession before the holiday. A problem arose with those whose businesses involved the ownership of *ḥametz*. What were they to do during the week of *Pesaḥ*? The rabbis, ever sensitive to making the law liveable, created a procedure by which such people could actually transfer ownership of their *ḥametz* to a non-Jew for the duration of Passover and then reacquire it following the holiday. Today, those families who have stores of *ḥametz* which they cannot use up before the holiday use the same procedure to "sell" their *ḥametz*.

Mekhirat Ḥametz (selling *ḥametz*) is based upon a notion of transference of ownership. Within rabbinic law, it is possible to transfer real property through the payment of money and the symbolic pulling of a handkerchief between the parties to the transaction. With *ḥametz*, the idea was to temporarily, but truly, transfer legal ownership to a non-Jew for the period of Passover, but then be able to easily regain possession of it after the holiday. In earlier days, individuals would actually sell whatever small amounts of *ḥametz* were left over to neighborly non-Jews who understood what was happening. Today, this is impractical, so we employ an official of the synagogue as our agent for the purpose of selling our *ḥametz*.

As complicated and curious as all this may sound, *Mekhirat Ḥametz* provides a fascinating insight into the intricacies and legal gymnastics of the Talmudic mind. Although the "sold" *ḥametz* may be sitting in a sealed cabinet in your home, it legally belongs to a non-Jew whom you most likely do not know. This is not a legal fiction. In fact, should the non-Jew want to use some of your *ḥametz*, he or she has every right to do so. (This, in fact, happened to the congregants of Lincoln Square Synagogue a number of years ago. The non-Jewish secretary who bought the *ḥametz* made a list of the more affluent members of the congregation, called for appointments, and then helped herself to the member's best whiskey, and there was absolutely nothing the startled *Pesaḥ* observer's could do about it!) In the end, this entire procedure once again makes clear the extraordinary lengths we take to remove *ḥametz* from our lives during these eight days of Passover.

OBJECTS

An agent, a handkerchief, a contract, and some money.

PRACTICE

All *ḥametz* in your possession should be sold before 10:00 A.M. on the morning before Passover begins. However, if the first Seder is on Saturday night, the *ḥametz* is sold on Friday morning. Here's how to sell your *ḥametz*:

1. Appoint your rabbi or *shammes* as your agent to negotiate the sale of your *ḥametz*. He or she is then authorized to act on your behalf. This may be done verbally or by signing the document described in the next step.

2. Transfer ownership of your *ḥametz* to your agent, the rabbi or *shammes*. This is done via a "*shtar harsha'ah*," an authorization symbolized by the pulling of a handkerchief. The agent will take hold of one corner of a handkerchief and ask you to take hold of an opposite corner. By pulling

on the handkerchief, the agent acquires ownership of your *ḥametz.* This is an ancient way of doing business. In addition, you will sign your name and address to a document which appoints the rabbi or *shammes* as your agent and indicates that this transference has taken place. Notice that many other individuals have signed the document, authorizing the agent to act on their behalf. It is also customary to donate some *Tzedakah* money to the synagogue, not as a cost of doing business, but as a philanthropic gesture in honor of the agent's work.

3. At this point, the rabbi or *shammes,* acting as agent for a large number of people, has the legal right to sell a lot of *ḥametz.* Now, he or she must sell the *ḥametz* to a non-Jew. This is done through a bill of sale contract between the agent and the non-Jewish purchaser which gives the person unconditional title to all the goods listed and full access to them. It is important to note that, according to Jewish law, the *ḥametz* need not be physically moved to the purchaser's property. The contract is signed by the agent and the purchaser and goes into effect as of 10:00 A.M. the morning of *Erev Pesaḥ*, the exact time we are no longer allowed to possess or use *ḥametz.*

4. When the non-Jew acquires possession of the *ḥametz,* he or she has the right of total access to the property and may use any of it as he/she pleases. That is why the agent tries to find a purchaser of good will, who understands the purpose of the transaction. The contract actually calls for the purchaser to buy the *ḥametz* for a large sum of money, on which he/she puts a small down-payment. The purchaser has eight days to come up with the balance. As soon as *Pesaḥ* is over, the agent contacts the purchaser and demands payment in full. When the purchaser cannot produce the money, the agent re-purchases the *ḥametz* and ownership reverts to the agent and thus to the individuals named in the power-of-attorney contract.

PRACTICAL QUESTIONS AND ANSWERS

What if I personally cannot sign the authorization document making the rabbi my agent?

In cases of great necessity, this can be done by letter or phone. Some congregations include a form giving the rabbi power of attorney in their pre-*Pesaḥ* bulletins.

What if I have disposed of all of my *ḥametz* and have nothing to "sell?"

You should still engage in *Mekhirat Ḥametz* given the possibility that you may have overlooked some product which might contain *ḥametz.*

Can I sell someone else's *ḥametz* for them?

Yes, as long as you are designated as a representative of that person. Then you can write their name and address on the contract with the agent. I have sold my parents' and in-laws' *ḥametz* for years.

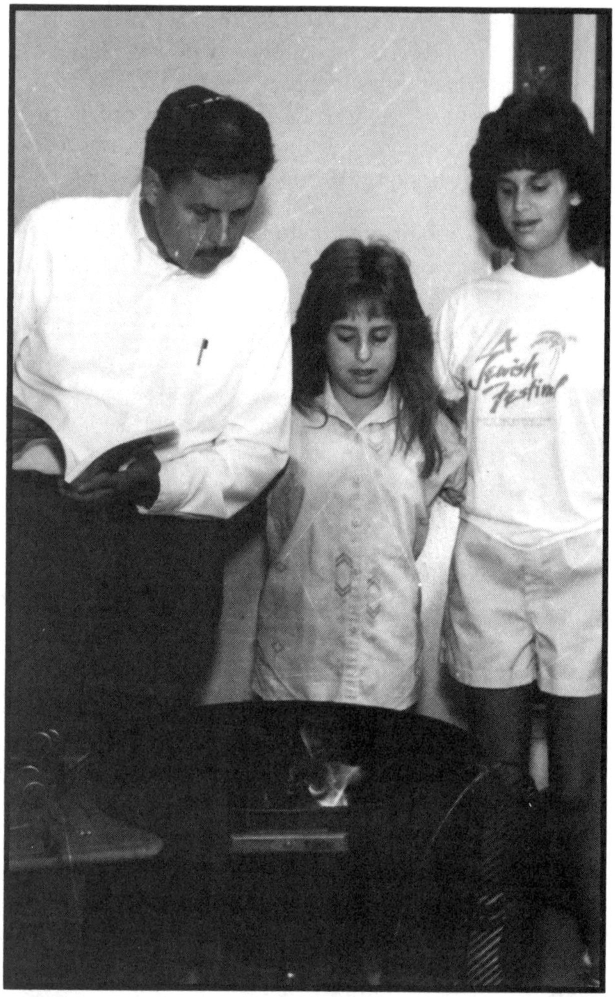

BI'UR ḤAMETZ

CONCEPTS

TOTAL DESTRUCTION OF *ḤAMETZ*

We are now at the end point of the process of eliminating *ḥametz* from our homes and lives. We have completed the Passover changeover, cleaned the home, searched for *ḥametz*, eaten the last *ḥametz* meal, and sold any *ḥametz* in our possession. Now, we must destroy the *ḥametz* we collected the night before and any leftover *ḥametz* from breakfast on *Erev Pesaḥ*. This is done through the ceremony of *Bi'ur Ḥametz*, literally, the burning of *ḥametz*.

OBJECTS

You will need a container or paper plate, a match, some fuel for a fire or lighter fluid.

PRACTICE

There is a debate among the rabbis as to whether the last of the *ḥametz* must be destroyed by fire or broken up into little particles and thrown into the wind or sea. Our custom is to burn the *ḥametz*, although if this is impossible, and there is no sea nearby to throw it in, the *ḥametz* can be flushed down a toilet.

The next question is at what time is this ritual to be done? *Bi'ur ḥametz* must take place within one hour of the last moment *ḥametz* may be eaten on the morning of *Erev Pesaḥ*. Generally, this point in time is calculated as one third of the length of the day or approximately 10:00 A.M. Thus, *Bi'ur Ḥametz* should be completed by 11:00 A.M. on the morning preceding the first Seder.

Here's how to perform *Bi'ur Ḥametz*:

1. Take the *ḥametz* collected in the search the night before, plus any leftover *ḥametz* from the morning's breakfast, and place it in an empty coffee can or similar container or in an outdoor

barbecue. It is also possible to place the *ḥametz* on a paper plate, but this option is messier.

2. Douse the *ḥametz* with lighter fluid or place some paper for fuel in the container with the *ḥametz.*
3. Have the pyromaniacs in your family ignite the *ḥametz.*
4. As the *ḥametz* burns, recite the *Bi'ur Ḥametz* formula in Aramaic and English.
5. Watch the *ḥametz* burn until it is totally consumed. Let the fire burn out or extinguish it with water, but only after all the *ḥametz* is nothing but ash.

BI'UR ḤAMETZ—BURNING *ḤAMETZ*

1. *Kol ḥamira va-ḥami'a d'ika vir'shuti,*	1. All *ḥametz* in my possession
2. *da-ḥamitei u-d'la ḥamitei*	2. whether I have seen it or not,
3. *d'va-aritei u-d'la va-aritei,*	3. whether I have removed it or not,
4. *livtil v'lehevei hefker*	4. is hereby nullified and ownerless
5. *k'afra d'ara.*	5. as the dust of the earth.

PRACTICAL QUESTIONS AND ANSWERS

Why must we recite the *Bittul Ḥametz* formula again?

Actually, the formula for *Bi'ur Ḥametz* is slightly different than the text for *Bittul Ḥametz* recited the previous evening. The *Bi'ur Ḥametz* formula contains a broader renunciation, including *ḥametz* "whether I have seen it or not," whereas the *Bittul Ḥametz* formula allows for *ḥametz* that "I have not seen."

What about the feather and spoon? Are they burned as well?

Yes. Anything that came into contact with the *ḥametz* during the search should be destroyed.

When Passover begins on Saturday night, when do we perform *Bi'ur Ḥametz*?

Because of the sanctity of the Shabbat, the *Bi'ur Ḥametz* ritual is completed on Friday morning.

INNOVATIONS

Some families save the *aravot* (willows) from the *lulav* of *Sukkot* to use as fuel for the fire of *Bi'ur Ḥametz*, again linking the *Sukkot* festival to *Pesaḥ*.

EIRUV TAVSHILIN

CONCEPTS

TWO CATEGORIES OF WORK

In Jewish law, there are different categories of *melakhah* (work) permitted on Shabbat and on *Yom Tov*. On Shabbat, no work is permitted and all preparations for the celebration of the holiday must be done before the day begins. On *Yom Tov* (a Festival such as *Pesaḥ*), categories of work which are prohibited on Shabbat are also restricted, with the exception of work which enables the Festival to be fully celebrated, such as preparing food, transferring a fire, and carrying. Specifically, on *Pesaḥ* it is permissible to cook (as long as the food is for that day's consumption) and use a fire.

1. כָּל חֲמִירָא וַחֲמִיעָא דְּאִכָּא בִרְשׁוּתִי
2. דַּחֲמִיתֵּהּ וּדְלָא חֲמִיתֵּהּ,
3. דְּבַעֲרְתֵּהּ וּדְלָא בַעֲרְתֵּהּ,
4. לִבְטִיל וְלֶהֱוֵי הֶפְקֵר
5. כְּעַפְרָא דְאַרְעָא.

Actually, the problem exists with the rule prohibiting the preparation of food on a *Yom Tov* for another day. When Passover is celebrated immediately before Shabbat, we may not prepare food on *Yom Tov* for consumption on Shabbat unless the preparation of the Shabbat food is symbolically started *before* the beginning of the *Yom Tov*.

AN *EIRUV* OF COOKED FOODS

The term "*eiruv*" refers to the process of setting apart a space or a period of time. The "*Eiruv Tavshilin*," literally "setting aside cooked food," is a legal device for reconciling two valid, conflicting claims: the enjoyment of Shabbat to its fullest and the prohibition against preparing food on one holiday for eating on the next. By setting aside some cooked food and *matzah* before *Pesaḥ* begins, and reciting the *Eiruv Tavshilin* formula, we establish that the process of preparing food for the Shabbat to come has begun, and thus, we can continue its preparation throughout the *Yom Tov*. This preparation includes all the things permissible during a *Yom Tov*, including baking, cooking, keeping dishes warm, etc.

OBJECTS

A cooked dish (e.g., a hard-cooked egg) and a piece of *matzah*.

PRACTICE

Put the cooked food and *matzah* on a plate, set it aside, and recite the *Eiruv Tavshilin* blessing and formula before Passover begins. This "meal" is kept intact throughout Passover until after Shabbat begins.

TEXT

You can find the text of the *Eiruv Tavshilin* ceremony at the beginning of most traditional *Haggadot*, including the Rabbinical Assembly *Haggadah*.

30

PREPARING THE SEDER TABLE

The day of the Seder is maddening. The plumbing breaks. The oven dies. I mean, everything seems to go wrong. But, it's also a good day, because your family is around. I look forward to it. I mean, it's a very busy day, it's hectic. But when you all sit down that night at the Seder table, there is a feeling of accomplishment, a feeling, you know, that it's all worthwhile. You're tired, but it's a special kind of feeling.

Marlene Horwitz

Miriam Prum I remember the first time I gave a Seder, I was a wreck. I mean, I kept saying to myself, "Can I really pull this off? Is it going to be good?" I still get nervous to some degree.

Judy Miller: It's the people that make a Seder great. I mean, you can cook and clean for weeks, and Lou can sit here and make notes and prepare whatever he wants to prepare, but if you don't have the right people...

Lou Miller: You've got to get everyone involved, to participate, to ask questions.

Mark Horwitz: I don't think it's a good day. No matter what Mother says about the post-pride of what she's accomplished, during the day she is like a chicken with her head cut off. People are running around like crazy... I mean, it's not fun. You've gotta do chores; you've gotta do this and that... Yeah, when you sit down, it's nice—but I wouldn't say it's a nice day.

Your Author (to Barry Horwitz): How many times do you go to the store?

Barry Horwitz: I can't count that high.

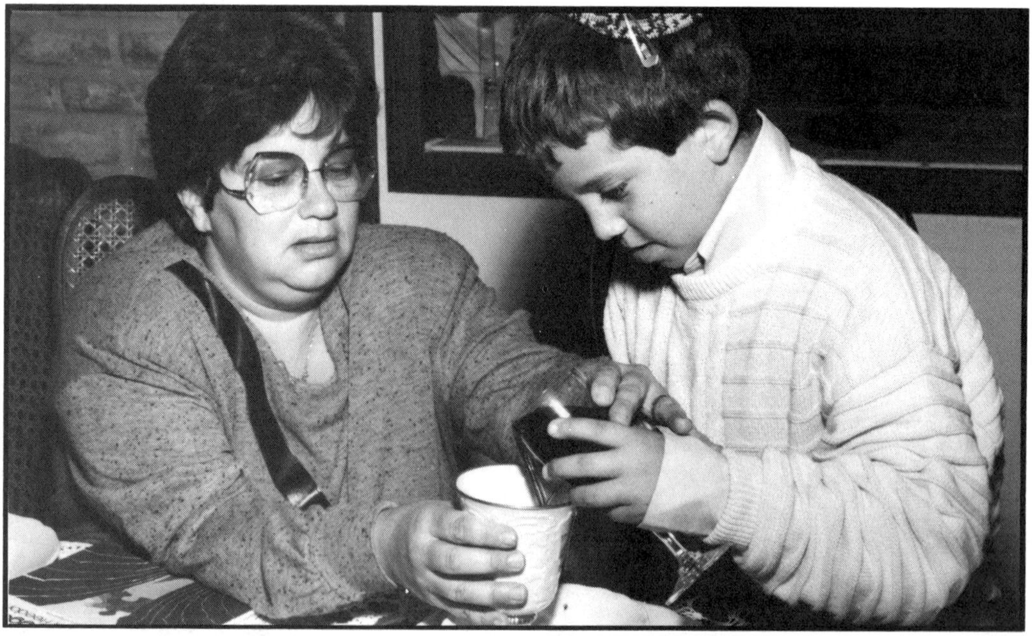

THE SEDER PLATE

The idea of the Seder Plate, the *K'arah*, is recent. A special plate is not mentioned in the Mishnah's account of the Seder, nor in the commentary on the Mishnah, the *Gemara*. In a commentary written around the year 1000, there is some mention of a basket into which all the symbolic foods were put. In fact, many Sephardic communities still use a basket for the Seder objects. The plate itself is probably an innovation of about the 5th century C.E.

The first actual description of how the plate should be arranged comes from a commentator named The Maharil. His arrangement became the standard which we still follow:

BAYTZAH **Z'ROAH**

MAROR

KARPAS **ḤAROSET**

ḤAZERET

Notice that two triangles can be deciphered. The top triangle (*Baytzah, Z'roah, Maror*) contains symbols that are known as "*mid'arytah*," literally "from the Torah," biblically ordained symbols. The bottom triangle (*Karpas, Ḥaroset, Ḥazeret*) consist of three symbols which are "*mid'rabanan*," literally, "from the rabbis," stipulated by the rabbis as they developed the form of the Seder ritual.

Let's examine each symbolic food—what it symbolizes, how it is used, and how it is prepared.

Z'ROAH

CONCEPT

The *Z'roah* represents the paschal lamb sacrificed by Jews from the time of the Exodus itself until the destruction of the Second Temple in 70 C.E. In biblical and Temple times, Jews made a pilgrimage to Jerusalem in order to slaughter a lamb as a sacrifice to God. There are historical indications that this sacrifice of a lamb was a very ancient rite, predating the Exodus. But, when the Exodus occurred, the historical memory of the people linked the idea of redemption to this sacrifice. When the Temple was constructed, the actual sacrifice itself was moved from individual family altars to the religious center in Jerusalem. Each family brought a lamb to the courtyard of the Temple, where the *Kohanim* (Priests) officiated and the *Levi'im* (Levites) sang praises to God, including the ancient verses of the *Hallel*. Each family took the slaughtered lamb back to their home where it was roasted whole and immediately eaten. There were to be no leftovers and no broken bones (the custom of poor people was to eat the marrow of broken bones). Once the Temple was destroyed, animal sacrifices came to an abrupt end. It was up to the rabbis to create a symbol as a reminder of these paschal sacrifices, and they chose the *Z'roah*.

Z'roah actually means "arm," a reference to the "outstretched arm" of God who saved the Israelites at the Reed Sea (see Deuteronomy 26:8).

OBJECT

The *Z'roah* is the shank bone of the lamb. The shank bone is the lower leg of the lamb. It is roasted or charred under a broiler, just as the ancient sacrifice was roasted. If a lamb shank bone is not available, a chicken leg (drumstick) can be used. Some vegetarians substitute a raw beet.

PRACTICE

The *Z'roah* is strictly a symbolic food. It is not eaten at the Seder. In fact, it is not even pointed at when described during the section of the Seder known as *Rabban Gamliel Hayah Omer*. The caution against using or pointing to the *Z'roah* is to avoid even the slightest indication that it is possible to engage in ritual sacrifice today. Without the Holy Temple, this is impossible.

It is a custom not to eat any roasted meat at the Seder meal, lest people think you are engaging in the now-prohibited sacrifices. Many Jews will not serve any roasted meat, certainly not lamb. Another view is that eating roasted meat may mean you are not motivated to return to Jerusalem to rebuild the Temple and reinstate the sacrificial system so that you will be able to eat roasted meat.

BAYTZAH

CONCEPTS

The *Baytzah*, a roasted hard-cooked egg, is the symbol of the *Ḥagigah* sacrifice in ancient times. There were a number of sacrifices brought in the Temple. We have just learned about the paschal sacrifice, unique to the Passover celebration. On each major pilgrimage Festival (*Sukkot*, *Pesaḥ*, and *Shavuot*), a special sacrifice was brought to celebrate the "*Ḥag*," the Festival. This sacrifice was known as the "*Ḥagigah*" sacrifice. Usually a lamb, the *Ḥagigah* generally functioned to provide enough food at the Festival for everyone at the table.

Why is a roasted egg chosen as the symbol of the *Ḥagigah* sacrifice? Many ideas have been suggested. The egg is the symbol of creation—birth and re-birth—the circularity of life. We see this when the egg is the food given to those who suffer a loss—the first food to be eaten by the mourner on returning home from graveside. Some even suggest that the egg may represent the future resurrection of the dead—the egg appears to be dead, but suddenly a chick pops out and starts the life cycle once again.

Why is the egg hard-cooked? This is to symbolize the hardness of the oppression in Egypt. It also suggests the Jewish people, who, it is said, like the egg, become harder and stronger as the pressure increases. For all the evils of the generations of oppression endured by Jews, it has often brought us closer together as a people than ever before.

OBJECT

The *Baytzah* is created by hard-boiling any size egg and then roasting it under the broiler. Here's how to prepare the *Baytzah*:

a. Boil an egg until it is hard, at least five minutes. Some boil the egg along with a tea bag or the skin of an onion which turns the egg a brownish color.
b. Puncture both ends of the egg with a peeler, the tip of a knife, or a needle. This relieves the built-up pressure inside the shell so it will not explode when it is roasted.
c. Place the egg on a broiler pan underneath the broiler. Roast it until at least one portion of the shell is brown.
d. Do not remove the shell. Place the whole egg on the Seder plate.

PRACTICE

The *Baytzah*, like the *Z'roah*, is strictly a symbolic food on the Seder plate. It is not eaten at the Seder. True, many eat hard-cooked eggs at the beginning of the meal, but not the *Baytzah* from the Seder plate, since it symbolizes the *Ḥagigah* sacrifice which we can no longer bring.

Interestingly, there is no reference to the *Baytzah* in the *Haggadah* itself. This is probably because the more general *Ḥagigah* sacrifice which it represents was not central to the celebration of Passover after the destruction of the Temple. It was certainly not as important as remembering the particular paschal sacrifice which was central to *Pesaḥ*.

MAROR

CONCEPT

Maror symbolizes the bitterness of the slavery in Egypt. In our attempt to simulate the conditions of Egypt, we taste the bitter herbs and remember.

Scholars have suggested that the first mention of *maror* in the Bible (Exodus 12:8), "and with bitter herbs they shall eat it (the paschal sacrifice)," may echo a previously established tradition among semi-nomadic shepherds who celebrated a pre-Exodus ritual lambing festival which featured exactly the same prescriptions as the Exodus night ceremony. This primitive seasonal rite consisted of sacrificing a perfect, unblemished animal, offered in exchange for the protection of the herd, a meal eaten in haste, and unfermented bread. At some point, the practice of eating certain plants was added to ensure ritual purity and to scare off evil demons believed to lurk in this season. We do not know the exact names of these plants; they were so well known to the people of the Bible that the simple designation "*maror*" was sufficient.

The practice of eating bitter herbs was codified in the Mishnah with specific plants listed: "These are the vegetables with which one fulfills the obligations on Passover: *ḥazeret, olshin, tamḥa, ḥarḥavina, maror*... (*Pesaḥim* 2:6)." Botanists have concluded that *ḥazeret* is compass lettuce (*Lactuca serriola*), *olshin* is chicory (*Cichorium pumilum Jac.*), *tamḥa* is sowthistle (*Sonchus oleraceus L.*), *ḥarḥavina* is eryngo (*Eryngium creticum*), and *maror* itself is centary (*Centaurea sp.*). Although these plants are known throughout the world, their growth cycle is different in the Middle East and therein lies the secret to understanding the symbolism of *maror*.

These bitter herb plants typically break through the earth in late fall or early winter. Then, the tender leaves of the plants are gathered and eaten in salads. But by Passover time, the five bitter herbs have changed dramatically—both in appearance, and more significantly, in taste. In the center of each plant, a stalk emerges which sprouts very small, very bitter herbs. These leaves are the *maror* which the Mishnah requires us to eat, leaves (read: lives) of our ancestors in Egypt which began as sweet but which became bitter in time.

Another interpretation of *maror* is taught by Zalman Schachter-Shalomi, a modern mystic and teacher, who points out that the root word of "*maror*" is "*mar*"—teacher. The *maror* teaches us that pain is sometimes purposeful. Like an alarm, a pain can be a warning of something amiss. Each of us experiences *Mitzrayim* in a variety of ways. The *maror* of *Pesaḥ*, like the *shofar* of *Rosh Hashanah*, comes to warn us, to teach us to learn from the bitterness which life hands us and to move on, ever on the road out of our personal *Mitzrayim*.

OBJECT

The food used for *maror* is, of necessity, a substitute for the actual "*m'rorim*" discussed in the Torah and Mishnah. Exiled from the lands where the native bitter herbs grow, Jews found only bitter lettuce, *ḥazeret*, available in the early spring. For the remnant left in Palestine and for the Sephardim living in southern climes, romaine lettuce became the *maror* of the Seder, the stalk being quite bitter to the taste. For Ashkenazim in the colder northern areas of Europe, lettuce was not always available and horseradish root, a dependable, indestructible plant became a popular substitute for *maror*. Today, either vegetable is acceptable for use as *maror* at the Seder. Many families use uncooked, unadulterated-with-beets, grated or slivered horseradish for *maror*, reserving romaine lettuce as the *ḥazeret* used in making the Hillel sandwich of *Korekh*.

PRACTICE

The ceremony of eating *maror* is described at that point in our explanation of the Seder. If you are using romaine lettuce, be sure the stalks and leaves are thoroughly cleaned. If horseradish is the choice, you can purchase kosher for *Pesaḥ* prepared horseradish or you can be adventurous and prepare your own.

Buy a piece of horseradish root in the produce section of your supermarket. Choose one that is especially hard and free of soft spots. If necessary, store the fresh root by wrapping it in a slightly dampened towel, then a dry one.

Here is Jerry Weber's No Fail Method of Preparing *Maror*:

JERRY WEBER'S HORSERADISH RECIPE

You'll need:

- Raw horseradish root
- salt
- sugar
- water
- Food Processor

Here's how:

"Peel the horseradish. Cut into small pieces and throw into a food processor. Process until your eyes tear. Add a little salt, a little sugar and a little water. That's it."

ḤAROSET

CONCEPTS

ANOTHER DIALECTICAL SYMBOL

Ḥaroset, like *matzah*, is a dialectical symbol, representing opposite ideas. On the one hand, *ḥaroset* (probably derived from the word "*ḥeres*" meaning "clay") is a reminder of the mortar with which the Israelite slaves made bricks during the days of bondage—a symbol of slavery. On the other hand, *ḥaroset* itself is made of sweet foods—wine, fruits, nuts, honey, and spices—and its purpose at the Seder table is to somewhat blunt the effect of the *maror*, the bitter herbs. Its sweetness is a symbol of God's kindness which made the bitterness of slavery easier to bear. We dip the *maror* into the *ḥaroset*, both symbols of bondage, yet the sweetness of the *ḥaroset* takes the edge off the bitterness of the herbs.

PRACTICE

Ḥaroset is also one of the few ritual items at the Seder which has no blessing. Why? Unlike *matzah* and *maror* which are commanded in the Torah, *ḥaroset* is a creation of the rabbis and, as such, does not require a specific blessing. Since it is also integral to the *maror* ritual, *ḥaroset* is not a separate obligation at the Seder, and thus, the blessing for *maror* encompasses it.

Ḥaroset, clearly the favorite symbolic food for most children and many adults at the Seder, is made from a wide variety of recipes. The basic ingredients of the most common type are chopped apples, chopped walnuts, sugar or honey, red wine, and spices, usually cinnamon. *Ḥaroset* is one of the few Passover symbols which lends itself to influence from the different cultures in which Jews lived. Ashkenazic *Ḥaroset* tends to be quite liquid in texture, heavy on the wine. Sephardic *Ḥaroset*, on the other hand, is more mortar-like in texture—there is usually no wine in the recipe.

The variations are endless, but here are two basic *ḥaroset* recipes:

ASHKENAZIC *ḤAROSET*

You'll need:

Apples (peeled and cored, then chopped or grated)
Nuts (chopped or ground)
Sweet red wine
Honey or sugar
Cinnamon

Here's how:

Combine equal amounts of apples and nuts. Add enough honey and wine to make a paste-like mixture. Season with ground cinnamon to taste. Make as much as you'll need for the Seder. Plan on a good sized bowl—this is a favorite!

SEPHARDIC *ḤAROSET*

Rica Sabah shared with us her version of Sepahrdic *Ḥaroset.* It contains dates and nuts, with apples and raisins for moisture:

You'll need:

1 lb. pitted dates
1/2 lb. shelled walnuts
1/2 lb. shelled almonds
1/2 lb. hazelnuts
1/2 cup white raisins
1 apple

Here's how:

Chop nuts until fine in food processor. Save nuts in bowl. Chop dates and raisins, a few at a time. Add nuts and continue chopping. Add slices of apple. Continue chopping until consistency of paste.

The use of these fruits by the Sephardim has been traced to verses in the Song of Songs, a book of the Bible read on the Shabbat of Passover:

Nuts: "I went down to the nut grove" (6:11)

Dates: "Let me climb the palm" (7:9)

Apples: "Under the apple tree I roused you" (8:5)

KARPAS

CONCEPTS

The meaning of *Karpas* is discussed when it is used in the Seder.

OBJECTS

Karpas can be any vegetable for which the blessing "*borei p'ri ha-adamah*" is recited, but traditionally, it is a green leafy vegetable such as parsley. Celery is also a good choice, and some families use radishes. Jews in the cold climates of Eastern Europe and Russia where green leafy vegetables did not appear before *Pesaḥ* used boiled potatoes for *Karpas*.

If your decision is to use parsley, choose several large, fresh bunches, clean thoroughly, and place in a plastic bag in the refrigerator before serving. If you cut a quarter inch off the stems and stand it up in a jar with a little water in the bottom, the parsley will get somewhat crisper. Try not to put the parsley on the table until the last minute; it wilts very quickly.

PRACTICE

The ritual use of *Karpas* is explained when it is used in the Seder.

ḤAZERET

CONCEPTS

Ḥazeret is a second version of bitter herbs. The rabbis speak of *ḥazeret* as the *maror* to be used in creating the Hillel sandwich of *Korekh*. Hillel's custom was to combine (*korekh*) *maror* and *matzah* together in a kind of sandwich (*ḥaroset* is considered optional). *Ḥazeret* is a type of bitter herb, again recalling the bitterness of the slavery in Egypt.

OBJECTS

Ḥazeret is most likely a type of bitter lettuce. Many families use the stalks of romaine lettuce for *ḥazeret*. Others use chopped, grated or prepared horseradish. Depending on what you use for *maror*, use something different for *ḥazeret* if a place for it exists on your Seder plate. Combinations could be:

MAROR	ḤAZERET
horseradish root	lettuce
prepared horseradish	lettuce
lettuce	grated horseradish root

Generally, whole horseradish root is not used for *ḥazeret*.

PRACTICE

Ḥazeret is used as the *maror* for the *Korekh* step of the Seder when making the Hillel sandwich. Place some *ḥazeret* (and *ḥaroset*, if you wish) between two pieces of the bottom *matzah* to create your version of the sandwich. There is no specific blessing for either *ḥazeret* or *Korekh*, simply a description of Hillel's practice at his Seder.

THREE MATZOT

CONCEPTS

We have discussed the concept of *matzah* at length in the chapter on *Matzah*.

OBJECTS

Three *matzot* are required for the ceremonies of the Seder. Some families set aside a fourth *matzah*, known as "The *Matzah* of Hope," a symbolic *matzah* dedicated to Jews who are still enslaved in countries which do not allow freedom of religion, particularly the Soviet Union. These *matzot* can be regular machine-made *matzot*, but many families try to acquire the special *matzah shmura* for ceremonial purposes. These *matzot* may not be egg *matzah*.

PRACTICE

Although not on the top of the Seder plate itself, the three ceremonial *matzot* are stacked one on top of the other and are wrapped in a napkin, placed in a special *matzah* cover consisting of three pockets, or inserted into skirted trays which make up the base of some Seder plates. In any case, the *matzot* need to be covered and uncovered as the Seder progresses, whenever a cup of wine is blessed.

A HELPFUL HINT

Since the leader and the few people seated next to him/her are the only participants at the table who have immediate access to the foods on the Seder plate itself, some families prepare miniature Seder plates at each setting. This saves a great deal of time otherwise spent passing bowls and plates of the various items. It can also act as a kind of appetizer plate for the children.

Each of these plates should hold portions of *karpas*, *maror*, *ḥaroset*, and perhaps a hard-boiled egg and a tiny cup of salt water. Put the *ḥaroset* and *maror* into small one-ounce souffle cups to reduce the mess of juices running together. It is not necessary to add a *z'roah* to these individual plates.

SETTING THE TABLE

Setting a beautiful Seder table is a goal many families strive for to enhance the celebration of Passover in the home. Yet, the rabbis were sensitive to the fact that throughout the generations there would be families who would not have the money to acquire elaborate ritual items. This explains the rather remarkable fact that the simplest plate can act as a Seder plate; a plain glass can be used as a Cup of Elijah.

Nevertheless, many families, even those of modest means, acquired the most beautiful Seder ritual objects they could. These items were often the most valuable property the family owned, and their use on *Pesaḥ* was anxiously awaited.

To spur this practice on, the rabbis also created the concept of ***hiddur mitzvah***, the embellishment of a commandment. They encouraged families to acquire the most beautiful ritual objects they could afford and to take other measures to enhance the celebration of the basic *mitzvah*. Thus, in addition to lovely ritual items, many families embellish the table with fresh flowers; fine china, silver, and crystal, a white tablecloth, even new clothes—in order to make the holiday celebration extra special.

Here are some tips for setting the Seder table:

a. COUNT how many people you need to seat, including everyone.
b. DECIDE how many tables and chairs you will need. Determine where they will come from if you don't have enough (It is a long-standing tradition to ask guests "can you bring four folding chairs?"). If you have to borrow or rent tables and chairs, be sure to do it well in advance of the Seder.
c. DETERMINE where the tables will be set. Many families cannot seat everyone in the dining room and furniture must be re-arranged to accomodate everyone.
d. Once the tables and chairs are arranged, SET THE TABLE.

SEDER TABLE ITEMS CHECKLIST

1. CANDLESTICKS: A minimum of two candlesticks is required.
2. CANDLES: Candles for *Yom Tov* are like those for Shabbat. They should be long enough to last at least 3-4 hours. Utility candles or long tapers are fine. White is the preferred, though not required, color.
3. *KIPPOT*: *Kippot* (skullcaps) should be provided for all males and for those females who may wish to wear one.
4. WHITE TABLECLOTH. Traditionally, this is the color of the evening. You may want to cover it with clear plastic to save it from the inevitable wine spills.
5. PLACE SETTINGS, one for each person.
6. FLOWERS or other centerpiece to brighten the table.
7. PLACECARDS, to avoid fighting over who sits where and to ensure that you have set enough places! (There is nothing more embarrassing than to sit down to a Seder table and find you have miscounted and one place is missing.)
8. SEDER CARDS, a wonderful idea for helping participants follow the order of the ceremony. Prepare an index card with the 15 steps of the Seder ("*Kadesh, Urḥatz*") to place at each table setting. Another idea is to prepare a large sheet of butcher paper or poster board with a list of the Seder steps for the leader to point to as the ceremony unfolds.

9. WINE CUPS: A wine cup for each person is required. Some place saucers under the cups to catch the spills.
10. CUP OF ELIJAH: This special cup reserved for Elijah (the Fifth Cup) should be the most beautiful cup in the home. Any material will do, and many special cups are designed just for this purpose in crystal, china, or silver.
11. WINE: And plenty of it. You will need enough for each person to fill four or five cups. According to strict interpretations of Jewish law, each cup should contain at least 3.3 fluid ounces. Have plenty of grape juice on hand as a substitute for the children and anyone who cannot drink wine. Traditionally, red sweet wine is the choice of the evening, but recent advances in *kosher l'Pesaḥ* wine-making allow for a variety of excellent wines to be served.
12. *MATZAH*: A minimum of three whole *matzot* is required for ceremonial purposes. Platters of *matzah* should be available around the table, enough for everyone to have at least one *matzah*.

    There are two choices for *matzah* at the Seder: *matzah shmura* (guarded *matzah*) or machine-made plain *matzah*. Egg *matzah* cannot be used for ritual purposes at the Seder. (See "Selecting *Matzah*" section for details on the differences between the kinds of *matzah*).

13. *MATZAH* COVER: The three ceremonial *matzot* are covered when other ritual objects are used at various points during the Seder. Special *matzah* covers are available with three compartments sown into the material. Any napkin can fulfill this need just as well.
14. *AFIKOMEN* HOLDER: A special cover or napkin for holding the piece of the middle *matzah* which serves as the *afikomen*. Again, beautifully embroidered *afikomen* holders are available for this purpose, but any napkin will do.
15. SALT WATER: Although not a formal part of the traditional Seder plate, a bowl of *mei melaḥ*—salt water—should be set near the Seder plate for the dipping of *Karpas* (and the hard-boiled egg of the meal, if it is your custom). Set several small bowls of salt water around the table for your guests to use, or place a small paper cup of salt water at each person's plate.
16. *HAGGADOT*: Have enough *Haggadot* so that each person at the table can have one. Uniform *Haggadot* are preferable.

17. WATER PITCHER, BASIN AND TOWEL: Have a full pitcher of water, a catch basin, and a towel available for the washing of the hands. If everyone will be invited to wash, you may need several set-ups depending on the number of guests.
18. HARD-BOILED EGGS: It is customary in some families to begin the meal with a hard-boiled egg dipped in salt water. Have a bowl of eggs available for this purpose.
19. PILLOWS: Since it is commanded that we recline at the Seder table, it is traditional to have a pillow set in the left side of each chair, although in some families, only the leader has a pillow. See Susie Wolfson's *Pesaḥ* Pillow Placecard idea in the Workbook.
20. SEDER PLATE: The ceremonial Seder plate is usually a specially-designed ornamental plate with five or six demarcated spaces for the symbolic foods. However, any plate is acceptable for use as the Seder plate. On the plate should be the following items:
    a. *Z'ROAH*—a roasted shank bone of a lamb or a roasted chicken leg.
    b. *BAYTZAH*—a roasted hard-cooked egg.
    c. *MAROR*—a piece of horseradish root, grated horseradish, or a stalk of romaine lettuce.
    d. *KARPAS*—a vegetable, usually parsley, celery or boiled potato.
    e. *ḤAROSET*—a mixture of fruit, nuts, honey, wine and spices.

    OPTIONAL:

    f. *ḤAZERET*—a stalk of lettuce or grated horseradish.

    The *Karpas, Ḥaroset,* and (optional) *Ḥazeret* are actually used from the Seder plate; the *Baytzah* and *Z'roah* are not touched. Nearby or underneath the Seder plate should be placed three ceremonial *matzot*: a top, a middle and a bottom *matzah*.

SEDER TIPS

1. Let the children help in preparing the foods for the Seder. They will love making *ḥaroset*, shelling nuts, decorating white pillowcases for the reclining pillows, creating placecards for the table, making salt water, even doing some baking.
2. Have several choices of wine on the table. Refilling the four cups goes more quickly and guests appreciate having a choice of wines.

With the availability of up-scale, gourmet wine selections (Weinstock, Hagafen, etc.), your Seder can become something of a wine-tasting affair.

3. Floral centerpieces are lovely on the Seder table. But, remember to keep them below eye level so they don't become obstacles to the conversation around the table. See Susie's Seder Centerpiece for a creative alternative to flowers in the Workbook.
4. Let guests and family help with the serving and clearing of courses during the meal. People will be anxious to help. Let them. But, you will want to organize this process in some way.
5. Use paper plates for miniature Seder plates at each setting or for the first course. This will speed your clearing of appetizers and facilitate the serving of the meal.
6. Many families serve the main course buffet-style rather than passing platters which can be quite difficult in cramped quarters.
7. Be sure to check signals with the Seder leader as the Seder progresses to gauge when the meal is about to be served.
8. Set the Seder table early. If you have changed your kitchen early, you can get a head start on setting the table. Put a light sheet over it to keep it free of dust and *ḥametz.*

SECOND SEDER TIPS

If you are conducting both *Sedarim*, here are some tips:

1. Make each Seder different. Several families we spoke to who conduct two *Sedarim* told us that hosting both evenings allows them the freedom to structure each for different purposes.
2. Invite different guests. One of the concerns most often spoken is finding the right mix of people to invite to the Seder. If you have family who are not particularly interested in a fairly traditional Seder, have them one night for a Seder which is more abbreviated. Then, invite guests who you think would enjoy a more analytical Seder the next night. The Millers call this their "Super Seder." Miriam Prum has one Seder for friends and one for family.
3. Try new things at your second Seder. Look upon this evening as one of experimentation. Try new readings, different songs, any number of the Innovations we have suggested in this text.
4. Change things based on the experience of the first Seder. If you tried things that didn't go well the first night, here's your chance to change.
5. Even if you are not giving the second Seder, but are attending someone else's second Seder, bring with you insights heard at the first Seder. A good deal of teaching can go on if there is sharing of what the participants collectively learned the night before.

31

AFTER PESAḤ

Ending *Pesaḥ* is a breeze compared to setting up for it. Putting the stuff in boxes is easy.

Linda Fife

There are a number of interesting traditions with regard to ending the Passover festival. Many families have favorite ways to "break *Pesaḥ*," to end the Passover dietary restrictions imposed throughout the holiday. Usually, these involve eating foods with high grain content, such as pizza, pasta, and bread.

On a more serious note, the Sephardic communities developed a number of interesting traditions which are still observed in their home countries and in Israel. The Moroccan community celebrates an end-of-*Pesaḥ* ritual called "*Maimuna*." The term is derived from the Hebrew "*emunah*," and the celebration is a combination "breaking *Pesaḥ*" and rejoicing over the new spring harvest.

Rica Sabah recalls a tradition on the last night of *Pesaḥ* that everyone would take in hand several stalks of wheat and symbolically beat each other with them, while simultaneously offering a greeting in Arabic: "*santak hadra*," "May you have a (literally: "green") fruitful year!" The ceremony is called "*Leil Ḥametz*"—"Night of *Ḥametz*". It highlights the fact that raw new wheat may now be eaten and expresses the hope for a year of plentiful produce.

AFTER *PESAḤ*

Well-organized *Pesaḥ*-makers prepare for next year's celebration at the end of this year's holiday. Consider this list of steps which, if done this year, can make next year's preparations much easier:

1. **Make a list of Passover leftovers.** Usually families find that they have not eaten all the *matzah*, salad dressings, ketchup, gefilte fish, macaroons, and assorted Passover foodstuffs they purchased for the just-finished holiday. Many of these products can be saved for use at Passover time the following year. Most canned goods and boxed foods that are unopened can be saved. DO NOT SAVE ANYTHING THAT HAS BEEN OPENED. Some families do not save any Passover foods for that length of time, preferring fresh-baked *matzot* (look for the ubiquitous label "Baked for Passover 57——) and other goods. Create a list of the foods you are saving as you place them in a storage cabinet or box destined for *Pesaḥ* utensil storage in your home.
2. **Label the *Pesaḥ* utensil boxes.** This takes a little extra time and effort, but it saves a lot of guesswork next year ("Where did I put the *Pesaḥdik* can opener?"). As you put the Passover items into storage boxes, create a list of contents. Don't forget to make separate boxes for utensils used for meat, dairy and pareve foods.
3. **Make a list of items that need replacing.** Inevitably, glasses break, silverware disappears, and you discover that the cheap can opener you bought is no match for a can of macaroons. Create a list of items you will need to replace next year, as well as a list of things you would like to have—a blender, a wine corkscrew, a new dishwasher (just kidding! Okay, we're not kidding.)
4. **Make a list of food items you used in bulk.** Take note of any shortages you experienced ("need more ketchup") or anything you overbought ("too much *matzah*"). This will help you gauge your shopping list next year.
5. **Create a Passover Notebook.** Use a loose-leaf, three-ring binder to save all the lists listed above, plus menus used for the *Sedarim*, recipes, guest lists, your Passover shopping list, any tips you want to remember, your Seder preparation materials, any hand-outs used at the Seder. You will find that when *Pesaḥ* comes around again, this notebook may be extremely valuable, saving you a great deal of time in next year's preparations for the holiday.

SELECTED BIBLIOGRAPHY

HAGGADAH TEXTS

There are dozens of *Haggadah* editions available and new ones seem to appear every year. There are four basic types of *Haggadah* texts: 1) those for use at the Seder table, 2) those whose commentaries provide excellent material to supplement your Seder experience, 3) those that are primarly art books, and 4) those written with a particular point of view. Here are some of the best we have found in each category:

HAGGADOT FOR TABLE USE

Passover Haggadah: The Feast of Freedom, edited by Rachel Anne Rabinowicz, The Rabbinical Assembly of America, New York, 1982.

The Conservative Movement's official *Haggadah* text, widely called the "RA *Haggadah*." Lucid translation of the traditional texts, beautiful graphics, and excellent commentaries make this a fine choice for a table text.

The Passover Haggadah, compiled by Rabbi Morris Silverman. Newly revised edition with transliterations edited by Jonathan D. Levine, The Prayer Book Press, Media Judaica, Inc., 1987.

A popular version of the text, the "Silverman *Haggadah*" is easy-to-follow, with good directions and instructive commentaries. The added transliterations make it attractive for families where there is little Hebrew fluency.

A Passover Haggadah: The New Union Haggadah, edited by Herbert Bronstein, drawings by Leonard Baskin, Central Conference of American Rabbis, New York, revised edition, 1985.

The Reform Movement's official *Haggadah*, known as the "Baskin *Haggadah*" or the "Union *Haggadah*." Stunning illustrations and a superb layout characterize this text, shaped by the ideology of the Reform Movement.

The Passover Seder: Pathways Through the Haggadah, arranged by Rabbi Arthur Gilbert, augmented by Florence Zeldin, edited by Patricia Singer Golden, KTAV Publishing House, Hoboken, N.J., 1985.

A basic text for beginners with clear instructions.

HAGGADOT WITH COMMENTARIES

The Family Haggadah, edited by Rabbi Nossom Scherman, Mesorah Publications Ltd, 1981.

Known as the "Art Scroll *Haggadah*," this traditional text of the *Haggadah* features extensive commentaries written from an Orthodox perspective.

The New Haggadah, edited by Mordecai M. Kaplan, Eugene Kohn, and Ira Eisenstein, Jewish Reconstructionist Foundation/Behrman House, NY, revised edition, 1978.

"Kaplan's *Haggadah*," this text reflects the ideology of the Reconstructionist Movement.

The Passover Haggadah, edited by Adin Steinsaltz, Carta Publishers, Jerusalem, 1983.

This traditional text is enhanced with perceptive commentaries by one of the leading Talmudists of our time. Yes, it is called the "Steinsaltz *Haggadah*."

The Passover Haggadah—Legends and Customs, Rabbi Menachem Hacohen, Adama Books, 1987.

A beautiful compilation of traditional texts, commentaries, and art.

HAGGADOT AS ART

The Polychrome Historical Haggadah for Passover, edited by Jacob Freedman, D.D., Court Square Press, Inc., Boston, MA, 1974.

The Copenhagen Haggadah—1739, First Facsmilie Edition, introduction by Chaya Benjamin, Rizzoli Publishers, NY.

The Sarajevo Haggadah, text by Cecil Roth, Izdavacki Zavod "Yugoslavia," Beograd, Nemanjina 34, 1975.

Haggadah Shel Pesach, illustrated by Arthur Szyk, edited by Cecil Roth, Massada Press, Jerusalem, 1980. Known as the "Szyk (pronounced 'Shick') *Hagggadah*."

HAGGADOT WITH A PARTICULAR POINT OF VIEW

Haggadah for the Liberated Lamb, Roberta Kalechofsky, Micah Publications, 255 Humphrey Street, Marblehead, MA, 01945, 1985.

A *Haggadah* for vegetarians.

The Shalom Seders, compiled by the New Jewish Agenda, introduction by Arthur Waskow, Adama Books, 306 W. 38th St., NY, NY, 10018, 1984.

A *Haggadah* (actually three) for those who lean to the left.

San Diego Women's Haggadah, Second Edition, Women's Institute for Continuing Jewish Education, 4079 54th St., San Diego, CA, 92105, 1986.

A feminist *Haggadah*.

RESOURCE BOOKS

Many books have been written about Passover and the Seder. Here are a few of the most useful:

The Passover Anthology, Philip Goodman, Jewish Publication Society of America, New York, 1973.

The first, and still one of the best, compilations of information about Passover.

A Feast of History, Chaim Raphael, Gallery Books, 112 Madison Avenue, NY, NY, 10016, 1972.

An excellent historical survey of the Passover Seder.

Seasons of Our Joy: A Handbook of Jewish Festivals, Arthur Waskow, Summit Books, New York, 1982.

A superb guidebook by one of the leading Jewish spiritualists of the past two decades.

The Jewish Festivals, Michael Strassfeld, Jewish Publication Society of America, Philadelphia, 1985.

A fine survey of Passover by one of the authors of *The Jewish Catalogue.*

Living the Jewish Way: Observing Jewish Holidays, Irving Greenberg, Summit Books, New York, 1988.

How to Run a Traditional Jewish Household, Blu Greenberg, Simon and Schuster, New York, 1983.

A wonderful guide to creating a home filled with Jewish observance.

PASSOVER RESOURCES FOR CHILDREN AND FAMILIES

Mah Nishtana? A Passover Haggadah for Children, Shai Publishers, P.O.B. 45075, Tel Aviv, Israel, 1985.

Lovely illustrated *Haggadah* text with linear Hebrew and English transliterations.

A Family Haggadah, Shoshana Silberman, Kar Ben Copies, Inc., Rockville, MD, 1987.

Designed for the family with young children, this text offers some terrific ideas for Seder celebration. An audiotape, "Songs for the Family Seder," by Cantor Robert Freedman, is available in conjunction with the book.

The Feast of Freedom Coloring Book, Rachel Anne Rabinowicz, The Rabbinical Assembly, New York, 1984.

The New Model Seder for School and Home, edited by Rabbi Sidney Greenberg and S. Allan Sugarman, The Prayer Book Press of Media Judaica, Inc., 1986.

A fine basic text geared for families with children.

My Very Own Haggadah, Judyth Robbins Saypol and Madeline Wikler, Kar Ben Copies, Inc, Rockville, MD, 1983.

A *Haggadah* for pre-schoolers.

The Animated Haggadah, a videotape produced by The Gesher Foundation, available from Scopus Films, 150 5th Avenue, Suite 1102, N.Y., N.Y., 10011, 1985.

A delightful story of a Passover Seder featuring claymation figures. A story book is also available.

The Joy of Passover, a videotape by Institute for Creative Jewish Media, 1987, P.O. Box 426, West Simsbury, CT. 06092.

A fine overview of the Seder ritual.

Only Nine Chairs: A Tall Tale for Passover, Deborah Uchill Miller, Kar Ben Copies, Inc., Rockville, MD, 1982.

The all-time favorite read-aloud book at Passover time.

The Carp in the Bathtub, Barbara Cohen, Kar Ben Copies, Inc., Rockville, MD, 1972.

The delightful Passover equivalent of "we can't kill the pet turkey for Thanksgiving," only this time it's a fish.

We Tell It To Our Children: A Haggadah for Seders with Young Children, Mary Ann Barrows Wark, Mt. Zion Hebrew Congregation Rabbi's Publication Fund and Mary Ann Barrows Wark, 1588 Northrop Street, St. Paul, MN, 55108, 1988.

A unique puppet *Haggadah* Seder for very young children, featuring song parodies and puppets that tell the Exodus story.

Passover, Malka Drucker, Holiday House, New York, 1981.

A Picture Book of Passover, David A. Adler, Holiday House, NY, 1982.

An introduction to Passover for elementary school children.

Ask Another Question, Miriam Chainkin, Clarion Books, New York, 1985.

Together: Passover, Melton Research Center, 3080 Broadway, New York, 10027, 1985.

A booklet of parent-child activities for Passover learning.

Building Jewish Life: Passover, Joel Lurie Grishaver, Torah Aura Productions, 4423 Fruitland Avenue, Los Angeles, CA, 90058, 1988.

A parent-child read aloud resource for grades 1-3.

Building Jewish Life: Passover Activity Book, Torah Aura Productions, 1988.

A reading and activity book for grades K-1.

My Exodus, a video tape by Torah Aura Productions, 1985.

Six children tell their own stories of the Exodus from Egypt.

PASSOVER COOKBOOKS

Matzah Meals, Judy Tabs and Barbara Steinberg, Kar Ben Copies, Inc., Rockville, MD., 1985.

A Passover cookbook for kids.

The Passover Gourmet, Nira Rousso, Adama Books, New York, 1987.

The Complete Passover Cookbook, Frances R. Avrutick, Jonathan David Publishers, Inc., Middle Village, NY, 11379, 1987.

Check your local Jewish bookstore or synagogue gift shop for the constantly changing array of Passover cookbooks published by Sisterhoods, schools, and individuals.

AFTERWORD

Ḥasal siddur Pesaḥ—we have completed our journey through the Passover . We have described the steps to prepare for the holiday. Now, it is up to you to enact the "art" of Jewish living by painting your own composition of Passover in your home.

We wish you *Yasher Koaḥ*, "may you be strengthened," to continue the work you have begun by learning about *Pesaḥ*, to continue to "make *Pesaḥ*" in your family, and to continue to explore the many avenues of Passover celebration.

As you do, please share with us your experiences in creating *Pesaḥ*. Of all the Jewish holidays, Passover is perhaps the one holiday that most invites creativity in expression. We would love to hear about your family traditions, both new and old, so that we may share them in future editions of this volume and the Workbook which accompanies it.

Please send your comments and ideas to:
Dr. Ron Wolfson
University of Judaism
15600 Mulholland Drive
Los Angeles, CA 90077

Thanks and *Ḥag Sameaḥ v'Kasher!*

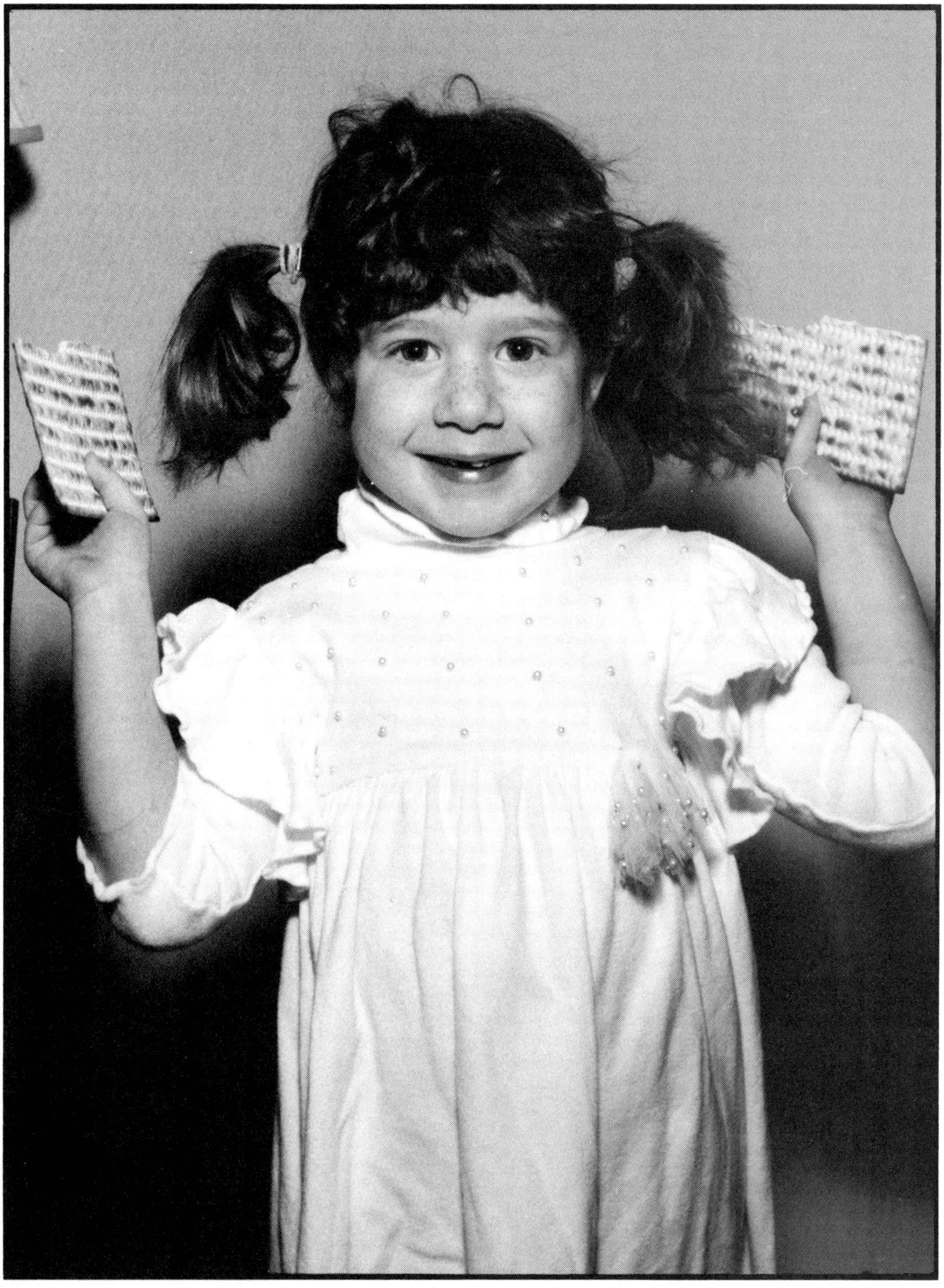

Ideas for Our Seder

Ideas for Our Seder

Ideas for Our Seder

Ideas for Our Seder

Ideas for Our Seder

About JEWISH LIGHTS Publishing

People of all faiths and backgrounds yearn for books that attract, engage, educate and spiritually inspire.

Our principal goal is to stimulate thought and help all people learn about who the Jewish People are, where they come from, and what the future can be made to hold. While people of our diverse Jewish heritage are the primary audience, our books speak to people in the Christian world as well and will broaden their understanding of Judaism and the roots of their own faith.

We bring to you authors who are at the forefront of spiritual thought and experience. While each has something different to say, they all say it in a voice that you can hear.

Our books are designed to welcome you and then to engage, stimulate and inspire. We judge our success not only by whether or not our books are beautiful and commercially successful, but by whether or not they make a difference in your life.

About
The Federation of Jewish Men's Clubs

The Federation of Jewish Men's Clubs works to improve the quality of Jewish life, to enhance Conservative Jewish identity locally and world wide, to strengthen and build Men's Clubs, and to support and encourage family education, leadership training, and social and community activities.

Founded in 1929, The Federation of Jewish Men's Clubs represents Men's Clubs and Brotherhoods in Conservative congregations throughout North America. Current programs focus on:

Remembering those who perished in the Holocaust through the Yom HaShoah Yellow Candle Program™;

Sensitizing high school students to the dangers of messianic churches;

Teaching Jewish skills, such as synagogue Hebrew (through the Hebrew Literacy Campaign), holiday observance (through the Art of Jewish Living Series), comforting the mourner (through *A Time to Mourn, A Time to Comfort*), the meaning and history of the *pidyon haben* ritual, having a Jewish housewarming (including a brief service of putting up a mezzuzah), teaching people how to pray based on the maariv service, advice to parents in dual-faith families, and how to participate in the Torah Service (videotape);

Training synagogue and Men's Club leaders to serve their clubs, congregations, and communities more effectively.

THE FEDERATION OF JEWISH MEN'S CLUBS

Art of Jewish Living Series

THE PASSOVER SEDER

by *Dr. Ron Wolfson*

Explains the concepts behind Passover ritual and ceremony in clear, easy-to-understand language, and offers step-by-step procedures for Passover observance and preparing the home for the holiday.

Easy-to-Follow Format: Using an innovative photo-documentary technique, real families describe in vivid images their own experiences with the Passover holiday. Representing the diversity of Jewish life—families with young children, families with teenagers, Jews by Choice, empty-nesters, single parents, singles, Ashkenazim and Sephardim—their stories bring to life the thrill and challenge of fashioning a joyful and rewarding family Passover.

Easy-to-Read Hebrew Texts: The Haggadah texts in Hebrew, English, and transliteration are presented in a three-column format designed to help celebrants learn the meaning of the prayers and how to read them, whether they can read the original or must depend on transliterations.

An Abundance of Useful Information: A detailed description of the procedures involved in performing rituals is included, along with a section of practical questions and answers. "Innovations" offers imaginative ideas and customs for Seder celebration.

"A creative 'how-to' for making the Seder a more meaningful experience."
—*Michael Strassfeld, co-author of* The Jewish Catalog

7 x 9, 336 pp. Quality Paperback, ISBN 1-879045-93-1 **$16.95**

Also available are these helpful companions to *The Passover Seder:*

•Passover Workbook	ISBN 1-879045-94-X $6.95
•Audiocassette of the Blessings	DNO4 $6.00
•Teacher's Guide	ISBN 1-879045-95-8 $4.95

HANUKKAH

by *Dr. Ron Wolfson*

Edited by *Joel Lurie Grishaver*

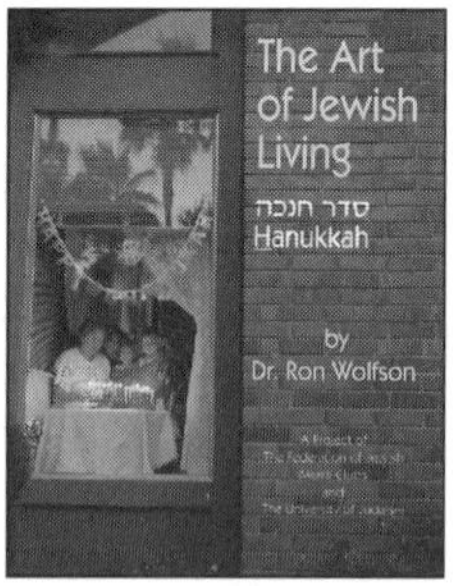

Designed to help celebrate and enrich the holiday season, *Hanukkah* discusses the holiday's origins, explores the reasons for the Hanukkah candles and customs, and provides everything from recipes to family activities.

There are songs in English, Hebrew, and Yiddish (with clear transliterations), recipes for Hanukkah foods—particularly all sorts of luscious latkes—useful information on the arts and crafts of Hanukkah, the calendar and its relationship to Christmas time, and games played at Hanukkah. Putting the holiday in a larger, timely context, "December Dilemmas" deals with ways in which a Jewish family can cope with Christmas.

Throughout the book, representative Jewish families explain their customs and ideas about observing Hanukkah, while vividly expressing their personal feelings about the holiday.

"This book is helpful for the family that strives to induct its members into the spirituality and joys of Jewishness and Judaism...a significant text in the neglected art of Jewish family education."
—*Rabbi Harold M. Schulweis, Congregation Valley Beth Shalom, Encino, Calif.*

7 x 9, 192 pp. Quality Paperback, ISBN 1-879045-97-4 **$16.95**

THE FEDERATION OF JEWISH MEN'S CLUBS

Art of Jewish Living Series

THE SHABBAT SEDER

by *Dr. Ron Wolfson*

The Shabbat Seder is a concise step-by-step guide designed to teach people the meaning and importance of this weekly celebration, as well as its practices. The activities of the Friday evening ritual are set out in a straightforward, simple way, along with instructions on how to perform them, and the information is presented through an exploration of the Shabbat ceremonies of real families representing a cross section of modern Jewish life.

Each chapter corresponds to one of ten steps which together comprise the Shabbat dinner ritual, and looks at the *concepts, objects,* and *meanings* behind the specific activity or ritual act. *The Shabbat Seder* is designed in a unique, easy-to-read format for people with varying degrees of Hebrew skills; the blessings that accompany the meal are written in both Hebrew and English, and accompanied by English transliteration. Also included are a question and answer section and a "Shabbat Gallery" offering craft projects, recipes, discussion ideas and other creative suggestions for enriching the Shabbat experience.

"A how-to book in the best sense...."

—*Dr. David Lieber, President, University of Judaism, Los Angeles*

7 x 9, 272 pp. Quality Paperback, ISBN 1-879045-90-7 **$16.95**

Also available are these helpful companions to *The Shabbat Seder*:

•Booklet of the Blessings and Songs	ISBN 1-879045-91-5	$5.00
•Audiocassette of the Blessings	DNO3	$6.00
•Teacher's Guide	ISBN 1-879045-92-3	$4.95

A TIME TO MOURN, A TIME TO COMFORT

A Guide to Jewish Bereavement and Comfort

by *Dr. Ron Wolfson*

A guide to meeting the needs of those who mourn and those who seek to provide comfort in times of sadness. While this book is written from a layperson's point of view, it also includes the specifics for funeral preparations and practical guidance for preparing the home and family to sit *shiva*.

Advice is given for attending a Jewish funeral, how to help during *shiva*, what to say to the mourners, and what to write in a condolence letter. Special sections deal with specific situations of modern life, including deaths from AIDS, helping young children grieve and understand *shiva*, and mourning the death of an infant or child.

"A sensitive and perceptive guide to Jewish tradition. Both those who mourn and those who comfort will find it a map to accompany them through the whirlwind."

—*Deborah E. Lipstadt, Emory University*

"Speaks in many voices: the voices of those who have endured grief, the voices of rabbis who deal daily with tragedy, the voices of those who are spiritually searching, and the voices of those who have found their own path through dark times."

—*Dr. David J. Wolpe, author of* Healer of Shattered Hearts

7 x 9, 320 pp. Quality Paperback, ISBN 1-879045-96-6 **$16.95**

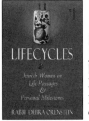

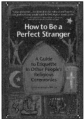

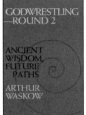

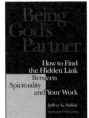

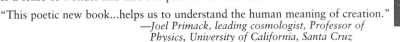

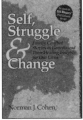

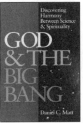

Add Greater Understanding to Your Life

JEWISH LIGHTS Classic Reprints

TORMENTED MASTER
The Life and Spiritual Quest of Rabbi Nahman of Bratslav

by *Arthur Green*

Explores the personality and religious quest of Nahman of Bratslav (1772–1810), one of Hasidism's major figures. It unlocks the great themes of spiritual searching that make him a figure of universal religious importance.

6" x 9", 408 pp. Quality Paperback, ISBN 1-879045-11-7 **$17.95**

YOUR WORD IS FIRE
The Hasidic Masters on Contemplative Prayer

Edited and translated with a new introduction by *Arthur Green* and *Barry W. Holtz*

The power of prayer for spiritual renewal and personal transformation is at the core of all religious traditions. From the teachings of the Hasidic Masters the editors have gleaned "hints as to the various rungs of inner prayer and how they are attained." These parables and aphorisms of the Hasidic masters pierce to the heart of the modern reader's search for God.

6" x 9", 152 pp. Quality Paperback, ISBN 1-879045-25-7 $**14.95**

THE EARTH IS THE LORD'S
The Inner World of the Jew in Eastern Europe

by *Abraham Joshua Heschel*

Powerfully and beautifully portrays a bygone Jewish culture.

"Re-creates the mind and character of a whole people and of an entire era. Not only Jews, but all who regard the culture of the inner life as important will find this book moving and meaningful."

—Virginia Kirkus

5.5" x 8", 128 pp. Quality Paperback, ISBN 1-879045-42-7 **$12.95**

A PASSION FOR TRUTH
by *Abraham Joshua Heschel*

In his final book, completed a few weeks before his death, one of the most beloved religious leaders of our time gives us a personal exploration of the tension between despair and hope in Hasidism and of how great religious teachers of tradition affect and shape our own personal spirituality.

5.5" x 8", 352 pp. Quality Paperback, ISBN 1-879045-41-9 **$18.95**

THEOLOGY & PHILOSOPHY...Other books:

Israel: An Echo of Eternity
by Abraham Joshua Heschel

5.5 x 8, 272 pp, Quality Paperback, ISBN 1-879045-70-2 **$18.95**

Aspects of Rabbinic Theology
by Solomon Schechter

6 x 9, 440 pp, Quality Paperback, ISBN 1-879045-24-9 **$18.95**

The Last Trial: On the Legends and Lore of the Command to Abraham to Offer Isaac as a Sacrifice
by Shalom Spiegel

6 x 9, 208 pp, Quality Paperback, ISBN 1-879045-29-X **$17.95**

Add Greater Meaning to Your Life

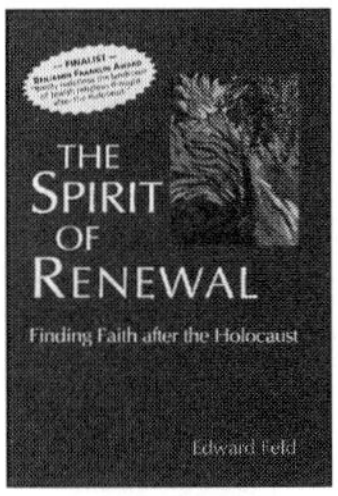

• Award Winner •

THE SPIRIT OF RENEWAL
Finding Faith After the Holocaust

by *Edward Feld*

"Boldly redefines the landscape of Jewish religious thought after the Holocaust."
—Rabbi Lawrence Kushner

Trying to understand the Holocaust and addressing the question of faith after the Holocaust, Rabbi Feld explores three key cycles of destruction and recovery in Jewish history, each of which radically reshaped Jewish understanding of God, people, and the world.

"A profound meditation on Jewish history [and the Holocaust]....Christians, as well as many others, need to share in this story."
—The Rt. Rev. Frederick H. Borsch, Ph.D., Episcopal Bishop of L.A.

6" x 9", 224 pp. Quality Paperback, ISBN 1-879045-40-0 **$16.95** HC, ISBN-06-0 **$22.95**

•Award Winner•

SEEKING THE PATH TO LIFE
Theological Meditations On God and the Nature of People, Love, Life and Death

by *Rabbi Ira F. Stone*

For people who never thought they would read a book of theology—let alone understand it, enjoy it, savor it and have it affect the way they think about their lives. In 45 intense meditations, each a page or two in length, Stone takes us on explorations of the most basic human struggles: Life and death, love and anger, peace and war, covenant and exile.

"A bold book....The reader of any faith will be inspired, challenged and led more deeply into their own encounter with God."
— The Rev. Carla V. Berkedal, Episcopal Priest, Executive Director of Earth Ministry

6" x 9", 132 pp. Quality Paperback, ISBN 1-879045-47-8 **$14.95**
Hardcover, ISBN 1-879045-17-6 **$19.95**

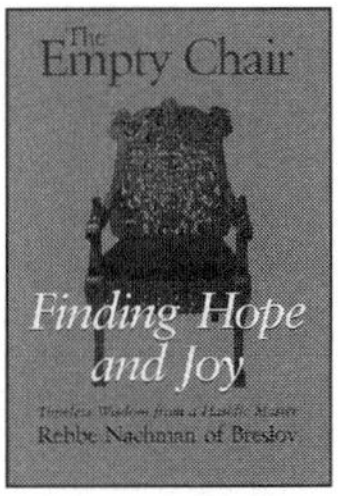

THE EMPTY CHAIR: FINDING HOPE & JOY
Timeless Wisdom from a Hasidic Master, Rebbe Nachman of Breslov

Adapted by *Moshe Mykoff* and *The Breslov Research Institute*

A "little treasure" of aphorisms and advice for living joyously and spiritually today, written 200 years ago, but startlingly fresh in meaning and use. Challenges and helps us to move from stress and sadness to hope and joy.

Teacher, guide and spiritual master—Rebbe Nachman provides vital words of inspiration and wisdom for life today for people of any faith, or of no faith.

"For anyone of any faith, this is a book of healing and wholeness, of being alive!"
—Bookviews

4" x 6", 128 pp. Deluxe Paperback, 2-color text, ISBN 1-879045-67-2 **$9.95**

FINDING JOY
A Practical Spiritual Guide to Happiness

by *Dannel I. Schwartz* with *Mark Hass*

Searching for happiness in our modern world of stress and struggle is common; *finding* it is more unusual. This guide explores and explains how to find joy through a time-honored, creative—and surprisingly practical—approach based on the teachings of Jewish mysticism.

6" x 9", 192 pp. Hardcover, ISBN 1-879045-53-2 **$19.95**

Motivation and Inspiration for Recovery

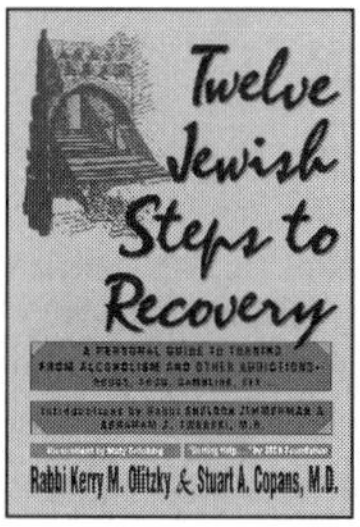

TWELVE JEWISH STEPS TO RECOVERY
A Personal Guide To Turning From Alcoholism & Other Addictions...Drugs, Food, Gambling, Sex

by *Rabbi Kerry M. Olitzky & Stuart A. Copans, M.D.*
Preface by *Abraham J. Twerski, M.D.*
Introduction by *Rabbi Sheldon Zimmerman*
Illustrations by *Maty Grünberg*
"Getting Help" by *JACS Foundation*

A Jewish perspective on the Twelve Steps of addiction recovery programs with consolation, inspiration and motivation for recovery. It draws from traditional sources, and quotes from what recovering Jewish people say about their experiences with addictions of all kinds. Inspiring illustrations of the twelve gates of the Old City of Jerusalem.

Experts Praise *Twelve Jewish Steps to Recovery*

"Recommended reading for people of all denominations."
— *Rabbi Abraham J. Twerski, M.D.*

"I read *Twelve Jewish Steps* with the eyes of a Christian and came away renewed in my heart. I felt like I had visited my Jewish roots. These authors have deep knowledge of recovery as viewed by Alcoholics Anonymous."
— *Rock J. Stack, M.A., L.L.D. Manager of Clinical/Pastoral Education, Hazelden Foundation*

"This book is the first aimed directly at helping the addicted person and family. Everyone affected or interested should read it."
— *Sheila B. Blume, M.D., C.A.C., Medical Director, Alcoholism, Chemical Dependency and Compulsive Gambling Programs, South Oaks Hospital, Amityville, NY*

Readers Praise *Twelve Jewish Steps to Recovery*

"A God-send. Literally. A book from the higher power." —New York, NY

"Looking forward to using it in my practice." —Michigan City, IN

"Made me feel as though Twelve Steps were for me, too." —Long Beach, CA

"Excellent—changed my life." —Elkhart Lake, WI

6" x 9", 136 pp. Quality Paperback, ISBN 1-879045-09-5 **$13.95** HC, ISBN -08-7 **$19.95**

RECOVERY FROM CODEPENDENCE
A Jewish Twelve Steps Guide to Healing Your Soul

by *Rabbi Kerry M. Olitzky*
Foreword by *Marc Galanter, M.D., Director, Division of Alcoholism & Drug Abuse, NYU Medical Center*
Afterword by *Harriet Rossetto, Director, Gateways Beit T'shuvah*

For the estimated 90% of America struggling with the addiction of a family member or loved one, or involved in a dysfunctional family or relationship. A follow-up to the groundbreaking *Twelve Jewish Steps to Recovery.*

"The disease of chemical dependency is also a family illness. Rabbi Olitzky offers spiritual hope and support."
—*Jerry Spicer, President, Hazelden*

"Another major step forward in finding the sources and resources of healing, both physical and spiritual, in our tradition."
—*Rabbi Sheldon Zimmerman, President, Hebrew Union College-Jewish Institute of Religion*

6" x 9", 160 pp. Quality Paperback Original, ISBN 1-879045-32-X **$13.95**
HC, ISBN -27-3 **$21.95**

Motivation and Inspiration for Recovery

RENEWED EACH DAY
Daily Twelve Step Recovery Meditations Based on the Bible

by *Rabbi Kerry M. Olitzky* & *Aaron Z.*

VOLUME I: Genesis & Exodus
Introduction by *Rabbi Michael A. Signer*
Afterword by *JACS Foundation*

VOLUME II: Leviticus, Numbers & Deuteronomy
Introduction by *Sharon M. Strassfeld*
Afterword by *Rabbi Harold M. Schulweis*

Using a seven day/weekly guide format, a recovering person and a spiritual leader who is reaching out to addicted people reflect on the traditional weekly Bible reading. They bring strong spiritual support for daily living and recovery from addictions of all kinds: Alcohol, drugs, eating, gambling and sex. A profound sense of the religious spirit soars through their words and brings all people in Twelve Step recovery programs home to a rich and spiritually enlightening tradition.

"Meets a vital need; it offers a chance for people turning from alcoholism and addiction to renew their spirits and draw upon the Jewish tradition to guide and enrich their lives."
—*Rabbi Irving (Yitz) Greenberg, President, CLAL, The National Jewish Center for Learning and Leadership*

"Will benefit anyone familiar with a 'religion of the Book.' Jews, Christians, Muslims..."
—*Ernest Kurtz, author of* Not God: A History of Alcoholics Anonymous & The Spirituality of Imperfection

"An enduring impact upon the faith community as it seeks to blend the wisdom of the ages represented in the tradition with the Twelve Steps to recovery and wholeness."
—*Robert H. Albers, Ph.D., Editor,* Journal of Ministry in Addiction & Recovery

Beautiful Two-Volume Slipcased Set

6" x 9", V. I, 224 pp. / V. II, 280 pp. Quality Paperback Original,
ISBN 1-879045-21-4 **$27.90**

ONE HUNDRED BLESSINGS EVERY DAY
Daily Twelve Step Recovery Affirmations, Exercises for Personal Growth & Renewal Reflecting Seasons of the Jewish Year

by *Dr. Kerry M. Olitzky*
with selected meditations prepared by *Rabbi James Stone Goodman, Danny Siegel,* and *Rabbi Gordon Tucker*
Foreword by *Rabbi Neil Gillman, The Jewish Theological Seminary of America*
Afterword by *Dr. Jay Holder, Director, Exodus Treatment Center*

Recovery is a conscious choice from moment to moment, day in and day out. In this helpful and healing book of daily recovery meditations, Rabbi Olitzky gives us words to live by day after day, throughout the annual cycle of holiday observances and special Sabbaths of the Jewish calendar.

For those facing the struggles of daily living, *One Hundred Blessings Every Day* brings solace and hope to anyone who is open to healing and to the recovery-oriented teachings that can be gleaned from the Bible and Jewish tradition.

4.5" x 6.5", 432 pp. Quality Paperback Original, ISBN 1-879045-30-3 **$14.95**

Spiritual Inspiration for Daily Living...

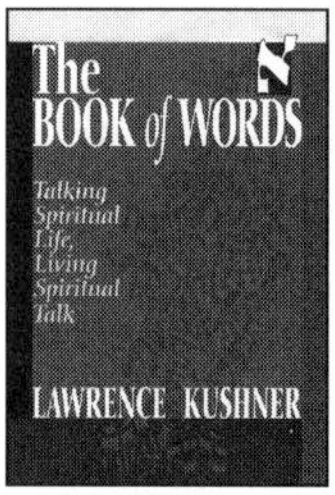

THE BOOK OF WORDS
Talking Spiritual Life, Living Spiritual Talk
by *Lawrence Kushner*

In the incomparable manner of his extraordinary *The Book of Letters: A Mystical Hebrew Alphabet*, Kushner now lifts up and shakes the dust off primary religious words we use to describe the spiritual dimension of life. The *Words* take on renewed spiritual significance, adding power and focus to the lives we live every day.

For each word Kushner offers us a startling, moving and insightful explication, and pointed readings from classical Jewish sources that further illuminate the concept. He concludes with a short exercise that helps unite the spirit of the word with our actions in the world.

"This is a powerful and holy book."
—*M. Scott Peck, M.D., author of* The Road Less Traveled *and other books*

"What a delightful wholeness of intellectual vigor and meditative playfulness, and all in a tone of gentleness that speaks to this gentile."
—*Rt. Rev. Krister Stendahl, formerly Dean, Harvard Divinity School/Bishop of Stockholm*

6" x 9", 152 pp. Hardcover, beautiful two-color text ISBN 1-879045-35-4 **$21.95**

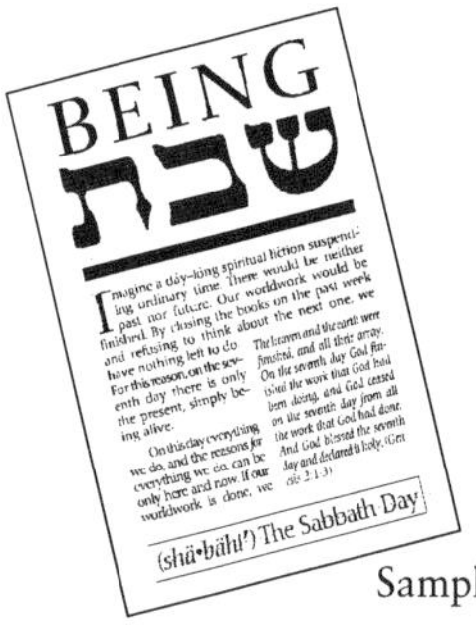

Sample pages from *The Book of Words*

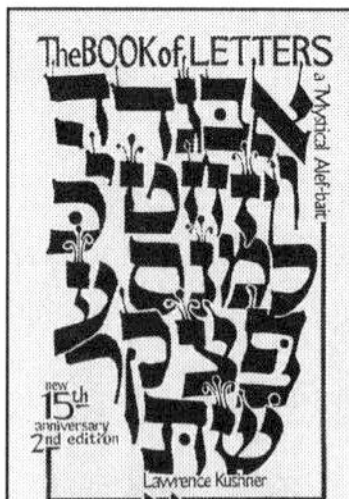

•Award Winner•

THE BOOK OF LETTERS
A Mystical Hebrew Alphabet
by *Rabbi Lawrence Kushner*

In calligraphy by the author. Folktales about and exploration of the mystical meanings of the Hebrew Alphabet. Open the old prayerbook-like pages of *The Book of Letters* and you will enter a special world of sacred tradition and religious feeling. More than just symbols, all twenty-two letters of the Hebrew alphabet overflow with meanings and personalities of their own.

Rabbi Kushner draws from ancient Judaic sources, weaving Talmudic commentary, Hasidic folktales, and Kabbalistic mysteries around the letters.

"A book which is in love with Jewish letters."
— *Isaac Bashevis Singer* ז״ל

• Popular Hardcover Edition
6"x 9", 80 pp. Hardcover, two colors, inspiring new Foreword.
ISBN 1-879045-00-1 **$24.95**

• Deluxe Gift Edition
9"x 12", 80 pp. Hardcover, four-color text, ornamentation, in a beautiful slipcase.
ISBN 1-879045-01-X **$79.95**

• Collector's Limited Edition
9"x 12", 80 pp. Hardcover, gold embossed pages, hand assembled slipcase. With silkscreened print.
Limited to 500 signed and numbered copies.
ISBN 1-879045-04-4 **$349.00**
To see a sample page at no obligation, call us

....The Kushner Series

GOD WAS IN THIS PLACE & I, i DID NOT KNOW
Finding Self, Spirituality & Ultimate Meaning

Who am I? Who is God? Kushner creates inspiring interpretations of Jacob's dream in Genesis, opening a window into Jewish spirituality for people of all faiths and backgrounds.

In this fascinating blend of scholarship, imagination, psychology and history, seven Jewish spiritual masters ask and answer fundamental questions of human experience.

"Rich and intriguing."

—*M. Scott Peck, M.D., author of* The Road Less Traveled *and other books*

6" x 9", 192 pp. Quality Paperback, ISBN 1-879045-33-8 **$16.95** HC, ISBN -05-2 **$21.95**

HONEY FROM THE ROCK

"Quite simply the easiest introduction to Jewish mysticism you can read."

An introduction to the ten gates of Jewish mysticism and how it applies to daily life.

"Captures the flavor and spark of Jewish mysticism. . . . Read it and be rewarded."

—*Elie Wiesel*

"A work of love, lyrical beauty, and prophetic insight. "

—*Father Malcolm Boyd,* The Christian Century

6" x 9", 168 pp. Quality Paperback, ISBN 1-879045-02-8 **$14.95**

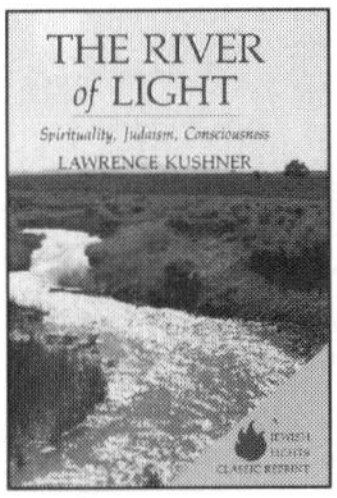

THE RIVER OF LIGHT
Spirituality, Judaism, Consciousness

A "manual" for all spiritual travelers who would attempt a spiritual journey in our times. Taking us step by step, Kushner allows us to discover the meaning of our own quest: "to allow the river of light—the deepest currents of consciousness—to rise to the surface and animate our lives."

"Philosophy and mystical fantasy...exhilarating speculative flights launched from the Bible....Anybody—Jewish, Christian, or otherwise...will find this book an intriguing experience."

—*The Kirkus Reviews*

6" x 9", 180 pp. Quality Paperback, ISBN 1-879045-03-6 **$14.95**

INVISIBLE LINES OF CONNECTION
Sacred Stories of the Ordinary

Through his everyday encounters with family, friends, colleagues and strangers, Kushner takes us deeply into our lives, finding flashes of spiritual insight in the process. This is a book where literature meets spirituality, where the sacred meets the ordinary, and, above all, where people of all faiths, all backgrounds can meet one another and themselves.

"Does something both more and different than instruct—it inspirits. Wonderful stories, from the best storyteller I know."

— *David Mamet*

"A wonderful collection of stories charmingly told by a gifted storyteller."

— Booklist (*American Library Association*)

5.5" x 8.5", 160 pp. Hardcover, ISBN 1-879045-52-4 **$21.95**

Spiritual Inspiration for Family Life

MOURNING & MITZVAH

• With over 60 guided exercises •

A Guided Journal for Walking the Mourner's Path Through Grief to Healing

by *Anne Brener, L.C. S.W.;* Foreword by *Rabbi Jack Riemer;* Introduction by *Rabbi William Cutter*

"Fully engaging in mourning means you will be a different person than before you began." For those who mourn a death, for those who would help them, for those who face a loss of any kind, Brener teaches us the power and strength available to us in the fully experienced mourning process. Guided writing exercises help stimulate the processes of both conscious and unconscious healing.

"A stunning book! It offers an exploration in depth of the place where psychology and religious ritual intersect, and the name of that place is Truth."
—*Rabbi Harold Kushner, author of* When Bad Things Happen to Good People

7 1/2" x 9", 288 pp. Quality Paperback Original, ISBN 1-879045-23-0 **$19.95**

WHEN A GRANDPARENT DIES

A Kid's Own Remembering Workbook for Dealing with Shiva and the Year Beyond

by *Nechama Liss-Levinson, Ph.D.*

Drawing insights from both psychology and Jewish tradition, this workbook helps children participate in the process of mourning, offering guided exercises, rituals, and places to write, draw, list, create and express their feelings.

"Will bring support, guidance, and understanding for countless children, teachers, and health professionals."
—*Rabbi Earl A. Grollman, D.D., author of* Talking about Death

8" x 10", 48 pp. Hardcover, illus., 2-color text, ISBN 1-879045-44-3 **$14.95**

HEALING OF SOUL, HEALING OF BODY

Spiritual Leaders Unfold the Strength and Solace in Psalms

Edited by *Rabbi Simkha Y. Weintraub, CSW, for The Jewish Healing Center*

A source of solace for those who are facing illness, as well as those who care for them. The ten Psalms which form the core of this healing resource were originally selected 200 years ago by Rabbi Nachman of Breslov as a "complete remedy." Today, for anyone coping with illness, they continue to provide a wellspring of strength. Each Psalm is newly translated, making it clear and accessible, and each one is introduced by an eminent rabbi, men and women reflecting different movements and backgrounds. To all who are living with the pain and uncertainty of illness, this spiritual resource offers an anchor of spiritual comfort.

"Will bring comfort to anyone fortunate enough to read it. This gentle book is a luminous gem of wisdom."
—*Larry Dossey, M.D., author of* Healing Words: The Power of Prayer & the Practice of Medicine

6" x 9", 128 pp. Quality Paperback Original, illus., 2-color text, ISBN 1-879045-31-1 **$14.95**

SO THAT YOUR VALUES LIVE ON

Ethical Wills & How To Prepare Them

Edited by *Rabbi Jack Riemer & Professor Nathaniel Stampfer*

A cherished Jewish tradition, ethical wills—parents writing to children or grandparents to grandchildren—sum up what people have learned and express what they want most for, and from, their loved ones. Includes an intensive guide, **"How to Write Your Own Ethical Will,"** and a topical index. A marvelous treasury of wills: Herzl, Sholom Aleichem, Israelis, Holocaust victims, contemporary American Jews.

"While the book is written from a Jewish viewpoint, its principles can easily be adapted by people of other faiths."
—*The Los Angeles Times*

6" x 9", 272 pp. Quality Paperback, ISBN 1-879045-34-6 **$17.95**

Spiritual Inspiration for Family Life

THE NEW JEWISH BABY BOOK
Names, Ceremonies, Customs—A Guide for Today's Families

by *Anita Diamant*

A complete guide to the customs and rituals for welcoming a new child to the world and into the Jewish community, and for commemorating this joyous event in family life—whatever your family constellation. Includes new ceremonies for girls, celebrations in interfaith families, and more.

"A book that all Jewish parents—no matter how religious—will find fascinating as well as useful. It is a perfect shower or new baby gift."
— *Pamela Abrams, Exec. Editor,* Parents Magazine

6" x 9", 328 pp. Quality Paperback Original, ISBN 1-879045-28-1 **$16.95**

BEST RELIGION BOOK OF THE YEAR

PUTTING GOD ON THE GUEST LIST

•AWARD WINNER•

How to Reclaim the Spiritual Meaning of Your Child's Bar or Bat Mitzvah

by *Rabbi Jeffrey K. Salkin*

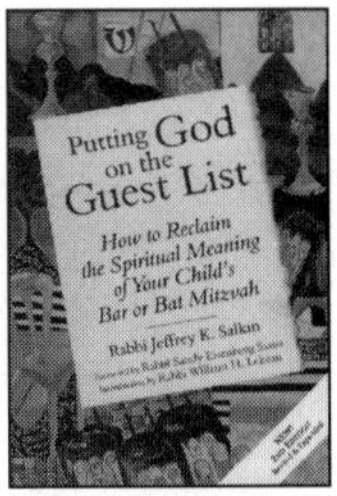

Joining explanation, instruction and inspiration, helps parent and child truly *be there* when the moment of Sinai is recreated in their lives. Asks and answers such fundamental questions as how did Bar and Bat Mitzvah originate? What is the lasting significance of the event? How to make the event more spiritually meaningful? New 2nd Edition.

"I hope every family planning a Bar Mitzvah celebration reads Rabbi Salkin's book." — *Rabbi Harold S. Kushner, author of* When Bad Things Happen to Good People

New! 2nd Ed.

6" x 9", 224 pp. Quality Paperback, ISBN 1-879045-59-1 **$16.95** HC, ISBN -58-3 **$24.95**

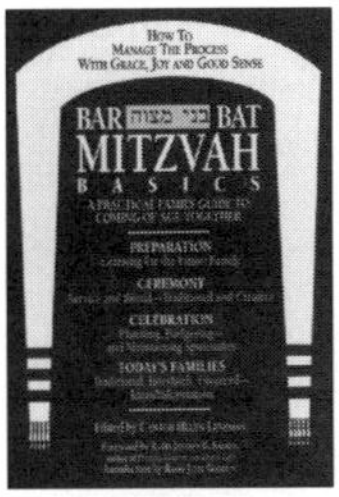

BAR/BAT MITZVAH BASICS
A Practical Family Guide to Coming of Age Together

Edited by *Cantor Helen Leneman;* Foreword by *Rabbi Jeffrey K. Salkin, author of* Putting God on the Guest List*;* Intro. by *Rabbi Julie Gordon*

A practical guide that gives parents and teens the "how-to" information they need to navigate the bar/bat mitzvah process and grow as a family through this experience. For the first time in one book, everyone directly involved offers practical insights into how the process can be made easier and more enjoyable for all. Rabbis, cantors and Jewish educators from the Reform, Conservative and Reconstructionist movements, parents, and even teens speak from their own experience.

"Out of her vast experience as Cantor and educator, Leneman has written an important guide that strengthens and solidifies the family through the wisdom and warmth of Judaism."
—*Rabbi Harold Schulweis, Valley Beth Shalom, Encino, California*

6" x 9", 240 pp. Quality Paperback, ISBN 1-879045-54-0 **$16.95** HC, ISBN -51-6 **$24.95**

EMBRACING THE COVENANT
Converts to Judaism Talk About Why & How

Edited & with Introductions by *Rabbi Allan L. Berkowitz* and *Patti Moskovitz*

This book is a practical and inspirational companion to the conversion process for Jews-by-Choice and their families. Written primarily for the person considering the choice of Judaism, it provides highly personal insights from over 50 people who have made this life-changing decision. But it also will speak to their families—the non-Jewish family that provided his or her spiritual beginnings and the Jewish "family" which receives the convert—and help them understand why the decision was made.

"Passionate, thoughtful and deeply-felt personal stories....A wonderful resource, sure to light the way for many who choose to follow the same path."
—*Dru Greenwood, MSW, Director, UAHC-CCAR Commission on Reform Jewish Outreach*

6" x 9", 192 pp. Quality Paperback, ISBN 1-879045-50-8 **$15.95**

Children's

BUT GOD REMEMBERED
Stories of Women from Creation to the Promised Land
by *Sandy Eisenberg Sasso*
Full color illustrations by *Bethanne Andersen*

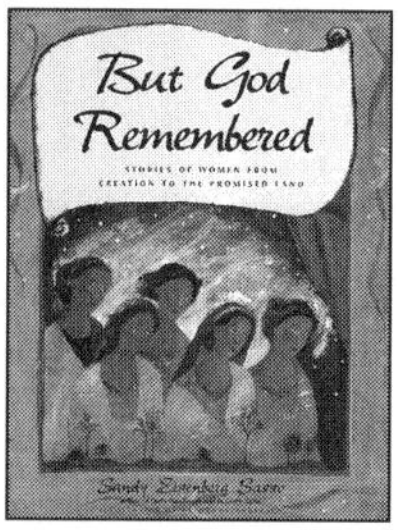

For ages 8 and up

NONSECTARIAN, NONDENOMINATIONAL.
A fascinating collection of four different stories of women only briefly mentioned in biblical tradition and religious texts, but never before explored. Award-winning author Sasso brings to life the intriguing stories of Lilith, Serach, Bityah, and the Daughters of Z, courageous and strong women from ancient tradition. All teach important values through their faith and actions.

"Exquisite....a book of beauty, strength and spirituality."
—Association of Bible Teachers

9 x 12, 32 pp. Hardcover, Full color illus., ISBN 1-879045-43-5 **$16.95**

AWARD WINNER

IN GOD'S NAME
For ages 4-8

by *Sandy Eisenberg Sasso*
Full color illustrations by *Phoebe Stone*

MULTICULTURAL, NONSECTARIAN, NONDENOMINATIONAL.
Like an ancient myth in its poetic text and vibrant illustrations, this modern fable about the search for God's name celebrates the diversity and, at the same time, the unity of all the people of the world. Each seeker claims he or she alone knows the answer. Finally, they come together and learn what God's name really is, sharing the ultimate harmony of belief in one God by people of all faiths, all backgrounds.

"I got goose bumps when I read *In God's Name*, its language and illustrations are that moving. This is a book children will love and the whole family will cherish for its beauty and power."
—Francine Klagsbrun, author of *Mixed Feelings*

"What a lovely, healing book!"
—Madeleine L'Engle

Selected by Parent Council Ltd.™

9 x 12, 32 pp. Hardcover, Full color illus., ISBN 1-879045-26-5 **$16.95**

For ages 4-8

GOD'S PAINTBRUSH
by *Sandy Eisenberg Sasso*
Full color illustrations by *Annette Compton*

AWARD WINNER

MULTICULTURAL, NONSECTARIAN, NONDENOMINATIONAL.
Invites children of all faiths and backgrounds to encounter God openly in their own lives. Wonderfully interactive, provides questions adult and child can explore together at the end of each episode.

"An excellent way to honor the imaginative breadth and depth of the spiritual life of the young."
—Dr. Robert Coles, Harvard University

11x 8½, 32 pp. Hardcover, Full color illustrations, ISBN 1-879045-22-2 **$16.95**

Children's

A PRAYER FOR THE EARTH
The Story of Naamah, Noah's Wife

For ages 4-8

by *Sandy Eisenberg Sasso*
Full color illustrations by *Bethanne Andersen*

NONSECTARIAN, NONDENOMINATIONAL.

This new story, based on an ancient text, opens readers' religious imaginations to new ideas about the well-known story of the Flood. When God tells Noah to bring the animals of the world onto the ark, God *also* calls on Naamah, Noah's wife, to save each plant on Earth. *A Prayer for the Earth* describes Naamah's wisdom and love for the natural harmony of the earth, and inspires readers to use their own courage, creativity and faith to carry out Naamah's work today.

"A lovely tale....Children of all ages should be drawn to this parable for our times."
—*Tomie dePaola, artist/author of books for children*

9 x 12, 32 pp. Hardcover, Full color illustrations, ISBN 1-879045-60-5 **$16.95**

THE 11TH COMMANDMENT
Wisdom from Our Children

For all ages

by The Children of America

MULTICULTURAL, NONSECTARIAN, NONDENOMINATIONAL.

"If there were an Eleventh Commandment, what would it be?"
Children of many religious denominations across America answer this question—in their own drawings and words—in *The 11th Commandment*. This full-color collection of "Eleventh Commandments" reveals kids' ideas about how people should respond to God.

"Wonderful....This unusual book provides both food for thought and insight into the hopes and fears of today's young."
—*American Library Association's* Booklist

8 x 10, 48 pp. Hardcover, Full color illustrations, ISBN 1-879045-46-X **$16.95**

# of Copies **Order Information** $ Amount

# of Copies	Title	$ Amount
______	Aspects of Rabbinic Theology (pb), $18.95	______
______	Bar/Bat Mitzvah Basics (hc), $24.95; (pb), $16.95	______
______	Being God's Partner (hc), $19.95	______
______	But God Remembered (hc), $16.95	______
______	Earth is the Lord's (pb), $12.95	______
______	11th Commandment (hc), $16.95	______
______	Embracing the Covenant (pb), $15.95	______
______	Empty Chair (pb), $9.95	______
______	Finding Joy (hc), $19.95	______
______	God & the Big Bang (hc), $21.95	______
______	God's Paintbrush (hc), $16.95	______
______	Godwrestling—Round 2 (hc), $23.95	______
______	Hanukkah (pb), $16.95	______
______	Healing of Soul, Healing of Body (pb), $14.95	______
______	How to Be a Perfect Stranger Vol. 1 (hc), $24.95	______
______	How to Be a Perfect Stranger Vol. 2 (hc), $24.95	______
______	In God's Name (hc), $16.95	______
______	Israel: An Echo of Eternity (pb), $18.95	______
______	Last Trial (pb), $17.95	______
______	Lifecycles, Vol. 1 (hc), $24.95	______
______	Lifecycles, Vol. 2 (hc), $24.95	______
______	Minding the Temple of the Soul (pb), $15.95	______
______	Mourning & Mitzvah (pb), $19.95	______
______	NEW Jewish Baby Book (pb), $16.95	______
______	One Hundred Blessings Every Day (pb), $14.95	______
______	Passion for Truth (pb), $18.95	______
______	Passover Seder (pb), $16.95	______
______	Putting God on the Guest List (hc), $24.95; (pb), $16.95	______
______	Prayer for the Earth (hc), $16.95	______
______	Recovery from Codependence (hc), $21.95; (pb), $13.95	______
______	Renewed Each Day, 2-Volume Set (pb), $27.90	______
______	Seeking the Path to Life (hc), $19.95; (pb), $14.95	______
______	Self, Struggle & Change (hc), $21.95; (pb), $16.95	______
______	Shabbat Seder (pb), $16.95	______
______	So That Your Values Live On (hc), $23.95; (pb), $17.95	______
______	Spirit of Renewal (hc), $22.95; (pb), $16.95	______
______	Time to Mourn, Time to Comfort (pb), $16.95	______
______	Tormented Master (pb), $17.95	______
______	Twelve Jewish Steps to Recovery (hc), $19.95; (pb), $13.95	______
______	When a Grandparent Dies (hc), $14.95	______
______	Your Word is Fire (pb), $14.95	______
______	Other:______________________________	
	• The Kushner Series •	
______	Book of Letters (hc), $24.95	______
______	Book of Words (hc), $21.95	______
______	God Was in This Place...(hc), $21.95; (pb), $16.95	______
______	Honey From the Rock (pb), $14.95	______
______	Invisible Lines of Connection (hc), $21.95	______
______	River of Light (pb), $14.95	______

Check enclosed for $____________ *payable to:* JEWISH LIGHTS Publishing
Charge my credit card: ❒ MasterCard ❒ Visa
Credit Card #______________________________ Expires ______________
Name on card ______________________________
Signature ______________________ Phone (_______)______________
Name ______________________________
Street ______________________________
City / State / Zip ______________________________

Phone, fax, or mail to: JEWISH LIGHTS Publishing
P. O. Box 237, Sunset Farm Offices, Route 4, Woodstock, Vermont 05091
Tel (802) 457-4000 *Fax* (802) 457-4004 **www.jewishlights.com**
Credit card orders **(800) 962-4544** (9AM–5PM ET Monday–Friday)
Generous discounts on quantity orders. ***SATISFACTION GUARANTEED.*** *Prices subject to change.*

AVAILABLE FROM BETTER BOOKSTORES. TRY YOUR BOOKSTORE FIRST.